# The Sociology of Education

## Canada and Beyond

**Frank J. Mifflen**
**Sydney C. Mifflen**

Detselig Enterprises Limited
Calgary, Alberta

**Frank J. Mifflen**
**Sydney C. Mifflen**
St. Francis Xavier University
Antigonish, Nova Scotia

**Canadian Cataloguing in Publication Data**

Mifflen, Frank J. (Frank James), 1927-
The sociology of education

Bibliography: p.
Includes index.
ISBN 0-920490-23-9

1. Educational sociology. 2. Educational
sociology — Canada. I. Mifflen, Sydney C.
(Sydney Clarence), 1933-    II. Title.
LC191.8.C2M54    370.19'3    C82-091115-1

*48,584*

© 1982 by Detselig Enterprises Limited
P.O. Box G399
Calgary, Alberta T3A 2G3

Printed in Canada                                    ISBN 0-920490-2

# Contents

# *Preface*

This book is intended as a general text in the sociology of education for use in colleges and universities at the undergraduate level in Canada. It is designed so that it may be used for both one-semester and full-year courses. The format has been developed from the extensive experience of the authors in teaching courses in both the sociology of education and the social psychology of learning. The topics presented are such that they are both interesting to students and comprehensively cover the major variables explaining the institutionalized intergenerational inequality which is found in schooling but which has mhny of its roots in social issues pertaining to the broader society.

The sociology of education is in no way limited to national boundaries. We have kept that in mind in the presentation of theory and the inclusion of landmark studies for commentary. At the same time, we wanted to give attention to the contributions of Canadian scholars and to studies of particular relevance to the sociology of Canadian education. This is a Canadian text, for a Canadian market. Scholars from this nation have made important contributions to the field, both in Canada and beyond. The bank of knowledge in this area is reaching significant proportions. This was well illustrated at the 1981 meeting of the Canadian Society for the Study of Education, where the program included many more presentations on the sociology of education than ever before. While it is incorrect, in our view, to speak of a Canadian sociology of education, it is quite appropriate now to speak of the sociology of Canadian education. We have chosen to call the text *The Sociology of Education: Canada and Beyond* to acknowledge the growth of the field in Canada. The presentation is also illustrated and substantiated by reference to studies done outside Canada, particularly in the United States, Britain and France.

When research concentrates on entire societies and the structural variables that explain social reality within them, it is referred to as a *macro* level study. When it is concerned with smaller units within societies, and especially with the interaction of individuals within these units, it is called a *micro* level study. In our presentation we are concerned with both, and it is our position that no thorough understanding of the discipline may come about in any other way. However, we do emphasize macro level studies, both theoretical and empirical. This is based on our view of what is most important for and most interesting to students in a general or introductory course. Macro or societal wide influences such as class shape the reality of smaller or micro units to a substantial extent, even though the definition of the situation may vary, within limits, from unit to unit and from individual to individual. This has led to some compromise of our intention to reflect current activity in the sociology of

Canadian education, for much of that activity at the level of individual studies is focused on micro analysis. As we will point out rather clearly in the appropriate places, our choice is not meant to minimize the importance of this activity.

As writers and researchers we tend to follow a Weberian perspective in social analysis. We have tried to present other views faithfully and to avoid polemics in support of our own. We appreciate and are quite sympathetic to much of Marxist theory. However, we do not really share the hope for a society which eliminates imposed inequality, as much as we would like to see that goal achieved. Perhaps Marxists do not expect that either. But it is our view that even if class, in the relational meaning of that word, were to be eliminated, structured inequality would remain to a substantial extent, and it would flow over into market ability and become or remain intergenerational. We find many problems with the concept of equality of opportunity no matter how it is defined or restricted. Without being merely cynical or overly pessimistic, we believe that inequality among social groups, on a social basis, is virtually inevitable.

Although this text treats the implications for social policy of the various theoretical views, we do not here do much to suggest what specific social policy for educational change should be. We are very interested in this topic, but believe that it is mainly beyond the scope of the sociology of education, especially at this level. However, we do point out certain alternatives and try to make apparent the results which will inevitably follow when one is chosen before another.

A glance at the table of contents will reveal the book's organization, but a little explanation is appropriate here. A chapter on the history of Canadian education including social influences and consequences serves as an introduction in order to put the rest of the material in context. We feel that this is a particularly important chapter. It emphasizes those events that help explain the present structure of education in Canada, both its social structure and its organizational structure.

The remainder of the book is divided into five parts. The first main section concentrates on theoretical issues. Besides a chapter on general theory in the sociology of education, there are two other chapters that constitute departures from the usual format of texts in this field. We consider the topics, both with a social basis, of the meaning and measurement of intelligence and of learning theory to be very pertinent to this discipline, and have included treatment of these here. Parts II and III are largely descriptive, though theory and analysis are included where pertinent. More emphasis than usual is given to preschool influences on educational opportunity where we include chapters on socioeconomic status and family socialization. We have treated in a somewhat standard format three chapters dealing with organizational variables in the system of schooling. These include such topics as the school as a formal organization, the managers of education and the teachers, the clients of education and the adolescent 'subculture', the student value system and the factors which pertain to the organization of schools and classrooms for teaching.

Parts IV and V of the book are mainly analytical. Here we deal with the functions schooling performs both for the student and for society at large. We try to point out the consequences of educational attainment for adult life, particularly as this pertains to occupational prestige and lifetime earnings. We define more specifically the meaning of inequality and the contradictions which result from social policy which is based on a confused understanding or interpretation of that concept. Our presentation concludes with an analysis of the role of ideology as it affects the institution of schooling.

We have alluded to the omission of reference to many current micro level studies. One of the problems we were forced to face is the lack of a unitary theme in the results of such research. As might be expected, studies at the classroom, school or community level are affected by so many variables which depend on the specific unit that they produce different and sometimes conflicting results. With but few exceptions, or with exceptions in a much narrower range, this is not generally the case in macro analysis. We have said little about the sociology of educational innovation, although there is activity in Canada in this area. It is inevitable when using any text that individual professors and students will note the omission of favorite topics. We can only say that our choices had to be limited, and we trust that they will complement our presentation with references or material of their own. In general we have concentrated on issues and problems. We tried to strike a balance between failing to substantiate our presentations and inundating the reader with references to series of studies which differ mostly in detail or, conversely, arrive at conflicting conclusions. We have not been particularly concerned with that because it is our opinion that at this point the student needs most general knowledge in the broad range and the ability to research a specific topic in greater detail.

We have chosen to include within the main body of the text discussion of relevant statistical procedures. We have successfully resisted the temptation to relegate this material to appendices, although individual professors may choose to treat it in class or not. This is consistent with our conviction that the student must understand the meaning and use of these procedures, although not the mathematics on which they are based. We feel that no student can properly understand the literature, and particularly the journal articles, without this general statistical background. The alternative, which we did not wish to choose, is to suggest as a prerequisite a course in statistics. Our answer to this dilemma is to proceed in this way. We are aware of individual biases about the value of quantitative and qualitative research. We hold that the student should be generally familiar with both.

We have experienced the frustration of English language authors in dealing with gender-related pronouns, and have in most instances fallen back on the older practice of using the generalized masculine form. We do this only to

4

avoid the awkwardness of the alternative, and intend no slight or disrespect for either sex.

We have made no attempt to provide study questions, problems or other such supplementary material, believing that professors generally develop their own in any case.

We want to acknowledge the encouragement and financial support provided by St. Francis Xavier University, particularly through its University Council for Research. We are grateful to those, unnamed here, who have read the manuscript and made helpful suggestions to us. We owe a special debt of thanks to Mrs. Frances Baker, who spent many hours beyond the normal work day in preparing the manuscript for publication. We express the hope that our work may provide a challenge for many students, just as our own students have challenged us and contributed so very much to our development, both personal and professional.

# *Introduction*

We have chosen to introduce this text with a chapter which presents a brief social interpretation of the evolution of schooling in Canada. As we proceed through subsequent chapters we shall see that schooling in this nation is characterized by a great deal of inequality. It is our opinion that an understanding of the historical development of the institution will help to situate many of the mechanisms and practices from which unequal educational attainment results. We are convinced that a realistic understanding of any existing institution may come about only if it is built on an appreciation of earlier social factors which contributed to the structure it now has and the functions it performs.

# 1

# A Social Interpretation
# of the Evolution
# of Schooling in Canada

## The Contemporary Scene:
## Schooling as a Reflection of Social Class Differences

The principal emphasis in the sociology of education, whether in Canada or on an international level, is an attempt to investigate and explain the inequality which exists in the formal education system. That inequality manifests itself not only in unequal rates of achievement, so that one or another goes farther in school, or receives higher grades, but also in unequal results in later life for what appears to be the same amount of schooling. People have become accustomed to viewing the causes of this inequality as originating with the individual student, resulting from differences in such variables as ability or motivation, but investigation makes it clear that there are other causes involved. There is virtually as much inequality in educational achievement between individuals with comparable talent, at least according to our ability to measure it, as there is between students of different ability levels. This inequality which exists in the institution of schooling mirrors a comparable or even greater inequality which exists in society at large.

There are several theories which attempt to explain this phenomenon which we will subsequently investigate more thoroughly. The one, often referred to as the functionalist or consensual model, requires unequal rewards and holds that it is an essential component of social life. At most, the inequality is exaggerated, it is too great. Social policy is designed to reduce rather than eliminate it. In general terms those who hold to this model will admit that the excessive inequality which exists, and that alone, is the result of some form of power. It is imposed by individuals and groups who are in a position to channel off excessive privilege for themselves. The important point is that some degree of inequality is required, perhaps even desirable, in society and it is to be found also within the institution of schooling, which is one of its more important component parts.

The other theoretical view is generally referred to as the conflict model of society. In this case inequality exists for arbitrary reasons, and is the result of power alone. It is not essential in order for society to function and it exists because individuals and groups, for whatever reasons, get themselves in advantageous positions and take for themselves, against the will of their neighbours, excessive shares of those things which are valued by the social group.

In either view, inequality among social classes is taken to be a fact, and one which we shall see is important in the understanding of the evolution of Canadian education. As the formal educational institution unfolded historically in Canada, the influence of special groups helped to determine the form it would take. Generally this influence was based on the arbitrary use of power, no matter how it was hidden or legitimated. This was to result in the evolution of specific kinds of educational structures which were designed to give advantage to certain groups.

The inequality which today characterizes and in part results from the contemporary structure of schooling is, then, one manifestation of privilege — whether required but excessive, or not required at all — which exists in the broader society. From our perspective it is a particularly important one. It shows itself especially in inequalities between groups: social class, gender, ethnic and religious groups, and racial groups. There are *social* reasons for the kind of discrimination which exists against native people in Canada, or against females, or working-class children. Similar kinds of social influences explain the discrimination experienced by Black Canadians, recent immigrants and members of certain religious groups such as Catholic minorities in some areas of the Atlantic provinces, Ontario and the West, or Jehovah Witnesses in Quebec. Clement (1975) holds that the inequality of opportunity existing, among other places, in our schools, is the result of the inequality of condition which pre-exists in the broader society. Whatever the cause, there is virtually unanimous agreement that the institution of schooling plays an important role in preserving and perpetuating inequality.

In the remainder of this chapter we will attempt to relate the principal historical factors which bear on the development of the structures and functions of schooling in Canada. As a nation emerging from colonial status Canada was greatly dependent on external influences, particularly those emanating from Britain and France, and later the United States. We will point out some of the more important of these influences. In our interpretation of them, we will concentrate on the happenings in anglophone Canada, and especially Ontario, with a more limited commentary on the development of schooling in Quebec. Little will be said specifically about the West, where development took place considerably later. We proceed in this way for two reasons. This is a relatively new area of research, and much of the published material is restricted to the domain indicated. Moreover, the development of schooling in Ontario has had substantial influence on other areas of the nation, and certain generalizations may be made validly without distorting the reality of the development of Canadian education as a whole.

## Early Influences on Canadian Education

At the time of early colonization in Canada the institutions most responsible for socialization were the family and the church. Apprenticeship was important for occupational training although much of this was performed either through the family or under its watchful eye.

As society evolves towards a more complex level some of the functions of its institutions tend to be differentiated or specialized out. In line with this phenomenon, in the period preceding the twentieth century some of the functions of the family, especially occupational and political socialization, were passed over to the school (Porter, 1969). The capitalist economy which developed strongly first in England, then in Germany and the United States, was responsible for bringing Canada into that level of societal complexity which required the introduction of mass education. As Reimer (1971) has indicated, there is an important distinction between learning and schooling. Schools have other functions to perform, functions sometimes regarded as more important than learning, or different than that learning which results from mastering a specific curriculum. Bleasdale (1978:13) notes that emerging industrial technology requires more than knowledgeable workers. "(P)oor and working-class children had to be protected from 'pernicious opinions' about the prevailing social order and their rightful place." One of the more important functions of schooling was social control, including the reproduction and legitimation of social class differences and other invidious differences which are frequently related. This was so not only in Canada but in Britain (Blyth, 1972) and in the United States (Katz, 1971) as well.

### The Development of Schooling in England

Turner (1960) made the distinction between sponsored and contest mobility. Until this most recent decade, and even today to a considerable extent, formal education in England followed the sponsored mobility model. Students advanced, were *sponsored* through the system, primarily on the basis of social class. Britain in the eighteenth and nineteenth centuries had strong vestiges of an aristocracy, and there were firm boundaries between the upper and upper middle, the middle, and the working classes. As the system of formal education developed in England to the point where it became a mass institution it was the children of the upper classes who were sponsored through the system. Middle and especially working-class children were quickly weeded out, and this was an open and generally accepted procedure.

Blyth (1972:273-328) provides interesting and useful information on the history of educational development in England which we shall very briefly summarize here. Before the middle of the nineteenth century education was restricted very much to the upper classes. The *public* schools were private indeed and have remained fee-charging institutions to this day. They received that name because they selected a small number of *king's scholars*, children from working-class families who were admitted on the basis of excellence and subsidized from the royal or public purse. The *grammar* schools were those that corresponded to our public school system, and these began to develop only as England became highly industrialized. Universal education only really became established after the first world war and even then was severely class biased. There was much conflict of a religious nature, as there had been in Britain since the Reformation. The Anglican denomination was the Established Church. England had a long history of laws and customs which restricted many forms of privilege to members of this Established Church. This overflowed into the emerging educational system and was to some extent transferred to the Canadian scene even though there was never an official established church here.

After 1834 the state in England was made responsible for the education of pauper children. In 1833 the passage of the Factory Act placed a number of restrictions on child labour which had been very seriously abused. This made it illegal to employ a child more than forty-eight hours a week and required employers to permit the child to attend school for two hours a day. Ragged schools were soon introduced. Cognitive or substantive elements of the curriculum were weak and minimal but the ideological or indoctrination function was strong.

As a result of this, early schooling in England was very strongly class biased and this was rather universally accepted. A classical curriculum was provided through the misnamed public schools and these were restricted to the elite. Education for social control was the strongest component of the schooling provided to the children of the working classes.

England had been the leader in the emerging industrial revolution, but late in the nineteenth century technological advances in Germany and the United States were relegating it to an inferior position. Both of these nations had a more highly developed educational system. As a result strong emphasis was now given to technical and vocational education as England tried to catch up, and this aspect of the system of schooling was rapidly expanded to provide practical skills to those 'destined' to manual work. This was the beginning of a strong and open system of streaming, which had a class basis, eventually resulting in academic, general and vocational tracks. This has never really disappeared although there have been major efforts to reduce or eliminate the sponsored aspect of this streaming in the past decade or two.

After 1914 education was compulsory for children up to age 14 and remained free for those who chose to continue until age 18. Blyth (1972) reports that by the mid-twenties only 12 per cent of those in the elementary schools ever reached the secondary grammar school level and only four in a thousand went on to university. In 1926, as a result of recommendations of the Hadlow Commission, primary education was required for all until age 11, at which time tests were to be given to determine the track or stream students were to follow from then on, a system often referred to as the *eleven plus*. Age 11 was chosen because psychologists insisted that a child's intelligence could be reliably tested at that time. The privilege of a child choosing the stream upon maturity does not seem to have been given serious consideration. At this stage the streams included grammar, modern and vocational units corresponding to academic, general and vocational tracks. These were generally separate units; England did not develop the comprehensive school which became so familiar in Canada and the United States.

The post-secondary educational level also developed along class lines. The universities, especially the elite ones like Oxford and Cambridge, were open principally to the graduates of the fee-charging public system. In the earlier years admission was generally restricted to members of the Anglican Church. (This had important results in Canada at a later date because many of the instructors in early secondary schools in Upper Canada were recruited from Britain.) Much emphasis was later given to technical education at the post-secondary level, including degree granting privileges, but despite strong efforts by some advocates this never achieved the status of the regular university degree. Even with the international educational inflation which occurred after the second world war, participation rates at post-secondary institutions never approached the levels we have come to accept in Canada.

There were strong efforts to modernize and democratize schooling in England after 1950. More time is required to determine the degree of success being achieved, and much of the 'new' sociology of education which is very strong in Britain is directed along that line.

This brief and superficial summary of the evolution of schooling in England is important for the student who hopes to understand the parallel development in Canada. Especially in the earlier years the evolution of our institution was strongly influenced by the British sponsored model. That system, at least until the 1960's, was really a twofold class-related model. There was a classical education provided for the elites through the public schools and transferred to some small degree in this century to the secondary grammar school level. This led to entrance to the elite universities for those who wished to carry on. This was status-related in the sense that it established boundaries for a particular style of life. Such an education frequently led to a career in the established professions. There was also another streamed level for the children of the working classes, also status-related in the sense that it included indoctrination into a working-class style of life. In this way the existing class or stratification system was reproduced with minimal protest from those to whom advanced levels of education were denied. One of the principal functions of the entire institution was *social control*. This included especially the legitimation phenomenon which we will examine subsequently.

## The American Model

The evolution of public education has probably been more thoroughly studied and documented in the United States than it has been for any other nation with which we are concerned. In recent years scholars such as Michael Katz (1968, 1971), Bowles and Gintis (1976) and Bleasdale (1978), to name but a few, have done much systematic research in this area. More recently the fruits of this effort have overflowed to Canada.

Bowles and Gintis (1976:151-223), relying on many sources, have provided a good general overview of the development of schooling in American society. We will present a short summary of their presentation.

The early pilgrim settlers in the United States brought with them a great respect for literacy. This was especially so that they would be able to read the scriptures, something very important to them. Despite this early influence religion did not play the important direct role in the subsequent development of the public education system that it exercised in England and Canada. At the same time many of the colleges and universities were established by specific denominations and an elaborate parochial school system, privately financed, was established. The curriculum of these denominational institutions, both overt and hidden, was to follow the direction of the public schools or other institutions of higher learning, with the exception of specifically denominational or ethnic concerns. By and large the development of these institutions paralleled the public school system and at this level of analysis we will give little attention to specific differences.

Bowles and Gintis (1976), following Katz (1971) and many other educational historians, see the development of schooling in the United States as following the needs of the emerging industrial economy and being subservient to the capitalist class. They relate this development in three stages: the pre-industrial period where schooling was unimportant except for a few elites; the early industrial period which saw the introduction of free, compulsory, universal tax-supported education; and the mature industrial period which brought with it class-based tracking on the secondary level and eventually in post-secondary institutions. These periods very roughly correspond to the eighteenth, nineteenth and twentieth centuries.

Before the revolution, education for the public took place in the family, churches and through the institution of apprenticeship. Moreover, there were large numbers of Americans (the Blacks) to whom even basic literacy was denied, frequently by law. The schooling that did exist was given primarily through *dame schools*, often held in the home of a literate woman who for several hours a day, or some days, taught literacy to the children of her neighbours. Even in these early years most Americans, with the exception we have noted, were literate in the sense of being able to read, write and perform the basic arithmetic computations required in everyday life. At the same time there were *charity schools* for the poor, delinquents and untended orphans. These were very much institutions of social control, the principal function being to indoctrinate the students (inmates) to accept the prevailing value and normative system and hopefully to fit into lower level adult occupational roles.

The early industrial stage was ushered in with a gradual change over to a capitalist industrial economy, and this occurred first in the New England and mid-Atlantic states. Massachusetts was to become the model.

At the time of the American Revolution this new republic was largely a rural and agricultural society. The production of many consumer goods for sale was often accomplished through the *putting-out* system where an entrepreneur provided to a family raw materials (e.g., leather) which the members fashioned into the finished product (e.g., shoes) for a price. As long as this operation was performed in the home the emerging capitalist had little control over production, over the hours of work. Very quickly this process evolved into an early factory system. Quite simply, the entrepreneur gathered the producers into a central place, provided both raw material and tools, and paid a wage. Hours of work were now strictly established and the owner had strong control over the worker, including the power to discipline through firing. This emerging factory system spread rapidly, especially in the textile industries of New England, and the modern system of first family, then monopoly capitalism as we know it, was well established by mid-century. Large numbers of Americans left the farms and their numbers were swollen by increasingly large waves of immigrants who generally settled in the enlarging urban areas, becoming dependent on wage labour.

The early waves of immigrants were mostly Irish, with smaller numbers from Germany and other European countries. Because they brought with them their own customs, sometimes including a different language, and the ethnic differences were not always compatible with the emerging factory system, the early entrepreneurs gradually found it desirable to have an institution which would mould the culturally diverse children into a disciplined labour force. The factory required a normative system which stressed obedience, discipline, promptness and efficiency — characteristics which were of lesser importance in an agricultural economy. Schooling had very low priority in the first decade of the nineteenth century but by 1850 it had been well established, not without some degree of difficulty. As early as 1817 a Boston Town Meeting signed a petition for a system of free, public elementary schools. Those who signed were mostly artisans, shopkeepers, large merchants and entrepreneurs. Their concern was not merely for basic schooling for their own children but also, or especially, for the children of the now rapidly expanding working class. It took several decades for the system to become well entrenched, and even longer to complete its development.

In 1837 Horace Mann became Secretary of the Massachusetts Board of Education. A politician by inclination and experience and in some respects an

humanitarian as well, Mann was very much influenced by the early industrialization process. Interestingly enough, his salary was supplemented by large
industrialists. He felt that there was a strong need for an integrated culture,
especially for the newly arriving immigrants, and with it appropriate institutions of social control which would mould the people into a way of life supportive of the new urban-based economy. Mann viewed compulsory education as
a mechanism which would discipline potential workers, encourage thrift and
sobriety and eliminate the abuses of pauperism.

Mann was essentially a liberal. He was certainly a promoter of the new
industrial system, but not of its abuses. Blyth (1972) reports that one of his
first efforts was to establish a normal school where potential teachers could
learn to exercise their profession in a uniform way. He did not have smooth
sailing. Most of the opposition came from farmers and the factory workers
who viewed compulsory education as an institution with few advantages but
having unacceptable costs in taxation and the deferred income of their children. Mann also had to convince many industrialists and entrepreneurs that
the cost of schooling, paid through taxation, was well worth the return it paid
in a disciplined work force and, reputedly, in lower rates of delinquency.

Mann's perseverance paid off. By 1859, when he terminated his office,
elementary education in Massachusetts was free, tax-supported, and a system
of truant officers was well established. A secondary system of high schools
was beginning to emerge, principally for the middle classes, and in the next
stage this was to expand so that it also acquired a universal character. Katz
(1971:106) notes that at the conclusion of this period, by 1880, the system
had taken the form we know now. It ". . . had acquired its fundamental
structural characteristics, they have not altered since. Public education was
universal, tax-supported, free, compulsory, bureaucratically arranged, class
biased and racist."

We shall see subsequently that there are many functions of schooling.
Certainly the development of cognitive skills and substantive learning is one
of them, although particularly at this stage we are dealing mostly with the
specializing out of a process which had been accomplished in other institutions, especially the family. Bowles and Gintis emphasize the major importance of what today we so broadly refer to as the hidden curriculum. They
take great pains, quite convincingly, to demonstrate that it was the non-cognitive aspects of the emerging system of formal education which were the
principal concern of the elite. The goal was to control the masses, to teach
them to accept their *appropriate* place in society. This included respect for
those in authority, courtesy and politeness, punctuality, discipline and the view
that the capitalist system of industrialism was the best possible system. They
were to be subservient rather than original or creative and must not seriously
question the authority of their employers. Children who came from family
and cultural backgrounds which did not give high priority to those values,
perhaps did not accept them at all, were compelled by law to spend a number

of years in institutions whose principal purpose was to mould them, usually covertly, so that they accepted the general value and normative system of this new industrial order. Now, a century and a half later, students sometimes find it difficult to understand how large a change this was. Those who accept cultural relativism hold that one culture is not superior to another. A part of this compulsory system of schooling was the imposition of a uniform cultural system which supported the capitalist ethic and taught the working classes to accept the lower strata they occupied in a system of stratification character-ized by substantial inequality and, to a considerable extent, based on ascrip-tion.

By the year 1880 there was free and compulsory mass elementary edu-cation in the United States. It had its origins in the developing factory system of Massachusetts and the eastern seaboard and quickly spread to other areas of the developing nation. We accépt Katz's (1971) assessment that by this time public schooling had been implemented in a way which has remained substantially unchanged. Its principal function, according to Bowles and Gin-tis (1976), was a form of social control which they refer to as legitimation and allocation. Legitimation serves an ideological function. It presents the prevail-ing system as the most acceptable one, and reconciles those who are less priv-ileged to accept their lot. Allocation simply refers to designating people for their appropriate slot in the stratification system, mostly through the various rungs in the occupational prestige ladder. This appropriate position generally corresponds closely to the class position of the family of origin, although a limited amount of substantial mobility is permitted to fill vacant spots in the upper middle and upper classes not assumed by people of those class levels, who do not generally fully reproduce themselves.

The next stage in the evolution of schooling in the United States covers the modern era. Essentially it is a period of growth and innovation. The growth saw mass public elementary schooling spread to the secondary level in the first half of this century, and to the post-secondary level in this generation. The innovations included many liberal reforms advocated by John Dewey and the progressivists. Advocating student-centered pedagogy, the twentieth century saw the introduction of I.Q. and achievement testing and tracking.

Testing was used to separate out students who were judged, whether accu-rately or not, to be of inferior ability. (The meaning of intelligence, and the validity and reliability of intelligence testing, will be examined in chapter 3.) These students were directed into the lower level of an hierarchical tracking system which included academic, general, vocational and secretarial levels, only the first of which was not a terminal program. There was a strong positive relationship between tracking and social class background.

Bowles and Gintis (1976) take great pains to demonstrate that intelli-gence is not a scarce commodity. The point they want to make is that it is usually some other characteristic such as motivation or alienation which makes it difficult for some students to achieve well in school. Moreover, intelligence

(I.Q.) makes a minimal unique contribution to the economic success in adult life while length of schooling makes a substantial one. Why separate out some students for terminal tracks, particularly when this is done on the basis of social class? They try to demonstrate that the principal reason is to perpetuate the stratification system. The phenomenon which they refer to as IQism is a way of hiding the social class bias of a school system which is meant to allocate primarily to the elites the credentials so necessary for advancement in the occupational world today. The use of ability and achievement tests makes it appear as if the system is a meritocracy. In reality the dice are loaded from the the beginning but those in the lower social classes and minority racial or ethnic groups come to accept it as if it is appropriate, right and just. They then become reconciled to their inferior position in society and the process of legitimation has been accomplished.

Public education in the United States during this century has evolved in such a way as to incorporate large, comprehensive schools which include a variety of tracks. As the student body enlarged to include most of the relevant age cohort through the secondary level, large numbers were counseled into the lower tracks, mostly on the basis of ability and achievement tests which were indirectly class-related. Because these tracks were terminal, such students were prevented from going on to university and were directed to lower level occupational slots, thus preserving the more prestigious positions for members of the higher classes.

At the turn of the century only about four per cent of the relevant age cohort remained through high school. By the mid-thirties this had increased almost tenfold and by the 1960's virtually all of that group remained in high school. These changes unfolded against the backdrop of industrial expansion which saw the United States become perhaps the leading industrial nation of the world. Accompanying this was the educational philosophy of progressivism with John Dewey as its principal spokesman. Progressive education was equated with liberalism, an ideology which acknowledged abuses but regarded the structures as being basically sound. Dewey's democratic school of thought saw three general functions of the educational system: the integrative, egalitarian and personal development functions. It failed to recognize that the first was incompatible with the other two (Bowles and Gintis, 1976).

These liberal reforms brought with them a pragmatic or utilitarian emphasis, and this allowed in turn the introduction of vocational education. Contrary to popular opinion the growing labour movement was not an advocate of this form of tracking. In fact, many sections offered vigorous opposition, realizing that the children of working-class families would become locked in and impeded in mobility aspirations. It was the industrialists and organizations like the National Association of Managers who formed the strong lobby group, not only for reasons such as those already indicated but also to save in on-the-job training costs. This movement finally resulted in federal aid to vocational education in 1917 and in the comprehensive high school within a generation.

Meanwhile the ideology of equality of opportunity continued to prevail. As Blyth (1972) notes, text books were forbidden to present anything critical and most of the American population came to regard this expansion as reform.

The student should understand that there is nothing inherently undesirable about vocational or any other form of practical education. The problem relative to equality results from these being *terminal* tracks impeding advancement in the system beyond a certain stage. This problem is aggravated when students are tracked into terminal streams either against their will or at an age when it is too early for them to make a mature choice.

According to Bowles and Gintis (1976), in 1870 about 1.7 per cent of the 18 to 21 age cohort were enrolled in higher or post-secondary education. By 1940 this had increased to 25 per cent and by the seventies to over 50 per cent. The problem of too many high school graduates for the higher prestige jobs which had existed earlier and which was resolved through terminal tracks now expressed itself at the post-secondary level. As a result of the rapid educational inflation after the second world war, a mechanism was needed to duplicate this allocative and legitimation function at the next higher level. Consequently, there was a tremendous proliferation of community colleges. Large numbers of students were "tracked" into these institutions and through the cooling-out process described by Clark (1960) were denied the credentials which were required to advance to universities. In the meantime the nature of the American work force had changed so that most were employed in the tertiary or service level. Karabel (1972) notes that enrollment in community colleges had advanced from 153,970 in 1948 to 1,169,635 in 1968. Only about one-third of these were successful in gaining an academic diploma and fewer still actually transferred to four-year universities. The remainder were prepared to take up lower level positions in the intermediate range of the work force leaving the more prestigious positions to the university graduates, especially the more elite ones. As in the case of tracking at the secondary level this was strongly class-related (Pincus, 1978).

It is evident from this presentation of the evolution of schooling in the United States that the principal functions of this system were social control, allocation and legitimation. There are other functions of formal education which we will deal with in chapter 10. The point we want to emphasize here is that much of this development was a mechanism which was meant to perpetuate an hierarchical stratification system. The ideology stating that schools are democratic institutions, that there is equality and equality of opportunity, should not be accepted at face value. The moral and intellectual leadership provided primarily by the elites sometimes consciously, sometimes unconsciously helped to institutionalize inequality within American schools. As we shall see, much of this was adopted in Canada.

## The Development of Schooling in Anglophone Canada

### Religious Influence: The Struggle for Control

In 1841 the provinces of Quebec and Ontario were united into one political unit. The history of the development of schooling in anglophone Canada was thus inextricably bound to its development in Quebec. The situation in the Maritime provinces, which were separate political units, ran a parallel if somewhat distinct course. The gradual unfolding of the mosaic which led to universal public schooling in these five provinces is very complex. One social fact probably stands out more strongly than any other; that was the pervasive presence of religious strife. The primary purpose of the religious involvement was a political one: an attempt by the religious authorities to control the masses. Speaking of the developing system in the united Canadas before confederation Adams (1968:49) notes:"(O)ne fact stands out in the power struggle over the control of education in 1841: the interest and welfare of the general public were largely disregarded by governing authorities who did not consider the educational interests or needs of the mass of people."

Katz (1973:16), one of the more eminent educational historians of both Canada and the United States, is perhaps even more severe in his judgement:

> Unfortunately, the pietistic educational historians of earlier generations have left us with a singularly useless, as well as misleading, version of the educational past of both Canada and the United States. We are asked to believe a tale of sacrifice, heroism and triumph through which the contemporary public school came into existence as the great achievement of Western political culture. We are asked to believe in the essentially beneficent, egalitarian and ameliorating influence that public education has exercised in our societies for the past century. It is a story that simply does not fit the inadequacies of public education as we have come to know them in recent years.

Katz is here referring to the process of bureaucratization. His accusations of class bias are equally severe. "In one form or another training in behaviour and belief has always been more important to people in control of schools than the development of intellectual skills. . . . High schools helped the children of the middle class into white-collar jobs, while everyone, including the poor, paid the bills" (Katz, 1973:18). He also speaks out strongly against the conservative and elitist character of schooling. "Public schools have always represented conservative social forces expressing and reflecting the aspirations, the fears and the interests of the more affluent members of communities; that is what I mean when I say class bias" (Katz, 1973:18). Other recent analysts of the development of schooling in Canada more or less share this view, including Myers (1973), Prentice (1970,1977), Prentice and Houston (1975), McDonald and Chaiton (1978), Katz and Mattingly (1975), Bleasdale (1978), Wilson (1978), Lazerson (1978), French (1978), Audet (1970), Hamilton (1970), Magnuson (1980), Adams (1968) and Schecter (1977).

The fundamental religious affiliations which were struggling against one another in pre-confederation Canada included especially the Anglicans, the Roman Catholics and the Protestant dissenters who came in large numbers for some fifty years after the American Revolution. The Anglicans were the Established Church in England and that denomination held a similar though unofficial position in most of Ontario and the Maritimes in the early colonial period. The Catholics were the majority in Quebec and parts of southeast Ontario, among the French and Irish in the Maritimes, and among many of the highland Scots settlements in Nova Scotia. After the conquest the Anglicans became very powerful in Quebec as well, though numerically they were a small minority.

## The Strachan Influence

The most important name in the early period of the evolution of schooling in Ontario was John Strachan, a Scot and converted Anglican priest who came to Canada in 1799 and eventually became the Anglican bishop of Toronto. Strachan quickly worked his way into the primitive educational establishment, beginning first as a teacher. As early as 1791 there had been pressure to establish grammar schools, and the District Public School Act of 1807 authorized the establishment of eight such schools. Meant for the children of the middle and especially the upper classes (Blyth, 1972) these followed the classical curriculum of the British public schools. There was popular reaction against this exclusiveness and in 1816 under Strachan's influence the Common School Act authorized the establishment of common schools. Both kinds of schools received state subsidies but the difference soon was to become rather extreme. By 1839, 12 grammar schools with about 300 pupils received 18 dollars per pupil. There were by now some 650 common schools with over 14,000 pupils and these received assistance only to the extent of two dollars per pupil (Johnson, 1968). Moreover, after 1816, 100 pounds was contributed from public funds towards the salary of the grammar school teachers, but only 25 pounds was available for the teacher in the common schools (Wilson, 1978).

Early Canadian schooling thus followed closely the British model. The grammar schools emphasized the classics and prepared graduates for admission to the university if that was their wish. The common schools gave more emphasis to rote, appropriate behaviour and social control. The Lancaster system was introduced in this latter group. Adopted for Anglican use by Dr. Gordon Bell, it was first introduced in Halifax in 1814 and was soon transferred to Ontario. Described as a system where those who knew little taught others who knew even less, it never really became popular in Canada, though the fact that it was tried in common schools is itself important.

Under Strachan's influence there was a move towards local control from the very beginning, but with an element of centralization as well. Following the 1816 Act a centralized Board of Education was established with Strachan as its first chairman. Local authorities could establish a common school wherever a minimum of 20 pupils was assured. Very strongly associated with the Anglican dominated Family Compact which expected separate and superior schools for the elite, Strachan was most interested in higher education. Under his influence, but with some modification to his proposal of Anglican patronage, Upper Canada College was founded as a secular institution in 1831. It was from the beginning an elitist institution. King's College, Strachan's original proposal, was founded in 1843 and later became the University of Toronto. Strachan's denominational plans for this institution were officially shelved by his foe, Egerton Ryerson, whose star was now on the rise (Wilson, 1978). Unofficially, Anglican influence was pervasive.

The Scottish influence in higher education was strong. McGill was founded in 1836 by anglophone Protestants in Quebec. Nova Scotia by mid-century had King's College, Acadia, Dalhousie, St. Francis Xavier and a number of academies. Queens was established in 1841. French Canada had boasted of an institution of higher learning since 1633, a year before the founding of Harvard, and this was to become Laval in 1854. Virtually all of these institutions were established by a specific denomination even if, like Upper Canada College or Dalhousie, they were officially secular. This denominational character in many cases was to persevere for a century or more.

So it was that in anglophone Canada, before universal, tax supported elementary and secondary education was the rule, there was already a well established network of higher education institutions catering principally to the established families. While the British and Anglican influence was strong, so was that of the Scots and both dissenters and Roman Catholics (Blyth, 1972). The earlier 'reformers' concentrated on controlling or reducing the Anglican influence. Social class distinctions were more covert in a frontier society, but they were hardly less real because of this (Hamilton, 1970). Schooling was to act as an agent of political socialization. "The content of that socialization included a commitment to a Christianity that could accommodate most Protestants, to Canadians as loyal subjects of the Queen, and to social class harmony within an hierarchically ordered society" (Lazerson, 1978:4-5). A particularly important role of the emerging schools was to provide moral instruction, a function specialized out of the family and Church to some extent. More than anything education was to instill the correct value system, one which supported the prevailing stratification system and where there was to be no serious examination or criticism of the status quo (Lazerson, 1978).

## The Ryerson Influence

Egerton Ryerson became Chief Superintendent of Education in Upper Canada in 1846. Already a prominent influence for some time, Ryerson during a leave the previous year had travelled to the continent to study the system of education existing there. On his return he immediately called for a system of universal, free elementary education. Curriculum was to take into consideration modern industry and commerce (Johnson, 1968). A methodist, Ryerson was a reformer intent on diminishing the denominational and especially the Anglican control over schooling. Education should be very much involved in moral socialization but it should also be secular. Familiar with the policies of Horace Mann who occupied the equivalent position in Massachusetts, he soon introduced in Canada many of Mann's policies including elected school boards, a property tax for the provision of free schooling, secular schools which respected religious differences, and a strong centralized Department of Education which would standardize and supervise teaching and the curriculum and rather thoroughly implement bureaucratic policies which have remained ever since (Blyth, 1972). These policies which Ryerson regarded as reforms did not always come about easily. For years the property taxation in support of schooling met opposition from many quarters, particularly farmers and businessmen.

Following the Durham Report of 1839 Upper and Lower Canada were united in one government in 1841. A Common School Act was passed in that year attempting to give a uniform school system to Canada East and Canada West. It failed, principally because of religious differences. It gave the appointed municipal councils the right to build schools and levy taxes for them. They were eligible for state assistance to match the local levy. This was the act which introduced *the principle of dissent* allowing a minority in any township or parish to set up its own school for which it was eligible for state support. This was inserted at the insistence of the English Protestant minority in Canada East and eventually became the constitutional basis of separate schools (Johnson, 1968).

Another bill in 1850 introduced property taxation for school support at the option of the local district. Very few opted for this form of financing in the beginning. Separate schools were exempted from dual taxation and in 1863 they were given a share of the provincial and municipal grant, but subjected to inspection and appropriate teacher standards. Ryerson was not in favor of the principle of dissent, passed before he took office, but accepted the inevitable. He succeeded in bringing separate schools under state control. He was also instrumental in bringing reform to the Grammar Schools in 1853 and 1855, merging them into the provincial system in the same way as the separate schools. This system, consolidated by the Separate School Act of 1863, was basically incorporated in the British North America Act of 1867, and the formal education system of Ontario was substantially adopted in later years in the West. By the time of confederation Ontario, Quebec, Nova Scotia and New Brunswick — the four original provinces — were supporting both an elementary and a secondary school system through municipal property taxation, although in Nova Scotia especially this was still a volatile political issue. Towards the turn of the century Manitoba revoked the right to separate schools in the disposition of the famous Manitoba School Question (Blyth, 1972). Quebec had its separate but co-existing English-Protestant and French-Catholic systems. Ontario continued to allow separate schools especially for Catholics and, to a more limited extent, for the French. There was much strife in Nova Scotia which was to continue in some areas until after the second world war but a public school system which allowed denominational instruction eventually evolved so that separate schools were no longer required. While schooling was now generally free, the compulsory character was much slower in being introduced. Ontario established compulsory education in 1871. Prince Edward Island tried a brief experiment for 12 weeks in 1877. New Brunswick introduced compulsory schooling in 1905, Nova Scotia in 1915 and Quebec and Newfoundland in 1943.

Meanwhile the class bias described by Katz (1973) remained. In 1871 in Ontario the term 'public' was introduced to describe elementary schools, and secondary schools became known as 'high' schools. Changes were made in the curriculum to give less emphasis to the classics at the secondary level but more private schools were introduced to retain that characteristic. The high schools were forced to compete with the fee-charging collegiate schools, especially after 1876 when a system of government support depending on results was introduced along with intermediate exams along the lines of the British *eleven plus*. As a result of this 'payment by results' policy, which lasted only seven years, a new pattern began in all provinces giving emphasis to standardized examinations which determined entrance to high school. This effectively excluded many of the children of the poor and the working class. As a result the high schools, which were structured to permit entrance to the university at the sophomore level after graduation (senior matriculation) or after the eleventh grade or second last grade (junior matriculation) had disproportionately large numbers from the middle and upper classes. By 1900 only about 5 per cent of elementary pupils went on to the secondary level. Until 1920 secondary schools effectively were open only to the middle and upper classes because they alone could pass the entrance examinations (Johnson, 1968). The Canadian system fell midway between the British sponsored model and the American contest model. Class bias was less open than in England, less covert than in the United States. It was nevertheless very real. The religious and ethnic basis of so much strife over such a long period effectively hid much of the class discrimination. The ideology of equality of opportunity never attained the credibility in Canada which it enjoyed in the United States, but Canadians tended to be more aware of ethnic rather than social class differences.

**Post-Confederation Consolidation**

There remained after confederation only the need to consolidate the system into a formal, centralized bureaucratic structure. Because Section 93 of the British North America Act made education the responsibility of the provinces, this bureaucratization came about at the individual provincial level. Each province developed a Department of Education or its equivalent and an administrative staff which eventually became highly specialized. Normal schools were introduced and there was standardized certification for teaching, an occupation which was dominated by females. Commercial courses in high school were introduced in 1891 and manual training and domestic science in 1897. This was the beginning of tracking although it was to be some years yet before strict vocational and general tracks were to become the norm. A technical school was opened in Toronto in 1915 and this new development spread to other provinces after the first world war. Vocational schools now became very common, especially in Ontario. Unlike the case in the United States, the voice of labour favoring vocational education was strong, the principal spokesman being the Dominion Trades and Labour Council. The influence of Progressivism was felt less strongly in Canada, or less directly. Nevertheless, ability and achievement testing was introduced and the provincial high school examinations persevered for many years. Especially after the second world war bus transportation became common and this together with an increasing move towards centralization allowed for consolidation of senior and junior high schools and a more formalized and overt form of tracking along American lines. The little red school house became a thing of the past and small local school boards tended to become amalgamated into larger units. By the 1930's even secondary education was generally free and in the 1950's state aid to higher education became the norm. As in the United States community colleges began to boom, serving the same tracking purposes, and the great age of educational expansion was under way. By 1970, when the effects of the declining birth rate became noticeable, free and compulsory primary and secondary tax-supported education was the norm in Canada and post-secondary education was highly subsidized. As we shall see in subsequent chapters the social class bias was to remain.

## Schooling in Quebec: Background and Development

The Province of Quebec — Lower Canada or Canada East before confederation — fell behind anglophone Canada in the development of compulsory schooling. Early education there was influenced very much by the heritage which New France received from the mother country. Before the conquest in

1759-60 that heritage permitted, even encouraged a strong role for the clergy. Consequently, in its early years schooling in New France was dominated by the Catholic Church and that pervasive influence remained until the reforms in this past generation (Magnuson, 1980).

Durkheim (1977) shows how the influence of the Jesuit Order was so strong in the evolution of pedagogy in France. Medieval education emphasized rhetoric, the ability to overcome one's adversary in debate. With the Renaissance there was a revival in *form* and re-awakening of interest in the classical period of antiquity. This, along with the success of the Reformation, was perceived as threatening ecclesiastical control. The Jesuits, founded early in the sixteenth century, very early directed their efforts largely to the education field. The format they employed involved fierce competition and a tradition of excellence while promoting strong loyalty to the Church. At the time of colonization in New France the educated administrative staff was accustomed to ecclesiastical control, even though there was a history of strife between Catholics, Protestants and Jansenists. Hence the religious strife which arose in New France after the conquest was something with which the colonists had been familiar for a lengthy period of time.

The first schools in New France were the results of attempts to christianize the native people. The religious orders, particularly the Jesuits, were very prominent and made heroic sacrifices to bring their faith to these people. This was to set the tone for the evolution of schooling later. Even after confederation religious instruction continued to be the primary function of schooling well into this century (Magnuson, 1980).

Before the conquest formal schooling received very low priority in the colony. There were *episcopal* schools, *monastic* schools and also *charitable* schools for the orphans (Audet, 1970), but the level of literacy among the colonists remained low. The elites feared an educated public. The few who received a secondary education provided in the Jesuit colleges which sprang up in Quebec City and Montreal, and in the Grand Seminaire, also in Quebec, were trained in theology, philosophy and the classics for a preparation for the professions, especially the priesthood. In its earlier years there was no attempt to establish a permanent settlement; the colony was intended to be an intermediary fur-trading institution. As a result the number of settlers was very small. Even after permanent colonization the economy was a rural one and no substantial effort was directed at promoting schooling, with the exceptions noted above.

With the conquest in 1759 (Quebec) and 1760 (Montreal) and the Treaty of Paris in 1763 New France became a conquered colony of Britain. Anglicans dominated in many ways in the emerging educational system, especially in the first half of the nineteenth century. In 1801 the Royal Institution for the Advancement of Learning was established, supported by the Anglican Bishop, Jacob Mountain (Blyth, 1972). Adams notes that it was Protestants who received the benefits. Papineau was quoted in the Montreal Star of February

7, 1829 as saying that the ". . . object of the Institution was in the first place the proselytism of all to one belief and secondly to make it subservient to other civil and political views. It was evident that education was the least thing considered" (Adams, 1968:14). Most of the members of the Catholic establishment shared this view. Only schools of the Royal Institution could get government support and only Protestants (especially Anglicans) could teach in them. But while the Anglicans were in almost complete control in those years it was a losing battle because numerically they were so few. The Fabrique Act of 1824 permitted parish schools under local control, the beginning of district school boards. While this legislation was not successful in establishing many schools, it was very successful in breaking the stronghold of the Institution. The Assembly in 1829 passed an act giving the right to secular common schools under local control and this in turn eventually led to the separate denominational system (Adams, 1928).

There was much strife in the century before confederation. It had both a religious and a cultural basis and it is frequently difficult to separate the two. The conflict was to overflow into the arena of schooling and by the time of confederation there had arisen a tradition of denominational schools: English and Protestant (including Anglican), and French and Catholic. Popular education was not yet a reality by 1867, but denominational freedom was enshrined in the constitution, principally at the insistence of the Protestant minority under the leadership of Alexander Galt. In legislation passed in 1841, 1845 and 1846, the balance of power for education was given to local authorities. This included the principle of dissent. Public schools were to be developed along religious rather than language lines. Outside of Quebec and Montreal a local area could establish a school according to the religion of the majority (usually Catholic) which all children could attend. People of the dissenting faith then had the right to establish a second school for their own children. In the two major cities denominational boards provided schools for both groups (Magnuson, 1980). Thus there arose at first in practice and later in law separate administrative and supervisory bodies for the English-Protestant minority and the French-Catholic majority and with some exceptions these have coexisted without undue strife ever since.

It was not until 1943 that public education became compulsory in Quebec. There are complex reasons for the tardiness of this development. For many years the Catholic Church held that it was the right of the family and not the state to make such a decision, although ecclesiastical authorities began to emphasize after confederation the responsibility of parents to educate their children. At the same time Church authorities feared paying for universal schooling through taxation. They regarded state supported schooling as an undue incursion in the educational domain, something the Church habitually insisted on controlling itself. There had already been a degree of government intervention. As early as 1829 there were government grants to help erect school buildings (50 pounds), to help pay teachers' salaries (20 pounds) and to help defray the cost of indigent children (10 shillings). An Act of Parliament in 1841 (Common School Act) gave municipal councils the right to levy taxes for schools which were eligible for matching government grants (Johnson, 1968). Meanwhile education was not highly valued in the rural areas where most of the people lived. Parents often regarded schooling as something which interfered with the productive requirements of the family. An extra worker on the farm, even a young one, could provide a valuable contribution which many of them could not afford to forego.

And so it was that by the late nineteenth century the public education system in Quebec had achieved its final form up to the reforms of the recent Lesage and Levesque governments. There were two parallel denominational systems which provided an elementary education to all who wished to attend. While there was a centralized administrative and supervisory system there was also much local autonomy. The clergy were influential in both but especially, exceptionally perhaps, in the Catholic system where the local curé was very powerful. There was primarily lay control in the Protestant institutions and lay teachers there were the norm. In the Catholic system the presence of the Church remained a powerful one and the teaching staff included a high percentage of priests and religious orders. The curriculum provided for basic literacy through teaching of the three R's but exceptional importance was given to the teaching of religion. In the case of the Protestant schools this was more instruction in morals with scripture reading, bible stories and hymn singing. The Catholic system included to a higher degree doctrinal instruction as well. There was an attempt to instill strong loyalty to the respective denominations — something more difficult in the Protestant case because there were several denominations involved. This pluralism was enshrined in law although it applied only to these Christian groups. Others such as members of the Jewish faith were denied these rights. While the general population was slower than people in the rest of Canada to take advantage of the opportunity of schooling, by 1910 there were just as many children in elementary school on a per capita basis as there were in the rest of the nation. The retention rate however was lower, partly because secondary education was not free (Magnuson, 1980).

The secondary system which evolved in Quebec was somewhat different. While there were public high schools there were large numbers of private schools and classical colleges in both the Protestant and especially the Catholic system. These were fee-charging institutions and the students generally lived in residence. The Catholic classical colleges were usually run by priests, frequently members of religious orders. Besides strong emphasis on the classics they gave considerable importance to philosophy and theology. Those who finally received the baccalaureate were prepared for a career in the priesthood, the law, medicine, politics or teaching, but required further education for the professions. Contrary to popular opinion, there were tracks in some of these colleges which provided training in other areas as well — business and technical education especially (Magnuson, 1980).

The post-secondary level consisted especially of McGill and Bishops for the Protestant system and the University of Laval, University of Montreal, and major seminaries for the Catholics. The baccalaureate permitted entrance. Graduation from local high schools sometimes did as well.

The position of females in the Quebec education system was somewhat anomalous. Even in colonial days the religious orders of women, especially the Ursulines and the Congregation of Notre Dame, provided convent training for girls. Large numbers of women, compared to men, were literate (Johnson, 1968). However, it was not really until modern times that an integrated system of schooling which followed the regular curriculum was made available to women. The situation was somewhat different in the Protestant and Catholic systems. The Church was highly suspicious of higher education for Catholic girls. It was felt that their position should be in the home, and education would provide obstacles to this. Only in 1899 did the École Normale Jacques Cartier open its doors to female students, and the first classical college for girls, Collège Marguerite Bourgeoys, was not opened until 1908. Laval University would still not admit female students at that time.

In the Protestant system the situation was somewhat better. The McGill Normal School admitted females from its beginning in 1857, but only in 1884 did the university open its doors to women for degrees. Nevertheless, university preparation for females was more advanced than for the Catholic majority. For these reasons some young ladies left the province, going to the United States or France, for a university education (Magnuson, 1980).

> By the middle of the twentieth century Quebec had fallen below the national average in almost all educational criteria: money spent on education, qualifications of teachers, pupil-teacher ratios and pupil retention rates. In the lay areas of teacher qualifications and the percentage of children in school, Quebec was dead last among the ten provinces in 1958. Not only did Quebec fare poorly interprovincially, but Catholic Quebec was way behind Protestant Quebec in most categories (Magnuson, 1980:76).

There were complex reasons for this, including the unrelenting opposition of the Church to state control and the relative poverty of rural Quebec. The tide of public opinion began to change in mid-century and it was this which ushered in the Quiet Revolution.

The introduction of educational reform followed the final report of the Royal Commission of Inquiry on Education (the Parent Commission) in 1966. It was highly critical of the existing system, condemning ". . . the elitist character of education, the appalling lack of coordination in the administration of education, the overemphasis on literary knowledge at the expense of scientific and practical studies, the outdated and authoritarian classroom procedures and insufficient spending on education" (Magnuson, 1980:107).

In 1964 a Ministry of Education was created, the first for over a century. This resulted in centralization and radical lessening of the power of the Protestant and Catholic Committees. These were reduced to an advisory position restricted to the confessional or religious aspect of the schools. The reform which followed was pedagogical rather than curricular at the elementary level. "At the heart of the secondary school reform was the extension of education from four to five years and the remaking of secondary school from a differentiated to a comprehensive one" (Magnuson, 1980:110). As a result a new institution came into being, *collèges d'enseignement général et professionnél* (CEGEPs). These were designed as an intermediate stage between the secondary and university levels. They offered a two-year academic course designed for those aspiring to a university and a three-year vocational course for those who intended to enter the work force directly. Most of the existing specialized institutions including classical colleges were incorporated into this new institutional form, and only 20 per cent of the previously existing classical colleges remained by 1972. A student preparing for university admission was now required to take 13 years of school, the last two in CEGEPs. At the same time the universities reduced their undergraduate programs from four to three years (Magnuson, 1978).

It is still too early to evaluate the effects of the Quiet Revolution on schooling in Quebec. Almost certainly it will promote a reduction in inequality because any student prepared to do so may advance to the university level without paying a fee. The elitist character of secondary education, from that perspective, will have now disappeared. At the same time the prestige of the vocational or technical track probably will remain low and the enrollment therein of working-class children will likely be disproportionately large.

## Interpretation

By 1871 free and compulsory schooling had been introduced in Ontario, with some 85 per cent of the children attending (Davey, 1978). Schooling was free throughout the rest of anglophone Canada and in Quebec although the compulsory aspect had not yet been introduced. Before this time the absence of publicly financed education did not mean the absence of schooling or of literacy. Formal education was hardly required for upward mobility. The illiteracy which did exist was spread throughout the various classes although it may have been somewhat higher among the poor (Schecter, 1977).

The introduction of formal education may be regarded as a newly evolving form of social and cultural reproduction (Harp, 1980). The higher level of education was available only to a limited number of the more privileged members of society. For them it was largely a status variable, initiating a new form of status boundary. For the lower classes who occupied a position on the other side of this emerging boundary, schooling was to provide primarily the ability to read, write and cipher to a limited degree, abilities which had earlier been learned in the family and at work. Eventually it was to become a class variable in the sense that formal education became a condition for advancing in the occupational world, although as a boundary mechanism it would continue to remain important.

The early reformers, especially Ryerson and the school promoters in Ontario and Forrester in Nova Scotia were conscious of the potential for conflict between the two great classes. For them there was an important distinction not only between civilized and savage societies, but within a society between the respectable classes and the lower order (Prentice, 1977). There is no indication that schooling was being introduced in order to break down that barrier. On the contrary, the early reformers openly acknowledged that the basic purpose of education was for social control (Schecter, 1977), a process which would appease the members of the lower class and make manageable class conflict. This was the fundamental argument used by Ryerson for so many years in promoting free and compulsory schooling (Fiorino, 1978; McDonald, 1978), as it had been used in the United States. There was at least latent conflict between the classes, and with the evolution of industrialism, already well under way in Ontario, a new social institution was required to control such conflict. Ryerson, as cited by Graff (1978:198), spoke of the necessity of instilling moral principles (respect, obedience, acquiescence) in the students of the common schools to prevent them from ". . . hating those that are above them, and desirous of reducing all to (their) own level."

The schools then would be the promoters of peace in a one-sided campaign. They would encourage the workers to assume the values of the upper classes. There was economic, ethnic and sexually based inequality in the existing social order (Graff, 1978), and education was to promote integration without changing the system of power, privilege and prestige. Ostensibly to eliminate crime, indolence and poverty, schooling was to pursue this dream (and fail to attain it) without defining these issues or investigating their causes. Imposing on everyone a value system which gave privilege to the few and struggle to the many, it emphasized respect for property and authority, legitimating the prevailing political system and the highly ascriptive social order (Harp, 1980).

The family is the principal institution for primary socialization. It is in this informal setting that the early value system is learned. In a society characterized by marked intergenerational inequality the values and attitudes of families of one class may be considerably different from those of others according to their respective positions in the social hierarchy (Kohn, 1969). Schooling has become the primary agency of secondary socialization. One of its principal functions is to integrate different subunit (family, ethnic group, etc.) value systems into a functioning whole (Parsons, 1959; Bowles and Gintis, 1976). There is general agreement on this even if not on the problem of why this is so.

Schooling was to begin to replace some of the functions which had earlier been provided by the Church, especially this kind of integrative process which we have discussed. During the period of changeover there was much conflict between the Church and the state, the resolution of which took many years to complete, especially in the province of Quebec where Catholicism was so strong.

The emergence of mass education is more closely in accord with a conflict model than a functionalist model of society. With few exceptions it was imposed on society by a privileged elite, men especially who were assuming greater influence because of involvement in or support for a new economic base, that of industrial capitalism. One of the principal functions of the state in a capitalist society is to create a climate favourable to the economic elite (Panitch, 1980). As the institution of schooling grew, it was eventually dominated by the state through its bureaucratic structure. This process occurred rather rapidly in anglophone Canada, more slowly in Quebec.

In the functionalist theory the principal functions of schooling are integration and selection (Parsons, 1959). Integration refers to a process of socialization which instills in societal members a common value system. Selection is concerned with the process of choosing the most suitable candidates to fulfill various societal roles, especially though not exclusively in the adaptive or economic realm. In theory, this selection is performed on the basis of ability and merit, and those who are selected for roles which are more important for society or more difficult to fulfill are rewarded more generously (Davis and Moore, 1953). As this new institution of socialization emerged, it is not apparent that it did so in accord with this functionalist model.

In a conflict model of society the functions of formal education are quite different: legitimation and allocation along class lines. This terminology has been articulated more thoroughly by neo-Marxists but it suits a Weberian conflict model as well. Legitimation refers to the process of justifying the prevailing system of inequality which in Marxist thought has a class (economic) base. Allocation is the process of choosing societal roles in accord with one's class (Marxists) or socioeconomic status (Weberians) so that the more privileged positions remain or are kept for the more privileged group. Allocation is not based on ability or merit but on some ascriptive feature. Thus the children of antagonistic classes or status groups receive societal roles which are generally in accord with or parallel to the roles occupied by their families of origin. As schooling emerged in Canada it seemed more closely in accord with this conflict model, although in the sociology of education the matter is still open to debate.

We may categorize the socialization which the school promoters in Canada advocated for this new institution as political, economic and moral. In practice the three overlap and it is rather difficult to discuss one independently of the others.

We have seen that the establishment of universal compulsory schooling came about not without difficulty. As noted, early education in Canada was accompanied by much religious conflict. Religion tends to be a conservative institution, socializing into and legitimating the prevailing system. Conflict between denominations results from competing efforts at maintaining control. A denomination which is successful in this struggle is in a position of having considerable influence over members of society who are active in other institutional arenas, even if frequently the process is reversed.

John Strachan was the most important early figure in the evolution of schooling in Ontario. A leading member of the Anglican establishment which itself was most influential in the political forum, Strachan was largely responsible for founding grammar schools primarily for the group of elites, and later, secondary and post-secondary institutions as well. It was partially because of the non-Anglican majority, made up largely of dissenters for whom Ryerson was to become a principal spokesman, that the District Public School Act of 1807 (authorizing the establishment of eight grammar schools) was followed by the 1816 Act authorizing common schools, the latter being less generously funded. The conflict between the Anglicans, who may be regarded as the remnants of the aristocracy — a class in decline — and the dissenters and Roman Catholics was more basic than that which appears in the promotion of schooling. There was political struggle for the control of the government as well. In the end the Family Compact lost its dominant position and it was the emerging class of entrepreneurs and industrialists which became most influential. In the Ryerson years this group came to control the state, or at least to have great influence on it, and with it, the educational bureaucracy.

In the Province of Quebec the religious conflict was between the English-Protestant minority and the French-Catholic majority. As in Upper Canada the dominant position of the Anglicans relative to other Protestant groups was in decline, but that group had become very powerful after the conquest and remained so for many years. The basis of the conflict there took much longer to resolve despite the co-existing denominational system which emerged. In some cases the conflict remains overt even today, more so than in most other areas of Canada, even if the basis has become more a linguistic-cultural one rather than religious. The essential point to bear in mind, for all of Canada as it existed in the nineteenth century, is that the religious institutions were involved not exclusively because religious values were so different (despite the rhetoric they were not), but largely because these religious factions were struggling for a controlling position in society. In Quebec the Catholics were overwhelmingly dominant in the rural areas. Schooling beyond literacy would not have strengthened the position of the institutional church. It is more likely that it would have encouraged larger numbers to migrate to the cities where the English-Protestant influence was stronger. Traditional Catholic strength was in the rural and agricultural base. Nor did the Catholic hierarchy encourage its people to read widely. The modern liberal ideas, often anti-clerical, which were becoming popular in Europe and America, were soon to be condemned by the official Church. Support for mass education beyond literacy would endanger this position. The system of classical colleges provided suffi-cient graduates for the professions, especially the clergy. There was little need for more than this in the rural areas. Traditionally basic literacy had been taught in the home during a more convenient seasonal schedule. At an early age the children were given many responsible chores which contributed signif-icantly to family income. Quebec did not experience the need of a disciplined work force in the same way or to the degree that it was being perceived as a requirement for industrialism in Ontario.

Economic socialization was tied to political socialization. The changing economy was to function within a political order and it was essential that the political system be sound. This was not the case in Upper or Lower Canada at the time of the 1837 rebellion. In Ontario at the beginning of the nineteenth century the economy was still closely tied to the land but change was in the wind. As the century moved on industrialism began to emerge, and after confederation the national policy was to give it added strength. Large numbers of immigrants, especially Irish, provided the essential labour for the emerging factory system. Two features were required if the transition was to be a smooth one: a stable and supportng political order and a passive or quiescent work force. Schooling was to contribute to both.

The changeover from a land-based economy with the remnants of an aristocracy to industrial capitalism required modified political values, espe-cially representative government in which the emerging middle class would have an appropriate influence. With the union of Canada East and Canada West after the 1837 rebellion, government was moving from a system of appointment to one of election. This transition became complete with confed-eration. The working classes, swelled by immigration, were numerically dom-inant and it was essential that their political clout correspond with factors favorable to the emerging industrial system. McDonald (1978) contends that Ryerson and the other school promoters understood this very well and that an integral part of their educational reform was to develop a system of schooling where the appropriate political socialization would come about.

Ryerson was concerned that mass support for the established political system was on the decline, especially after the rebellion of 1837. Fearing any form of republicanism such as the one existing in the United States, deeply concerned with a perceived diminishing respect for authority, he advocated a system in which the colony, with responsible government, would be a loyal handmaiden of the Crown.

The period of the 1830's and 1840's was a difficult one in Upper Canada. The influence of the appointed Executive or Legislative Councils was gradu-ally giving way to an elected Assembly and eventually to Parliament as we know it now. Ryerson and his followers felt that the authoritative function of political appointees was an important one. It would safeguard Christian morality as they understood it, and loyalty to the empire, factors conducive to the emergence of industrialism. Ryerson was a keen observer of political events taking place in Europe. Although anti-aristocratic, the last thing he wanted was popular democracy; he was anti-democratic as well. In a letter to Higgenson on April 30, 1845 (McDonald, 1978:88-89), he wrote: "My leading idea has been . . . not only to impart to the public mind the greatest amount of useful knowledge based upon, and interwoven throughout with sound Christian principles, but to render the Educational system . . . the indirect but powerful instrument of British Constitutional Government." Such a system would maintain a stable society without radical democratic ideas. This would have important results for the propertied classes. They would have a supportive political regime and a quiescent work force, one with 'sound Christian principles.' In return for their support for a free and then a compulsory school system, paid for by taxation where those with property would inevitably pay more, Ryerson promised a stable and loyal citizenry. The schools would not point out that the interests of working-class youth were in conflict with those of the propertied classes. In them these children would learn their 'place,' would become manageable. It was not the purpose of education, as envisioned by the school promoters, to guaranteee the working classes an effective democratic voice but rather to make them subjects in a political and economic setting which gave rewards disproportionately to someone else. The emphasis was on authority rather than reason. The last thing Ryerson wanted was to establish the practice of students questioning the system which was, for him, divinely ordained. There is overwhelming evidence which demonstrates "Ryerson's belief in the power of the school to mould character and support attitudes" (McDonald, 1978:95). He cried out for free and later compulsory schooling in which these values would be taught. It was essential to mould the minds of the young along the lines of Christianity as he, Ryerson, saw it, and in line with the wishes of the crown. "Clearly, from the outset, he saw the office of superintendent in a political context extending far beyond the parameters of his commission to structure a system of public education" (McDonald, 1978:85). The established system included the monarchy, the emerging middle class whose source of wealth was now becoming industrial investment, and a working class which frequently barely subsisted. The outcasts were the idle poor, the delinquents and criminals whose position, he felt, was the result of ignorance and improper family and ethnic socialization.

It is apparent then that the school promoters, at least in Ontario but almost certainly in other areas as well, viewed schooling as a necessary institution whose principal function was to exercise this measure of social control. Such a system should be an ". . . instrument to guarantee an orderly and stable society capable of containing any widespread acceptance of radical democratic ideas" (McDonald, 1978:91). Disagreeing with the earlier American model where schools were responsible to the community, Ryerson was to insist on a centralized element where they would be subservient to the state which, in Canada, has never been strong in providing benefits to the working class (Panitch, 1980).

There were other facets of existing society which the promoters of schooling soundly condemned. They included pauperism, vice and crime. These were opposed to disciplined work habits and respect for property, and the function of schooling was in part to overcome the ignorance from which, reputedly, these evils had sprung.

"In a period of massive social change, of urban-industrial modernization, education was increasingly seen as a dominant tool for social stability in societies where stratification by social class had replaced traditional paternalistic control by rank and deference" (Graff, 1978:187). In that system the position of the workers frequently was very difficult. In the urban areas there was little security. Employment was often temporary and sporadic. Income was low and many lived at a bare subsistence level. Under such trying circumstances it was essential to have institutions ". . . like the school, to aid in the inculcation of restraint, order, discipline and integration: the correct rules for social and economic behaviour in a changing and modernizing context" (Graff, 1978:187). If the appeal for the inculcation of good working habits (from the viewpoint of the industrialist) was not as direct as it was in Massachusetts it was no less real. The promoters continually waged war on idleness, indolence and crime, holding that schools would instill in the pupils industry, discipline and honesty with the appropriate respect for authority which would ensure that working-class children would fit easily and smoothly into the new industrial system (Schecter, 1977). In his early years Ryerson time after time thundered that poverty and crime were the result of ignorance. His claim was that mass education would overcome these evils, and he manipulated statistics from many nations to make his point. Later in his tenure, when it became more evident that the relationship was not so simple, he excused the schools and blamed the parents for not sending their children often enough, that is, a sufficient number of days and years.

The focus and overemphasis on schooling effectively obscured the role of other factors contributing to criminal behaviour. These included ethnic discrimination, especially against the Irish whether Protestant or Catholic, occupational level, and sex. Those who advocated schooling were less clear on how it would eradicate crime and delinquency if such other structural factors remained. It is correct that criminality was associated with literacy, as Graff (1978:202) notes, ". . . but the clearest patterns of successful prosecutions relate directly to ethnic affiliation, occupational class, and sex, when the effects of literacy are controlled." Moreover, at least around London, Ont., the well educated equalled the illiterates in number of arrests and it was inequality in the prevailing system of privilege which was the real basis of conviction for delinquency, vagrancy and crime. Neither Ryerson nor his followers accepted that there were structural factors such as economic inequality and the various forms of discrimination which were causal variables in explaining crime. Ignorance resulted in poverty, poverty in criminal behaviour, was the cry. And so the claim was that overcoming this ignorance would reverse these conditions and the benefits would go to all (Graff, 1978). Schecter (1977:376) aptly cites from an address by Forrester, Nova Scotia's Minister of Education delivered around 1860:

> . . . the real advancement of any country, depends on the intelligence, the skill, the industrial and moral habits of its inhabitants. . . . Or, to speak without a figure, pauperism, and vice, and crime will, to the extent to which these qualities are diffused, be comparatively unknown. . . . And the result of this . . . will be the increased and the ever increasing value of property . . . all will be benefitted — the labourer, the tradesman, the farmer, the manufacturer, the rich and the poor, the learned and the unlearned.

In retrospect it is easy to see how illusory these claims were, especially for Nova Scotia which has had an unusually high rate of poverty ever since.

In concluding this introductory chapter we would like to acknowledge that this interpretation of the development of schooling in Canada has not only been brief but has been restricted to the east, that part of the nation which first entered confederation. Eastern Canada, especially Ontario, in many respects served as a model for the evolving educational systems of the west, but there were and are regional differences which the specialist should pursue. The star of the western provinces shines with a bright light in this nation today, but that part of Canada was much more of a frontier society during the years with which we have been concerned. We have seen no evidence that our description of inequality is not applicable, in a general way, to all ten provinces and the Territories which make up this land.

Katz (1973) accurately noted that the introduction of free and compulsory schooling in Canada was not a reform meant to benefit the working classes, the poor and uneducated, the people in need. It was to legitimate a system of intergenerational inequality, and to control those who were being exploited by the developing industrial system of capitalism. It was imposed by those who, disproportionately, were reaping the rewards in order to render the system secure. Not until the second half of the century did even a minority of Canadians become conscious of the inequalities in formal education suffered by the working classes and the poor. Much of the remainder of this book will demonstrate that such systematic inequality remains.

# Part I

# General Considerations

In this second section we will deal with a number of general considerations which are basic in the study of the sociology of education. In a broad sense they are concerned with theoretical issues. In chapter 2 we present a resume of theory, covering especially the various paradigms which apply to the institution of schooling. We then deal, in chapter 3, with the meaning and measurement of intelligence, and with the reliability and validity of I.Q. testing. We are especially concerned with this issue because, as we shall see, intelligence is socially defined and we want to understand the implications this has for schooling. In chapter 4 we present some of the various theories of learning, and are concerned primarily with social learning theory. We also look at the meaning and importance of motivation, and comment on development and maturation.

We give much greater emphasis to the material developed in Part I than is traditional in a course in the sociology of education. It is our opinion that a foundation in these basic areas is a prerequisite to understanding the causes of social differences which occur in schooling.

*2*

# Theory
# in the Sociology
# of Education

## Introduction

### The Meaning and Importance of Theory

The student who is as yet unsophisticated in the discipline of sociology has a tendency to view the study of "theory" with some anxiety. In many cases the casual reader may have visions of complexity, a rigorous logic, and a high degree of abstraction which have little justification in fact. If such anxieties do exist, we would like to dispel them at once. The matter to be presented in this chapter is not complex and has a relatively low level of abstraction.

The science of sociology in each of its subdisciplines is concerned not only, and not especially, with a mere description of the relationships which exist in the pertinent area of interest. We are even more concerned with establishing the nature of the relationship and the causal components involved. When we come to observe that some particular behaviour or specific kind of interaction is regularly present we want to be able to explain *why* this is so. What is the *cause* of the regularity which is seen, and why are there exceptions (this is generally the case) to a general rule?

It is this aspect of sociology with which we are dealing in any consideration of theory. "A *theory* is a statement based on observed facts that explains what is supposed to be a causal relationship between those facts" (Spencer, 1979:30-31). Spencer quite properly inserts the conditional element "is supposed to be" because theory in sociology never has the certitude of law which is a universally correct and demonstrated relationship.

### Social Stratification and the Sociology of Education

The sociology of education is essentially the scientific study of social interaction as it pertains to the institution of education or of schooling. In that study, education, which takes place within the institutional setting, may be both a dependent and an independent variable. The nature of the institution, the process of learning, the topics which are deemed appropriate in the curriculum are all both the cause and the effect of broader social issues and social settings. Whatever else may be said about education being temporarily held in the background, that which is learned is some kind of an asset, in the sense that the subject did not before have this newly learned item, this new form of organization, this new style of life. Assets come to us not only as individuals but also as members of groups. In the history of virtually every known society assets are disbursed unevenly. It happens that more is usually distributed to one kind of position or group and less to another. It is also usual, in the sense of being the norm, of being regular, that this differential distribution is passed on in a patterned and socially constructed manner over a series of generations.

The study of the intergenerational distribution of whatever is of value in a society is that branch of sociology known as *social stratifications*. The sociology of education may be regarded as a subsection of this particular area of our discipline. Even though it has become very prominent in the last two decades, in many ways theory in the sociology of education is but a more specialized application of the theory of social stratification. It is essential then that the student interested in the sociology of education understand the basic concepts, distinctions, paradigms, models, which have been developed in the stratification area of the discipline.

Rossides (1976:15) gives a working definition of social stratification, noting that it ". . . is a hierarchical configuration of families (and in industrial societies in recent decades, unrelated individuals) who have differential access to whatever is of value in the society at a given point and over time, primarily because of social, not biopsychological, variables." Education is one asset which is valued in modern societies, usually quite highly. Families and other social groups which are hierarchically arranged do have differential access to the process of education and to the rewards it brings, and they do pass on these privileges to some extent to their children. We are interested in this broad range of theory on stratification, and we are particularly interested in refining it in the measure that it pertains in a special way to the institution of education. Why does this unequal distribution occur?

There are other areas of sociological theory which are important as well, but these will be treated somewhat superficially here. The institution of schooling may be viewed as a complex organization and that branch of theory is also pertinent. Some aspects of social psychological theory are also critical, such as the theory of the development of self-concept. At this point we will generally overlook such branches, where appropriate dealing with them in a particular chapter, and restrict ourselves principally to that aspect of sociological theory which is concerned with the intergenerational transmission of inequality, that is, of differential or preferential access to whatever is of value in society, with particular reference to the institution of education.

To put the matter more succinctly, the sociology of education has become a particularly important forum for the investigation of the social phenomenon of inequality as it manifests itself in unequal access to schooling. This results only partially from unequal ability, motivation and aspiration, and it causes unequal privilege, prestige, and power in later life as a result. In investigating those theories which deal with stratification, with the patterned intergenerational transmission of inequality, Murphy (1979) in an excellent recent work assesses that body of theory under three broad models, each of which contains overlapping, and at the same time, peculiar insights. This presentation, adopted also by many other authors, includes (1) functionalism, (2) conflict theory, and (3) interaction theory. We will generally follow that typology in the remainder of this chapter.

There are basically two models of society. The one (functional model) follows a liberal ideology which sees society as being good but not too good. Like a living organism, the social structure changes slowly, and not radically, and tends to adapt to the environment in such a way that long-term change leads to a somewhat higher order on an evolutionary scale. Society is not perfect; but it is integrated and in general it provides for its members in a satisfactory and continually improving way. The other perspective (conflict model) disavows any real similarity between the social structure and a living organism. The parts are not integrated, and in general the needs (or wants) of only the elites are met in a satisfactory way. This disproportionate distribution of privilege results because human behaviour is explained in terms of self-interest and coercion. The coercion is the result of the use of *power* which is sometimes legitimated (authority) and sometimes is not. Whether it is legitimated or not is relatively unimportant because the authoritative relationships themselves are merely the consequence of an earlier deception and the abuse of power (Scimecca, 1980:11-13).

There are, of course, many variations of the functional and conflict approach, and we will give attention more to similarities than to differences. Both approaches, however, have one important common factor. They regard social organization as something objective, something which is 'out there' and is real. It has a meaning in itself, and a life of its own, regardless of the position of the observer. There is another and much more subjective approach to the study of society which we may broadly refer to as *interactionism*. This view is concerned especially with the relationships which exist between society and the individual, and it views social organization in a much more relative or subjective manner. Here one is concerned with how members of a social group define a given situation differently, and with the methods used by one individual or group to determine that a given situation be defined in a specific way by another. This definition may vary from that which is being held by other members of the group. What specific meaning does it have? How did this come about, and why is this so?

These are some of the concerns to be found in the perspective which we broadly refer to as interactionism, and which includes *symbolic interactionism, ethnomethodology and phenomenology*. There have been exciting advances made in this broad area within the past decade, and this whole approach is sometimes referred to as *the new sociology of education*. In reality its roots are not new at all, and may be traced to such early thinkers as Simmel, Weber, Durkheim, James, Cooley, Mead, Park (Turner, 1978) and to others including Mannheim. Much more emphasis has been given to this perspective lately, especially in Britain. It had not been widely used either in stratification theory or in the sociology of education until this past decade. While important advances are being made, it is perhaps premature to regard interactionism as an integrated perspective. One may confidently expect that such an integrated presentation is not far away. Moreover these different approaches are not mutually exclusive. Sociology benefits from both.

In the remainder of this chapter we will examine first Functionalism, then the Conflict Model. We will then present the theory which we refer to as critical functionalism, which may be regarded as an attempted synthesis of the two. Finally, we will discuss briefly the perspective of symbolic interactionism. We will review the underlying stratification theory, then the more specialized application of this general theory to the institution of schooling. As a final note, we will indicate some of the more pertinent Canadian contributions to each position.

## Functionalism

### General Characteristics

Functionalism is a relatively recent body of theory of social stratification. Its more remote pioneers were early sociologists such as Comte and Durkheim, or social anthropologists such as Malinowski and Radcliff-Brown (Vanfossen, 1979:23). Often referred to as Structural Functionalism, it emphasizes the function played by the patterned structure of social roles. Sometimes, but less frequently, it is called the consensual model, because it emphasizes a consensus or agreement on the part of the members of society. Among the principal modern contributors are Talcott Parsons (1953) and Kingsley Davis and William E. Moore (1945) in the stratification area, and Parsons (1959), Parsons and Platt (1973), Clark (1962), Merton (1968) and Trow (1961) in the more specialized area of the sociology of education.

Functionalism, in practice, is not one simplified theory on which all contributors agree. There are variations, areas of overlap and of disagreement. In presenting its principal characteristics we must be aware of that and not assume that all theorists agree with any one presentation or any general survey. For example, Parsons' (1953) analysis, as well as that of Davis and Moore (1945), tends to be on an extreme macro level, very general, meant to apply to every known society. Robert Merton (1968), another important contributor, gives emphasis to a middle-range level of analysis, somewhat intermediate between Parsons' grand theory and individual empirical studies.

### The Meaning of Structure and Function

A general summary of functionalism would include the following characteristics. Society may be regarded somewhat as a living organism. The parts of that organism, especially those composed of institutionalized systems of roles called *structure,* tend to work in close conjunction with one another. The institutions of society, especially the major ones such as the family, religion, or the economy, have a cooperative or symbiotic relationship with one another in order to meet the needs of all. The provision of such needs is referred to as the *function* of the particular constellation of roles. Perhaps the institution of the family is one of the better examples. In it there are usually the roles of the father, mother, and child. Every society has some kind of family system, and its principal function is the socialization or enculturation of the newer members being born into the society. There must be some institution to fulfill this function, for without enculturation there would be no predictable patterns of interaction, and hence, society would be in constant confusion and turmoil, and could not survive. The other major institutions (the economy, the government) work in a cooperative relationship with the family and not in opposition to it, and vice versa. With change in the environment there is more or less smooth adaptation in each in order to meet the needs of all.

### Society as a stable organism

Society, in this theory, is viewed as a kind of organism which is basically stable. Functionalists do not deny instability but regard it in lesser light, and assume that every society tends towards equilibrium or homeostasis. The institutionalized roles or the culturally accepted pattern of roles provides for this stability, and the institutions in which these roles are set are continually evolving in a way which ensures such stability in a constantly changing world, at least over an extended period of time. The stability is not perfect, especially on a short-term basis, and this accounts for dysfunctions — interactions which move the social group away from equilibrium. Despite temporary stresses, in the long run, stability is maintained.

### Priority Among Roles and Inequality of Rewards

The members of society share values, and there is a generally regarded hierarchy of such values. This sharing is referred to as *consensus,* and is a part of the process of socialization. Some positions in society are regarded as being more important than others,or require more skill to fulfill, or longer periods of training, or greater risk or dedication, or have more people depending on them. In order to ensure that the roles which provide such functions are fulfilled well, by the more capable and more properly motivated people, society rewards these positionsin an unequal manner with those things which are acknowledged to be of value. As a result, some constellations of roles receive more of things which are universally valued than do others. The advantages which result from this, making some more privileged than others, may be differentially passed on to succeeding generations. This inheritance is not only a matter of the transmission of material advantage in the form of wealth but it includes with it the transmission of values, attitudes, life styles, and motivation. This in turn allows the succeeding generation to take up positions in society which also will be rewarded in a privileged way for the same reasons. Thus there arises the phenomenon of social stratification, the hierarchical ordering of groups who pass on their privileges intergenerationally. In the functionalist theory this social process of differential evaluation and reward, including intergenerational transmission, is a necessary feature of society because without it the more important or the more difficult and demanding roles would not be fulfilled. Hence, stratification is functional for all.

### The Meritocratic and Technocratic Perspective

In the funcionalist view the major basis for advancing to more highly evaluated roles is achievement. As society continually evolves into higher forms the requirements for fulfilling such roles are presumed to be more advanced, requiring greater levels of skill. Hence, in functionalist theory society is generally referred to today (in the more developed nations, like Canada) as meritocratic and technocratic. By meritocratic, we mean that a person merits his role on the basis of achievement rather than ascription, as the result of universalistic or impartial treatment. The technocratic society is simply one where role occupants are required to have a high level of technological skill.

It is through socialization that the members of society are prepared for their different roles. In this process, education may be viewed in a broad way — wherever there is teaching and learning in life — or in a more restricted sense. In this latter case, it is restricted to the formal domain of schooling, from kindergarten to the highest level of graduate or professional school. It is with this formal and specialized institutional setting that we are concerned in the sociology of education. The teaching and learning which occur here include the substantive elements of the curriculum, and also values, attitudes, and life styles which are considered to be appropriate for the particular adult roles which are to be assumed. There are various institutions through which this process may be accomplished, especially the family, but in modern society the responsibility for this element of the socialization process has been differentiated out of the family to a substantial degree and allocated to the institution of schooling. As society has evolved to a greater level of complexity formal education has assumed an increasingly important role. Today, in Canada, and in most of the industrial societies, it is virtually impossible for a member of society to assume an adult role which is highly rewarded without a substantial amount of formal education.

## Functionalist Perspectives in the Sociology of Education

Murphy (1979:13) points to four themes which are prominent in functionalist theory as applied to the sociology of education. These focus, first, on the role of formal education in the evolution of modern society from particularism to universalism and from ascription to achievement, and also the role of the school in selecting the more capable candidate for specific adult roles. A second theme investigates the dysfunctions of the formal education system for many groups in the perpetuation of some form of inequality. A third is the debate about the biological or biopsychological influence as opposed to the social or environmental one in the formulation of I.Q. This is the heredity-environment controversy (to be treated in a separate chapter), and includes problems of validity related to the theoretical versus the operational definitions of intelligence. The fourth theme, largely empirical in nature, is a study of ". . . the relative functional autonomy of the parts of a social system' (Murphy, 1979:13), and concentrates on the ability of formal education, as opposed to other societal institutions such as social class, to reduce inequality or, conversely, to enhance or replicate it. The theoretical issues involved in these themes are relatively straightforward but the validity of each body of theory is dependent on the validity of the functionalist theory on which it is based. In this chapter we will concentrate on the first two themes; the third and fourth will be treated in Chapters 3, 11 and 12.

### School: The Focal Socialization Agency

The most influential theoretician on the formal role of the school in society, particularly American society, is Talcott Parsons (1959), whose writings may be regarded as generally representative of the entire functionalist approach (Scimecca, 1980:7). Parsons does a masterful job of pointing out the fundamental function of both primary and secondary education as an intermediate institution between early family socialization and adult role selection and performance. In this regard, Parsons sees two overriding functions of the school: (1) leading the child from a particularistic to a universalistic and from an ascriptive to an achievement orientation, and (2) selection or differential allocation to unequally rewarded adult roles. He emphasizes especially the primary grades because the entire process begins there, and is not usually reversed at a later stage. Parsons' entire presentation is contingent on the validity of the functionalist assumptions in general and on the reality of equality of opportunity (but not of ability or motivation) in particular. This is a major problem in the entire functionalist perspective.

Parsons recognizes that there are other agencies which are involved in the socialization process during the school years, including the family and many voluntary organizations. But of them all, during that period from entry into the first grade to entry into the labour force, the school is the focal socializing agency. The entire socialization function ". . . may be summed up as the development in individuals of the commitments and capacities which are essential prerequisites of their future role performance" (Parsons, 1959:70). These commitments are (1) to the broad values of society, and (2) to a specific role within the social structure. Parsons' functional analysis is based on what he refers to as a common value system, and on the necessity of somehow allocating persons to specific roles in society some of which have, or are evaluated as having, a more important or more demanding responsibility to perform. The school is the primary structure for instilling this common value system during these years, and for directing the individuals to the kind of adult role slots for which they are competent or have the proper degree of motivation.

### From Particularism to Universalism and From Ascription to Achievement

Parsons (1951) earlier had outlined a series of five orientations, called pattern variables, which members of society must learn for performing specific roles and for understanding and fitting into the structures of society. Two of these orientations are particularly relevant for that aspect of socialization which is differentiated out to the school system. These are universalism-particularism, and ascription-achievement. The first of these, universalism-particularism, is concerned with the degree of objectivity or objective standard used in the judgement of role performance. If the standards are purely or perfectly objective then we judge such a role to be universalistic. If the standards are subjective and impartiality is not required, the role is said to be particularistic. Obviously no role is either completely universalistic or completely particularistic; it is a matter of degree or orientation. The early family roles of son, daughter, sibling are largely particularistic. Adult occupational roles tend to be universalistic. The second of these orientations with which we are particularly concerned is ascription-achievement. This refers primarily to the requirements for role performance. Such requirements may be based on criteria which generally are not earned or merited but come to a person because of some special relationship such as race, sex or social class; or they may be based on criteria which are earned or merited in a competitive situation. The first is ascription, the second achievement. These also are a matter of degree, but modern liberal society is reputed to be largely achievement oriented. Roles in the family are more highly ascriptive.

It is the special function of the school to socialize the child from the particularistic and ascriptive orientations he is accustomed to in the home to the universalistic and achievement orientations which are more generally required in later life. Hence, from the first days in class the child is gradually "moved" in the direction of universalism and achievement. He finds that he is not given preference over his classmates in school as he is at home. Judgements by both peers and adults are based more and more on objective criteria in a competitive situation. All entrants begin at the same place and are expected to learn the same material, at least before the selection process begins. This is an institutionalized competitive situation where all have an equal opportunity to succeed or excel from the perspective of educational inputs.

### Differential Selection for Adult Roles

It is a primary function of the school to select those students who, because of greater ability or greater motivation, are more likely to succeed in the more important or more difficult adult roles in society. This is done on the basis of achievement. The school also allocates individuals in general patterns to major categories of adult roles so that one or another such category would not be over- or under-represented when the students enter the work force. In this way, through the processes of selection and allocation based on universalistic and achievement criteria the more able or more willing students are selected for the more important and more difficult roles, and a suitable supply of candidates is directed at other, even if less demanding, adult roles. This is functional; it fulfills a need for society.

### Equality of Opportunity

Parsons is not naive enough to suggest that all children bring with them to school an equal chance to succeed — hence his stress on equality of opportunity. He understands that selective processes have already been working in preschool socialization. These are the results of other institutional inputs, such as social class. It is not so much the function of the school to overcome such advantages, where they accrue differentially, as to ensure that students are treated universalistically or fairly, and to provide the opportunity for whatever kind of success they might achieve, or might be willing to achieve, in accord with the advantages and limitations they have. Many such advantages or limitations (commitments, capacities, abilities) have a prior social basis, and it is beyond the scope of the school, except in a general way, to attempt to overcome them. Nevertheless, children of equal ability and motivation should succeed equally well.

## Problems with the Functionalist Model

Parsons' theory is frequently accused of being a teleological explanation. It describes what the school does and uses that as an explanation for why it does it. We will review the opinion of some other theorists on this subsequently. At this point, it is important to emphasize that there are serious difficulties inherent in this position, although the solutions suggested by many critics are not without problems either. The theory does not explain well the "function" which schooling performs. It is one thing to claim — whether accurately or not — that intergenerational inequality is required for society to function. It is a different matter to suggest that the selection which is produced through schooling is that which fulfills a necessary function (Murphy, 1979).

Hurn (1978:38-42) points to other problems. It is very difficult to test this theory, especially in the macro level stratification aspects, and one of the desirable criteria for any good theory is that it be testable. Functionalist stratification theory simply has too many assumptions which are not demonstrable (Tumin, 1953; Buckley, 1958; Wrong, 1959; and Roach *et al*, 1969. Even in its application to the educational institution there are difficulties which are somewhat crippling. If advancement in schooling and allocation to adult roles are even approximately universalistic (fair, just), how does one explain institutionalized sexual, racial, and ethnic discrimination? Although we are not aware of any attempt to measure this, the amount of talent, sometimes of the greatest potential, which has been wasted or shelved in this way is probably astronomical. In the area of job performance we now know that most pertinent skills are learned "on the job" rather than in school (Berg, 1970). It is not simply that educational achievement selects those who are generally more capable of learning on the job. There is little or no correlation between college grades and occupational status (Hurn, 1978:38) when other pertinent variables such as social class are controlled. Presumably such grades are some reflection of ability, especially for those who are similar in other ways. Bowles and Gintis (1976) have demonstrated that they have almost no predictive value when social class is controlled. But the opposite is not the case. For those of equal ability (I.Q.) and achievement, social class is highly influential and predictive. The functionalist assumption of equality of opportunity breaks down.

Another problem with this theory is that the great increase in educational achievement which has occurred in the past thirty years has not provided more intergenerational mobility (Hurn, 1978:41). Boundaries between status groups have not diminished despite the great amount of educational inflation, something we cover more thoroughly in dealing with the critical functionalists.

As we indicated earlier, there are numerous other sociologists who have written from a functionalist perspective. Turner (1960) has pointed to the distinction between sponsored and contest mobility, noting the increased emphasis now given to the latter (especially in the United States, and presumably in Canada as well). Trow (1961) has shown how the recent evolution in the role of the secondary school performs a useful function, and Parsons and

Platt (1973) have written in a similar vein relative to higher education. Clark (1962) has made a convincing presentation on what is often referred to as technological functionalism, and those who have written in the human capital tradition have pointed to the advantages, to both individual and society, of investment in advanced education. It is probably not productive to examine these and similar contributions at this level in our enquiry. Where pertinent, we will introduce them in later chapters.

At this point, we would like to bridge the gap between the functionalist and conflict paradigms by introducing briefly some thoughts of Robert Merton, one who gives more emphasis to conflict even within the consensual model.

## Dysfunctions of Formal Education: Robert Merton

Robert Merton, another distinguished American sociologist, is a significant contributor to functionalism. His writings are more in line with what he himself refers to as middle-range theory, with a stronger acknowledgement of the pervasiveness of conflict. Merton basically accepts the assumptions of the functionalist model, particularly its tendency towards social order and equilibrium, but notes that society is far from a perfectly coordinated organism. That which promotes most of the needs of most of the people neglects or is incapable of providing major needs for certain groups or aggregates. There is a price to pay for equilibrium and this falls heavily on particular subgroups. This is the basis of the explanation of dysfunctions.

One of Merton's more important contributions is the distinction between manifest and latent functions. A *manifest* function is one which is broadly recognized, intended, overt and apparent. A *latent* function (often but not necessarily dysfunctional) is one which is not so broadly intended or perceived; it is more covert and may be an inevitable consequence of certain aspects of social organization which is not intended at all. Merton's (1968) classic study on social structure and anomie brings this out well. Society sets goals which may be too high and not universally attainable, and also prescribes institutionalized means for attaining these goals. One aggregate — the conformers — strives for the goals and uses the socially acceptable means. Frequently this is the majority, but it is inevitable that certain members accept the goals but reject the means (innovators), reject the goals but accept the means (ritualists), or reject both (retreatists). Merton also includes a category of rebels. The important point is that these adaptations are an inevitable consequence of social organization and except for the conformers are generally regarded as dysfunctional. They are also latent because they are not widely recognized and not consciously intended.

This emphasis on dysfunctions has been picked up by many theorists. Applied to the institution of schooling it points out that the goals of education (maximum mobility, affluence, etc.) are not universally available to all. Besides the conformers, there may be innovators (cheaters), ritualists (career students accepting schooling as an end in itself), retreatists (dropouts, hippies), and even rebels (deschoolers). This is an inevitable, even if not an intended, consequence. Much of the remainder of this book is an attempt to understand and determine the social influences directing students to each of the various categories or adaptations.

Nevertheless, Merton does see this particular form of social organization — in our case, education — as something which is essential for the well-being of society as a whole, even if it does bring undesirable consequences for certain subgroups. Although the emphasis on conflict is noticeable, the structures of society do develop in a way that permits it to function reasonably well and move or evolve towards a higher form of social organization. There are many theorists who reject this model completely, who do not regard society as a smoothly functioning (even if not perfect) and integrated whole. These are members of the conflict school, and it is to this model that we turn our attention now.

## The Conflict Model

### Introduction

There has been a remarkable resurgence in conflict theory in the field of sociology in the past generation. The theory itself is as old as pioneers like Marx and Weber, and existed in embryonic form since early philosophers speculated on social order. The functionalist theory had been particularly influential and enjoyed wide popularity in the period between the two Great Wars. Although it has by no means disappeared, there was a shift in emphasis during the decade of the fifties, and this became quite evident by the sixties.

There is a lesson in the sociology of knowledge here, although it is not our intention to develop it extensively. Weber had long since pointed out that there is no such thing as a value-free social science. There is a limited social context in which our knowledge is developed and organized, determining the manner in which it is passed on (Mannheim, 1952). The decades of the thirties and forties, despite the tragedy of the Second World War, were comparatively tranquil in the United States where academic social science had finally reached adulthood. In the sixties with the increased visibility of class conflict and economic colonialism, with the spread of race riots and increasing attention to the Vietnam War, political stability decreased and young academics, many still in graduate school and alive with humanistic motives, wanted to become involved. During this same period, French Canada, particularly Quebec, planned and then began to enforce major educational change which was indicative of a new political consciousness and a search for equal partnership or self-determination. Britain and Western Europe had experienced the threat of a total and potentially annihilating war brought on by the increasing antagonisms between the Soviet Union and the West.

Given this social climate, one best characterized as based on feelings of fear and suspicion on both the national and international level, it is not surprising that the assumptions of functionalism or consensualism fell into disrepute. Many academics wanted to become "involved", but liberal educational reform appeared to have little success. Conflict theory was reviewed. The early dormant presentations of orthodox Marxists became more widely read, and taught. The academic, if not the political, content of the writings of Marx became more respectable, and new insights developed by an increasingly respectable New Left began to flood the social science literature. Weber also was rediscovered. The result is a very prominent conflict paradigm of society which to some considerable extent has relegated functionalism to the rear. In this approach the intergenerational inequality which is so apparent in society is not perceived as something which is generally beneficial to all. It is the imposition of those who are in positions of power. Society is not regarded as a smoothly functioning organism tending to equilibrium. It is an area of conflict in which victory goes to the strong.

## The Marxist Model

Karl Marx has probably had a greater influence on the study of society and especially social class than any other individual. Like other great social scientists, such as Freud, Marx was an innovator and any assessment of his work should be made with that in mind. Central to Marx's teachings are three prominent issues: the materialist conception of history, economic determinism, and the relationship between the substructure — the economy — and the superstructure, the other major institutions of society. This includes the role of ideology.

### The Materialist Conception of History

Marx's view of society was essentially an evolutionary one resulting from the perception and meeting of material needs. This provided a framework for the interpretation of all historical events, an approach to the understanding of historical facts. Every society is characterized by some cooperation among its members, beginning with the initial cooperation required for family formation. As perceived needs were met new needs arose, and new kinds of cooperation were called for to meet them. Among these are what Marx referred to as *the social relations of production.* These relations were comprised of a normative system, a system of expectations about the way society's members were to behave. Most basic among societal needs were those related to the economy which was characterized by a specific kind of organization, some state of knowledge, science, and technology. Marx referred to this as the forces or *the mode of production,* while the social relations included the conditions of labour, the principles or ownership and distribution, and ideologies and systems of thought. History, in retrospect, may be divided into a number of evolutionary stages, each of which is characterized by a peculiar mode of production: the ancient, the asiatic, the feudal, and the capitalist stages. The forces of production are more dynamic than the relations of production, and in each stage the two eventually come into such conflict that a new stage results. The later stage will not appear until the earlier one has contributed all it can in the evolutionary development. The final stage is that of the communist utopia, and when that arrives no further qualitative evolution will unfold.

Economic Determinism: The Polarity of Class Relationships

In this process of evolution every individual falls into one of two basic categories. These are identified by the relationships people have to the means of production. There are the owners and those who work for them (slaves, serfs, labourers), groups which Marx characterized as the Oppressors and Oppressed. This relationship is the basis of Marx's theory of stratification, really a theory of social class, and it was always the economic realm which determined on which side of the relationship an individual was to be placed. This emphasis on the role of the economy is usually referred to as economic determinism.

In the capitalist mode of production — the one with which Marx was primarily concerned — the fundamental class relationship was that between the capitalist (owner of land, equipment, and money) and the wage labourer who owned little more than his ability to work. The economic power of the capitalists, whom Marx referred to as the bourgeoisie, allowed them to exploit the insecurity of the workers, called the proletariat. These two groups or classes were in fundamental opposition or conflict with one another. This class conflict may be sometimes latent, sometimes overt, but eventually the proletariat will become sufficiently well organized and will rise in revolt against the capitalist oppressor. In Marxist theory this is the beginning of the final societal stage, the utopia of communism. In this final stage there will be no classes. Property and the means of production will be collectively owned and all members of society will have the same relationship to production. Each will contribute according to his ability and each will receive according to his need. Work will no longer be alienating and the various kinds of leisure will be open to all.

For Marx then, a social class is defined on the basis of the relationship to production. There may be temporary intermediate classes such as the intelligentsia or the *petit bourgeoisie,* but the enduring classes in the capitalist system are the bourgeoisie and the proletariat. The relationship is fundamentally an economic one, and none of the other institutions of society (education, religion, law, the state) will change the class relationship in any substantial way. In fact, they support it.

### The Role of the Superstructure

These other institutions are referred to as the superstructure, and they are all subservient to and supportive of the economy or substructure, that is, of the specific mode of production. The values and rules or norms, in fact the entire cultural complex which surrounds them, take their form in each stage of societal evolution in such a way as to support the fundamental class relationship. In capitalism the legal institution has evolved to support private property; in fact, justice is defined on the basis of private ownership. In another stage this need not be so because there may be a better or more suitable arrangement or pattern of social relations.

### Ideology and Legitimation

Marxists have written a great deal about the role of ideology. An ideology is a system of thought about the way things are, the way they should be, and what should be done about any disparity between the two. The prevailing ideologies in society are part of the overall social relations, and like those relations they support the fundamental class relationship which is exploitative. As an example, the ideology of democracy evolved to support the capitalist system, although there is really very little economic democracy or freedom in that system. These ideologies are imposed on the workers even though they do not usually recognize this. They are passed on through many institutions, such as the family, politics, or religion.

### The Role of the School

One of the more important institutions for this kind of indoctrination is formal education. In Marxist theory education is but another institution within the superstructure, though in capitalist society a very important one, which is controlled by the economic elite. Its purpose is to legitimate the exploitative class relationship which is characteristic of the particular mode of production.

Modern Marxist scholars (frequently referred to as neo-Marxists) almost universally share this general assessment of the purpose of schooling, although they may differ at the level of particular details. The school is an instrument of the bourgeois or capitalist class. Because of the nature of the class system the elites pass on the privileged positions they hold to their descendants. They hold this privilege primarily because of ascription, and it is based on usually covert but sometimes overt forms of exploitation. This must be made to appear necessary, legitimate, just, or inevitable. It looks as if it is based on merit and ability, but, in fact, it is not. Most people accept this myth and so become reconciled to an inferior position. The institution of schooling has two general functions: (1) to prepare the children of the elites to succeed their parents, and (2) to direct the children of the workers away from such positions and reconcile them to the inferior status which results. There is some quite limited room for mobility between classes because the elites do not fully reproduce themselves. The mobility which occurs is used as an example of the fairness of the system, and the ideology states that there is equal opportunity for all.

There is only a narrow band between some of the neo-Marxists and others who at least implicitly accept the functionalist model and concentrate on explaining the nature of the dysfunctions involved. Marxists hold that the failure of the school is inevitable. The more critical functionalists assume that even though there are many imperfections the school is moving towards a reduction of inequality, towards more humane ends (Hurn, 1978:46). In Marxist thinking no substantial reform is possible until there is a change in the social order. For the functionalist, school reform is possible within the capitalist system.

Two of the more important contributions made in the modern Marxist interpretation of schooling are those of Christian Baudelot and Roger Establet (1971) in France, and Samuel Bowles and Herbert Gintis (1976) in the United States. Their writings may be regarded as somewhat representative of this school of thought.

### Baudelot and Establet

Murphy (1979:88-89) notes that these French Marxists follow in the tradition of Althuser, a very strong structuralist among Marxist thinkers. For them, an examination of formal education must be treated on the basis of a forum for class conflict. There are intrinsic structural barriers which prevent the proletariat as a class from getting any real advantage from formal education. It is a mistake, a diversion, to look at individuals — one or a small number of whom might become substantially upwardly mobile. There is a basic collective (class) conflict in the school system which is a legitimating mechanism for the bourgeoisie. It is the role of the state in capitalist society to support the exploitative position of the bourgeoisie, and the state controls the institution of schooling. Education favours the capitalist class in two particular ways. In the first case it tracks students *on a class basis* into a vocational or a higher education stream: the proletariat in the one, the bourgeoisie in the other. There is considerable effort to mask this procedure; it is made to appear open, but in fact, it is not. The individual exception serves merely to legitimate the system. Students in the lower track are not really given a decent education at all. From a substantive point of view, what they learn is relatively useless. This ensures that they will take their adult roles among the workers and also, more insidiously, it fails to give them the kind of abstract thinking ability and conceptual clarity which is necessary if they are to understand class conflict and the nature of the exploitation imposed on them by the system.

This leads to the second point, the role of ideology, which holds such a strong position in Marxist thought. Noting again that schooling is a tool of the state, and the state of the capitalist class, Baudelot and Establet see the second basic function of the school as the inculcation of the bourgeoisie ideology. This ideology, which includes such myths as meritocracy, equality of opportunity, and reform liberalism, is presented in the school system in the same manner and with a similar kind of certitude as objective truth. There is a qualitative difference in the pedagogy used in the vocational and academic tracks, and students in the former are encouraged to be passive, non-thinkers who accept the system as morally just. Although the school pretends to teach the students in the lower track what their own needs are, in reality it is imposing on them the needs of their masters. It fails to analyze the nature of society, pretending that this would be of little interest or use for those who are destined to be workers. The end result is that students from the proletariat are programmed for failure in the occupational world, have little but an instinctive understanding of the kind of exploitation in which they are caught, and have little development by way of abstract thinking ability which would assist them in tackling their problem and obtaining objective justice.

The function of the school in capitalist society is to do precisely these things. Every stage in society must have some institution which is predominantly responsible for socializing the members in the dominant ideology. In the feudal era this was done by the Church, but responsibility in capitalist society has passed to the institution of schooling. This is a structural arrangement. The interdependence of the major institutions — family, state, education, religion — makes them a cohesive entity each with necessary functions which must be performed if capitalism is to survive. Baudelot and Establet have little hope for reform as long as the economic system remains a capitalist one. This lack of hope for substantial or meaningful change within the system is typical of those who hold to the Marxist theoretical point of view.

The data on which Baudelot and Establet base their conclusions are taken from the school system of France where there is a more pronounced elitist influence than in Canada or the United States. Following Turner's (1960) distinction, schooling in France more closely approaches the sponsored rather than the contest model. The basic theoretical assumptions of Marxism do not really vary that much. Bowles and Gintis (1976) have come to similar conclusions in the United States, even though education in that nation more closely approaches the contest paradigm.

*Bowles and Gintis*

Samuel Bowles and Herbert Gintis (1976) are two political economists in the United States who turned their attention some ten years ago to an analysis of the purpose of schooling in American society. Their book, *Schooling in Capitalist America,* is a popularized presentation of sophisticated statistical analysis based on data gathered from a variety of secondary sources. (The nature and results of their statistical analysis is presented in greater detail in chapter 11.) Their fundamental conclusion, similar to that of Baudelot and Establet, is that the institution of schooling in society in general and in the United States in particular can do nothing but support the exploitative capitalist or bourgeois class. Students are educated not to critically examine the nature of society but to support it.

Bowles and Gintis incorporate into their work the conclusions of certain recent American educational historians, especially Michael Katz (1971). This analysis presents the evolution of schooling in the past two centuries in the United States as a thoroughly successful institutional mechanism which supports the dominant class. Universal primary education was introduced primarily to discipline potential factory workers, to provide social control. Much later, when more and more students were entering secondary schools, tracking was introduced in order to direct the students on a class basis into higher or lower levels in the occupational world. Mechanisms such as testing and counselling were used ostensibly as an objective basis for tracking, but in reality they were always biased against the working class. Later still, in a third stage of development which is much more recent, this mechanism of tracking was introduced into the post-secondary level with the proliferation of community colleges. With the post-World War II period of educational inflation students from the lower and working classes could be directed to community colleges; students from middle-class backgrounds were directed to regular four-year universities, and students from elite backgrounds were directed to elite universities, such as Harvard, and to graduate schools.

These authors unleash a devastating attack on liberal educational reform, particularly relative to meritocracy. Using a sophisticated statistical analysis based on correlation and regression, they demonstrate that ability as measured by standard I.Q. tests has almost nothing to say about how well or how poorly a student will do in adult life. The intellectual ability required for advancement in the educational system falls within the normal range, and almost all students possess that ability. It is primarily social class which determines success or failure in the school system.

In the theory of these authors there are two principal functions of schooling: allocation along class lines, and legitimation.

Allocation refers to the process of selection which directs the students to particular levels of adult occupational roles. There are essentially three such levels. The lowest includes the unskilled and semi-skilled, primarily manual occupations. The intermediate level includes the highly-skilled manual workers and technicians, and the middle range, white-collar cohort. The elite level is made up of large owners and upper-level management. Students are selected for these different levels primarily on the basis of social class. Intergenerational mobility is low and is largely within a narrow range. Large scale mobility from the lower to the upper class is rare.

theory of stratification. In his now famous essay *Class, Status and Party* (1966), Weber insisted that stratification is the result of social power which emanates from three sources: economic power, prestige power, and political power. Of these, in the long run, economic power (class) has the greatest influence, but at a particular time prestige power (status), and political power (party) may override class determination. Moreover, economic power may be enhanced by the other two.

Power, for Weber, is the ability to impose one's will on another. This other may be willing to suffer the imposition (legitimated power, authority) or unwilling (raw or naked power). Economic power is the result of one's ability in the market place; this is earning ability, including wealth. Capital is only one kind of earning ability, albeit generally the most important kind. There is also earning ability based on accumulated knowledge and skill which is marketable. This is an intermediate level ability, but is important. At the lowest level there is earning ability which is based on sheer manual labour. Class situation results from one's market or earning ability. There may be a capitalist class, acquisition class(es) based on marketable knowledge and skills, and a labouring class. All three give power, though to a greater or lesser degree.

Status honor is the result of prestige offered by others as the result of life style, particularly one's occupation. Power of this kind may usually be translated into economic power as well. Status groups are communities; the members usually take communal action, while classes do not, or do so to a lesser extent. Status groups try to monopolize a certain life style, while classes do not.

Weber concentrated less on party which is political organization in its widest sense, but he did emphasize that such power is used to attain a planned goal. It may adhere to any kind of organization but is most prominent in politics.

Stratification is the result of social power which manifests itself in three ways: class, status, and party. One's socioeconomic status (a term not used by Weber) is the result of a mingling or a weighted average of these kinds of power (Rossides, 1976).

Education: A Class or Status Variable?

Those who follow the thinking of Weber may regard education as either a class or status variable. In the first instance its fundamental purpose would be to provide acquisition skills. Knowledge and skills acquired in school may enhance one's market ability and ultimately, if schooling is prolonged, lead to an intermediate or high class position. This is very much in accord with a modern technocratic perspective, the view that as society becomes more industrialized increased levels of technological knowledge and skills are demanded of larger numbers of people in the work force. This position is less popular today than it had been earlier.

As a status variable education leads to a style of life and a pattern of consumption which sets one group, or one level of status, aside from another. Here the emphasis is not on the knowledge and skills which are required for production but on an element in life which sets the group apart and makes it unique. This is what any status group does. It tries to monopolize a certain style of life and establish boundaries to keep other individuals or groups out. A college degree could do this very well without being particularly useful in the market place.

The Role of the School

Modern disciples of Weber are regarding education, particularly higher education, more as a status variable. They point out that the skills required for job performance are not usually difficult and, with but a few exceptions, may be learned more efficiently on the job. To our knowledge neo-Weberians have not yet thoroughly investigated whether such skills may be learned even more efficiently on the job by those with a higher level of schooling. It is probably beyond dispute that at least functional literacy is required, but it is also important to determine if additional general knowledge learned in school is an asset for on-the-job training in the sense that it could not have been acquired, or acquired as well, on the job. If it is, then formal education beyond literacy would have to be viewed as a class variable, although this would not preclude it being (at least partially) a status variable as well. This problem is not solved as easily as it might at first appear. Among other things, being overly educated or underemployed strengthens the relationship between work and alienation.

Recall that status is one source of social power. The power comes from the prestige that others somewhat voluntarily confer on the basis of a number of variables (style of speech or dress, religious affiliation, etc.). One of the more important variables is occupation, which tends to be ranked along a continuum of prestige. The credentials which are gained in school serve as boundaries, opening up higher level occupations to those who possess them, and conversely denying entrance to those who fail to gain this level of educational achievement. Once a person has entered a given occupation his education is not particularly useful, but it is very useful for opening the boundary door and gaining admission. Many studies have shown that those in a given occupation who have higher credentials do not, on average, perform better than those in the same occupation with a lower level of education. There may even be a slight negative correlation (Berg, 1970).

In this light the institution of schooling is controlled by elites who use it primarily to establish boundaries for status group membership. It serves to restrict credentials, making it more difficult for those of lesser status groups to achieve them. In this age of educational inflation the ante is being continually raised. The power of status groups may be and frequently is challenged by class and party groups. Class groups tend to be less organized (communal), parties more so. As a result of these competing sources of power (status inconsistency), education to some extent, even at the highest level, has become available even to those with a somewhat negative status, such as specific racial or ethnic groups which traditionally have been the object of discrimination. Even the most advanced degrees do not necessarily open higher status group boundaries, for there are other means of monopolizing life styles as well (especially race and ethnicity), but in the long run they tend to do so because status consistency prevails.

Until recently, it has been difficult to distinguish social theorists of the Weberian school from some functionalists, especially those who analyse the dysfunctional elements of social organization. It is certainly accurate to classify Weber as a conflict sociologist, but he never accepted the utopian visions of Marx. Marxists view class in a relative sense, depending on one's relationship to the means of production. They hold that it may be eliminated by collectivizing such ownership. Hofley (1980) points out well that there is much confusion because of different kinds of definitions (or the absence of a definition) of class by other theorists, and that even if class in the relational or Marxist sense could disappear it does not follow that inequality resulting from power would disappear as well. Hofley refers to this as the two problematics, and it is an issue which neither Marxists nor other theorists have resolved. But it is a very important issue in the sociology of education. Even if a classless society in the Marxist sense were possible social power may remain. Formal education could still contribute significantly to status honor. Clearly it is important to understand such a relationship and to determine why it is so. Weber's theory seems more capable of dealing with this problem. He devoted much of his energy to the analysis of bureaucracy and tended to view inequality more and more as the result of the ownership or control of the means of administration, and he felt that this would not be eliminated in any specific form of social organization. The traditional distinction between the Marxist and the functionalist, that intergenerational inequality may be *removed* because of a new kind of social organization brought on by revolution (Marxists), or may be greatly *reduced* through mechanisms of reform which would provide equal opportunity to all (functionalists) — this distinction tends to break down when dealing with the Weberian conflict model. Weber did not really have much hope that the effects of social power would disappear at all.

Empirical Validation: Randall Collins

Perhaps the most widely recognized sociologist of education in the Weberian tradition today is Randall Collins (1971, 1974). An American, Collins's major work is an empirical investigation of the increasing educational requirements for occupational roles in the United States. In general, he is testing the functionalist model, and to a substantial extent his evidence finds it lacking; it is not a model which fits American society well, although it does have some small degree of validity.

Collins's (1971) basic presentation is that the adequacy of the functionalist model of educational stratification rests on the requirement of increased formal education providing technical knowledge and skills which are more and more necessary in advanced industrial society. As Murphy (1979:98) notes, the theory presumes that the skill requirements for the same jobs need upgrading, and the proportion of jobs requiring higher-level skills is increasing. The institution of schooling must provide more training in order to prepare individuals to fulfill the roles which now have more advanced technological requirements. Bowles and Gintis (1976) refer to this as the technocratic perspective. Those who have higher levels of formal education will be in a better position to fill the more technically demanding roles of industrial society. Those who have greater ability and motivation will be the ones advancing farther in the school system on the basis of merit, and in turn will be rewarded proportionately. This is the meritocratic perspective.

On the other hand, if increased educational requirements are not a necessity in industrial society then this would substantiate the conflict model. There is no need for this increased education (from the point of view of job performance), and it is only because of the power of elite groups that such a requirement is imposed.

Collins has gathered evidence from a large number of studies and about a variety of occupational roles. Using this as the basis of his judgements he claims that there is some — but not much — support for the functionalist model. The level of education required for various occupations has been increasing considerably in the past thirty years, and continues to increase. Collins concludes that about 15 percent of this is required for job performance and about 85 percent for some other reason. Technical efficiency is generally not a prime requisite. There is no real relationship between level of education and adequacy of job performance. Very often, the better educated worker is not the most productive. Racial, ethnic, and sexual discrimination on the job market leads one to conclude that other variables often take precedence over formal education in determining job placement, and these variables are usually ascriptive in nature.

In typical Weberian tradition, Collins explains this kind of inequality on the basis of status group monopoly. A status group always tries to adopt a life style which is somewhat distinctive, thus creating boundaries between itself and other — especially lower — groups. Most jobs today exist within the framework of formal organizations. The elite members compete with those in other organizations and, even more important, they attempt to recruit lower-level personnel who have life styles which simultaneously maintain the boundaries between them and at the same time give a higher status appearance to the entire organization. Recruits for elite positions are normally from an upper status group so that they may easily fit into the expected life style. Those for intermediate and lower level positions are expected to have been socialized in such a way as to respect the differing life styles but at the same time to enhance the overall prestige of the organization. Hence the increased demand for higher educational credentials.

This position presumes that the elites have a virtual monopoly on the more advanced levels of education, a presumption we will demonstrate later on to be generally accurate but admitting of many exceptions. It also presumes that even as the average level of education increases, and increases considerably, the institution of schooling continues to be in a position to teach elite culture to the few and respect for that culture to many.

Collins presents considerable evidence for his position. The most important empirical results ". . . found educational requirements for white collar employees to be highest in organizations which emphasized normative control of employees and that educational requirements were more strongly associated with normative status conditions than with technical conditions" (Murphy, 1979:101). Normative control refers to or includes respect for the elite culture or life style and the boundaries which exist between the elite status groups and the lesser ones. Formerly, lower average levels of education were adequate, providing the requisite respect for the elite culture and also the level of skill required for technical efficiency. The increased level of education now required is only minimally called for by the demand for higher levels of technical skills — the functionalist position — and is primarily the result of a need to maintain the position of the elite group relative to others. It is sometimes referred to as educational inflation. Education is largely a status (85 percent) rather than a class (15 percent) variable.

There can be little doubt that Collins's presentations are very important. Murphy (1979) does point to several problems, but this line of investigation is relatively new and additional investigation should reduce if not eliminate them. Collins focuses on specific skills rather than general knowledge, despite the possibility of that general knowledge enhancing the ability to learn the requisite skills on the job, either more thoroughly, more quickly, or both. Karabel and Halsey (1977:31) suggest that the basic presumption of Collins's hypothesis may not be warranted. More educated workers, those who are over-educated or underemployed, may be in lower status jobs because they are less productive for other reasons. Technical knowledge and skill are necessary but not sufficient attributes for adequate job performance.

The function of the school in Collins's view is to teach particular status culture: the appropriate style of speech, dress, values, and manners. This provides the organizations with educated workers who have internalized the goals of the firm, including respect for appropriate social distance and the difference in life styles which are to be maintained between various levels of employees (Karabel & Halsey, 1977).

This concludes our investigation of both the functionalist and the conflict model. As we noted earlier, there are some scholars who do not fit easily into one or the other, but who subscribe to a position referred to as Critical Functionalism. Before proceeding to the Interactionists we would like to look a little more closely at this position.

# The Critical Functionalists

## Introduction

Viewed from one perspective it would seem more logical to insert this section as part of or immediately following Section 2 of this chapter, where Functionalism was covered. Yet, critical functionalism may usefully be regarded as following an intermediate road. It is not inappropriate to suggest that these theorists have a foot in both camps, and this not in a pejorative sense. They tend to accept intergenerational inequality as necessary and inevitable for social organization but at the same time they emphasize that degree of inequality which is the result of social power. The influence of Weber is strong, but so is that of Durkheim, a progenitor of modern functionalism. Education does have important functions in modern society, whether capitalist or socialist. These are usually manifest functions. There are also latent functions, less universally intended or understood. These tend to be dysfunctional or discriminatory against certain groups and are largely, if not completely, imposed by elites. Although we have treated Merton and Collins within the functionalist and conflict paradigms respectively, as most authors do, it would not be stretching logic too far to insert them here. Critical of the classical functional approach, they find it difficult also to adhere very closely to a power model, particularly the economically based model of the Marxists. Other theorists in a similar position include Pierre Bourdieu and Christopher Jencks.

## Cultural Capital: Pierre Bourdieu

Bourdieu's (1966) presentation is often referred to as the cultural capital theory. His evidence is restricted to France but the findings probably apply to a substantial degree throughout the western world. He begins by rejecting the theory that the higher educational achievement of the middle and upper classes is due to any genetic superiority or difference, claiming it is socially determined by advantageous cultural characteristics which the children of such groups learn at home and already enjoy when they begin their schooling. These advantages may be referred to as cultural capital and the greater investment of this capital in the institution of schooling accounts for the greater return in achievement. Murphy (1979:23-31) underscores Bourdieu's claim that for parents of the same income level, their level of education over two generations predicts the achievement of their children. When social status of the fathers was the same, the status of the grandfather was useful in predicting success. It is the cultural level of the family of origin which best explains the success of the children in school and later in adult occupatonal roles. This includes especially language superiority, general culture, and heightened awareness of the mechanics of the school system and its value as a means to an end. The kind of language skills learned by the children of the upper and middle classes are those that are rewarded in school (see chapter 6, Section 2, below). Such children possess an advantage — cultural capital. They are more skilled in abstract thinking, in the manipulation of abstract symbols, and in school-related problem solving. When they begin school they bring with them more of this capital to invest.

General culture includes more broadly based knowledge, an appreciation of the "correct" way to act,and a more sophisticated understanding of the means to be used to achieve the desired goal. It is manifested by higher rates of participation in those aspects of culture which are considered to be on a "higher" level: attendance at the theatre, museums, concerts, appreciation of the "finer" music, and other prestigious elements of a higher life style.

Those who enjoy disproportionate amounts of this cultural capital also have, because of this, an advantage relative to the mechanics of the school system and the normative ethos or system of expectations which exists there. They understand better the distinctions between different kinds of schools and the various tracks found within the school. They are more conscious of the value of certain aspects of the system as a means to an end, and of the importance of deferring gratification in order to achieve at least up to minimal expectations. They are more aware of and more practiced in the deportment and kinds of behaviour expected in school. Murphy (1979:24) refers to "an intuitively experienced ethos that varies among socio-economic groups" and which is reinforced by one's peers and, even if unconsciously, by teachers and counsellors who take social background into consideration. All of this too is cultural capital, or a rewarding of it, and gives to the student with such a background a greater chance of success. Bourdieu essentially sees students of working-class origin as deficient in a higher, more acceptable culture, which is here to stay. His suggestion for reform is a remedial one. The school should concentrate more on providing cultural capital to these deficient groups. But unless the boundaries of socio-economic status groups are diminished or destroyed — something Bourdieu does not really see happening — the inequality of opportunity will remain.

## The Unexplained Variables: Christopher Jencks

Christopher Jencks (1972;1979) falls very much within the school which Karabel and Halsey (1977) refer to as methodological empiricism. Like Bowles and Gintis (1976), Jencks and his colleagues at Harvard use very sophisticated statistical techniques in analyzing a great deal of secondary data in the United States. (More detailed analysis of these techniques will be presented in chapter 12.) In 1972 their publication, *Inequality,* attempted to interpret the importance to be attributed to major institutions, especially family and schooling, for the phenomenon of inequality in the United States. To the surprise of all, the analysis showed only minor association among such dimensions of inequality as cognitive ability, educational achievement, occupation, and income. Neither family of origin nor education was able to explain much of economic success (Yankelovich, 1979; Murphy, 1979).

The cluster of variables with the greatest predictive power relative to economic success Jencks and his colleagues described as *luck.* This is primarily a residual category including variables left out of the original equation, and the study has been criticized on those grounds. To be fair to the authors, they could only discover the influence of variables included in their data sources. In subsequent work, Jencks (1979) indicates that from one-half to two-thirds of the variance in earnings for the sample is explained by switches between jobs and careers, annual changes in circumstances, and lucky or unlucky breaks. Family background, ability, education, and teenage personality characteristics explain most of the rest; i.e., the one-third to one-half not explained by the other set of variables (Yankelovich, 1979:33).

We will examine these findings in greater detail in chapter 12. Jenck's formulations so far really are short on theory, or theoretical considerations, which is our principal concern at present. It is nevertheless important to point out here his (negative) findings, that family background and educational achievement are far less influential in explaining economic success than scholars have been suggesting. At the same time, we should be conscious of the limitations of the study. It has a narrow data base. The reliability of the work to this point has not been determined. It is a responsible but, at the same time, limited work.

## The Interactionists

The distinction between macro-level and micro-level analysis is frequently misunderstood. It is important to grasp its meaning if we are to understand the contribution of the interactionists to the sociology of education, a contribution which, although not new, is becoming particularly important at this time.

"A macro analysis is one in which the explanatory factors are the characteristics of whole societies rather than the characteristics of micro units (individuals, schools) within them (Murphy 1979:199)." It is the initial emphasis which is given either to the broad societal characteristic or to the individual and individual motivation of the unit which is the basis of the distinction. An analysis of the relationship between social class and educational achievement in Canada, such as that provided by Porter (1965) is macro-level analysis. But when the direction of enquiry changes to an individual school, or family, or community, given that the results are not necessarily applicable to society at large, the level of analysis then becomes micro. Here the focus is on individual components with the expectation that peculiarities make this inter-action unique.

In any discipline the distinction between macro and micro analysis is often ambiguous and there is frequently overlap. Large-scale theories include an interest in how change occurs through aggregate variables, and micro-level studies tend to include an interest in how the interaction of units is shaped by component variables in social interaction (Abrahamson 1981:2-3). The two types of analysis are not mutually exclusive and valuable results will almost certainly emerge from contemporary efforts to integrate the two approaches. We tend to generalize to the societal level when a sufficient number of case studies which may be regarded as representative produce the same results.

Max Weber was a great pioneer in micro-level analysis and also in its integration with macro-level theory. Indeed his definition of sociology included the concept of the *interpretive* understanding of social action (Hagedorn 1980). It is to this that his insistence on *verstehen* applies. We must understand the motives of individuals in the social interaction in which they are involved. Pioneers such as Weber, Cooley and Mead saw quite clearly that social action frequently includes a *bargaining* process which may vary in accord with an actor's understanding of the expectations of others with whom he or she is involved.

Interactionist analysis attempts to acquire an understanding and expla-nation of these largely subjective elements in social interaction. This broad school includes the micro-level theory of symbolic interactionism, ethnometh-odology and phenomenology. While our treatment of these theories here will be brief, sufficient simply to indicate their meaning and differences, we should note that most research in the sociology of education in Canada falls within the framework of such micro-level analysis.

Interactionist theories ". . . focus on the micro rather than the macro level, on humans as creative, active beings instead of on forces external to them, on the negotiation of meanings, and therefore on processes that need to be interpreted rather than on structures (Murphy 1979:141)." Hagedorn (1980) points out that interactionist theory rests on the basic assumption that social life has meaning only at the individual level or in social interaction. From this point of view there would be no such thing as objective *social* reality in the same sense that there is an objective existence to this book. When the book acquires a social meaning it is the result of how individuals view it or define it. For one, depending on earlier social influences, a book might be regarded (defined) as an interesting, even exciting companion which opens up new knowledge which is rewarding in itself. For another, as the result of different social influences, the same book might be perceived as a boring challenge which must be mastered before a final exam, the contents of which, mercifully, might soon be forgotten, being of little practical use in later life.

For the interactionists then, there is little point in studying structures of social life as if they have some universal or common meaning. Their meaning varies with each individual, and so structures may not be dealt with as if they are distinct from the people involved. These sociologists are interested in the subjective meanings and intentions of the actor and the way such states vary as the result of social learning.

*Symbolic interactionism* was refined as a distinctive sociological approach by Herbert Blumer, who himself was a student of the great American pioneer George Herbert Mead. Both regard human beings as thinking, feeling individuals, who attach meaning to the situation in which they find themselves,and who react not only to an objective situation but also to their interpretation of the intent of the one with whom they interact. This intent is recognized especially through the interpretation of symbols, or communication made through symbols, which includes language but is not restricted to it. A smile, a frown, some other display or indication of emotion, an earlier communication, these and other symbols give meaning to a situation and help the actor to define it. The interaction takes into consideration how the other will respond. There is always consideration of the future, some process of anticipation. Each party in social interaction interprets or defines the meaning of the other's actions instead of merely reacting to stimuli.

A symbol stands for something else. People share the meaning of symbols, and they anticipate the responses of others in interaction using symbols. Subsequent behaviour is based on this anticipation. As Mead taught, every person has a self-concept which is based on, or is the result of, how he perceives others viewing him. We feel that others label us as popular, unpopular, good, bad, quick, slow, and in many other ways, and we interact with others in a way which includes self-presentation determined in this way. All of this is based on role-taking, whereby we place ourselves in the position of the other and anticipate his actions or responses (Hagedorn, 1980:12-14).

*Phenomenology,* as treated within the discipline of sociology, is in some ways similar to symbolic interactionism, and rests on similar assumptions. It is particularly concerned with the sociology of knowledge, with how our consciousness is formed. Phenomenologists hold that we never know reality directly but only as it is interpreted by our consciousness (Murphy, 1979). To understand society we must be aware of the influences which form our consciousness, which define our knowledge. Social interaction is determined by the kind of knowledge we have and its meaning for us. Phenomenology studies the acquisition, meaning, and interpretation of such knowledge or consciousness and the action/interaction which results from it.

*Ethnomethodology* is the study of the methods people use in their interaction. If social interaction does not have an objective meaning but depends on the individual's perceptions, then it is important to understand how individuals influence the perception of others. Ethnomethodology studies the methods people use in determining the perceptions others will have (Murphy, 1979).

A thorough integration of these areas of study in sociology has yet to be presented, though important steps within this framework are being taken. Bernstein is one who has made a significant contribution from this perspective. His works on language, class and control include an attempt to integrate interactionist analysis with global characteristics such as social class. Later in this chapter mention will be made of Canadians who take an interactionist position, and the work of one of them, Wilfred Martin, will be reviewed. A global analysis of micro-sociological approaches is made impractical at this time by the fact that they vary so much among themselves (Hagedorn, 1980:12). This should not be taken as an indication that they are unimportant; indeed, we will refer extensively to the work of interactionists in later chapters.

## Canadian Influences

We will conclude this chapter by examining briefly the contributions of Canadian sociologists to theory in the sociology of education. That contribution is not large in comparison with that of the United States or Western Europe. Canadian scholars have tended to concentrate much more on issues which are peculiarly ours. We pointed out in our social interpretation of the history of education in Canada that formal education here was strongly influenced by the British, French, and American policies. We have a multi-cultural nation, and studies have tended to concentrate on cultural differences in aspiration and achievement.

There are exceptions. Murphy (1979) discusses Belanger and Rocher, and Porter among the functionalists, and Clement and Escande within the conflict camp. Finally, Martin and Mark Novak are discussed within the interactionist paradigm. We shall borrow heavily from that presentation in discussing these theorists.

### Canadian Functionalists

Belanger and Rocher

Belanger and Rocher (1975), with special emphasis on Rocher (1975), are a rare breed of functionalist who give particular emphasis to struggle and change within an orderly, or functional society. Based on the existing political experience in Quebec, their analysis provides useful insights for that province.

Murphy (1979:52-67) points to a number of specific characteristics of this rather mainstream functionalist presentation. In typical Parsonsian fashion, society is viewed as a complex organism which may be analytically divided into four institutional complexes or subsystems, each of which in turn may be further subdivided in a similar manner. There is always tension in the society not only because of specifically different individual goals, but because there are different collectivities such as ethnic groups and social classes which have varying interests. It is characteristic of global societies to allow or even encourage pluralistic perspectives and at the same time to provide for the integration of the totality. Integration includes maintaining social control with emphasis on a common overriding culture which, at the same time, permits a substantial amount of diversity. The different elements are agents of innovation. As such, they are not necessarily opposed to the *status quo;* they may enhance or improve it. Nevertheless, there is a certain amount of tension, the result of plurality of interests and of change. Society must provide institutions for tension management, and in modern times these include family, education, the media, and voluntary organizations such as the church. These are socialization structures. In Parsonsian system analysis, the socialization or enculturation function includes both pattern maintenance and tension management.

Each of these structures — and we are concerned particularly with education — may be analyzed from two points of view: as an open system where it is perceived as influencing and being influenced by the other subsystems, and as a closed or autonomous system. It is the function of education to bridge the social with the cultural, to provide the appropriate motivation to members of society in accord with the values, norms and rules of the cultural system so that these members take their appropriate roles in the adaptive, goal attainment, and integrative subsystem. In earlier societies this function was performed primarily by other institutions, particularly the family. In modern industrial society it is performed principally by the school.

With the increase in universal education the school is expected to provide a general type of socialization including the appropriate motivation, and instruction in society's value and normative systems. It also provides special education for different collectivities such as ethnic groups and social classes, and for specific occupational roles. This democratization of schooling takes its toll. The educational structures were originally created for a minority, or elite. Now universally available to all, they are inadequate to serve the majority. There is tension and conflict, especially between teachers and different publics who have different interests — parents, students, ethnic groups, and others of the kind.

Rocher (1975) speaks of two different kinds of cultural change now occurring in society in a more or less orderly fashion, neither of which is necessarily dysfunctional. One is the circulation of knowledge which was formerly provided to the minority or elite. The other is the development of new knowledge, especially a radical change in thought. The institution of schooling contributes to both, and society benefits from it. There are tensions as this evolution comes about, and there may be dysfunctions as the result of holdovers from earlier structures. Principal among these is credentialism, an exaggerated importance given to diplomas. Many people occupy adult roles in accord with a diploma they hold but wherein they are not very happy or successful. Others may have greater motivation or ability but are excluded because of the absence of the credential. In the area of social policy, Rocher recommends a closer relationship between the school and the work place, and an emphasis on proper motivation for a role rather than ability, especially of the intellectual kind, which is not really scarce. Virtually everybody has the ability to perform occupational roles, but not the interest. This problem could be reduced by encouraging closer association between schooling and work, and by permitting mobility between roles regardless of credentials.

In summary then, the school is an agent of socialization which has assumed particular importance in modern society. Educational structures include dysfunctional holdovers from an earlier day when they served primarily an elite. In preparing individuals for adult occupational roles the school should concentrate on motivation. Intellectual ability is not scarce, and the selection process should be more concerned with the student who is interested in or motivated for a specific role. A closer association between schooling and the work place would assist in this process. All students are to be given the general knowledge which was at one time restricted to an elite, and specialized knowledge which is peculiar to the chosen occupational role.

The contributions of Belanger and Rocher do add to systems analysis, and as such represent a Canadian contribution of some importance in macro-level theory. They are based on the assumption of the functionalist model, the problems of which we have earlier discussed. However, it is not at all established that schools provide common general knowledge to all. These authors do not effectively refute the claim of conflict theorists that much of the educational system is still specifically reserved for the elite in the form of a different kind of learning even at the lower level. This contribution to functional analysis has not assisted in overcoming the problem of functionalism as such.

John Porter

Let us turn now to the work of John Porter, perhaps the most eminent of all Canadian sociologists. Porter's major work, *The Vertical Mosaic* (1965), is an analysis of the Canadian stratification system, and it is a work of great importance. Murphy (1979:67-80) accurately describes Porter as a functionalist because he views society as an organism made up of subsystems which are integrated. At the same time he gives major importance to the place of power within that system. He is a critical functionalist at heart.

To begin with, Porter (1970, 1971) very much accepts a meritocratic-technocratic perspective of society. The meritocracy is as yet an ideal. The technocratic element is already present in industrial society. Higher-level education is required or functional for the increasingly complex roles existing today, and will be required to an even greater extent with further development. There is no indication of any empirical basis for this latter assumption.

It is in the tension between the not-yet-realized meritocracy and the technological requirements of modern society that the power struggle unfolds. In *The Vertical Mosaic,* Porter notes the special advantage which elites have. For our purpose here it is sufficient to note that these elites, with less than perfect success, attempt to monopolize higher education. Because of ascriptive advantages they have a higher achievement rate than do other groups in society, and this is dysfunctional. The educational institutions must change in order to accommodate increasing technological requirements, but powerful groups in society do not take this proposed change lightly. Porter *et al.* (1971) show that financial considerations are the largest factor impeding higher educational attainment for the non-elites and especially for females and the lower classes in Canadian society. Specific social policies, including free tuition, grants for students from lower-income families, and redistribution of income through progressive taxation, are advocated.

One of the groups experiencing the greatest amount of discrimination in Canada relative to the cost of education is the female student population. Parents are less willing to make financial sacrifices for their daughters, feeling still that the occupational utility of advanced education is less for females than for males. Another major form of financial discrimination results from structural constraints which prevent females from earning as much as males in vacation and part-time employment.

In summary, Porter holds to a meritocratic ideal but a less than meritocratic practice in education and in the stratification system in Canada. Elites benefit from this and will not eagerly respond to change which takes away their advantage. At the same time the technology of a rapidly developing economy requires higher education for all (or more), and the elites will use their power to impede progressive change. The tension will likely be reduced in favour of more universal higher education on a more meritocratic basis, because society requires this. Of course, the elites may transpose their advantage in some other way. The institution of schooling has an important functional role to play in society, and will evolve in a manner which allows it to fulfill that function.

## Canadian Conflict Theorists

### Wallace Clement

It might be well to bridge the gap between the functionalists and conflict perspective by referring to Wallace Clement. Clement (1975) is a conflict sociologist who has concentrated on an analysis of the Canadian Corporate Elite, the title of his principal book. Not primarily interested in the sociology of education, he replicated much of Porter's earlier work on elites and points to a number of ways in which this group maintains its power. One of these is elite education.

Clement makes a distinction between inequality of opportunity and inequality of condition. The latter refers to the reality of stratification in society, the hierarchical arrangement of rights, privileges and power, which exists in some established concrete form. Unequal opportunity refers to differential access to this hierarchical arrangement of rewards on an ascribed basis. Opportunity would be equalized if society were strictly meritocratic. In Canada, and in many other modern societies, it is not. One's ability and motivation are not decisive factors. Far more influential is the ascribed group from which one comes. The influence that such ascription brings opens doors of power which are hardly accessible to the non-elites, or to only a limited number who receive special attention. The elites control structural aspects of society which allow them to maintain their power. One of these is education.

In Clement's presentation it is the ascribed characteristics of one generation which leads to inequality of opportunity in the next. Differential educational achievement does not cause the inequality of condition, but rather is a result of it. The elites use formal education — particularly elite private schools and a few universities — to maintain a social network which is relatively exclusive. Education is one of a number of structures used to maintain exclusiveness, a monopoly on a certain life style including class opportunity. C. Wright Mills (1956) and E. Digby Baltzell (1958) had earlier shown the same set of structural arrangements in the United States. The critical point which Clement suggests is that because unequal educational opportunity is a result of stratification rather than its cause, equalizing it would simply mean a rearrangement of the structures which maintain the elite social network. Other structures, such as private clubs, would perpetuate the elite position.

Clement's empirical findings deal with the corporate elite — approximately 1000 positions — which dominates power positions in Canada. The related educational structures, such as private schools and elite universities, are only one link in a structural chain meant both to socialize in and restrict others from the dominant class values. But this exclusive education does not cause the inequality which results from ascriptive features. It simply maintains and enhances solidarity within a status group.

Claude Escande

A second Canadian sociologist in the conflict group who has made a significant contribution in the area of our concern is Claude Escande (1973). Described by Murphy (1979:122-135) as one who writes from a Marxist perspective, Escande begins his book by presenting the typical Marxist analysis of capitalist society and its division of labour which creates two enduring classes, the bourgeoisie and the proletariat. In this society education is an institution which is controlled by the bourgeois class through the mediation of the state. Its purpose is to reproduce and reinforce the prevailing social relations of production, the entire cultural complex which supports the prevailing system, and its class division. Education and the inequality which results is the effect of class inequality rather than the cause of it. As a result, Escande is not optimistic that reform in the institution of education will succeed in altering the fundamental nature of class society. Somewhat in the manner of Bowles and Gintis, he sees schooling as a mechanism of legitimation which depoliticizes the issue of inequality and prevents the working-class youth, except in special circumstances, from developing political consciousness.

In the second part of his book, Escande presents data which he has gathered pertaining to recent attempts at reform in Quebec society. In his analysis he compares the present CEGEP structures, which were established following the Parent Commission, with the earlier classical colleges. These latter were primarily middle and upper class, generally preparing their graduates for careers in law, medicine, the priesthood, or the state bureaucracy. They were not institutions which favoured the working-class youth, who were the majority in Quebec and who generally accepted their assigned place in the prevailing division of labour.

The purpose of the reform instituted following the Parent Commission was to increase educational opportunity for those who were earlier deprived. The CEGEP was the post-secondary institution established to do this. It had two main components: a two-year general course leading to university, and a three-year technological course leading directly to the labour force.

Unfortunately, in the analysis of his data Escande largely abandons his earlier theoretical framework of bourgeois/proletariat class structure. Instead, he refers to upper, middle, working, and farmer classes, and he divides the middle class into those who are bourgeoisie-oriented and those who are not. This is all quite confusing and is difficult to defend from a methodological viewpoint if one accepts the earlier Marxist perspective. Nevertheless, in his analysis Escande clearly refutes the contention that CEGEPs have democratized education. They have failed to give prestige to diplomas received in the technological stream and, like the earlier classical college system, they continue to be middle-class institutions. The inequality remains hidden by the distribution (albeit unequal) of students from every class. It may be discovered only if one looks to the underrepresentation of working-class youth, especially in the university preparatory course. It may be perceived less directly if one notes that education for the middle and upper classes (in the CEGEPs) is a consumption variable, not particularly important for eventual career choice where family background is more determining; while for working and farmer class youth it is more an investment (frequently a difficult one) which provides a diploma that tends to ensure the pertinent career but provides little opportunity for mobility.

Escande's presentation is typical of one who writes from such a perspective. What is special about it is twofold. It examines Canadian, particularly Quebec, society and notes that the rapid education change (presented as reform) which occurred there in the past generation has not democratized education. It continues to serve the interests of the privileged classes, although this is usually well hidden. The second special characteristic is an attempted integration of American empirical-style analysis with the typical European Marxist theoretical presentations which generally lack an empirical basis (Murphy, 1979). Although Escande has not been entirely successful, from the point of view of theory any advance in this direction would be a valuable contribution.

## Canadian Interactionists

Several Canadian authors have made contributions in the area of microsociological theory in the sociology of education. These include Martin (1975, 1976), Loosemore and Carlton (1977), Stebbins (1971, 1977), and Novak (1974, 1975). We will examine the work of Martin briefly, following our pattern of not reviewing thoroughly interactionist theory.

Wilfred Martin (1975, 1976) gathered data from open and closed planned schools in Canada which use team teaching. An open planned school, according to Martin (1976:15) is one which may include several or variable physical areas, each with a team of teachers. A closed plan school has no such physical openness, and when team teaching is employed usually only one teacher is active with the students at one time.

Martin gathered data from both of these kinds of settings. Using a symbolic interactionist perspective, he analyzed teacher-teacher and teacher-pupil interactions. Where goals were not identical or only partially coincided, a process of negotiation usually ensued. Essentially this was a process of ordering or trading to make the interests more complementary. Negotiation may include bargaining, a process of exchange which the parties, or at least one party, considers favourable.

Martin delineates five parts of the negotiation process, and the extent of negotiation is measured by substantive content (important or unimportant), direction (who initiates the negotiation), and intensity. The entire process is an attempt to change the definition of the situation which is held by the other party, usually through the process of bargaining and exchange. The exchange may take any form: material or symbolic rewards which have a meaning to the recipient. In the process it is usual for each party to compromise, to redefine the situation, although it sometimes happens that one prevails completely. The other actors involved may be defined as non-negotiables, intermittent negotiables, or continuous negotiables, and the process of negotiation may be between equals or non-equals (Murphy, 1979:168-171).

It is non-equals primarily who are defined as either non-negotiables or intermittent negotiables, and equals who are usually continuous negotiables. In teacher-teacher interaction, negotiation and bargaining are usual. In teacher-student interaction, there are situations which are non-negotiable. The superior would simply impose without bargaining, but because the classroom is expected to represent a somewhat cooperative situation, the process of negotiation is usually experienced.

The definition of the situation, especially the perception of the students by the teacher, is very important. Some students, usually the ones who are evaluated highly, who have a good record, are defined as continuous negotiables. The teachers usually interact or negotiate with them successfully with the result that students, or student and teacher, redefine the situation. Other students are perceived as non-negotiables. These are usually the poor performers. Most are intermittent negotiables. Students, in turn, may see a particular teacher as more or less negotiable than another. It is beneficial to both parties to have the strategies of the other party identified, and the learning of the entire process in the schooling situation is an important aspect of socialization which is to be applied continuously in later life.

Murphy (1979) points out that there are problems with Martin's analysis, particularly how an actor defines whether others are negotiable or not, and also with the stages of negotiation. The student who is interested in detail should review Martin's book, *The Negotiated Order of the School,* (1976). It is a most interesting presentation. More to the point here is a recognition that this analysis by a Canadian author has added significantly to the body of microsociological theory. It is a serious and praiseworthy attempt at viewing the process of schooling, and of teacher-student interaction, in a different and illuminating way. Martin is currently engaged in research in the area of knowledge control within the classroom.

There is another Canadian author, Mark Novak (1974, 1975) who has added to interactionist theory. Novak's analysis deals with the Free School phenomenon, to be treated later, and we will present his findings then.

This brief presentation may mislead the reader into thinking that little is happening in Canada in the sociology of education. On the contrary, research in this area is expanding rapidly, particularly in the centres such as the Ontario Institute for Studies in Education, but theory construction is proceeding more slowly.

There is one additional important area of theory which we have not yet touched. It deals with the definition, meaning measurement and advancement of intelligence. This is a somewhat disputed area and as yet has few definitive findings. It is not usual to deal with this topic thoroughly in a general text, but it is our contention that it is an area of major importance. For that reason we have set aside a separate chapter for it, and we will move on to that fascinating and important consideration now.

# 3

# I.Q.
# and the Meaning
# of Intelligence

## Introduction

It is not usual to include a chapter or a large section on the development of the concept of intelligence and its measurement in a text in the sociology of education. If the problem is treated at all in a separate section, it is much more usual to present a brief history. Practical conclusions which pertain to social policy are frequently presented throughout the text, sometimes with a brief description of empirical data on which they are based. This kind of approach does not lend itself to any thorough or integrated treatment of the problem. As a result students, teachers and parents are often unfamiliar with a global view of the biological and social influences on intelligence and with the educational policy which has a bearing on this.

We suggest that the omission of this aspect of our discipline is a serious error. The study of intelligence itself is usually regarded as more properly belonging to the discipline of psychology. Yet the social influences on intelligence are both real and substantial; and the relationship between I.Q. and educational achievement is so important and so often misunderstood that this entire subsection of our discipline rightly falls within the scope of the sociology of education.

Most of the contributions made within the scientific community in this area in recent years have come from the United States and Britain. Breton (1972) has added substantially to our understanding of social factors leading to career decisions of Canadians, although this is only indirectly related to this problem. Trevor Williams (1972, 1973, 1974, 1975a, 1975b, 1975c, 1976, 1977) is a Canadian based scholar who has made a significant contribution in this field using Canadian data. Our approach in this chapter will be to investigate the problem in a general way. We will present some Canadian data but are more interested in a global approach.

There is probably no area in the entire field of social psychology which is as controversial as this one. The reasons for this will become much more apparent shortly, but principally it is because some of the scientists who favor

79

a strong heritability component to intelligence have taken the position that just as there are individual genetic differences which provide one *person* with a higher intelligence than another, so there are individual genetic differences which provide distinctive *groups* (racial groups, social class groups, national groups) with a higher (or lower) average intelligence. As Williams (1977) so perceptively notes, intelligence is a socially valued trait. People *care* if one takes a stand that one individual has an advantage over another genetically in the development of such a trait, even if they have come to accept it. People *care even more* when this advantage, because of such social factors as inter-marriage or selective mating, is attributed to an entire group such as the American middle class, the Japanese citizens or the Eskimos. No such problem seems to arise when the trait under consideration is not a socially valued one, or not valued to a particularly strong degree, such as height.

The student then must be aware that this entire problem is beset with non-scientific influences which are the result of ideological positions. Weber long ago pointed out that the social scientist cannot eliminate biases but he can know and control them. In examining the evidence to be presented — and we will come to no hard conclusions — it is essential for all of us to know our biases, our ideological positions, and control them. Evidence, not feeling, is the key to scientific development.

Differences, on average, between groups is quite pertinent to the sociology of education, for obvious reasons. Because of this we will present a summary of the heredity-environment debate and the kind of social policies which have been suggested by proponents of both sides.

In the presentation which follows we will first try to explain the meaning of the concept of intelligence and the development which has come about in our understanding of that concept in recent years. We will then investigate the meaning of I.Q. testing, which is an attempt to measure intelligence in some way. There are problems related to the reliability and validity of I.Q. tests which we shall note. Finally, we will review the heredity-environment or nature-nurture controversy in an effort to understand the relative influence of genetic versus environmental inputs in the development of individual and group intelligence. We shall also investigate social policies which have been advocated as a result of this discussion.

Much of the controversy involved in the nature-nurture debate centers around the methodology which has been used, including the assumptions behind various statistical models. If the assumptions are not valid then the statistical inferences will likely be invalid as well. There has been a great deal of newly developed quantitative analysis employed in this field in recent years. This brings with it a number of problems. Many sociologists are not familiar with this type of analysis and hence find it very difficult to assess recent work critically. Moreover, the underlying assumptions of a particular statistical model sometimes are only *nearly* met, yet the results may be offered as if they were present. We do not know how much this departs from accuracy or leads to invalid conclusions.

For these reasons we think it is important for the student dealing with this topic to have some limited familiarity with the related statistical techniques. In the discussion which follows we will attempt to limit the statistical concepts involved to the level of the sophomore or junior sociology student. We will present a review of the meaning of mean, standard deviation, the normal distribution, correlation, reliability and validity. We will also explain the procedure of factor analysis, all in a simplified manner with a relatively low level of complexity. We have relied on many sources in the preparation of this chapter and they are cited where appropriate. There are two sources to which we returned time after time. One of these is pertinent because of the nature of the investigation, it being the principal contribution of Arthur Jensen (1969) in opening up this entire matter to intense social scientific enquiry. The other source which we have relied on so heavily is Hans J. Eysenck's book *The Structure and Measurement of Intelligence* (1979). It is one of the best presentations (in the sense of lack of complexity) we have seen on this entire matter. It reduces a very complex problem to a level which is quite manageable for an undergraduate student. We cite these scientists frequently and would like to acknowledge that in a special way now. But for the problem of repetition perhaps more frequent references to them would be in order. At the same time, in order to prevent one-sidedness in our presentation we constantly looked to the material provided by many of their critics.

## The Meaning of Intelligence

### Theoretical Definitions

The social scientist routinely attempts to define conceptually the variable he is dealing with in his work, and then find an appropriate indicator so that he can measure it when conducting his empirical research.

Perhaps no variable in these overlapping disciplines has proven so difficult to define theoretically as intelligence. What does this concept *mean?* It was introduced as a technical term in psychology about a century ago, and since has become a common word in our language. Jensen (1969:8) in his controversial article on I.Q. and Scholastic Achievement, borrowing from E. G. Boring, states that intelligence is, by definition, what intelligence tests measure. Any one who tries to attribute more to the concept than this is going beyond the point of scientific accuracy. The man-in-the-street understanding of intelligence refers to some capacity or ability to learn, to organize learning and to solve problems. This is certainly not precise enough to satisfy the requirements of scientific accuracy. For the moment, however, it will have to do. We can get a clearer idea of what intelligence means by seeing how our understanding of it developed.

## The Development of the Concept

Eysenck (1979) gives an excellent presentation of the development of this concept and of tests which are meant to measure it. Jensen's (1969) article is more concise and perhaps more complex. Both of these scholars stand on the heritability side of the nature-nurture debate, but there is nothing controversial about this part of their writings.

Eysenck (1979) notes that intelligence, in the mind of the layman, refers to some capacity to organize learning and to solve problems. There is such an ability or capacity in humans which has some physiological base and which, like other physiological traits of the human organism, is subject to now well established scientific laws of genetics, although like other traits (colour, height, weight) it is subject to other influences as well. There is differentiation or unequal endowment relative to this genetic component just as there is for height, and the capacity or ability *develops,* or may develop, at least up to the point of maturity.

Discussion on the nature of intelligence goes back at least as far as Plato and Aristotle, both of whom distinguished between intellect, which guides and directs, emotion, which feels or experiences, and the will which supplies the motive power, the encouragement or decision to act. Aristotle made another important distinction between observed activity and an underlying capacity on which this is based. This implies that intelligence is an ability which may or may not be used in practice, or which may not be used to its maximum potential.

Herbert Spencer was perhaps the final great contributor to the theory of intelligence prior to the modern era. Regarded by some as a pioneer in social thinking, Spencer held that all cognition involves an analytic (discriminative) and a synthetic (integrative) process. Moreover, as the human develops from infancy to maturity this capacity of cognition develops or differentiates into specialized abilities. Spencer used the term intelligence to refer to these abilities. It was borrowed from the Latin *intelligentia* used by Cicero to translate the earlier Greek concept of cognitive ability. Spencer, although he may have been regarded somewhat as a liberal in his day, was a strong advocate of social Darwinism. He held that remedial help for those who were less advantaged would be counterproductive because it would interfere with the evolutionary process and the survival of the fittest. Nevertheless, his contributions were substantial, particularly his introduction of biological considerations and his insistence on empirical evidence (Eysenck, 1979).

Meanwhile physiologists came to understand more about the structure of the brain and the functions of its different parts. The early psychologists, as a result of knowledge gleaned from other disciplines, came to regard intelligence ". . . as *innate, all-around cognitive ability* . . ., an ability which had important social consequences" (Eysenck, 1979:10). This all-around ability was considered to have special components such as verbal, perceptual, spatial and numerical aspects and it would be the role of modern psychology to substantiate this perception, or refute it, with empirical evidence (Eysenck, 1979:8-11).

This brings us to the beginning of the modern era in psychology. Up to this point, which corresponds approximately with the beginning of this century, intelligence had been distinguished from the emotions and the will, was regarded as an innate, all-around cognitive ability which had a physiological base in the cortex of the brain, included certain specialized abilities, was a capacity which developed as the human organism grew, and was one which had important social consequences. This corresponds fairly well with the idea that the layman has even today, three-quarters of a century later. To this point there had been no real effort made at measuring the concept or testing for degree of intelligence, although this was the next step, beginning in France at about the turn of the century. We will cover this in the section dealing with measurement.

Since that point in time psychometrics has made very rapid strides and become a sophisticated part of the discipline. New and advanced statistical and mathematical techniques have continued to evolve, many in fact directly because of work in this area. These techniques were to be used not only for the measurement of intelligence but, more to the point here, for the distinction or separation of special abilities from the all-around cognitive ability which was the general understanding of intelligence up to this point. Two scientists particularly influential in this regard were C. Spearman in England and L. L. Thurstone in the United States.

These and other researchers made the important distinction between mental ability and knowledge, and they investigated the level of complexity or difficulty for a problem or range of problems. For some kinds of mental tasks the solution depended upon a store of acquired knowledge, but for others the answer does not come from simple learning or memory. Greater breadth or scope of knowledge seemed to be correlated with intelligence but was somewhat different from it. It was assumed that for a given population there was a reasonably high correlation between intelligence and (1) learning, (2) the storing of knowledge (memory), and (3) the reduction of this knowledge to general principles which might be applied in parallel areas. It was also assumed that, when dealing with problems of an increasing level of complexity, those only who were more highly intelligent could solve the more complex problems, and could solve them more quickly. All of this was later established empirically.

Spearman introduced the designate g to denote a common or general factor of intelligence which he had been able to isolate in his empirical testing.

It was noted that there were problems the solution of which called for acquired knowledge, and others for which the answer seems to have little relationship with simple learning and memory. As the process of measurement advanced, tests which were designed to measure this ability based on acquired knowledge and memory were referred to as *culture-bound,* and those measuring an ability largely independent of this were termed *culture-fair* tests. Cattell (1971) later introduced a different terminology for these capacities: *crystallized ability* for that responding to culture-bound, tests with the designate $g_c$, and *fluid ability* for that responding to culture-fair tests, with the designate $g_f$.

To this point three analytical constructs seem to have been isolated:

(1) *general intelligence* (g) which is an underlying mental ability to learn, store knowledge, reduce it to general principles, and solve problems.

(2) *crystallized intelligence* ($g_c$) which refers to the ability to learn, store knowledge, and use it for appropriate problem solving.

(3) *fluid intelligence* ($g_f$) which refers to the ability to solve increasingly complex problems independent of stored knowledge other than that which virtually everybody (of any culture) possesses.

There is a strong correlation between these abilities, or these aspects of intellectual ability. When a large number of different tests are applied to a random population, those who score well (poorly) in g do so also in $g_c$ and $g_f$. Those who score well on one test of $g_c$ score well on other tests of $g_c$; they also score high on tests of $g_f$ but not quite so consistently. The scores of culture-bound tests are more consistent among themselves than they are with culture-fair tests. The reverse also is true. Those who score well in one $g_f$ test score consistently well in other $g_f$ tests. They also score well, but not as well, with $g_c$ tests, and they score high in g. That which is common to all tests, regardless of the kind of ability, is the general factor g which Spearman had isolated (Eysenck, 1979:10-24; Jensen, 1969).

We are at the point now where we have some idea of what intelligence means, at least in terms of these three concepts. It remains to try to be more precise about the nature of the capacity which these abilities entail, and to determine if there is a real or only an analytical distinction between them.

Spearman (1927) formulated three laws governing the development of new knowledge which he referred to as the laws of neogenesis — from the Latin for new birth. Jensen reports that when Spearman was examining the many tests which were most heavily loaded for general intelligence (g) he described the general processes which they involved as the ability to adduce relations and correlates. This refers to the ability to distinguish the general from the particular, and to see the particular as an instance of the general category to which it belongs. "These are essentially the processes of abstraction and conceptualization" (Jensen, 1969:9). Jensen notes that tasks which call for the ability to solve problems with these processes are the best measure of g. He also warns that g should not be reified because it is an hypothetical construct which explains covariation among tests. In a large number of tests of different types why is it that variance in (any) one of a group is accompanied by variance in others of that group? It is because of this construct, g, which Spearman isolated.

Spearman's three laws of neogenesis were called (1) the apprehension of experience, (2) the eduction of relations, and (3) the eduction of correlates. The first of these refers to the fact that a person knows or is aware of what goes on in his own mind. If he strives for something he is aware of what it is he is trying to get. If he feels, or knows, he is aware of what it is that he feels, or of what knowledge he experiences. This law may seem very basic, as indeed it is, but it is important because it is upon this that subsequent abilities are built. The second law (eduction of relations) states that ". . . when a person has in mind any two or more ideas . . . he has more or less power to bring to mind any relations which essentially hold between them" (Eysenck, 1979:25-26). If a piece of cork floats on water, and a piece of wood does the same, then cork is related to wood at least to the extent that both are lighter than water. There are two points to bear in mind about this law: that it speaks of essential relations, and that this ability is a matter of degree. Some people are better at, or have a greater ability than others to deduce such relations.

The third law (eduction of correlates) states that ". . . when a person has in mind any idea together with a relation, he has more or less power to bring into mind the correlative idea" (Eysenck, 1979:26). Again, this is a matter of degree. Thus, if a person knows that tigers are members of the feline family, and that cheetahs are related to the species 'tiger,' then cheetahs belong to the feline genus as well.

It should be pointed out that most of this information was uncovered in the process of using tests which attempted to measure intelligence or mental ability. First came the observation that humans have this ability generally designated as intelligence and that it exists in varying degrees, then came a large number of tests or groups of test items which tried to measure the ability, then came an understanding of the kinds of abilities which the tests measured. This latter information resulted because some out of a large number of test items seemed to measure a certain kind or certain aspect of the overall ability rather consistently. We have come to understand the nature of the ability (intelligence) through the use of tests which are designed to operationalize or measure it. It is for this reason that many people define intelligence as that which intelligence tests measure. Of course there are two problems remaining, the task of defining intelligence tests in a different way than merely tests which are designed to measure intelligence, and of understanding if there are other mental abilities which are useful for problem solving and complex reasoning which are not measured by such tests. These problems will become increasingly important when we discuss the validity of these tests and the social policy involved in determining the limits of their use or application.

The final task for us before we leave this section is to determine if g, $g_c$ and $g_f$ are real and distinct from one another. We are especially interested if $g_c$ and $g_f$ are really different even if related abilities, and if each in turn is really distinct from g.

It is necessary to introduce this part of our presentation with a brief discussion of the statistical technique known as factor analysis. We have chosen, in this general text, not to relegate this to an appendix. We consider an understanding of what factor analysis *does* (but not the mathematical theory on which it is based) as an integral part of this presentation. The same approach applies to certain other statistical procedures. Factor analysis was developed by Spearman precisely to determine the nature and meaning of the abilities to which we refer. Again we rely on the presentation made by Eysenck (1979). It is a remarkably simple explanation of a relatively complicated technique. At this level our presentation will be somewhat oversimplified and the student who is particularly interested would do well to go to the source.

Factor analysis is essentially the analysis of sets of correlation coefficients. A correlation ranging in strength from zero to plus or minus one (-1 to 0 to +1), is a quantitative measure for the strength of the relationship between two variables. It has nothing to say about why the variables are related, or about which variable has a *causal* influence on the other one. If the correlation (symbolized by r) is greater than zero (either positive or negative) this indicates that there is some common overlapping element in the two variables. A correlation of .50 or greater is rather high in sociology. We do not often get them in a range which is very close to 1.00. The sign of the correlation (plus or minus) has nothing to do with its strength. It simply tells the direction in which the elements vary. If the correlation is positive, then as one variable gets larger (or smaller) so does the other one. If a correlation is negative then as one variable gets larger (or smaller) the other changes in the opposite direction.

As an example, there is a correlation of approximately .55 between I.Q. and economic success. It is rather obvious that there is some relationship between these two variables. Those who are more intelligent seem to receive a greater share of income in our economic system, although we will see later on that there are other important considerations as well. Nevertheless the relationship is far from perfect. It is not always the case that those who are the most intelligent are also the most successful economically. This is a rather general rule which has many exceptions. The strength of the relationship is indicated by the size of the correlation (r = .55), stronger than .40, weaker than .65. Notice that correlations of .55 and -.55 are of equal strength, although the relationships are in different directions.

If we square the correlation ($.55^2$ = .30) the result tells us the percentage of causal factors that one variable has (often written *explains*) of the other. In our example it is obvious that I.Q. is the independent variable, actually *causing* some part of the variance of the dependent variable, economic success. (It is not always so apparent which variable is the independent one, and in some cases neither one is; the relationship is spurious, or partly spurious). In our case we notice that about one-third (30 per cent) of the variance in economic success is the result of causal factors in I.Q., or working through I.Q.

The student should recall that correlations are meaningless except for data gathered for *groups*. They deal with variance, and there can be no such thing as variance for an individual. Moreover, if the size of the group is small (let us say, 25 or less) then our confidence in the meaning of the correlation is not strong, or the size of the correlation would have to be larger to be considered significant. If the group is the result of a random selection, and is fairly large, then we can usually generalize from it to the larger population which it represents.

Now let us imagine that we are conducting an empirical study. We have selected a fairly large random sample of our population, and we have collected data on fifty different variables which we have reason to believe have some bearing on our dependent variable, economic success. It is onerous to figure out a correlation manually, but the computer will do it for us almost instantaneously. Using the computer, we can quite easily get the correlations of all of our variables with one another. Let us say that we number the variables. We can easily construct a table which is numbered from one to fifty along the top, and also down the side. The computer tells us the correlation of variable 1 with all the others from 2 to 50. We can write each one in our table, and repeat the operation for all the other variables. Notice that there are 2500 cells in our table (50 for the variables along the top, multiplied by 50 for those down the side). Actually we only need half of these because each relationship is there twice. The correlation between variable 1 (on the top) and variable 3 (on the side) would be identical to the correlation between variable 3 (on the top) and variable 1 (on the side). If we imagine a diagonal line from the top left-hand corner to the bottom right-hand corner then all of our correlations would be included once in each half of our table.

This table is known as a *correlation matrix*. It includes the correlations of all the independent variables (vars 2 to 50) with the dependent variable, economic success (var 1). It also includes the intercorrelations of all the independent variables with one another. Each of these intercorrelations between the independent variables is composed of two elements: (1) that which they have in common with the variable, economic success, and (2) the specific relationship which they have with one another. There may be, and quite likely are, certain clusters of variables which have a similar type of specific relationship with one another. This is not immediately apparent. The specific kind of relationship is hidden because the correlations include not only that specific relationship but also the general relationship that each has with the variable economic success (or, for that matter, with any other common variable).

The statistical technique known as *factor analysis* is a procedure which separates out from a group of variables specific relationships which they have with one another after the common relationship they have with a general factor or variable has been eliminated. This may be stated in another way. When we study the intercorrelations between a number of variables which correlate with a particular variable (common or general factor), if we remove from each that part or amount of the intercorrelation which is due to the relationship with the common factor we are left with residual correlations which represent, or may represent, a specific relationship which they have with one another. Moreover, when dealing with a fairly large number of variables (in our example, 50) there are usually clusters of variables the members of which have the same type of specific relationship with one another. The technique of factor analysis isolates these clusters whose members share a similar specific relationship. Actually, the process may be repeated a number of times, each time separating out first the common relationship with the general factor, next the first special relationship which is proper to a cluster of variables, next another special relationship, and so on. Each of these is called a factor (the special relationship among the members of a cluster of variables which is over and above the general relation each has with a common variable or factor). We do not usually draw out a large number of factors because the strength of relationship with each succeeding factor is always weaker. With each step a larger amount of the variance has been explained — hence a smaller amount left to be explained.

There is one other important matter. The factors which are extracted indicate real relationships, but if they are going to be useful to us they must make sense theoretically. We can not emphasize this too strongly. Let us go back to our original example. Imagine that there are five separate variables which logically could be united to form a scale for *fatalism*. We may not be aware of that in the beginning. If each of these variables has a specific relationship with the others over and above that which they have in common with our dependent variable, economic success, then the technique of factor analysis will point that out. We have a cluster of five variables which *hang together,* and when we examine them thoroughly it may become readily apparent that they make sense theoretically — they seem to combine logically to form a factor which we now name fatalism (because this label seems to describe the particular cluster of variables). We can now treat this scale (fatalism) as a separate variable, and this makes sense logically or theoretically. We can understand why these variables form a factor.

All of this is an oversimplification — a rather gross oversimplification — of a very complicated procedure. The mathematical logic behind it, the rules which must be followed to ensure validity, these and other considerations are beyond the scope of this book. However, before our readers are converted into good operative sociologists who conduct empirical research and perform analysis they will have to understand the way factor analysis works to a greater extent, receiving this training probably in an advanced statistical course in graduate school. As an example, we have not even mentioned *rotation,* whether *orthogonal* or *oblique,* and these are critical elements of factor analysis. At present we simply want the student to understand *what is being* (a "factor" which represents a real relationship is being isolated) and to be able to read intelligently literature which includes analysis based on this technique. At this point in time and training the student must take it on "faith" (really on external evidence) that this procedure is a valid one.

Now we can return to our consideration of the meaning of intelligence and to the problem of determining if there is a real distinction between general intelligence (g), crystallized intelligence ($g_c$), and fluid intelligence ($g_f$). Bear in mind Spearman's laws of neogenesis and that our general interpretation of intelligence to this point is a mental ability or capacity to perform these operations to a greater or lesser degree. Early psychologists developed a large number of tests which were designed to measure this ability, and these have become more refined over the years. We are not concerned here with the validity of these tests (that will be discussed later) so long as we understand that they are designed to measure some mental ability, at least an approximation of g. Some will be culture-fair, some culture-bound tests. They are attempting to measure g, or aspects of g which are independent of special knowledge. If we examine the results of a large number of these tests which have been applied to a large randomly selected population, regarding each test as one variable, we can establish a correlation matrix for the relationship which exists among them. If for our sample two tests come up with identical results then they would correlate perfectly (something we would not expect). The size of the correlations are quite high but not perfect, on the average. Remember, test A and test B would have a high correlation if, and only if, they produce nearly the same results.

Examining all of the intercorrelations between the items (test score correlations) in our matrix, we should recall that they all have a common factor, that which they are measuring (whatever this is) — an approximation of g. *It has no meaning to say that they may be measuring different things* because if this were the case the correlations would be zero. The common causal factor which they have is the result of their measuring the same thing. The fact that they do not correlate perfectly is the result of their measuring, on an individual basis, something else besides g. Recall from our previous example that each intercorrelation contains the general relationship which each test has with g, and also any special relationship they may have with one another.

It is here that our technique of factor analysis becomes particularly valuable. Applying it to our correlation matrix (via the computer) it will isolate for us two principal factors, over and above g. These correspond closely to our special abilities, $g_c$ and $g_f$. Moreover, we can continue the process for each of these specific factors and break them down into even more specific abilities of which each is composed.

Eysenck (1979:46-49) reports on additional empirical work done by Vernon (1965) to define further these factors. This analysis indicates the general factor g and two first level or primary factors which correspond roughly with

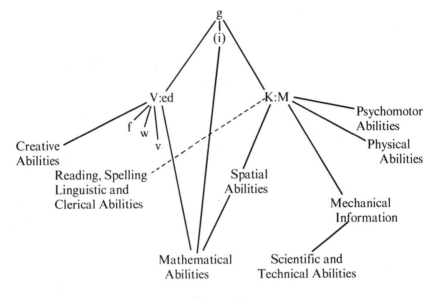

Figure 3-1

Vernon's model of the main general and group factors underlying tests relevant to educational and vocational achievements. Source: Eysenck (1979:47).

$g_c$ and $g_f$ which Vernon labels V:ed (verbal-educational), and K:M (spatial-motor ability). Each of these in turn may be broken down into even more special abilities. V:ed includes creative abilities, fluency (f), verbal-literary (w) and verbal-linguistic (v) abilities, and numerical abilities (n). The factor K:M includes perceptual ability (p) and various spatial, mathematical, scientific and technical, mechanical, physical and psychomotor abilities.

At this point the student in the sociology of education should not be too concerned with a detailed examination of the second level special abilities. This belongs more to the specialist in psychology. From our point of view it is sufficient, although extremely important, to understand what intelligence is. It is an ability, corresponding to Spearman's laws of neogenesis, to experience (and manipulate) knowledge, feelings, reality, *which is socially defined* and which allows one, to a greater or lesser degree, to adduce correlates and relations. Together with this general ability there are the two primary level special abilities, corresponding with $g_c$ — an ability to store, reduce to general principles, and manipulate acquired knowledge, and $g_f$ — a special ability which is largely independent of acquired knowledge other than that which everyone, regardless of culture, is deemed to hold. Each of these primary level special abilities in turn contains other special abilities with which we are not particularly concerned at this time. We can regard $g_c$ and $g_f$ as real, different but highly correlated abilities, but we should be careful about making a real (as opposed to analytical) distinction between them and g. The best way to understand intelligence is as a mental ability (experienced in degrees, i.e., more or less) which corresponds with our description of general intelligence (g) which may be regarded as containing crystallized intelligence ($g_c$) and fluid intelligence ($g_f$), each of which contains more highly specialized abilities. We may regard this as a working definition of intelligence, adequate for our purposes at this level of study. We should regard intelligence as a continuum of these abilities. Remember always that people who possess a high degree of one aspect of this ability possess also a high (but not necessarily equal) degree of the other aspects. They are highly correlated. Stated in another way, those who score high (or low, or in the middle range) of g score in a similar (though not identical) manner in $g_c$ and $g_f$, and in the special abilities each in turn contains.

We have given a good deal of attention to this development of the meaning of intelligence. The reason, as we indicated already, is that *intelligence is socially defined*. Our definition is one which corresponds with the social/cultural reality of the western world in this industrial age. It is probably not significantly different from a definition which would be quite useful in a much different culture, because these abilities which are measured are (or seem to be) almost universally valued. Yet there may be, and almost certainly are, at least minor differences in the degree to which they are valued among cultures, especially cultures which are widely separated on a primitive-modern scale.

This is not to say that these abilities are not real. They are real indeed. They are mental abilities which are analytically separated out on the basis of a wide variety of tests of ability. But we do not know that we have exhausted the supply of such kinds of tests, although to this point we have pretty well exhausted the supply of those we can think of. One of the principal reasons determining the kinds of tests we have developed is that they measure, out of a range or variety of mental abilities, those that we value in a particular and recognized way. This is not to say that there are not other such abilities which we have not come to value, or which we value less overtly. It is the view of the authors that we have tested for most of these abilities and the work of social scientists of the future will be more in the area of refining them than of discovering new ones. This, however, is a judgement on our part and, like many other such judgements, could prove to be wrong.ep In all of this discussion we have been considering intelligence as a trait which does not change qualitatively with age and development. This is the way in which those who discuss I.Q. and intelligence tests normally consider it. Some psychologists, notably Piaget, speak of intelligence as something which changes qualitatively through several distinct stages, so that intellectual ability at one stage is something different in kind and not simply in degree from what it had been at an earlier stage. Since this view of intelligence does not have the same implications for social policy as the one we have been discussing (though it may have in the future), we merely take note of it here and leave further consideration of it to chapter 4.

## Operational Definition

Whereas a theoretical definition denotes the conceptual meaning of a variable, an operational definition, often referred to as an indicator, is the concrete measurement or representation of the theoretical or abstract variable. We come to understand conceptually what a variable means. In conducting our research we must gather empirical data, and this data is meant to represent and to measure the conceptual abstraction. In dealing with intelligence there might appear to be a special problem because we have taken the position that intelligence is that mental ability which intelligence tests measure. This might appear to be circular reasoning or begging the question. The problem, fortunately, is more apparent than real. We do have a conceptual idea of the meaning of mental ability. We have selected out, from the entire potential range of mental abilities, certain ones which we have come to understand as intelligence, and we are able to define these conceptually. The fact that we have used a large variety of tests to assist us in the *selection* process does not prevent us from *conceptualizing* this ability, nor does it prevent us from using an operational definition which is based on such tests.

While some have operationalized intelligence on the basis of the kinds of tests we have discussed, others have attempted to do so on the basis of occupational achievement or prestige. Jensen (1969:13-16) points out that there is a high correlation among various independent scales which measure occupational prestige. The estimate made by psychologists of the intelligence demands of occupations correlates highly with the public's estimate of the prestige of such occupations ($r = .90$). Jensen quotes from Duncan (1969:90-91) who concludes that

> . . . intelligence is a socially defined quality and this social definition is not essentially different from that of achievement or status on the occupational sphere. . . . When psychologists came to propose operational counterparts to the notion of intelligence, or to devise measures thereof, they willingly or unwillingly looked for indicators of capacity to function in the system of key roles in the society.

The tests used to separate the mental abilities defined as intelligence came to rely very highly on measuring abilities which lead to occupational achievement. Duncan continues: ". . . so that what we now *mean* by intelligence is something like the probability of acceptable performance (given the opportunity) in occupations varying in social status." A man-in-the-street theoretical definition of intelligence refers to an ability for abstract thinking and problem solving. A similar type of operational definition refers to the kind of ability which leads to achievement in the occupational and, we might add, the educational world. These are *social* definitions, as we have already pointed out. They are arbitrary. In a different kind of society they could very well be defined in a different way. Again this gives us an opportunity to emphasize the reason for our concern about this entire matter in the sociology of education. There is a strong correlation in our society between educational achievement and occupational prestige. The mental abilities required for both are the result of a socially defined and arbitrary selection process, and are called intelligence. They might very well be different, in which case people with another set of abilities would be the ones who were defined as being more intelligent. In our educational system students are rewarded for the possession and use of certain abilities which we feel important, and other students who might possess different but real abilities are not rewarded in the same way.

## I.Q.: The Measure of Intelligence

It is virtually indisputable that there are real differences among individuals' psychological traits, including intelligence in the way that we have defined it. It is also apparent that some of these differences exist on the basis of genetic endowment, and some on the basis of training or environment. To this point we have not established the degree of importance of each of these components in individual variability in intelligence. We will investigate some of the evidence pertaining to that problem shortly. In this section we will summarize evidence about the kinds of tests with which intelligence is measured. It has already been pointed out that (1) intelligence is socially defined, (2) the abilities which this definition delimits are real, and (3) they have a genetic and an environmental base. Here we are concerned specifically with measuring this trait quantitatively, and subsequently with the reliability, validity and use of such tests.

### Intelligence Tests

Eysenck (1979) points out that we are now in the third generation of intelligence testing, a little less than a century after the process of testing began. Each generation represents an improvement on the earlier one.

We will not concern ourselves here with a description of each of the many varieties of intelligence tests. Some are group tests, others individual; some are more heavily related to achievement, others to ability; some are verbal, others are non-verbal performance tests. Such treatment belongs more properly to a course in psychometrics. In keeping with the nature of our earlier presentation on general intelligence (g), crystallized intelligence ($g_c$), and fluid intelligence ($g_f$), and remembering that the latter two at least include even more specialized abilities, we will try to present a summary of the historical development of testing. We will attempt to understand not only what such tests measure, but how this is done. Later we will allude to problems of reliability and validity.

### The First Generation: The Intelligence Quotient

The first generation of intelligence tests was developed in France by Binet and Simon at the turn of the century. They were not designed to measure "intelligence" as such but were meant to be a selective process which would help predict who would be (more or less) successful in a particular school system. The best way to understand the meaning of those early tests is to hold implicitly that intelligence was defined *at that time* as the set of mental abilities which were required for achievement in the French school system. At a very early date the kinds of tests that evolved were changed somewhat, and refined, especially in the United States, so that they soon came to measure other abilities as well. But even today these abilities are virtually the same. Those that lead to success in school usually lead to success in other areas of life as well, or at least to those other areas in life — such as occupation — with which the testers are concerned.

Binet — he was the principal pioneer — noticed that intelligence increases with age, at least up to about age 15-16 when the *ability* seems to be mature even if there is a cumulative increase in knowledge as the result of the use of this ability in later years. He and his colleagues studied the distribution of intelligence in the population, and they found that it was approximately normal, i.e. , it generally followed the distribution found in the standard distribution or normal curve. In such a distribution approximately two-thirds (68.26%) of the scores fall within one standard deviation of the mean, and 95.4% fall within two standard deviations. In the case of intelligence (as defined by Binet) the curve was slightly skewed at both ends. The student can review the meaning of standard deviation in the section on point scales immediately following this one.

After they had determined the nature of this distribution, Binet and his co-workers experimented with a variety of tests and test items with various levels of complexity for each year from age 7 to age 15 in order to determine the level which the average person of each age group could meet: no more, no less. They could do this fairly easily with sufficient experimenting because in the normal distribution the median corresponds with the mean. We will indicate the formula they used momentarily. Mathematically, because the place each percentile occupies in a normal distribution is precisely known, it is possible to rearrange the items in such a test experimentally until the distribution of test scores matches the distribution of the normal curve. This is roughly what Binet did for each age group.

In any of these specific age groups from 7 to 15, the child of average intelligence would be expected to answer so many test items and no more. The child of superior intelligence could answer more and the child with less than average intelligence would not do as well. Let us take as an example the age 10 group. It was relatively easy experimentally to determine the degree of complexity which the average child in this group could master — no more, no less. This was established at the mental age of 10. Children of a higher mental age could answer more, and those of a lower mental age would answer less. The *chronological* age at which the child could match exactly this ability was divided into the mental age. If the intelligence of the child was average at age 10 the result would be unity, by definition. If a child reached this mental age earlier, the result would be greater than unity, say 1.13. If he or she arrived at it later, the result would be less than unity, say .92. Binet multiplied the result by the constant 100 (effectively removing the decimal point) and he referred to this measure as the Intelligence Quotient (I.Q.). The formula is:

$$\text{I.Q.} = \frac{\text{mental age}}{\text{chronological age}} \times 100$$

Because this distribution matches (approximately) the normal distribution and the mean score by definition equals 100, with a standard deviation of 15, these early French psychologists could tell exactly where a child would fit, compared with other children, on the scale. This was so except for a very small number of children at the upper and lower ends where the distribution was skewed.

As indicated earlier, other psychologists modified these first generation I.Q. tests considerably in the ensuing years so that they included most of the abilities we have already discussed. The most serious problem associated with this quotient is that it is only effective between ages 7 to 15. At approximately age 15 these abilities are fully developed. This is the mental age of 15. As a person increased in age chronologically beyond 15 the mental age would remain stationary. Hence the size of the I.Q. would decrease. There were ways of compensating for this although they were not completely satisfactory. But even if this scale was somewhat less than ideal this was a very important beginning, the first step towards the much more reliable testing which is available today (Eysenck, 1979:56-61; Jensen, 1969:5-8).

There is another problem associated with the formulation of this quotient. Recall from the previous chapter the reasoning of Pierre Bourdieu on cultural capital, assets which receive special value because of the influence of the middle and upper classes. If the test items used by Binet and his associates were correlated with such cultural capital which is arbitrarily given special value in society, then this quotient would be operationalizing precisely that. Similar types of problems relative to the meaning and measurement of intelligence will be indicated subsequently. We do not feel that this particular difficulty is a meaningful one because of lower correlations of any other ability or behaviour with g, $g_c$ and $g_f$ as already explained. This is not an attack on Bourdieu's presentation. Knowledge and behaviour which is valued in a particular school is not necessarily either restricted to or included in the tests which have been used to measure intelligence.

### The Second Generation: Point Scales

Before describing the second generation of intelligence measures, it could well be useful to review briefly what is meant by *mean* and *standard deviation,* two extremely important descriptive statistics.

The arithmetic mean, usually referred to simply as the mean, is the total of all scores divided by the number of scores. It is the principal or highest measure of central tendency, that is, it is the one statistic which best describes an interval distribution (at least a normal one) from the point of view of the average or central tendency. Most students intuitively understand the mean; they have been using it all their lives, calling it the *average*.

The standard deviation is a little more complicated but it is still relatively easy to understand what it does. It is a measure of *dispersion,* giving us some kind of indication of how the scores in a distribution are distributed around the mean. There are other measures of dispersion but it happens that this one has certain mathematical properties which are unique, and very convenient. In order to get a "feel" for the meaning of the standard deviation we should always compare its size to the size of the mean. If it is large, say 20 per cent of the mean, or more, this tells us that the group is quite heterogeneous with a lot of scores spread some distance from the mean in both directions. If the standard deviation is relatively small compared to the mean, say 10 per cent or less, this tells us that the group is rather homogeneous with the scores generally confined rather close to the mean. Actually this is an oversimplification and presumes that all the scores are positive — something which is easily "arranged" by transposition. The standard deviation is a statistic which gives us a special kind of "average" indicating how individual scores are spread around the mean, the average of all scores.

We have already mentioned the normal distribution or normal curve. This is a bell shaped distribution which is perfectly symmetrical, as indicated in Figure 3-2. If we look at one half of this bell shape we notice that it curves first in one direction, then in the other. It just so happens that the point where the curve changes direction is the point indicating one standard deviation from the center of the entire curve, the place where the mean is located. The normal curve corresponds to a precise mathematical formula.

We will not explain here the probability distribution which the normal curve represents. For our purpose now it is enough to note that this distribution is perfectly described by these two statistics, the mean and the standard devia-

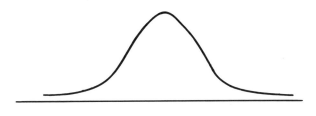

Figure 3-2

General Form of the Normal Curve

tion. We can locate any point on the curve representing a specific percentile if we know the mean and the standard deviation.

We can take any normal distribution for which we know the mean and the standard deviation and *transpose* it to a curve which has a mean of whatever size we desire (say 100, where the mean before was 80) and a specific standard deviation, provided that our curve still meets the mathematical properties of the normal curve. This is exactly the type of procedure which was followed in the second generation of intelligence testing, the so called point scales. Tests which may have mean scores of any size with varying standard deviations are transposed mathematically, still maintaining the shape and properties of a normal curve, to a curve which has a mean of 100 and a standard deviation of 15. This can be done by administering large numbers of different kinds of tests to a fairly large representative sample of the population and determining the mean and standard deviation for each. It is a fairly simple procedure to transpose each distribution to one which has a mean of 100 and a standard deviation of 15. This is then a *point scale* and the scores are equivalents rather than actual quotients. The real unit of measurement has become the standard deviation, each point representing one-fifteenth of this measure. A transposed score of 90 is two-thirds (100-90)/15 of a standard deviation below the mean. Because the distribution is (approximately) normal we know exactly what this means and precisely where this individual fits relative to the entire population.

These point scales are the ones which are generally in use now. There are many of them with a fairly high degree of reliability, and they may be made suitable for any age group except the very young and the very old. There are objective rules for such testing, and if these scales are designed in such a way that they follow such rules, particularly with reference to degree of complexity and spread, then they are valid measures. The results of such tests correlate highly with g and with one another (Eysenck, 1979:71-66).

### The Third Generation: Rasch Scales

There is a new and third generation of intelligence scales now being developed, called Rasch scales. These are still being refined and are not yet in general use, though Eysenck predicts that they soon will be.

One difficulty with point scales is that segments on the scale that are numerically equal are not really equivalent. A score of 50, therefore, does not necessarily indicate a respondent who is half as intelligent as one with a score of 100, as a person three feet tall is half as tall as one six feet tall. The difference between a score of 60 and 70 may be more than the difference between a score of 90 and 100. Rasch scales try to overcome this difficulty. Fundamentally, they try to formulate a test in such a way that all items on it discriminate along the same ability line and none other. They assume that people have a unidimensional quality which alone determines their score on a test and that this ability is independent of the ability of others who take the same test. If all requirements are met, the resulting scale is one in which numerically equal segments refer to equal amounts of the ability measured. This is called an interval-ratio scale, and does not require standard deviation transposition. In an intelligence scale of this sort, the difference between 60 and 70 would be the same as that between 90 and 100, and a person with a score of 50 could be said to be half as intelligent as a person with a score of 100.

The student should not, at this point, be too concerned with the mechanics of how these scales work, other than to understand this ratio properly. They are scales-of-the-future, and if they can be developed properly they will add considerably to the meaning and significance of testing (Eysenck, 1979:66-68).

We have been discussing up to this point the theoretical and operational definition of intelligence and the categories of tests (indicators) which have been used. Before we pass on to the heritability-environment controversy, we must investigate the validity and reliability of such testing.

### The Validity of Intelligence Tests

Eysenck (1979:68-100) reviews the entire matter of both reliability and validity of intelligence tests and speaks very favorably of them. McClelland (1976) is more skeptical and we may say that he represents a substantial number of investigators. Jensen (1969) and those who support him in the heredity-environment dialogue generally approve such tests, or at least the better ones, and impute high coefficients of both reliability and validity to them.

*Validity* refers to the degree of agreement between the theoretical and the operational definition (indicator). In our case it answers the question: do these tests really measure what we want them to measure? It is obvious that if they are measuring something else to a substantial degree they are, at least partially, indicators of something other than intelligence.

There are a number of points already alluded to which we must bear in mind. The first is that intelligence is socially defined. From a large range of mental abilities we have selected out certain ones which we call intelligence. This is a general ability (g) which includes more specific abilities ($g_c$ and $g_f$) each of which includes a wider range of still more specific abilities. This range of abilities enables us to perform mental operations, to a greater or lesser degree, which correspond to Spearman's laws of neogenesis.

A second point of major importance is that tests which measure this range of abilities find high correlations between g, $g_c$, and $g_f$ and all the other still more specific abilities. If they do not then they are measuring different things. They would not be valid indicators. Moreover, in the third place, the results of scores of such tests should correlate highly with one another,indicating that they are pointing to some common ability or range of abilities. Different tests have uniform results. And finally we must always bear in mind that social scientists have developed firm objective criteria for good testing. Tests which do not follow such criteria must be rejected, but it is relatively easy to determine if such criteria are met. They will then satisfy these three points just mentioned, and they then have a high coefficient of validity, in the range of .90 - .91 (Eysenck, 1979:79).

In the social sciences we rarely get coefficients which are much higher. This is because, among other reasons, there are measurement errors involved. We have learned how to make allowance for such error in quantitative computations, but we probably never will learn how to control such error perfectly.

There are a number of specific objections to intelligence testing which should be noted, and to which we should respond in a general way. The first of these is that such tests are biased in favor of the upper and middle classes. We must make a distinction here, or answer this objection in two ways.

Intelligence is socially defined, as we noted already. When we hear claims that the tests are biased towards specific social classes we should determine if the claim is that they are measuring abilities which may be found to a higher degree in such classes. If that is what is meant, then we are really referring to the range of abilities being measured, that is, to the definition of intelligence itself and not to the tests. The answer is probably affirmative, in this sense: intelligence is defined on the basis of certain abilities which are found (on average) to a greater extent in the middle and upper classes (regardless of the cause). Such classes are, on average, more "intelligent" then the aggregate of the remaining classes, because of reasons to be discussed below. If we could catalogue the entire range of mental abilities and separate out those which we use in the definition of intelligence we would be left with certain abilities which we may term *residual* abilities. We have no substantial knowledge of the nature of such residual abilities, or if they correlate highly with one another, or if their measurement would favor certain classes. But if the traditional objection is taken in this sense it has no real meaning. The objection should be that the (arbitrary, social) definition favors the upper and middle classes, recognizing at the same time that there are valid tests for measuring this variable.

The second way of viewing this objection is to interpret it as meaning that the tests themselves are biased. They are composed by middle-class psychologists, rely on knowledge which is ordinarily familiar to people reared in a middle-class environment. We shall see subsequently that there is an as yet undetermined (but substantial) environmental factor which explains some of the variance in intelligence, as there is a genetic component. The objection is that the tests are couched in terms of a vocabulary found in such an environment, and present problems of a type already familiar to people reared in such an environment.

The response to this objection must be qualified. There are tests to which this objection is applicable to a substantial degree, and such tests would be invalid — failing to correspond with the criteria required for validity, especially that the scores of all tests correlate highly with one another. But there are also tests to which this objection does not apply, or applies to such a limited extent that it still allows for a high coefficient of validity.

There is a second important point to be noted relative to this objection. Tests which are designed to measure fluid intelligence ($g_f$), which does not or which hardly depends on an ability related to the accumulation of knowledge, are among the best predictors of scores for crystallized intelligence ($g_c$). The objection would be more valid if there were not a high correlation between these two specific kinds of tests. Moreover, this is a problem which those who design the tests are aware of, and one which is met by the criteria established for good testing. One could challenge these criteria, claiming that they themselves are biased, but such a challenge breaks down when it comes to the high intercorrelations between $g_f$ and $g_c$, or between tests which are designed to measure different and more specific kinds of ability.

Both Jensen and Eysenck in responding to this objection note results relating to certain groups which are just the opposite of that expected by the accusation of bias. For example, Eskimos and Inuit have an average intelligence equal to that of Canadian citizens at large. Yet as a group they rank among the poorer Canadians, have a low level of formal education, and have hardly been exposed to a middle-class environment, to formal language, or to puzzles and problems of a middle-class background. If such tests are substantially biased against these people, then in reality they would have an average intelligence substantially higher than that of the average Canadian. The same situation exists for Japanese people. As a national group they have the highest average measured intelligence ever recorded (about 106). Yet when compared to Canadian or American standards, especially before this generation, they hardly experienced an enriched environment on the basis of class standards (Eysenck, 1979:68-69).

To this point we have been discussing internal validity. There is also *external* validity, the correlation between measured intelligence and other indicators which themselves correlate with intelligence, such as educational achievement and occupational success (Jensen, 1969; Eysenck, 1979). There is a middle range correlation between these variables and measured intelligence. The reason for this lower correlation is that intelligence in these cases is a threshold variable, a necessary but not a sufficient condition for educational achievement or occupational success. We know that there is a very high correlation between advanced educational achievement at the graduate school level and measured intelligence. There is a similarly high correlation between intelligence and occupational prestige, partly but only partly because of the correlation with educational achievement. Bowles and Gintis (1976) state that I.Q. has only a very modest *independent* contribution (Beta = .13) to make to economic success while educational achievement as measured by years of schooling is a much better predictor (Beta = .56) as is social class (Beta = .45). We shall examine this more carefully in chapter 11 and try to explain there the reason for this relationship. For the present let us note that the reason for the higher contribution made by years of schooling is that there are other variables such as motivation, persistence, and personality characteristics which affect both. Many of the variables required for economic success are considerably different from and not necessarily highly correlated with intelligence. The knowledge and abilities required are generally within the range of normal intelligence, although persons with high intelligence may gain this knowledge more quickly or easily. But as one advances through the school system and comes to the higher level, especially the graduate school level, the degree of complexity is much higher and competition much more fierce. Hence the higher correlation with I.Q. at this level. For this reason those who recruit college graduates for positions in industry and commerce are generally interested in a minimally adequate level of academic performance and then in other variables such as personality and degree of participation in extracurricular affairs. But high grade point average is generally a prerequisite for entrance into graduate school, and it is an excellent predictor of measured intelligence.

In summary, intelligence tests which follow the objective criteria established for sound testing possess a reasonably high coefficient of validity, about .90. There is also a substantial though lower correlation, for reasons indicated, between intelligence and both educational achievement and occupational success. This means that the sophisticated kinds of testing now in general use, the second generation or point scales, have a degree of validity which is quite high and compares well with that which is generally found in the social sciences.

## The Reliability of Intelligence Tests

Reliability refers to the consistency of an indicator. It responds to the question: does the operational definition measure the same variable each time it is applied regardless of extraneous conditions? A clock which is consistently five minutes fast would possess a high degree of reliability, although it would not be perfectly valid because it is always making at least a small error.

The reliability of intelligence testing, when controlled for measurement error, is quite high, generally between .90 and unity for people beyond age 8 (Jensen, 1969:18).

There are two points to be noted here. The first is that I.Q. is not stable in early life, before age 8, but it becomes consistently more stable over time. This should not be surprising. Intelligence is a trait which is developing, especially in the early years, just as height is. By the time a child reaches age 9 or 10 most of "fixed" intelligence has been developed just as by age 15 most of the height trait is fixed. There is a reasonably high correlation between measured intelligence at age 10 and at subsequent stages in life, and I.Q. at age 9 or 10 is an excellent predictor of adult I.Q.

A second important point is that intelligence tests may vary considerably for subjective reasons, i.e., because of the state of the subject at the time the test is administered. Illness, depression, fear, intimidation — these and other variables may introduce considerable variation for the same person over a relatively short period of time. One of the rules of good testing is that the subject be in a "normal" condition at the time of testing. The best approach is to take an average of the scores of several tests administered over a short period — a few months or so — after attempting to control any subjective feelings or emotions which would significantly depart from normal. A test administered when a subject is sick, hung over, is intimidated by the tester or in a variety of situations similar to these is almost certain to be less reliable.

We have now concluded our inquiry into the nature and meaning of intelligence, the process of measurement, and the reliability and validity of such testing. Providing that investigators are consistently speaking the same language and are talking about the same thing there is really nothing very controversial about the material we have covered up to this point. However, there is a controversial aspect to most of what follows, particularly the relative importance of heredity and environment in the formation or development of intelligence, and the social policy which is to be used or, in the opinion of some, should be used in the educational system as a result of the knowledge (or lack of knowledge) we have on these and related matters.

## The Heredity-Environment Controversy

Williams (1977) refers to the development of intelligence as a biosocial process. There is virtually unanimous agreement throughout the literature that this is so. The mental ability or set of abilities which we have defined as intelligence is a product of a biological or genetic component which one inherits from his or her parents, and of environmental factors. If the environment is severely deprived, the development of intelligence will be retarded or arrested. If the environment is enriched, just the opposite may be expected to occur. The interaction of the genetic component and the environment varies for every individual.

## History of the Nature-Nurture Debate

Williams (1977:250-251) gives a brief history of the nature-nurture or heredity-environment debate, one which is certainly not new in the social sciences. "Explanations of human behaviour have generally reflected the prevailing Zeitgeist (250)." In the first thirty years of this century following a period in which the social Darwinists were influential, the prevailing explanations tended to have a strong biological component. The influence of Herbert Spencer was strong, and there was a generally conservative and traditionalist climate in the prevailing literature. This resulted in discriminating policies. Spencer himself, with his survival of the fittest attitude, advocated social policies which were not to interfere with social advantages held by "superior" individuals and groups. The madness of Hitler with his belief in the biological superiority of the Aryan race cost the lives of more than six million members of minority groups, mostly Jews.

During the Great Depression and especially following World War II an increasing emphasis was given in social science literature to an environmental explanation. Inequalities in education, in occupational achievement, in income — these and many other such phenomena were attributed primarily to a social or environmental factor. Inequalities in group and individual intelligence were also seen primarily in this light.

## Within-Group and Between-Group Differences

There are differences in any physical trait between individuals. Such differences always have some genetic or biological component. Again height is a good example. We are born with a certain biological determination for height, and this component represents a range. Each one of us will find a personal point in that range depending on the kind of environmental stimulation we have. Such factors as diet, disease and physical mobility are likely to affect our height considerably. As a result the height each one of us attains at his twenty-first birthday is a result of a genetic component and an environmental one. This is obvious.

There are differences in height, or in any other trait, within a population. This is what is technically referred to as the *within-group* variance. If we can gain sufficient information we can explain the relative importance of the variables involved in determining this variance. Again this is obvious.

There may be many subgroups in any population: males-females; anglophones-francophones; blacks-whites, and many others. There may also be average differences in a trait such as height between such groups. It is quite apparent to us for males and females, and it may have both a genetic and an environmental component. This is technically known as *between-group* variance, and again if we have sufficient information we can explain the relative importance of variables which determine this variance. The explanation may be somewhat different than that which explains the within-group variance.

**Recent Developments**

In 1969 Arthur Jensen, an American psychologist, published an article entitled "How Much Can We Boost I.Q. and Scholastic Achievement?" Much of the article followed the quite acceptable format of explaining the meaning and development of the concept of intelligence, methods of measurement, and theoretical considerations on the heritability of intelligence. As long as this was meant to explain variations in intelligence among individuals there was no great problem. But Jensen carried the investigation one step further. Pointing out that certain groups in American society (social groups, racial groups, ethnic groups) have been consistently exposed to a lengthy pattern of intermarriage or selective mating, and on average have an I.Q. which is considerably lower than the American average, Jensen suggested that this average between-group difference which probably began with environmental restrictions may have been transmuted after many generations to the point where it had a genetic basis. He was speaking specifically about Black American citizens only who, as a group, had an I.Q. of one standard deviation or 15 points below the national average.

At this point a storm of controversy arose, much of it in the public media rather than in scientific investigation. To be fair to Jensen, he had not made the definitive assertion that this average difference was due to a genetic component but rather ". . . that it is a not unreasonable hypothesis that genetic factors are strongly implicated in the average Negro-White intelligence difference" (1969:82). He was suggesting that the investigation be opened up to the scientific community, that if his hypothesis turned out to be accurate as his preliminary investigations had indicated, then specific social policies might be adopted which would help to compensate for this difference. Among other vilifications Jensen was accused — quite unfairly in our opinion, even if his hypotheses were proven incorrect — of being racist, and of opening up an investigation or stating a hypothesis which was quite unethical.

Belief is always unsubstantiated empirically; otherwise it is fact or knowledge. We mentioned earlier in this chapter that belief and ideology have very much entered into this controversy and have encouraged people to make assertions which cannot be or have not been substantiated. We advise students to examine their own position on this matter and if there is bias involved to attempt to know it and control it. Jensen's position has not yet been definitively proven or disproven, and the issue remains an important one in the sociology of education where perhaps our major concern is with institutionalized inequality. It also has major implications in social policy in our schools and institutions. Group differences in average intelligence do exist in Canada. It is a *social* problem, at least in the manner in which we deal with such differences, and also in the manner in which such differences came about. Williams (1977:258-259) notes a considerable difference in measured intelligence in Canada between English-Canadian and French-Canadian high school students, and also on a regional basis with students in the Atlantic area having a much higher proportion of scores in the low I.Q. range and a much lower proportion in the high I.Q. range. Why is this so?

In the pages which follow we will try to summarize and simplify this rather complicated problem of the genetic and environmental components of intelligence on both an individual and a group basis. For a more thorough treatment of the matter we refer the reader especially to Jensen's (1969) article and to subsequent presentations made by him and listed in our bibliography, to Williams (1973, 1974, 1975a, 1975b), Eysenck (1979), Eckland (1967, 1971), Black and Dworkin (1976) and Montagu (1975).

We will present Jensen's model in three stages: the genetic component, the environmental component, and the explanation of group differences. We will then present the environmentalist response, i.e., the response of the critics, under two headings: Estimates of heritability for the general population, and heritability as a component of group differences. Jensen's suggestions for pedagogical reform and the response of the critics will be reserved for the section dealing with social policy.

**The Jensen Model**

The Genetic Component

It is difficult to present a simplified summary of Jensen's writings on the heritability of intelligence. It is couched in technical terms and mathematical formulae which are generally familiar to the geneticist but not to the sociologist. We will try to bypass the mathematical complexities, noting that the main problem related to the issue is the inability to measure or estimate accurately the environmental variance. The technical procedure follows well the demands of genetics.

There are several technical terms with which we must become familiar. These include phenotype, genotype, variance, and heritability.

A *phenotype* refers to some trait of an organism (in this case, intelligence) without any reference to the causal influence in the development of that trait. A *genotype* refers to the genetic element in any phenotype, and is established once the egg is fertilized by the sperm. *Variance* is a technical measure of the degree in which a particular variable (in this case, the phenotype, intelligence) changes or varies within a given population. Statistically it is the standard deviation squared. *Heritability* (abbreviated h²) refers to that part of the variance in a population's phenotype which may be explained by or is the result of the genotype. Both variance and heritability always refer to a group or population, never to an individual case.

In addition to these technical terms, we should understand that in any measurement such as the ones with which we are concerned there is always some error (measurement error) which is generally unknown but may be estimated and included in the computations.

The phenotype (P) is always some function (f) of the genotype (G) and the environment (E). We may express this mathematically: $P = f(G + E)$.

The actual formula used by geneticists in their calculations is quite complex because it includes some technical aspects of G or E or a combination (interaction) between the two. Also included are considerations of assortative mating, dominance deviation, epistasis, covariance and interaction, each of which is included in the calculation of the variance of G or E. We will overlook this very technical formula because it is not needed for our understanding of what is going on. In general the variance of the phenotype ($V_p$) is some function of the variance of the genotype ($V_G$) plus the variance of the environment ($V_E$) plus the variance of the measurement error ($V_e$) where these other variables we just referred to (assortative mating, etc.) are included in the computation. An oversimplification of the formula (which is technically incomplete) would then be: $V_P = V_G + V_E + V_e$.

The most difficult variable to measure directly is $V_E$, and in practice it is estimated on the basis of the variance which is left over after all others are computed. This is not an ideal situation and is the principal reason why the calculations are so seriously challenged.

We should also understand the meaning of covariance and interaction. In the instance with which we are concerned, covariance refers to the phenomenon that children with better than average genetic endowments have a better than average chance of coming from parents who provide an enriched environment. Interaction refers to the fact that different genotypes respond to the same environment in different ways.

The formula used to calculate heritability (h²) which we do not give here, includes some aspect of all of those variables. Essentially the other variables modify or make more accurate the calculation of $V_G$ and $V_E$.

Jensen's (1969) calculations were based on an extensive number of studies (mostly from western Europe) of identical twins (MZ), fraternal twins (DZ), siblings, and unrelated individuals. In some cases the children were raised together, in some they were raised apart, sometimes by their parents, sometimes separated from them. Some were raised in environments which were quite similar, others being quite dissimilar. Some of the data were provided by the British psychologist Sir Cyril Burt, part of which was invalid, but subsequent analysts do not think that would change the results significantly. Using correlations of the intelligence of parents and children, and of children with one another, Jensen was able to solve for all of the unknown factors in his equation. The result was that his estimate of heritability ($h^2$) was that it explained about 80 per cent of the variance in intelligence. Jensen was not the only one who had made such calculations, but his estimate was generally higher than that made by others.

The Environmental Component

In his estimates of kinship correlations in intelligence Jensen tries within very broad limits to control for environment, i.e., to study relatives who have the "same" environment. For each individual or pair, environment may be broken up into common environment and specific environment. The *common* environmental factors are those that have a similar influence on the pair; the *specific* environmental factors have a unique influence on each. Moreover, it is critical for sound methodology that the total environmental factor, both common and specific be *representative* — like a random sample — of the entire range of environments. Considering the relative scarcity of large studies and the lack of control by the researcher, Jensen, on the methodologies of these independent studies, it is easy to understand that this is probably the largest source of error in his calculations. Jensen is not unaware of this, and tries to make allowances for it. But if the environments are not truly representative it is likely that the variance ($V_E$) is underestimated, in which case the calculation of heritability ($h^2$) would be unduly high.

Jensen's estimate that $h^2$ accounts for 80 per cent of the variance in intelligence leaves 20 per cent to be accounted for by other factors. Remember that these predictions refer to the average for a population where intelligence is normally distributed. In applying these estimates one must avoid the conclusion that an enriched environment may increase I.Q. *only* 20 per cent in an individual case. This is nonsense. We are talking about averages, not individuals. It should be apparent that individuals or even subgroups who have been exposed to an extremely deprived environment (and who make up only a small percentage of the population) may make dramatic gains without changing the average to any great extent. However, it is not likely that those who are (merely) culturally deprived (not extreme deprivation) would make such dramatic gains if the environment were improved, because there is much less room for environmental variation.

Jensen employs the concept *reaction range*, one often used by geneticists, to point out the range for variation in a phenotype (intelligence) for four hypothetical genotypes. There is genotype variation ($V_G$) in every population. This is represented by the four genotypes, A-D in Figure 3-3. There is also environmental variance ($V_E$ ranging from restricted to enriched. The reaction range (RR) varies for each genotype. The mean I.Q. (phenotype) may vary from low to high to a different degree for each genotype. Taking phenotype D as an example, the mean (phenotypic) I.Q. may vary from a low of approximately 65 to a high of approximately 160 as a function of the environment. This would be a truly exceptional case but serves as a good illustration. The reaction range for the other genotypes is considerably smaller, and only a small percentage of the population falls any substantial distance to the left or

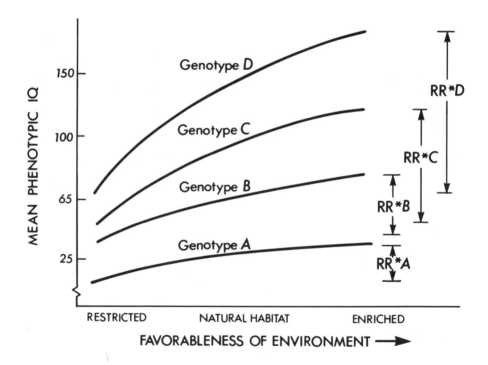

Figure 3-3

Scheme for the reaction range concept for four hypothetical genotypes. RR denotes the presumed reaction range for phenotypic I.Q. *Note:* large deviations from the "natural habitat" have a low probability of occurrence. (From Gottesman, 1963). Source: Jensen (1969:64).

right of the natural habitat. Environment is a social factor and we must emphasize again its importance in the development of intelligence. This social factor includes not only personal interaction between the child and the parents or other significant others. It also includes such things as diet and nutrition (which usually have a social base), poverty, socioeconomic status, the organization of preschool learning, the formation of values and attitudes and many other important elements.

### Explanation of Between-Group Differences

Jensen then moves on to examine the possibility of a substantial genetic component being a causal factor in mean subgroup differences in I.Q. found in the general population, specifically between American Blacks and Whites. The mean I.Q. in the United States is 100, but for the Black Americans it is 85, about one standard deviation lower. Why? Is it because Black people there live in a less nourishing environment? It is probably the case that they do, but even those in the highest class division among the Blacks have a similarly lower average I.Q. than the corresponding subgroup of whites. Jensen proposes that a heritability factor explains this, or at least that this is a not unreasonable hypothesis.

We should note that we are dealing with subgroups where intelligence is distributed normally, i.e. , in full range according to the properties of the normal curve. We are not talking about individual differences. The full range of behavioural characteristics is found in every subgroup which is distinguishable on a racial, ethnic, social class or national basis, and as background factors these are irrelevant when dealing with or comparing individuals.

It is only when different groups are compared with one another as groups that differences in a phenotype have meaning. Jensen's main reason for suggesting the possibility, even the likelihood, of a genetic component to I.Q. differences among races is the assertion that "(a)ny groups which have been geographically or socially isolated from one another for many generations are practically certain to differ in their gene pools, and consequently are likely to show differences in any phenotypic characteristic having high heritability" (1969:80). He has already shown (although with limited evidence and hardly conclusively) that intelligence has high heritability. It is an historic fact that Black people in the United States have been socially isolated for many generations. It has been demonstrated in the laboratory for certain animals, especially rats, that behavioural characteristics may be inbred after as few as six generations. Black people in the United States have been practicing assortative mating for many generations.

Perhaps an oversimplification of what this is leading to is that when a subgroup has been socially isolated for a number of generations and has practiced selective breeding or assortative mating, and when there has been environmental deprivation on a consistent basis during that time, then the resulting difference in the mean of some behavioural characteristic or phenotype such as intelligence which originally had an environmental basis may now, through transmutation, be subject to genotypic explanation. This is precisely the position that Jensen takes. Moreover, he suggests that it has serious social consequences and he is rather severe in dealing with the scientific community if it continues to ignore it. He notes that ". . . the possible importance of genetic factors in racial behavioural differences has been greatly ignored, almost to the point of being a tabooed subject, just as were the topics of venereal disease and birth control a generation or so ago" (1969:80).

As noted, the mean I.Q. of black people in the United States is about one standard deviation (15 points) below that of whites. When social class is controlled this reduces to about 11 points (Shuey, 1966). Moreover, these black citizens have an even lower mean on culture-fair tests, and also scored about one standard deviation below whites in tests of scholastic achievement. Clearly, Jensen suggests, there is the possibility of more than an environmental factor explaining this.

## The Response of Critics: The Environmentalists

In general the responses of critics with which we are concerned fall into two broad categories. They object to:

1. Estimates of heritability of intelligence for the general population, including the validity of measurement of intelligence.

2. The hypothesis that it is generally a genetic factor which explains differences in I.Q. scores between groups, specifically between Blacks and Whites in the United States.

We shall see a third set of objections when we deal with Jensen's pedagogical proposals in the concluding section on social policy.

Estimates of Heritability for the General Population

Kagan (1975) isrepresentative of critics who still challenge the validity of I.Q. testing. He claims that intelligence as defined by I.Q. tests is an artificial construct, that in reality it is more plastic and more substantial even if we have not yet learned how to measure it properly. Lewantin claims that the technique of factor analysis is too subjective; ". . . (it) does not give a unique result for any given set of data. Rather it gives an infinity of possible results among which the investigator chooses according to his tastes and preconceptions of the models he is fitting" (1975:178). It is not valid to move from a subjective interpretation of factors to an objective concept of intelligence. Moreover, Jensen fails to note which parts of I.Q., made up of specific abilities, are inherited and to what extent.

Kagan (1969, 1975) insists that I.Q. tests continue to be white, middle class, and biased. He does not accept the assertion that there are objective rules for removing potential bias or that such tests have a high correlation of reliability. Unfortunately, he provides little empirical evidence for his assertions. His position is rather extreme, going farther than other critics as far as the validity and reliability of the tests are concerned, and he then rejects all of Jensen's findings on this basis.

In the minds of most critics the problems in dealing with Jensen's methodology are regarded as being much more serious. Most are willing to accept that intelligence has a substantial genetic basis (Bronfenbrenner, 1975a; Elkind, 1969). Yet they insist that Jensen's estimate of heritability is too high, and the principal reason for this is the homogeneous nature of the environments of the twins, siblings and parents in the studies used by Jensen. For valid methodology the variability of these environments must be as great as it is for the general population (Bronfenbrenner, 1975a) and critics claim with good reason that this simply is not the case. The heritability estimate would be much lower if the environments fell along a normal distribution. Jensen's assertion that it is only in the extremes of environmental differences that serious consequences are to be found cannot be substantiated (Bereiter, 1969; Gould, 1975). Brace and Livingstone (1975) note that in animal studies deprivation need not be extreme for substantial differences to result, and there is no reason to suspect that it is different for humans. People with the same genes could easily have differences in the range of 25 I.Q. points (Cronbach, 1969). Jensen fails to give proper consideration to affective variables such as solicitude and warmth (Biesheuvel, 1975).

Jensen's attempt to control for environment is primarily a cross-sectional rather than a longitudinal one, and this is a serious error. Hunt (1969:131) notes that ". . . I.Q. of successive ages constitute increasing proportions of I.Q. of the criterion age." Something environmental may preclude development in an early stage which has very large results at a later stage. This is in accord with the Piaget model in which the sequence of the successive components of development is invariant, one stage being an organizer for the next. This is a different kind of genetic model, involving both determination and freedom. Mental growth involves the formation of new and successive mental structures, and Jensen's model does not take this into account well (Elkind, 1969).

In summary, Jensen's critics, with exceptions, are willing to accept the validity and reliability of I.Q. tests, and they agree that genetic determination plays a substantial role in the development of intelligence. They disagree sharply with the reliability of the Jensen methodology, specifically the attempts to control the environmental factor. His estimate of heritability, because of the phenomenon of selective placement in adoptions, is not generalizable to the population at large. It is almost certainly too high, perhaps by as much as 20 to 40 per cent. The problem of genetic difference between groups in the development of intelligence is a valid one for scientific investigation, but our methodology so far is not sufficiently sophisticated to measure it accurately. As Bronfenbrenner (1975a:140) notes, ". . . the heritability coefficient should be viewed not solely as a measure of the genetic loading underlying a particular ability or trait, but also as an index of the capacity of a given environment to evoke and nurture the development of that ability or trait."

### Estimates of Heritability for Between-Group Differences

Jensen's hypothesis about a genetic basis explaining the 15 point difference in average I.Q. between Blacks and Whites in the United States is the part of his presentation which is most thoroughly rejected by his critics. Lewantin (1975) sums up this response. He states that there is no evidence that this difference is largely the result of heritability, nor is there evidence that it is largely environmental.

Many of the critics would agree that it is possible, even likely, that when a subgroup is geographically isolated for a long period of time, causal factors involved in explaining differences between this and other subgroups may evolve from an environmental to a genetic base. But the matter is a little different for social isolation, at least for that degree of social isolation found in this particular case where, despite legal and social sanctions there has always been a considerable amount of breeding between the groups. "My assessment of the evidence . . . — and this is an assessment that we share with many of our geneticist colleagues — is that we simply do not have enough evidence at present to resolve this question. . . . We simply maintain that currently available data are inadequate to resolve the question in either direction . . ." (Bodner, 1975:284).

Another important problem is confusion over the meaning of the term "race." Race may be defined sociologically or culturally as well as biologically, but it is the biological meaning of the term to which the laws of genetics apply. Jensen is not at all clear on this, and in the United States the extent of interracial breeding has been sufficiently high so that the biological concept no longer has meaning (Montagu, 1975). Moreover, even if gene pools affecting intelligence differ considerably between races, as they do within races, there is no *a priori* reason to suspect one race to be superior to another genetically. Heredity theory would suggest just the opposite (Bodner, 1975). It is highly likely that cultural elements related to the use and expression of intelligence is the best explanation.

An even more serious problem is Jensen's suggestion that heritability components within a population may be used to explain differences between populations. This is unsound methodology, and Jensen is not unaware of the problem. Kagan (1969:127) notes: "(t)he essential error in Jensen's argument is the condition that if a trait is under genetic control, differences between populations on that trait must be due to genetic factors. It is important conceptually to distinguish, as Jensen does, between *interaction* of heredity and environment (as when a good genotype gets more of a boost from a good environment than a poor genotype does) and *covariation* of heredity and environment (when a good genotype tends to be located where the environment is good)" (Crow, 1969:155). We have serious problems in the precision of our measurement of these variables, and it is more than possible that interaction explains most of the variation between Blacks and Whites as far as average I.Q. scores are concerned.

The final point to be noted is that if Jensen overestimates the importance of heritability of intelligence for the general population, as he almost certainly does, the effect of this error would be cumulative. The carryover of this overestimation into the between-group part of his theory would confound his estimates there even more. This would be in addition to the difficulties already mentioned pertaining to between-group differences.

## Social Policy

### The Range of I.Q. and the Requirements of Schooling

Here we will deal with social policy only as it is related to the problem of the development, measurement and meaning of intelligence on an individual and group basis, and the use of intelligence tests.

Perhaps one of the first points to note, as Bowles and Gintis (1976) do, is that the range of difficulty of the substantive content which is to be learned in the formal institution of schooling is such that it is within the grasp of all students with a normal intelligence. Problems in learning are more attitudinal and motivational than they are the result of intellectual deficiency. There is a reasonably strong relationship between intelligence and educational achievement, especially at the level of higher education and with reference to grade point average. It is best to interpret this as meaning that superior intelligence allows one to learn the material more quickly and more easily. It does not mean that the material to be mastered is beyond the ability of students who fall within the normal range of intelligence. Moreover, much of what is learned in school is irrelevant, except in a general way, for occupational proficiency. There is little relationship between grade point average and success within an occupation.

If it is the *expectation* that those who have lower I.Q.'s will do less well in school, then it is likely that I.Q. testing, even if it has high coefficients of reliability and validity, discriminates against students who fall within the lower half of the normal range. Many other variables are important, even more important, for educational achievement. We shall be dealing with the meaning of self-concept, teacher expectations, and the self-fulfilling prophecy in other sections of this book. The measurement of intelligence for the use of teachers and administrators confers little advantage to the student except in the case of those who fall beyond the normal range. Moreover, intelligence consists of selective kinds of mental abilities. It is for reasons such as this that I.Q. testing has been abandoned in many areas of the United States, at least for use in the school system, and its use has been qualified to a considerable extent in Canada.

Students who fall within the normal range of intelligence should not be placed in tracks (unless they are interchangeable) at least until the time arrives when they are able to decide in a general way their own occupational future. If they are, then this almost certainly means there is discrimination. From the point of view of ability, students should not be "tracked out." They themselves should make this decision. It is likely that a significant part of the rationale for tracking is for convenience in teaching and administration rather than for the benefit of the student.

The problem, then, is with the interpretation of the practical meaning of measured intelligence rather than with the testing itself. Social policies should be formulated with this in mind.

## Remedial Education: The Jensen Proposal

There is little doubt that there are substantial differences, on average, between individuals and groups in measured intelligence. This has been demonstrated empirically in many cases, along racial, social class and institutional (e.g., orphanage) bases. Jensen's assertion that this, at least in some cases, is the result of a high heritability factor has not been substantiated. But the proposals Jensen makes for pedagogical reform are worthy of consideration regardless of the validity of his heritability assertion.

Jensen (1969) makes an appeal to educational authorities to change the pedagogy of the schools in such a way that they make use of the kinds of strengths which children on the lower end of the I.Q. continuum possess. Looking at studies which attempted to evaluate the massive number of remedial programs in the United States, costing billions and billions of dollars, he claims they have not helped the more deprived students, at least in the long range, to any substantial extent. A similar claim, even if on a smaller scale, could be made for Canada.

Jensen makes a distinction between *associative* ability and *conceptual* ability, or what he refers to as Level I and Level II types of learning. Associative learning is primarily the registration of inputs (i.e., new facts) and the formation of associations, and does not depend to any considerable extent on what the children have learned before except in normal socialization. It is in conceptual learning, which involves transformation of the stimuli and appropriate responses, where children in the lower I.Q. range tend to be at a particular disadvantage. This is because there are differences in patterns of learning and patterns of ability. Jensen simply invites educators to learn more about these differential patterns and to strengthen techniques designed to take advantage of a relatively superior Level I type of learning for children in the lower range of I.Q. He is not suggesting a sacrifice of conceptual ability for those who are strong in the Level II type of learning.

### Remedial Education: The Response of the Environmentalists

The environmentalists acknowledge that Jensen's main point is that children who fall at the lower end of the I.Q. continuum have both strengths and weaknesses, and that the strengths are disproportionately associated with Level I type of learning, the associative ability. They are in full accord that pedagogy should take advantage of one's strengths, so in general they have no argument with a social policy which would do that. The one outstandingly loud caveat is that this not be based on or lead to any discriminatory process, particularly the selection of students on the basis of some criterion other than learning potential, such as on the basis of social class or racial background. There is strong historical evidence of discriminatory processes being used in the past. The first thing social policy must effectively control is this kind of discrimination. *Then* such programs may have much to offer.

### Conclusion

This brings to an end our considerations on the meaning and measurement of intelligence. We have given more attention to this topic than is normally done in a text in the sociology of education. This is a matter of considerable importance, and as we have noted, there are strong social and environmental factors involved. We feel that this kind of enquiry is very much to the advantage of the student, and has very strong implications for educational policy not only in the areas we have so far discussed but also from the point of view of other relevant areas which will continue to turn up as we advance through the text.

As we have noted, there are other variables besides intelligence which have a strong association with educational achievement. In the concluding chapter of our general considerations we would like to investigate some of these, particularly as they are related to theories of learning and development and their relationship to education.

# 4

# *Learning and Schooling*

## Introduction: Social and Psychological Perspectives

Learning may be viewed as both a social phenomenon and a psychological one. It will be defined more precisely below, but for now learning may be considered simply as the growth in knowledge or understanding due to experience. Hence, because it is the result of experience, and experience for individuals usually arises in group or social situations, learning may be dealt with as an effect of social situations upon the individual, and to that extent is the concern of sociology. On the other hand, it is the individual who learns, and it is appropriate to study the dynamics of learning accordingly, that is, as a psychological phenomenon. Clearly the two perspectives are related.

Let us take a simple example. If Johnny has learned to raise his hand to show his intention of answering a question in class, one does not fully understand how Johnny learned this until he understands the process by which Johnny translates the signals from his environment (i.e., rules stated by the teacher, behaviour of others in the class) into a change of behaviour on his own part. These processes are loosely and variously referred to by such terms as perception, understanding, storage, retrieval, execution, etc. The psychologist is particularly interested in studying these processes. At the same time, in order to comprehend what Johnny has learned, one needs to know how Johnny's change in behaviour arose from his experience within the group situation. For example, were the relevant signals those produced by the teacher or those produced by his peers? What value do "rules" have for him? Does the teacher influence his behaviour outside of school as well as in school? What effect do group norms and expectations have on whether or not Johnny will learn to raise his hand before answering a question? The answers to these questions are more often the concern of the sociologist. However, it is obvious that the two concerns merge considerably. In fact, a field of study has arisen which concerns itself especially with this area of mutual concern to the two disciplines. It is called *social psychology*, and it is interesting to note that in universities social psychology may be taught either in the sociology department or in the psychology department, and frequently in both.

The same point may be made for the study of human development. The term 'development' in this context usually refers to the evolution of human capabilities that are more or less genetically determined. The physical ability to walk or to focus one's vision are examples of development, as is the intellectual ability to use logical categories such as classes (Inhelder and Piaget, 1969). Though these are largely determined by heredity both in degree of perfection and in time of manifestation, their evolution is to some degree triggered by the environment, though not as dependent on it as learned capabilities are. For example, the ability to use language is an inherited human capability, subject to development. The ability to speak a particular language, say English rather than Japanese, is a learned capability. The latter is more dependent on experience than the former, but even the general language capability needs to be triggered by environmental stimulation. There is, then, a social and cultural dimension to development as well as to learning and an area of overlap between sociology and psychology.

The sociological and psychological perspectives on learning and development are complementary; neither is comprehended without some consideration of the other. While this chapter will deal primarily with the psychology of learning, it will be restricted as much as possible to what is clearly related to the major themes of the sociology of education. The treatment of major theories of learning will be sketchy. Emphasis among them will be given to *social learning theory* as the view that seems most relevant to sociology. The relationship of motivation and human development to learning will be alluded to, and reference will be made to some of the concrete instances wherein the application of learning principles is practical for the sociologist.

The content of this chapter is particularly important for the understanding of the process of socialization, which will be treated at length in chapter 6. We will see that socialization within our society leads to the acceptance of conditions of inequality and inequity among social groups. To understand why this is so, we must know how children learn, for socialization is by and large a process of learning. This learning begins long before the child goes to school, but it continues there as well. The degree to which a youngster can take advantage of the opportunities provided by schooling is determined to some extent by his early learning, particularly in the areas of language, attitudes and values. The advantage that accrues to children of middle and upper classes is partly a result of the fact that *what* they learn, *how* they learn, and *why* they learn before going to school is more in tune with the content, manner, and purpose of learning in school than is the case for lower-class children. To appreciate this, one needs to know something about the dynamics of learning.

## The Nature of Learning

### Definition

The description of what constitutes learning has always been a major concern of scientific psychology. There have been two basic approaches taken.

One approach has been to emphasize the functions of environmental stimuli and observable responses in the description, and to define learning as an observable change in behaviour. This approach considers factors internal to the learner simply as a medium; what is important is the change in behaviour that the learner manifests as a function of events external to him. Thus, if Billy hears a word that is new to him spoken by the teacher, and later repeats that word, he is said to have learned. The principal advantage of describing learning in this way is that the variables involved in the description can be measured, and there is then the possibility that the study of the relationships between changes in environmental stimuli and learner responses may result in an *explanation* of learning as well as a description. This approach is known as *behaviourism.*

The other basic approach to describing learning is to emphasize the functions of variables *internal* to the learner: variables like sensory channels, memory, cell assemblies in the brain, and so on. When learning is thus described, the change involved may not be observable. In this case, Billy may learn the new word spoken by his teacher, store it in memory, and use the concept so expressed when he thinks, without ever repeating the word aloud or in writing. He has, indeed, learned the word. It is claimed that this is a more realistic approach, that learning does result primarily from internal processing, even if it is more difficult to measure and describe this processing than is the case with external events. This approach is called *cognitivism.* Both cognitivism and behaviourism have many particular variants and sometimes it is difficult to categorize a theory of learning as distinctly one or the other. It is important to remember that they are distinguished mainly in what they *emphasize.* Both approaches recognize the existence of both sets of variables.

Because psychologists have been thus split in their approaches to the description and explanation of learning, definitions of learning tend to be unsatisfactory to one group or another. Gagne (1977:3) has given perhaps the best synthesis to date. He defines learning as "*a change in human disposition or capability, which persists over time, and which is not simply ascribable to processes of growth.*" The processes of growth referred to are maturation and development. Therefore, the change which occurs in the infant that allows him to focus at a distance of ten feet is not due to learning but maturation. The phrase 'which persists over time' also excludes from the definition transitory changes due to fatigue or the use of drugs, and so on.

**Types of Learning: Cognitive, Affective and Psychomotor**

Most people, when talking about learning, will refer to changes in knowledge or understanding; or they will point to the learning of some new physical skill, like swimming or skating. Less often they will refer to learning that results in a change in their feelings or attitudes or values. People are more apt to say, especially in relation to school learning, that they learned geometry or biology or an English sonnet than they are to say that they learned *to enjoy* history, or *to value* scientific problem-solving, or *to tolerate* frustration, or *to despise* certain types of people. There are many reasons for this, not the least of which is that it is easier to measure or determine a person's learning in relation to cognitive and psychomotor products than it is to measure or determine his learning of attitudes and values, which are often referred to as *affective* behaviour (Bloom, 1956; Krathwohl *et al.*, 1964).

Paradoxically, lists of goals of school systems typically give importance to the learning of values, attitudes and "character," but these are seldom specified in ways that allow such learning to be tested. As a result, when school boards say that attitudes and values are being learned by students, there is little they can do to specify *what* attitudes and values are being learned or to what extent. The statements about affective learning contained in lists of educational goals are typically very broad and subject to wide variations of interpretation, and statements about the fulfillment of these goals through schooling can seldom be empirically justified. This point will be taken up again in the last section of this chapter.

The distinction between cognitive, affective and psychomotor learning is not at all new, although the effort to evaluate school learning in terms of these distinctions is quite recent and not widespread. The same distinctions were intended by those who said that the school has for its purpose the physical, intellectual, emotional and moral development of the child. Regardless of the labels used, and regardless of Durkheim's proposition that the school is the agent of moral socialization for the state, it is probably true that the emotional-moral or affective development of students has been subject to much less systematic effort than was their cognitive and physical development.

## Explanations of How Learning Occurs

The two basic approaches to the description of learning provided above correspond to two ways in which psychologists attempt to *explain* learning. These ways are generic: each includes a number of specific variants. The generic psychological theories are called behaviourism and cognitivism.

At this point we advise the reader who wishes to find a detailed presentation of learning theory to consult a more specialized text in psychology.[1] The brief and selective coverage that space allows here is restricted to those areas which have most immediate relevance for our theme, and to contemporary learning theory, which is better understood when its historical roots are known.

## Behaviourism and Conditioning Theories

In attempting to explain learning, behaviourists focus on the relationship between environmental events and observable learner responses, minimizing the role of organic factors within the learner. If it can be shown that, as environmental stimuli change systematically so also do learner responses (behaviour), and if this relationship can be set down as a comprehensive set of scientific principles or laws, then behaviourists feel that learning will have been explained. Consider the example suggested at the beginning of this chapter, that of Johnny learning to raise his hand. If one can know all the events in Johnny's environment that affect him at this time, and how they change so that Johnny's hand-raising behaviour under particular conditions either increases or decreases, then Johnny's learning of this behaviour is felt to have been explained. No recourse has been made to organismic entities like perception, memory, or even intelligence to achieve this explanation.

Because the learned behaviour that results from this process is a function of the establishment or manipulation of certain environmental conditions, the process itself is frequently called *conditioning,* and this term is closely associated with behaviourism.

Conditioning theories tend to be set forth with the aid of paradigms using terms like *stimulus* and *response*. The stimulus may be *antecedent* or *consequent,* depending on whether it comes before or after the response.

There are three conditioning theories which have particular relevance for socialization and school learning: associationism, connectionism, and operant conditioning.

## Associationism

We know from ordinary experience that, when we make a particular emotional response to something, we often generalize that response to whatever is

---

[1]For example: Hill, W.F. *Learning* (3rd ed.), New York: Crowell, 1977; Hilgard, R., and Bower, G.H. *Theories of Learning* (4th ed.), New York: Appleton Century Crofts, 1975. Most introductory psychology texts provide more than adequate coverage of the topics we are concerned with.

closely associated with that thing. If a person is afraid of the pain of getting a tooth out, even the dentist or the dentist's office becomes an object of fear. This secondary fear has been *learned,* because the conditions in which the original fear is evoked always involved a dentist and a dentist's office, and the person has *associated* the environmental stimuli such that the secondary stimuli have taken on the properties of the primary one, and now act independently of it. Using the symbols $S_1$ for tooth extraction, $S_2$ for dentist, and R for fear, the paradigm for this learning is shown in Figure 4-1.

This kind of learning accounts for the acquisition of many attitudes and emotional responses in the process of socialization. For example, the student's attitude to the subject of mathematics might have to be learned by associating mathematics with a particular teacher.

## Connectionism

When we want to learn the vocabulary of a new language, we sometimes do so by having someone say the English word to which we quickly respond with its translation in the second language, and repeat this many times. We are establishing a connection between the words in the two languages, so that when one is presented the other will automatically come to mind. (We are not suggesting that this is the ideal way to learn new vocabulary, but the example is familiar.) The connection, or bond, between the stimulus and response has been stamped in or learned. The learning is made easier if the correct response is followed by some pleasant consequence such as praise; it is made more difficult, or less likely to occur if the response is followed by an unpleasant consequence. Readers will probably recognize this as the explanation of learning by drill or rote. It accounts for much learning that occurs when the meaning of the response is either irrelevant or not understood. Children are often

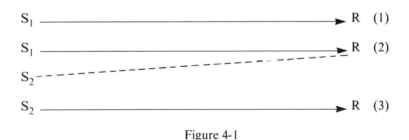

Figure 4-1

Paradigm for Associationist Explanation of Learning

thus conditioned to the learning of rules and, unfortunately, it also occurs in the learning of reading when the student is not developmentally ready to read.

## Operant conditioning

By far the best known contemporary behaviourist learning theory is operant conditioning, associated primarily with B. F. Skinner.

It is common experience that if we are rewarded for a particular behaviour, it becomes more probable that we will repeat that behaviour than if we are not rewarded. In more technical terms, the response that is followed by a reinforcing stimulus will more probably recur than one that is not. If the teacher pays attention to Johnny when he raises his hand, and the teacher's attention is something Johnny likes, then Johnny's hand-raising will probably become more frequent. If the teacher simply ignores Johnny when he raises his hand, then the hand-raising activity will probably decrease in frequency. The teacher may even establish particular conditions when, and only when, hand-raising on the part of students will be attended, e.g., after but not during a presentation by the teacher. In this case the teacher is controlling or conditioning the behaviour of the students by manipulating both the reinforcement (attention) and the conditions under which reinforcement is available. The behaviour of hand-raising at appropriate times is then learned, and that learning is explained by factors external to the learner.

The kind of behaviour subject to this type of learning is *operant* behaviour, that is, any behaviour of which the learner is potentially capable but which does not necessarily follow a particular stimulus (as a knee-jerk follows a tap on the patella). This covers the vast majority of normal motor responses. Skinner would say that it also covers language and thinking, as well as most affective behaviour. Operant conditioning theorists attempt to explain almost all socialization and school learning in this way.

Let us again use a paradigm to show the general application of operant conditioning theory. Again R will represent the behaviour of the learner; $S_R$ will represent the reinforcing stimulus, which follows R. $S_D$ will represent the

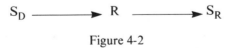

$$S_D \longrightarrow R \longrightarrow S_R$$

Figure 4-2

Paradigm for Operant Conditioning

conditions that signal the availability of reinforcement for a particular behaviour; it is called the *discriminant* stimulus. Thus we have the paradigm presented in Figure 4-2. The paradigm may be stated in words as follows: If the discriminant stimulus is present and the appropriate behaviour is exhibited, then that behaviour will be reinforced. From this relationship, and from observing episodes which variations within the relationship led him to set up in the laboratory, Skinner was able to derive a number of principles of operant conditioning, to the point where he thought that the learning of virtually all non-reflexive behaviour could be thus explained. We repeat that such an explanation of learning virtually ignores variables like intelligence as it is usually defined and places the causal explanation in variables external to the learner; not only that, but those variables (reinforcing and discriminant stimuli) are subject to manipulation by others. There is in this explanation of learning a high potential for *behaviour control* as opposed to individual freedom. Neither the processes of conditioning nor the issue itself are quite so simple as they have been made to appear here, but it should be clear that behaviour control is an important issue and that it has relevance for schooling and socialization in general.

Examples of the application of operant conditioning theory in modern schooling are abundantly available. They fall roughly into two categories: classroom control (often called 'discipline') and instruction. Teachers often manipulate reinforcement contingencies to control the behaviour of their students, especially to reduce disruptive behaviour and replace it with more appropriate behaviour. For example, a teacher might notice that Billy is being particularly annoying today, distracting his classmates with weird noises and paying no attention to his assigned tasks. She has spoken to him several times, but his behaviour has become more disruptive. Suddenly realizing that the very thing that is reinforcing Billy's behaviour is the attention he is getting from the teacher and his classmates, she begins to ignore Billy and manages to have the rest of the group do the same. Frustrated, Billy sits sullenly for a while and then, for something to do, turns to his assigned task. At this point the teacher pays attention to Billy, either by smiling at him or offering words of encouragement. Finding that the teacher's attention is available to him in this way, Billy continues with his work.

In the foregoing example, two global responses on Billy's part were conditioned: disruptive classroom behaviour and assigned task performance. The teacher withheld reinforcement to eliminate the former and provided it to encourage the latter. Though the example is somewhat simplistic, it does illustrate how operant conditioning theory underlies some techniques of classroom control. The application of this theory in school can become much more sophisticated in the hands of a teacher trained to use it. The systematic use of operant conditioning to influence the conduct of others is often called *behaviour modification,* though this term embraces the use of other theories as well.

For instructional purposes, operant conditioning theory is applied in what is called *programmed instruction* which, through the use of technology, has now begun to be implemented through *computer assisted instruction.* We will not attempt to describe programmed instruction here except to say that it is based on two principles: that a learning task should be broken up into components small enough so that the learner can achieve success in almost all his attempts to learn the components; and that knowledge of having completed a task successfully is reinforcing to the learner. Programmed instruction is used in schools primarily to make it possible for an individual learner to work at his own pace in a given task. Besides its sophisticated computer form, it can be implemented in written materials or in so-called teaching machines. It is less directly relevant for sociology of education than is behaviour modification.

## Cognitivism

Parents, teachers and other adults can often be heard to say, in reference to a given youngster, "I wonder what's going on in his head." This might refer to how the child thinks as he does, or why he is having difficulty learning, or where he gets his creative ideas, or similar processes and products of what-goes-on-inside-his-head. Psychologists who ask in a serious way about what goes on inside a person's head when he is learning, and who systematically attempt to answer the question so as to explain that learning, are often called cognitive psychologists. As was said above, cognitivists emphasize factors internal to the learner in their attempt to explain how learning occurs. They also insist that the behaviour change that occurs as a result of learning may be covert and unobservable.

Contemporary cognitivism has its roots in early structuralism and later Gestalt psychology. Again we refer the interested reader to psychology texts for a summary of the related historical developments. Today there are two main branches of cognitivism: *cognitive-field theory* and *information processing.*

Cognitive-field theory, while presenting a view of how learning occurs, also includes the areas of motivation and personality development. We will by-pass it here, not because it is an unimportant perspective but because what there is in cognitivism that is relevant to our theme can probably be understood better by looking at the information processing view; indeed, although the two views differ somewhat, they have virtually the same implications for and applications in the sociology of education.

Many of the factors that cognitive psychologists see as explaining learning are only indirectly measurable. Some are only hypothetical constructs; that is, they cannot be observed or measured, but some entity answering to the description given must be there (within the learner) to explain behaviour that can be observed. If this seems abstract, remember that intelligence itself is an hypothetical construct which is assumed to exist to explain what we call intelligent behaviour. Because they deal with such factors, cognitive psychologists frequently use models of different kinds to make their descriptions of learning processes more concrete. Three types of models frequently used are (1) *sensory perception* as a model of understanding (this is used even in ordinary language as when a person says "I see what you mean"); (2) *flow charts* to illustrate the temporal sequence and causal relations among elements of information processing; and (3) the *computer program* which, in this case, is constructed to resemble as nearly as possible the process involved in human thinking and problem-solving.

*Information processing* is the term used by many cognitive psychologists to comprehend all the steps that occur from the time a stimulus impinges on a learner's senses to the time when it results in some cognitive product such as a stored image or concept, a new relationship to assist in problem-solving a creative idea, and so on. Information processing theorists do not all agree on the steps involved, but a typical view is illustrated by the flow chart in Figure 4-3. This chart emphasizes the steps leading to memory storage, indicated by the solid arrows. Most cognitivists distinguish between short-term and long-term memory, but this is not universal. Steps 4 and 5 involve the use of mnemonic devices to facilitate storage and retrieval, such as when a person reduces a telephone number by chunking its segments into two sets and storing the sums of the numbers in these sets. This model assumes that once information is stored in long-term memory, it is never forgotten, even though retrieval may be difficult.

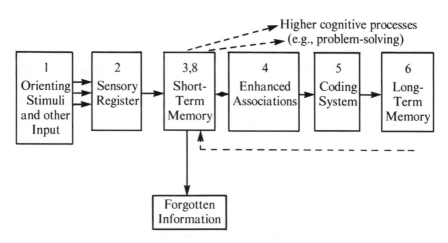

Figure 4-3

The flow of information that results in learning involves both *mental structure* and *cognitive processes* that operate on the content of these structures. It is generally held that the flow starts when a stimulus or stimulus situation impinges on one or other of the senses. Not everything which is thus perceived in the senses is attended to, however, but a process of *selection* operates. What is selected is transmitted through the *sensory register* to short-term memory and held briefly while it is *coded* for *storage* in the *long-term memory,* which storage lasts indefinitely. If and when the information is needed, it is *retrieved* to short-term memory and used as before in relation to some response. When that response involves the activity of relating this particular information to other information just received or similarly retrieved, the behaviour is referred to variously as understanding, thinking, problem-solving, creation of new forms or ideas, and so on. When it involves no such activity, we have simple recall. The responses of recalling, understanding, thinking, etc., are externally manifested through symbols, usually spoken or written language but including mathematics, graphic arts, music and so on.

There is evidence (Neisser, 1967) that at each stage of the processing of information, the information itself may undergo change, so that what is eventually represented may be a more or less severe distortion of what was originally presented. It is safe to say that all of us have experienced this phenomenon, whether it be manifested in the writing of exams or the telling of stories or whatever. The distortion may occur in the process of sensation, encoding, storage, or retrieval. For example, when we are recalling (retrieving) something from memory and our recall is less than perfect, we make inferences about the temporarily forgotten elements of information, and in the process distort the information that was originally stored in memory. In this we *construct,* or reconstruct, what we know, and the cognitive explanation of learning is seen to involve continuous mental activity and interaction in a process far less mechanistic than that proposed by behaviourists. Furthermore, our constructions are often related to our affective states so that at times we perceive what we *want* to perceive rather than what is really there, and recall what we want to recall. So, although we have only barely referred here to motivation and personality, it is clear that cognitive and affective states and processes are not at all independent of one another, but intimately related.

It may also be seen that, in this explanation of learning, stimulus situations may be internal as well as external, not only in terms of primary drives like hunger which prompt us to behave, but in relation to the various cognitive constructions we produce, which then become the objects for further internal processing. Learning is, therefore, more self-activated than in behaviourist explanations.

An example might help at this point. Suppose Tom is a student in a high school history class where the topic is the Bolshevik Revolution. The teacher is at the moment providing basic factual data about that event. Tom "perceives" this information through the visual and auditory channels. (For the sake of illustration, we will treat the words used as simple physical stimuli, though the process is much more complex.) The information is registered, and placed in memory, at which point Tom glances at his text to see if the particulars given by the teacher are the same as those recorded there. Remaining attentive, he then codes the new information and stores it in long-term memory. When the teacher subsequently asks students to compare the Bolshevik Revolution with both the French Revolution and the American Revolution, Tom retrieves from long-term memory the recently stored data as well as information stored earlier about the other two wars. Retrieval at this point may result in distortion; the information recalled is not exactly what was originally received or stored. Distortion may result, for example, from the fact that Tom feels favorable to socialist causes, and he may pay attention to those aspects of the information that would support his leanings. Further, the analysis and synthesis that he makes when called upon by the teacher may be considerably different from that given by a classmate who was exposed to exactly the same information but is more aristocratically inclined. Tom may even perceive this difference and examine his own 'understanding' of the topic, which illustrates that the object of perception taken in this sense may be something not directly derived from the observable environment.

As a follow-up to this example, it is appropriate to observe here that social groups which have systematic differences in their life experience will probably differ in the way in which they perceive or understand new information. This is because, as illustrated in the example, information is filtered through experience with its concomitant motivational implications. The same objective message will probably be understood differently, for example, by children from lower and middle classes to the extent that the message relates to different class experience, and similarly for different racial, ethnic and religious groups, and even for males and females. For the same reason, some students may simply block out or fail to attend to information or stimuli which other students find interesting, and systematic social class differences may be reflected here as well.

Cognitive psychologists continue to try to analyze the information processing sequence and, together with neurophysiologists, to identify and describe mental structures and their operations. To the extent that their purpose is achieved it would seem that schooling (particularly instruction) could be made more effective. Cognitive psychology seems to hold more promise than strict conditioning theory for application to the areas of concept attainment, problem-solving and creativity (though it clearly does not deal with psychomotor learning in any comprehensive way). Instruction based on this explanation of learning would tend to give more emphasis to these areas without denying the importance of the learning and retrieval of basic information.

Before leaving our treatment of the cognitivist explanation of learning, it might be appropriate to raise several questions relevant to our principal theme. What would the cognitivist explanation imply for the practice of intelligence testing, which relies on manifest behaviour? Does school teaching attend sufficiently to the distinctions among recalling, understanding, thinking, problem-solving and creative activity? If it does, *who* is taught to recall and *who* is taught to engage in the higher cognitive processes? In relation to these questions, the reader might recall Jensen's suggestions related to level I and level II learning, outlined in chapter 3.

We will now turn to a learning theory which seems to have the potential for integrating the behaviourist and cognitivist explanations, though as yet that potential is far from having been realized.

## Social Learning Theory

Because experimental psychology in the behaviourist tradition had emphasized the phenomena of learning as their object of study, and because almost all behaviour was seen by them to be a set of learned (rather than instinctive) responses, behaviourist experimental psychology was often called simply "learning theory." The term was used in a very broad sense and not simply with the connotation given it in ordinary language, i.e., classroom learning, etc. Most behaviourists in the first part of the twentieth century, however, had concentrated on explaining phenomena that involved only one individual at a time or, if it involved two, the other was there to control the learning of the first by arranging stimuli or controlling reinforcement.

The term *social learning theory* is given to the explanation of learning and learned behaviour proposed by those behaviourists who, in the first place, are concerned with learning as it occurs in groups of two or more, whether or not there is a deliberate effort on the part of one or more members of the group to influence the learning or the behaviour of the other(s). They concentrate on phenomena variously referred to as imitation, observational learning and vicarious learning, and they also deal with the aspect of mutuality or reciprocity in learning, that is, the influence that members of a pair or a group have on one another in a learning situation involving two or more. They deal with all kinds of learning — psychomotor and affective as well as cognitive (Rosenthal and Zimmerman, 1978:77-79) — and claim to do so more adequately than conditioning theory or cognitive theory, incorporating elements of both of these in their approach. The most prominent psychologists in the development of social learning theory have been Neal Miller and John Dollard (Miller and Dollard, 1941; Dollard and Miller, 1950), Robert Sears (Sears, 1951; Sears, Maccoby and Levin, 1957), Albert Bandura (Bandura and Walters, 1963; Bandura, 1969; 1971; 1973, 1977), and most recently, Ted Rosenthal and Barry Zimmerman (Rosenthal and Zimmerman, 1978). The earlier social learning theorists dealt mostly with the development of motor and affective responses; Rosenthal and Zimmerman, following Bandura's lead, have recently extended the social learning analysis to the area of cognition.

It is important to realize that in the social learning framework, imitation has a broad reference. Besides the copying of a model's exact behaviour (e.g., in learning to dance), it includes abstractions from modeled behaviour, as when rules or principles are learned from the observation of others' behaviour, and the learning of novel behaviour through extension and generalization of an observed response. Furthermore, modeling (the behaviour of the one(s) being observed) refers not only to directly observed behaviour but also to symbolically mediated behaviour (e.g., behaviour described through language symbols). Therefore, modeled behaviour may be transmitted in books, tapes, etc.)

How, specifically, does social learning theory account for learning? To answer this question it is necessary both to describe the evolution of this theoretical framework from earlier behaviourist approaches, and to introduce several distinctions fundamental to the theory.

Recall that behaviourists insisted on dealing with overt or measurable variables only, which they called stimuli (objects or events which instigated behaviour) and responses (the resultant behaviour). Skinner elaborated the notion of reinforcing stimulus, the consequence of the response which had the effect of increasing the likelihood of occurrence of that response. None of these psychologists was willing to deal with variables internal to the organism whose behaviour they were studying, since these variables were not directly observable or measurable and, they thought, had no *determining* effect on learning. A school of behaviourists arose in the thirties whose adherents, led by Clark Hull (1943), were reluctant to accept this rigid position. They were called the neo-behaviourists, and they were willing in their attempt to explain learning to point to internal organismic variables which could be at least *indirectly* measured. They spoke especially of *drives,* which could rise or fall in urgency and which, having reached a particular level of urgency, could stimulate behaviour. Thus hunger, which could be measured in terms of the number of hours of food deprivation, is a drive which can be an internal stimulus for behaviour. Fear was regarded similarly, being measured in terms of its correlative physiological signs (galvanic skin response, etc.) Furthermore, the reduction of urgency of such a drive (e.g., satiation of the hunger appetite) was regarded as pleasant and, therefore, reinforcing for any behaviour which resulted in such reduction. Now then, we have an internal stimulus, called a *stimulus drive,* and an internal reinforcer, called *stimulus drive reduction,* both of which can be related to external, measurable events or objects. This behaviour in terms of not only natural or primary drives such as hunger, but also of learned or secondary drives such as need for affiliation, need for achievement, or even the need for affection. Many of these drives are most often satisfied in social or group situations. Also, insofar as it dealt in organismic variables, it was a step in the direction of cognitive theory, presaging current attempts to integrate behaviourist and cognitive explanations of learning.

Normally, when we think of learning as being influenced by or under the control of reinforcement, we think of that reinforcement as directly affecting the learner. Social learning theorists, applying behaviourist theory to imitation and observational learning, showed that reinforcement could be indirect or *vicarious*. In this case, an observer seeing a model reinforced for a particular response, might himself learn that response, or might be induced to emit the same response previously learned.

Social learning theorists make an important distinction between *acquisition* of learning and *performance* of learned behaviour emphasizing that the two may not only be separated in time, but differentially related to both stimulus and reinforcement conditions. They point to this distinction to support their claim that though the *performance* of a learned behaviour may be affected by the observed reinforcement of the model's response, the *acquisition* of learning may not; and that, in fact, the stimulus role alone of the model may produce (covert) learning in the attentive observer, regardless of whether reinforcement is observed or anticipated.

An example may help here. Rosenthal and Zimmerman (1978:71-72), to illustrate this distinction, summarize a study done by Bandura (1965). Three groups of children were exposed to a modeling sequence. One group saw the model being punished for his actions; for a second group, the model was neither punished nor reinforced but ignored for the same actions; for the third group, the model was rewarded. The children were then placed in the same setting and their imitative behaviour was recorded. As might be expected, the group that viewed the rewarded model showed the most imitative behaviour; the ignored model group was intermediate, and the punished-model group displayed the least imitation. Then, without further training, all of the children were promised rewards if they would demonstrate what they had learned. All three groups displayed comparable levels of acquisition.

The study demonstrates that the anticipation of rewards (called *incentive motivation*) affects the presence or absence of imitative performance, but that learning occurs separately from such incentive motivation.

The use of words like 'attentive' and 'anticipated' in this context betrays the leaning of social learning theorists towards an incorporation within their framework of cognitive processing, including perception, storage and retrieval of information. Rosenthal and Zimmerman (1978:74-77) indicate that cognitive processes of attention and selection intervene between the presence of physical stimuli (the model's behaviour) and the acquisition of learning, and that it is the cognitive representation of the reward rather than its actual occurrence in the past that is significant in determining responses.

Meanwhile, it may be helpful to note here that to the extent that social learning theory is valid in its explanation of learning, *it bears upon practically all of the elements of socialization,* whether in the home or school or any other group setting, and whether related to explicit objectives, incidental learning, or the hidden curriculum. Social learning theorists are, in our view, probably correct in claiming to provide the best potential for the integration of behaviourist and cognitive approaches to the explanation of learning, and relating that explanation realistically to human interaction. Douglas Hintzman, himself a cognitive psychologist, states:

> Social learning theory, as developed by Bandura and others, is compatible with most of the work that has been done on behaviour modification; at the same time, it recognizes the role of cognitive processes in complex social behaviour. It provides a framework within which both 'behaviour modifiers' and 'information-processing psychologists' can fit. Furthermore, it directs attention toward important questions of how cognitive processes and behaviour interact (Hintzman, 1978:405).

This concludes our description of representative theories of learning. From what we have said, it should be clear that learning can hardly be understood independently of human motivation. We will turn briefly to this topic now.

## Motivation for Learning

The topic of motivation is a very, very broad one. Motivation psychologists attempt to answer the question, "Why do people (or animals) as individuals or groups, behave as they do; and why don't they behave differently?" Let us say from the start that it is our intention to treat only a very small part of the answer to that question, and to treat even that only superficially. However, because learning, and here we are confining the term to its naive, traditional meaning of setting out to learn something, is a human activity, we can speak of it as being motivated, and we can ask what motivates it.

### Innate Motives

One position in psychology is that learning satisfies a natural or innate, genetically related need. This is variously referred to as curiosity, the need for exploration, or competence. In this view, learning carries with it its own reward, and we learn one thing rather than another at a given time because at that time and in those circumstances that particular learning is especially related to our curiosity. It may be noted that to this point we have more of a description than an explanation of motivation. It does not allow us to predict what a person will want to learn in the future, nor how to change things so he will be curious about some particular learning. However, there is evidence that when, in relation to a particular learner, a stimulus situation possesses characteristics like novelty, incongruity, surprisingness, complexity or ambiguity, what we refer to as curiosity will tend to be aroused (Berlyne, 1960;1965).

**Learned Motives**

We are more concerned here with the type of motivation for learning which is itself learned rather than innate. Part of the socialization process involves the development in children and adolescents of socially approved goals, wants and desires. These wants and desires (motives) and the disposition to pursue these goals are learned; we think their learning is best explained through social learning theory as elaborated above.

Since motives can be learned, it is theoretically possible that such learning could encompass a very broad range of motives and that even such motives as curiosity, which many hold to be innately human, are learned. Having said this, we will confine our discussion of learned motives to two: the need for achievement and the fear of failure. These will serve as examples relevant to our concerns from which a degree of generalization might acceptably be made. We will also allude to the construct 'locus of control' and make passing mention of attribution theory, two areas of motivation theory related to our theme.

At the risk of redundancy, we repeat our caution here about the ambiguous use of the word 'learning.' When we speak of *motives being learned* we are referring to their being acquired through experience in a manner described by one or other of the theories of learning treated earlier in this chapter. When we speak of *motivation for learning*, we are using the term 'learning' in its non-technical sense, normally referring to the activity of students in school or other more or less formal instructional setting.

The Need for Achievement

Henry Murray (1938) developed a lengthy taxonomy of human needs, among which he included one called the *need for achievement*. This he defined as the need "to overcome obstacles, to exercise power, to strive to do something difficult as well and as quickly as possible" (Levy, 1970:137). David McClelland (1951, 1961) gave impetus to the study of this motive. He was largely concerned with the degree to which the need for achievement was manifested in large populations, and how its presence affected economic development for that population (national group). However, other researchers (Atkinson, 1965; Atkinson and Feather, 1966; Alschuler, 1973) attended more to the development of achievement motivation in the individual and to its relationship to success in school learning. Vidler (1977) gives a review of this research. In his work, Vidler describes the need for achievement in terms of an internalized standard of excellence and says that, while this may result in notable observable accomplishments, "it is the attitude toward achievement that is important, not the accomplishments per se" (p. 67).

Fear of Failure

Another learned motive is *fear of failure* or, as Atkinson (1965) calls it, *motive to avoid failure*. He defines it as "a capacity for reacting with humiliation and shame when one fails" (p. 33). That such a motive explains some general behaviour is hardly in dispute. That it may explain or account for a significant element of the motivation for school learning is at least disturbing. In school, failure is socially defined, or at least it is customarily defined by someone other than the learner. It is even institutionalized, as manifested in expressions like "failing a grade" or, from a teacher, "I failed three students" In the adolescent, fear of failure may be augmented by pressure from university-bound peers. It is obvious that if there is such a thing as the pursuit of learning for its own sake, the fear of failure in the activity of learning would seem to negate it in persons susceptible to such fear. Beyond this, it is easily perceived that fear of failure can be a very strong motive for cheating in school.

### Locus of Control and Attribution Theory

The term *locus of control* "refers to the perceived causality of behavioural outcomes. At one extreme (internal), the individual thinks of himself as being responsible for his own behaviour. At the other extreme (external), the individual sees others or luck or circumstances beyond his control as responsible for his behaviour" (Fanelli, 1977:45). Persons differing in locus of control, therefore, differ in the degree of blame or credit they accept for outcomes consequent upon their behaviour. Hence, to the degree that a person sees these outcomes as the result of his own effort, and to the degree that the outcomes are desirable, he may be expected to work towards them.

School learning and achievement is more likely to be valued by the person with an internal locus of control rather than an external one, provided he values the outcomes to which such achievement appears to him to lead.

A construct related to locus of control is *attribution of responsibility*. The theory connected to this construct is often called *attribution theory*. This theory extends the concept of locus of control to differentiate four elements of causality or responsibility: ability, effort, task difficulty, and luck (Fanelli, 1977:52). Ability and task difficulty are seen as stable characteristics; effort and luck as unstable characteristics. These are related to locus of control in that those with internal locus of control are more likely to attribute responsibility for success or failure at a task to either ability or effort; those with external locus of control will attribute responsibility in terms of task difficulty or luck.

Locus of control and causal attributions may be found differentially among different social groups. Coleman (1966) pointed out that sense of control (i.e., internal locus of control) was more important for Blacks in relation to educational achievement than even self-concept of educational ability. Henderson (1972), cited by Brookover and Erickson (1975:330), found that a sense of control was decidedly lower among Black than White elementary students. There is indirect support for this in an unpublished study by Masters and Peskey, cited by Fanelli (1977:58-59), but other studies cited there provide conflicting evidence. Racial differences have been found in causal attribution (Frieze, 1980:59) indicating that Blacks have a greater tendency to external attribution. The data on social class differences is inconclusive (Fanelli, 1977:59). We may note that the personality correlates of internal locus of control (Fanelli, 1977:47-51) are in large measure those which are differentially characteristic of persons in middle and upper classes, and that a similar relationship appears to hold between the personality correlates of external locus of control and the characteristics of persons of the lower social class.

## Effects of Punishment

Punishment still finds frequent use in our schools; while the use of corporal punishment may have diminished considerably, other forms of punishment such as ridicule, detentions, withdrawal of rights or privileges, and undesirable allocations continue to be found. It is normally used by the teacher for two purposes: to eliminate disruptive behaviour or to *punish a student for failure to learn.* We wish to stress that our concern here is with the latter, and is primarily with the motivational effects of such punishment.

Punishment is normally used to change behaviour, usually to suppress something undesirable so that another, different behaviour can replace it. However, when punishment is used for failure to learn, it results not in the suppression of a behaviour (failure to learn is the opposite of "behaviour" in this sense) but in an avoidance response; the student who was otherwise unmotivated to learn may now do so to avoid further punishment, much as the man on a bed of hot coals will keep jumping to avoid (or escape) pain. But what happens to the learner in the process? He undergoes a process of aversive conditioning whereby the particular learning in which he is engaged is associated with an unpleasant stimulus, in which case it will begin to take on its properties, as the reader will realize by recalling the earlier treatment of stimulus association. Such learning, therefore, becomes unpleasant in itself. Furthermore, once the threat of punishment for failure to learn is removed, the likelihood of the person engaging in similar learning is lessened, and this may generalize to other forms of "school learning." It would seem likely, also, and consistent with learning theory, that such learning would be less well retained and less effectively transferred than learning that had occurred under pleasant circumstances.

The issue of punishment for failure to learn is important for sociologists, since what is involved may be related to the use of measures for social control. Punishment as to both type and degree is used differentially in families of different social classes (Kohn, 1969). Teacher expectations and perceptions of the effectiveness of punishment also seem to vary in terms of the social status of the recipient, leading to its more frequent use with students from the lower class. If this is the case, then the desire for scholastic achievement will, for this reason alone if not for others, be less likely to thrive in lower-class students. Paradoxically, teachers who use punishment would normally say that they are simply trying to "get them to learn." Their error may be in assuming that, since punishment *can* be effective in suppressing undesirable conduct (i.e., disruptive behaviour) in students, it can also be effective in eliminating failure to learn. However, it may be a case of winning the battle but losing the war.

One school practice that is not normally thought of in terms of punishment for failure to learn, but often has the same effects for students, is the negative evaluation of student performance on examinations, term papers, etc. , and the refusal to "pass" the student to the next grade. This is a complex issue and at this time we wish merely to note that it is frequently perceived by students as punitive, regardless of the intention of the teacher or school administrator. The topic of grading and evaluation will be considered in chapter 9.

We have dealt briefly with several aspects of motivation to learn, including innate curiosity; the learned motives of need for achievement and fear of failure; the concepts of locus of control and attribution of responsibility; and finally with the effects of punishment on motivation to learn. There are many other concepts in motivation theory related to motivation for learning, but these have appeared to us the most relevant to our theme because of their sociological implications.

## Interaction of Learning and Development

It has been seen in chapter 3 that a student's intelligence is usually measured in terms of intelligence quotient or I.Q., and that this is age-related in that the expected performance for the person of "average" intelligence increases with age. A superficial interpretation might lead one to believe that progression here is smooth and nearly rectilinear. This belief would tend to be supported if all learning could be explained in terms of factors external to the learner, to which the learner simply reacted. As we have seen, such an explanation of learning, common among early behaviourists, is no longer widely held; most of those who study learning today appeal at least partly to internal factors through the medium of which the learner interacts with his environment. Variations in the functioning of these internal structures would, then, affect learning, both in process and content. It is the view of many that such variations occur in a somewhat systematic way so that the structures grow in complexity and serve as the basis for qualitatively different functions as the individual develops. Furthermore, the progression in intellectual development is not rectilinear but is best represented by an upward-directed, curved line with rises and plateaus. The plateaus represent the more-or-less distinct developmental stages, and the rises represent the transitions from one stage to another.

## Developmental Stages

Developmental stages are understood, in this context, as qualitatively different levels of organization for (human) functioning, such that the functioning at one level cannot be explained merely as *more* of the functioning characteristic of a lower level, but as of a *different kind*. The novelty in functioning results from a new organization of the elements of the structure basic to that functioning. The new organization results in turn from an interaction among those elements stimulated by but not determined by environmental events (cf. Lerner, 1976:30-33).

To attempt to simplify this rather complex statement, we will turn to one type of human functioning, thinking or intellectual functioning, and use an example to illustrate the concepts involved. Developmentalists would hold that intellectual functioning is based on cognitive structures, which are complex organizations of single elements. The structure that is basic to pre-logical thinking cannot, by simple accumulation, result in logical thinking However, practice in pre-logical thinking and attempts to accommodate apparent contradictions may lead to a state of readiness upon which the cognitive structure, over a short period of time (maybe months) reorganizes itself and becomes structurally capable of supporting first-order logical thinking. The reorganization is not produced by the accumulation of the products of earlier functioning, but occurs in a prepared structure in response to environmental demands. If the cognitive structure is not adequately prepared, then reorganization will not occur.[2]

The position that there are developmental stages in intelligence or any other human functioning is far from universally held by psychologists. The contrasting view which allows for continuous, cumulative rather than discontinuous development is referred to by Lerner (1976) as the unity-of-science view and is held generally by behaviourists. Social learning theorists generally do not hold to developmental stages as more than a useful device for describing change (Rosenthal and Zimmerman, 1978:30).

---

[2]This description is the authors' interpretation and oversimplification of the position of Jean Piaget and his colleagues. Piaget has been a very prolific researcher and writer, but the part of his theory to which we refer can be found in his book *The Origins of Intelligence in Children* (1963) and his and Inhelder's *The Early Growth of Logic in the Child* (1969). Both of these books appeared somewhat earlier in the original French.

## Stage Development and Cognitive Learning

If stage development reflects the reality of human functioning then assessment of intelligence and academic achievement in the standard fashion will be at best misleading. To say that people differ in the rate at which they pass through the stages of intellectual development is not to say that they differ in the ultimate ability for intellectual achievement. At the same time, if a student is relatively late in reaching the stage of intellectual development required for, say, beginning reading, but finds himself in the "grade" where reading is expected, he is likely to be labeled as lacking intelligence and certain negative expectations will develop concerning his performance. These expectations may function then as self-fulfilling prophecies. On the other hand, if his stage of development is recognized for what it is, and he is allowed to function without negative sanction in a manner consistent with that stage, probably he will in time learn to read and learning may remain a source of excitement for him. This is not at all to suggest that students should not be challenged to learn, but only that, like anyone else, they should not be required to exhibit performance of which they are as yet incapable. No one would think of reprimanding a six-month old baby who hasn't yet learned to walk (or even a two-year old; rather, one would seek the source of what might be termed a developmental disorder).

## Stage Development and Socialization

Socialization is clearly a learning process, and we have already said that we believe social learning theory offers the best promise for explaining the learning that is involved. At the same time, the existence of developmental stages, both in intellectual or cognitive and affective development, would appear to place certain constraints on socialization.

One area in which this might be illustrated is that of value formation, an important aspect of socialization. Value acceptance and value formation are here regarded as distinct; value acceptance does not entail the justification of the value, while value formation does. Value acceptance may be based on identification with a model (parent or other) or simply on authority, and is within the range of competence of a three-or-four-year old. Value formation involves formal reasoning with hypothetical conditional propositions. The person must be able to say, concerning a value that up to now he had accepted, "If (honesty) were not worthwhile . . .," and be able to complete the statement by indicating a logical consequence. He must then compare this to the proposition he has held up until now (presumably, that honesty is worthwhile) and reach a justifiable conclusion. The point to note is that this process requires a stage of intellectual development not normally acquired until adolescence (Inhelder and Piaget, 1958; Erikson, 1968).

Kohlberg (1964), elaborating and extending Piaget's views on moral development, has suggested that moral judgement is constrained by developmental stages and is much less subject to socialization than social learning theorists would have it. Although he recognizes the effects of punishment and identification, he suggests there are limits to such effects related to the stages of cognitive development. His position is a controversial one and not yet adequately based on data, but the general thrust appears sufficiently valid to support the point we are making here.

In summary, then, it would appear that there is an interaction between learning and development that is relevant to schooling in that an assessment of a student's ability or performance without consideration of developmental stages could result in false labeling and negative expectations. This might preclude the student's achievement of normal scholastic goals, either because of the effect of the labeling on his self-concept and motivation, or because of the operation of self-fulfilling prophecies related to the negative expectations.

## Teaching, Learning and Schooling

What has been said in this chapter will provide background for the understanding of much of what is to follow in the discussion of issues in the sociology of education. It would appear useful, however, to mention here in summary form some of the more comphrehensive issues which must be viewed in terms of the psychology of learning, motivation and development.

### Teaching and the Formal Goals of Schooling

The following is a list of the "aims of public education" as provided by a provincial education department. It is used here for illustrative purposes only, on the assumption that it does not differ very much from lists of aims provided in other provinces.

> Public schools in Nova Scotia should provide all students with a series of learning experiences that will help them to contribute to society and to live lives that are personally rewarding and fulfilling.
> Students should master knowledge and skills, develop a set of values, mature attitudes toward society, self-discipline and positive work habits, and be encouraged in initiative, spontaneity and creative effort through intelligent teaching.
> More specifically, the aims of public education are:

1. To develop competence in effective written and oral communication, with emphasis on clarity and precision in use of language.

2. To develop competence in arithmetic and understanding of basic principles of mathematics.

3. To develop knowledge and understanding of history particularly of the history of Canada, so that the students may be aware of the cultural diversity of their country and its relation to other countries and peoples, and have a basis upon which to assess current values.

4. To develop the habits and methods of critical thinking and to foster the natural desire to learn and understand.

5. To provide opportunity to all students to learn the second official Canadian language and to enable those with ability and interest to achieve bilingualism.

6. To provide opportunities in school programs and activities for students
   a) to be creative and to exercise originality and imagination;
   b) to develop civic, social, and moral responsibility and judgement;
   c) to have their curiosity encouraged and to develop knowledge, understanding and appreciation of themselves, their fellow beings, their environment and the relationship among the three;
   d) to acquire habits, attitudes and intellectual skills that will be helpful in employment and in training for employment;
   e) to develop knowledge, habits and skills related to achieving and maintaining good health and physical fitness (Nova Scotia Department of Education, 1979).[3]

This is a very broad statement of aims. The Nova Scotia Department of Education also publishes a large number of curriculum guides for various subjects each of which suggests specific objectives for instruction in these subjects, presumably consistent with the above statement. Teachers are free to select from or alter these objectives, but again they are to be consistent with the broad statement of aims.

There is no intention here to fault this statement of aims, nor to defend it. We use it merely to illustrate a number of issues of particular concern to us.

It will be observed that the statement of aims is comprehensive in that it refers to goals in all three of the areas of learning: cognitive, affective and psychomotor. As people in the field of education are wont to say, "The school must be concerned with the whole child." However, the aims are to be achieved

---

[3]Alberta, in contrast to Nova Scotia, distinguishes between the goals of education and the goals of schooling, listing separately the respective goals as adopted by its Legislative Assembly (MACOSA, 1979:883-85).

through instruction, and if one is to be satisfied that the aims have been met there must be assessment of some kind. Instruction implies the holding of some theory about how learning occurs, whether it is explicit and well articulated, or implicit and replete with inconsistencies. We are at this time unable to support the following statement with hard data, but it is the authors' view, based on experience in observing teachers in classrooms as well as teaching them in courses in sociology and educational psychology, that the typical teacher espouses a *cognitive* learning theory *as the basis of instruction*[4], even though he or she may acknowledge that learning may occur otherwise. In such a case the teacher will almost inevitably emphasize the attainment of cognitive objectives, and will treat affective objectives as if they are to be attained in the same way. Furthermore, when it comes to the assessment of achievement of objectives, there is general agreement among educators (Krathwohl *et al.*, 1964) that it is more difficult and time-consuming to assess the achievement of affective objectives than of cognitive objectives. (How do you *know* that a student 'appreciates her environment,' as the above statement of aims suggests she should?) The result is that the achievement of affective objectives is less carefully assessed, and often left to the teacher's subjective judgement. That being the case, teachers tend again to emphasize in their formal instruction explicit objectives the attainment of which can be objectively measured or assessed. (Interestingly, the same argument can be made for the preference for lower-level to higher-level cognitive objectives.)

## Incidental Learning and the Hidden Curriculum

If the above argument is valid, then much of what is stated in terms of affective objectives for school learning is not taught formally, and its achievement is not assessed. It is reduced to the level of incidental learning. This means that not only are those attitudes, values, and appreciations that the school system claims to be teaching its students not necessarily learned, but that what is learned in this area of attitudes will likely be an effect of the non-verbal behaviour of others rather than of what they say. 'Others' here includes groups and systems as well as individuals. The learning of roles and expectations as conveyed to students by the school system may well incorporate attitudes and values contrary to those that the system claims explicitly to be teaching. Thus the elements of social control referred to so prominently in chapter 1 are meant to be learned in school (differentially), even if through

---

[4]Paradoxically, many of the same teachers use methods of classroom control consistent with conditioning theories.

the hidden curriculum. We shall see in chapter 11 the claim of Bowles and Gintis (1976), with some empirical validation, that differential and hierarchically valued personality characteristics are passed on in this way to people belonging to different social classes, again through the hidden curriculum. The same may be said of sex stereotyping.

It might be noted that in the illustrative list of the public aims of education, explicit mention is made of curiosity as a motive for learning, while nothing is said of the learned motives to which we have alluded in this chapter. Yet it would appear that these learned motives have a great deal more to do with socialization processes to the extent that these are a part of school learning. To some degree, the differential learning of motives themselves is a part of the hidden curriculum.

## Conclusion of Part 1

This brings us to the conclusion of Part 1, Theoretical Considerations, which we think are especially important in the sociology of education. We have presented highlights of the general body of theory concerning the nature of society and the purpose to be (or being) fulfilled by the institution of schooling within that system. To this point that theory has been unable to resolve the problem of why students are *systematically* treated inequitably. We are aware of systematic discrimination, of course. Our concern is to establish or understand the basis of such discrimination. Is it because these students are qualitatively different in ability or motivation? Or is it simply because they are allocated inequitably to inferior positions in life?

One very meaningful variable which is especially important in the selection process which occurs (whether it is equitable or not) is intelligence together with its operational measurement. We have tried to demonstrate the meaning which intelligence has for the social scientific community and the evolution of intelligence testing up to the present day. We have made the point that intelligence is not a scarce commodity. At this point we hope the reader will understand how variance in measured intelligence has the potential for allocating students to different avenues to achievement — or failure — in the educational system, and in later life.

We also feel it important to include a chapter highlighting various theories of learning and related principles of motivation and development. Although this is related more closely to the discipline of psychology, it should be apparent that social factors are extremely important not only in the early years at home, but also at school and among one's peers. The mechanics of learning are not our particular concern, but the social factors involved in learning and development explain much of the variance in educational achievement. The motivation to learn is critical. Students learn, even those who may be described as the most dismal "failures." The problem is that they are often motivated to learn something other than that which is in accord with the goals of the school, and the personnel in school have much to do with this.

Much of the rest of this book is concerned with identifying and explaining these social factors which have such a strong influence on a student's achievement. Some of these factors exert their greatest influence in the preschool years, especially within the family or as the result of differences in life chances emanating from socioeconomic status or social class differences. It is to these which we turn our attention in the following section.

# Part II

# Preschool Influences

The inequality which is so characteristic of schooling has its roots in social processes which occur before the child comes to school for the first time. In Part II we attempt to enquire into several structural and macro-level variables which have a significant relationship with educational opportunity and attainment. In chapter 5 we deal with social class, sex stratification, and the position of the Native People in Canada, much of this in a descriptive way.

Many of these structural factors are mediated through the family and the socialization which occurs therein. Chapter 6 presents material on values, norms and attitudes which develop within the family and are themselves related to social class. They are most important in explaining unequal educational attainment for, as we shall see in Part III, the intergenerational inequality to which schooling contributes is a result of both external and internal stratification variables. It is the external variables with which we are concerned in this section. Much of their influence even in the educational domain comes about before the child begins school.

# 5

# Socioeconomic Status
# and Educational
# Opportunity

Perhaps the single most important direct and indirect relationship in the sociology of education is the one between social class, distributively defined, and educational opportunity. A student's social class of origin affects virtually every educational variable: ability, environment conducive to the development of intelligence, aspiration, motivation, self-concept of ability, achievement as measured both by grades and length of schooling, type of track pursued, ability group assignment, participation in athletics, student government and other extracurricular activities, truancy, discipline and dropping out. The relationship is such that it generally holds even when other important variables are controlled, and it almost always favors those in what is regarded as the superior class position.

We have presented certain important aspects of the theory of social stratification in chapter 2, and we will return to this again in chapters 11 and 12 when we consider the relationship between education and lifetime earnings, and the results of schooling. It is important to be conceptually clear on the meaning of our terms. Social stratification ". . . is a hierarchical configuration of families (and in industrial societies in recent decades, unrelated individuals) who have differential access to whatever is of value in the society at a given point and over time, primarily because of social, not biopsychological variables" (Rossides, 1976:15). One of the most important characteristics of that definition is the designation: *over time.* The privileges which accrue to people in a superior social stratum are such that, at least to some extent, they may be passed on to succeeding generations. One of these privileges is formal education, or achievement in schooling, and the intergenerational transmission of that privilege, by whatever mechanisms, is responsible for the relationships between social class of origin and the variables related to schooling that we indicated at the beginning of this chapter. When we speak of the relationship between class and educational opportunity it is to this that we refer.

The terms class, social class, social status and socioeconomic status are often used interchangeably, although they do not always have precisely the same meaning. *Class* refers to one's position in the market place, that is, one's ability to earn, or to receive income from wealth (Weber); or to one's relationship to the means of production (Marx). These are not the same thing. Weber is referring to class in the *distributive* sense, to one's possessions (more or less) as a result of earning ability. Marx is referring to class in the *relational* sense, to one's position relative to the means of production (owner or non-owner, oppressor or oppressed). This is a much more complex relationship. It is likely that if class in the relational sense were to disappear with the abolition of private ownership, class in the distributive sense would remain (Hofley, 1980); or at least intergenerational inequality which results from one's position in the market place and from other factors would remain. Because of the qualitative difference in the meaning of the term, when Marxists discuss the inequality (including that related to educational opportunity) which results from class they are usually concerned with different causal components than are those who define class in a distributive way. We are sympathetic to the Marxist position, and it will become increasingly apparent in subsequent chapters that this kind of analysis has much to offer which is not contained in another viewpoint. Despite that position, in this chapter we are primarily concerned with the relationship between social class in its distributive meaning and certain specific educational variables.

Unfortunately, the confusion relative to stratification terms does not end here. Weber refers to *status* or social status which is prestige accorded for social reasons to a person as occupant of a specific position. Such prestige is another form of privilege, though not strictly an economic one even though it may be translated into economic privilege in many cases. Functionalists often refer to *social status* in this way but are much less clear about excluding the economic variable or one's position in the market place. Weber also refers to *power*, the ability to impose one's will on others. We suggest bearing that in mind as a third and different dimension although it is frequently overlooked in the sociology of education. Power also may be translated into economic privilege, and prestige. The term *socioeconomic status* refers to one's position in a hierarchically ordered series of strata which is a weighted average of those things which are valued in a society, usually designated as privilege (wealth, income, consumer goods), prestige (status, with accompanying style of life) and power. There is even debate as to whether socioeconomic status in this sense is made up of discrete categories or is a continuum. Sometimes, but less frequently and less precisely, the terms social status and social class are used in this meaning as well.

We have entitled this chapter *socioeconomic status and educational opportunity* in order to make it clear that we are concerned here with the relationship between one's position in the various social strata, and educational opportunity. One of the major problems in sociology is the operational definition of socioeconomic status. That definition is frequently restricted to occupation, education and income, all of which are highly correlated. Occupation is usually the result of education and is the principal though by no means the only determinant of earnings. Education may be considered as both a class variable (required for a superior position in the market place) and a status variable (life style, pattern of consumption). It is also correlated with power. More educated people are usually more highly organized for the pursuit of collective goals.

There is another complicating factor to which we must allude. Many of the community studies conducted in early stratification research by American scholars such as the Lynds, Warner, Hollingshead and Reddick, and Havighurst asked respondents to rate the social position of community members without specifying the criteria to be used in this judgemental process. The researchers then frequently tried to determine or form some kind of index which could be used to measure operationally the social positions which were subjectively described. The variables employed sometimes went beyond occupation, education and income to such factors as type of dwelling and area of residence. Race, ethnicity, and even the number of generations since the founding one in the specific society were also considered or involved.

Martin and Macdonell (1978:213-218), in an apparent attempt to simplify this rather complicated matter, refer to sociologists' categorizing people along social class lines. "A social class is a social grouping of individuals who have certain common characteristics concerning some objective attributes, and who behave differently from those with other characteristics of those attributes" (p.213). This description has the great advantage of simplicity. The authors note that the principal operational variables are education, occupation and income, but that other variables such as ethnicity and language (and, we might add, sex) are also influential.

In discussing socioeconomic status we must make the distinction between social class of origin and social class of destination. The former refers to the socioeconomic position of the family of origin, in our case the family from which the student arises. The latter refers to the socioeconomic position the student will occupy as an adult when independent of the family of origin. We shall refer to this again when we review the status attainment process in chapter 12. When discussing educational opportunity we avoid the various meanings of equality (to be considered in chapter 13) and are concerned with the general or average ability to achieve in the educational domain in accord with specific characteristics.

In the presentation which follows we shall be concerned with socioeconomic status as a descriptive variable, particularly with the greater or lesser possession of educational attainment, occupational prestige, and income. We shall try to show the relationship between these variables (in class of origin), and educational opportunity. Occupation, education and income are highly correlated. We will tend to be more thorough when dealing with parental educational attainment and the child's educational opportunity because there is more descriptive material, and especially more recent material, available. We will also discuss occupational prestige and income, and their relationship with educational opportunity. We will then deal with some special relationships, particularly sex stratification and educational opportunity, and we will comment on the position of native people in Canada.


## Social Class and Educational Opportunity: Some General Comments


We have already pointed out that social class is related to virtually every variable pertaining to educational attainment in industrial societies. Breton *et al.*, (1972:524 footnote) have demonstrated that the ". . . correlations recently obtained in Canada between SES and educational performance items such as aspirations and expectations show high consistency with American findings." The literature is replete with studies demonstrating a similarly high consistency in other industrialized nations, including the Soviet Union (Heyneman, 1976; Dobson, 1977). The relationship, which is so pervasive, works through many intervening variables. However, in studying this relationship in less developed nations, and specifically Uganda, Heyneman (1976) shows that it is less strong. There, he notes, the preschool influence explains less of the variance in achievement. The schools themselves (in Uganda) have a stronger effect on cognitive achievement than one would expect in industrialized society. Heyneman's study was of primary school pupils, presumably the most pertinent group because of the importance of a good start.

Many authors have noted that schools are middle-class institutions. Richer (1974:521), citing Collins (1971), explains that this generally means that ". . . they provide for the continuity of the stratification system by transmitting the values and life styles of the middle class." Observing teachers in a small Ontario school, he found that "working-class children received significantly less than their share of teacher interactions when classrooms were highly teacher-centered. In student-centered classrooms, they received significantly more of their share of teacher interactions" (Richer, 1974:521). We can say that such differential treatment is typical in the class relationship.

"Educational achievement may be represented in simple form as an effect of three variables: ability, aspiration, and opportunity" (Hansen, *et al.*, 1972:573). Each of these, in a wide variety of empirical studies, is related to social class. The crucial question is whether class distinction ". . . results in differential encouragement of educational abilities and aspirations and/or in unequal opportunities to apply those abilities and realize those aspirations" (p.574). The findings of the study by these authors conducted among 6,000 high school students in San Diego were that intent was very important relative to college entrance, and that it in turn was strongly related to both ability (I.Q.) and social class. Social class is very important for and is mediated through the intention to enter college. Ability, itself dependent on class, is important as well. There is a noticeable absence of a direct link between social class and college entrance. The relationship is less direct, being mediated especially, and being disguised we might add, by ability and intent. In this context intent is similar to or identical with aspiration. While this study was limited to college plans among high school students, we can presume that in general it would also apply to plans for educational attainment at a lower level.

In studying educational access in Ontario, Marsden and Harvey (1971) have shown that father's education is a better predictor of post-secondary education than is combined family income. It is a better indicator of socioeconomic background, and of values and knowledge about higher education. This is probably because the combined income, usually of father and mother, may hide lower parental educational attainment and occupational prestige. These latter variables almost certainly would be higher when there is only one earner with an equivalent income.

Breton (1973), in a Canadian study which is national in scope, makes the point that a student's class of destination depends on stratification which is external to the school (class of origin), and also on internal stratification variables, those which are internal to the school such as program of study, ability grouping, system of evaluation and expectations of teachers. We will be dealing with these variables more extensively at a later point, especially in chapter 9. Breton notes that these internal stratification variables explain as much or more of the variance in class of destination as does class of origin. However they are themselves correlated with class of origin which, we may say, has a relatively strong indirect effect on both aspiration and attainment through internal stratification mechanisms.

Breton also found, not unexpectedly, that one of the most important internal stratification variables is the system of program of study: tracking. Allocation to tracks is usually based on some indicator of ability such as previous grades (rather than I.Q. tests), on the assessment of that ability by teachers or the principal, and on the guidance of counselors. The student's expressed interest, while not insignificant, is less important than this estimate of ability. It is important to note that the estimate of ability is based on both objective (earlier grades) and subjective elements (teachers', principal's, counselor's assessment) and that the latter especially is related to social class.

There is, of course, an important relationship between measured ability and both class of origin and class of destination. Williams (1977:257) notes that "correlations between the IQs of children and the SES of their family of origin fall in the 0.3 to 0.4 range (Jensen, 1969:75); and correlations between the IQs of individuals and their later social and economic attainments range from around 0.3 for income, to about 0.5 for occupational status (Duncan, Featherman and Duncan, 1972:89; Jencks, *et al*, 1972:337). Relationships of similar magnitude are found in Canadian populations." Measured ability is related to grades or earlier achievement which is part of the basis of allocation to different tracks. O'Reilly (1975) notes that in Canada home factors, which is roughly equivalent to socioeconomic status, account for about 65 per cent of the variance in standardized tests, and pupil aptitude and scores on I.Q. tests account for about 50 per cent of the variance in school achievement.

Many studies have established a strong relationship between social class and measured intelligence over the entire range of classes. In an interesting variation of such research performed in Regina, Kennett (1972) found that such systematic differences are to be found even within narrower categories of the middle class. In a parallel study performed in Sydney, Nova Scotia, Kennett (1973) also found a negative correlation for lower-class categories between measured intelligence and family size, but the relationship disappeared for the higher-class categories, suggesting that it was at least partly an artifact of social class.

Another very important variable is academic failure, itself related to social class. It is reasonable to suppose that students in both elementary and second-ary schools who fail individual courses are less likely to aspire to post-second-ary schooling. Breton's (1973) research established this to be the case. Even more significant is the finding that the failure rate in the school has a signifi-cant effect on the plans of all the students, even those who do not fail. This is the result of the influence of another social class variable, social context, and of social climate. These will be further discussed in chapter 8. The relationship relative to post-secondary education is a negative linear one: the higher the failure rate, the lower the rate of planning to attend college. The relationship holds even when level of mental ability, social class, and program of study are controlled. Despite this finding when controls are introduced, there is a direct relationship between social class and both social context (aggregate variables such as family background, ethnicity, class) and social climate (the value and normative system). Reporting on an American study, Bowles (1971) notes that in 1966 about 53 per cent of the students graduating from high school did not subsequently attend college. Of those whose family income was less than $3,000 about 80 per cent did not attend; of those whose family income was above $15,000 only about 13 per cent did not attend. The reason for the lower achievement of the lower income group is not merely a lack of money, important as that is. Context, and especially climate variables including ear-lier failure rates are also involved.

We do not wish to belabour this general social class relationship with educational achievement. Boocock (1980:40) notes that "(t)he family char-acteristic that is the most powerful predictor of school performance is socio-economic status (SES); the higher the SES of the student's family, the higher his or her academic achievement." This achievement is an effect of three variables, or three groups of variables: ability, aspiration and opportunity (Hansen *et al*, 1972). The relationship between class and achievement is pri-marily an indirect one, working through or mediated by these groups of vari-ables, and individual factors within them. We discuss these in their direct influences in other chapters where we consider their treatment more appro-priate. We would like now to turn our readers' attention to a description of the relationship between three of the principal components of social class — education, occupation, and income — and educational achievement. These components of class of origin are highly correlated so that, in a general way, one may serve as a proxy for another. One of the best ways to understand the strength of the class relationship with educational opportunity is simply to view the distribution of these parental characteristics together with the distribution of the educational attainment of the offspring. Obviously, if parental characteristics which themselves are components of socioeconomic status, and which are enjoyed or possessed differentially, are indicative of greater or lesser achievement on the part of the children, then the relationship is clearly established even if the causal factors are not.

## Parental Education and Educational Attainment

Table 5-1 presents the education distribution of the fathers of full-time undergraduates in Canadian post-secondary institutions for 1974-75. At the same time it shows, for comparative reasons, the educational attainment of the 45 to 64 male population cohort, the statistical aggregate to which most of these parents belong. The lack of educational opportunity for offspring of fathers who have only elementary education is clearly apparent. While these parents made up 44.2 per cent of the particular male population aggregate, i.e., of all men aged 45 to 64, their sons made up only 19.8 and their daughters 17.0 per cent of the full-time undergraduate post-secondary population. The offspring had less than half of their proportional representation in this group, the presumption being that adjusting for family size would make the disproportion even greater. Clearly, for whatever reasons, the opportunity for a higher education is being denied to this group.

While attendance at the post-secondary level of schooling is the best available descriptive indicator of educational opportunity, we also know that this group are lower achievers at the elementary and secondary levels and, as we shall indicate in chapter 8, are disproportionately represented among dropouts. At the post-secondary level the disadvantage is even greater for females.

The position reverses itself completely for the children of fathers who have some post-secondary education, 26.6 per cent of the appropriate male population. Their sons make up 40.6 and their daughters 43.4 per cent of the full-time undergraduates, an overrepresentation of more than 50 per cent. A similar but weaker advantage falls on the sons and daughters of fathers with some secondary education; they have an overrepresentation of approximately 33 per cent.

Table 5-2 presents information on full-time and part-time enrollment of terminal and undergraduate students for 1974-75 according to parental education. Several matters which have a significant bearing on educational oppor-

Table 5-1

Educational Attainment of Fathers of Full-Time Undergraduates
Compared with the 45-64 Male Population, 1974-75

| Level of Study | Father's Educational Attainment of Full-Time Undergraduates | | Educational Attainment of the 45-64 Male Population |
|---|---|---|---|
| | Male | Female | |
| Elementary | 19.8 | 17.0 | 44.2 |
| Some Secondary | 24.3 | 24.8 | n/a |
| Secondary | 15.3 | 14.9 | n/a |
| Secondary Sub Total | (39.6) | (39.6) | 29.6 |
| Other Education or Training | 10.0 | 10.9 | 9.4 |
| Post-Secondary Non-university | 1.6 | 1.7 | 6.7 |
| Some University | 7.3 | 7.7 | 4.4 |
| University Degree(s) | 21.7 | 23.3 | 5.7 |
| University Sub Total | (29.0) | (31.0) | (10.1) |
| Post-secondary Sub Total | (30.6) | (32.7) | (16.8) |
| | 100.0 | 100.0 | 100.0 |

Source: Statistics Canada, 1979b:55 (adapted)

tunity are immediately apparent. We will point out in chapter 7 that post-secondary education at the community college level, both terminal and transfer, does not have the monetary return or does not provide graduates with the occupational prestige equal to that of the four-year college or university. But as Table 5-2 indicates, students whose parents have only elementary education are overrepresented at the terminal level and underrepresented at the undergraduate level. This relationship also holds, although to a lesser extent, for students whose parents have some high school only. For students whose parents have completed high school the relationship begins to reverse itself, with a hardly significant overrepresentation at the undergraduate level. And at the post-secondary level (of parental education) full-time students are now overrepresented at four-year college or university, particularly full-time students whose fathers have a college degree.

There is also an important difference in representation in full-time as opposed to part-time studies. The offspring of parents whose education is at the elementary level only are overrepresented in part-time studies, and this is

Table 5-2

Educational Attainment of Parents of Full- and Part-Time Terminal and Undergraduate Students, 1974-75

| Parent's Educational Attainment | Terminal | | | | Undergraduate | | | |
|---|---|---|---|---|---|---|---|---|
| | Father | | Mother | | Father | | Mother | |
| | Full-time | Part-time | Full-time | Part-time | Full-time | Part-time | Full-time | Part-time |
| Elementary | 31.9 | 37.2 | 29.8 | 31.9 | 19.8 | 36.3 | 17.4 | 33.1 |
| Some High School | 29.0 | 26.2 | 31.4 | 29.5 | 23.8 | 25.0 | 24.9 | 23.3 |
| Completed High School | 14.4 | 12.4 | 17.0 | 19.6 | 15.1 | 13.4 | 21.1 | 17.2 |
| Sub-Total Secondary | 43.5 | 38.5 | 48.5 | 49.2 | 38.9 | 38.5 | 46.0 | 40.5 |
| Total Elementary and Secondary | 75.4 | 78.5 | 78.3 | 81.1 | 58.7 | 74.8 | 63.4 | 73.6 |
| Post-secondary non-university | 13.0 | 12.4 | 17.5 | 14.3 | 12.5 | 11.4 | 24.8 | 20.1 |
| Some University | 3.9 | 5.8 | 2.0 | 1.5 | 7.1 | 4.1 | 4.4 | 3.3 |
| University Degree(s) | 7.6 | 6.0 | 2.2 | 3.2 | 21.7 | 9.7 | 7.5 | 3.0 |
| Sub-total University | 11.5 | 11.8 | 4.2 | 4.7 | 28.8 | 13.9 | 11.8 | 6.3 |
| Total Post-secondary | 24.6 | 24.2 | 21.7 | 19.0 | 41.3 | 25.3 | 36.6 | 26.4 |
| Grand Total | 100.0 | 100.0 | 100.0 | 100.0 | 100.0 | 100.0 | 100.0 | 100.0 |
| Number Reported | 93,195 | 9,613 | 94,968 | 9,774 | 189,275 | 52,258 | 191,272 | 52,089 |

Source: Statistics Canada, 1978b:30.

especially so at the more prestigious undergraduate institutions. Conversely, at the post-secondary parental level and especially where a degree is involved, the students are vastly underrepresented in part-time studies. Clearly, there are significant differences in full-time as opposed to part-time post-secondary education in Canada, and this has an important bearing on educational opportunity.

These class differences in post-secondary education in 1974-75 became even more extreme at the graduate school level. Only 21.7 per cent of graduate students have fathers with only elementary education, yet these men make up 44.2 per cent of the age 45-64 male population. But 42.1 per cent of graduate students have fathers with post-secondary education or other training while these fathers make up only 16.8 per cent of the 45-64 male population (Statistics Canada, 1979b:55; 1978b:43).

In the five year period from 1967-68 to 1971-72 the full-time enrollment rate in the post-secondary non-university sector increased by 74.8 per cent; in the university sector it increased by 27.4 per cent. We might presume that this gave an added advantage to those of lower socioeconomic status, but this is far from certain. It did improve the position of females, although not to the point where they had equal representation with males. When the student population of full-time undergraduate programs is related to the 18-21 age group, the male rate of enrollment increased from 21.5 to 22.9 per cent; the female rate increased from 11.3 to 15.8 per cent. There was a more dramatic rate of increase for post-secondary non-university students, almost doubling from 7 to 12 per cent for both males and females (Statistics Canada, 1978b:15).

The educational background of fathers of full-time undergraduate students corresponds closely to that of fathers in graduate and professional schools. The background of fathers of part-time undergraduate students corresponds more closely to that of full-time terminal students. The educational attainment of mothers was not as high as that of the fathers, but the marked differences in that attainment between mothers of full-time undergraduate, graduate and professional students compared to part-time undergraduate and terminal students remains. The one major exception is for the professional students in education or teacher training programs. While the educational attainment of fathers is important for educational opportunity for both sons and daughters, that of mothers is more important for daughters than for sons (Statistics Canada, 1978a, 1978b).

The background of fathers of full-time undergraduates did not change significantly between 1968-69 and 1974-75. The marginal change that did take place is in the direction of greater inequality of educational opportunity (Statistics Canada, 1978b) even though there are greater absolute numbers of students of all class backgrounds. Thus the accessibility of university education did not change in favor of families in the lower socioeconomic status ranges. If there was any change it was in favor of the more privileged groups. Community colleges draw their students disproportionately from the more disadvantaged groups. During that five-year period the proportion of such students with fathers having university degrees rose 3 per cent, compared to a 5 per cent raise in the case of university students whose fathers had a degree.

There are significant differences in post-secondary attendance rates for both non-university and university institutions among the provinces. Table 5-3 presents these rates for all of the ten provinces, and for Canada as a whole for 1976-77. There are some anomalies in provincial rates. The attendance rates for the Atlantic provinces, with the exception of Nova Scotia, and for Saskatchewan, as might be expected, are quite low. These are the poorer provinces in Canada. Nova Scotia has the highest rate of attendance for the relevant age group at the university level. While we do not have specific details, there are several contributing factors to this. That province has long had a special love for higher education, even in pre-confederation days. It is overrepresented in four-year colleges and universities, there being one for approximately every 100,000 population cohort in the province. Another important factor is the underrepresentation there, especially compared to Prince Edward Island, Quebec, Ontario and Alberta, at the non-university level. Quebec is overrepresented at the non-university level, a reflection of the increasingly

Table 5-3

Regional Differences in Full-Time Post-Secondary Enrollment
by Type of Study and Province, 1976-77

| Province | Post-Secondary non-university (18-21 age group) | University (18-24 age group) | Total (18-24 age group) |
|---|---|---|---|
| Newfoundland | 4.5 | 8.8 | 11.5 |
| P.E.I. | 8.2 | 10.0 | 15.1 |
| Nova Scotia | 4.3 | 16.9 | 19.4 |
| New Brunswick | 2.9 | 11.8 | 13.5 |
| Quebec | 10.8 | 16.7 | 23.1 |
| Ontario | 9.6 | 15.4 | 21.1 |
| Manitoba | 4.4 | 13.7 | 16.3 |
| Saskatchewan | 4.1 | 12.1 | 14.7 |
| Alberta | 9.3 | 13.3 | 18.7 |
| British Columbia | 5.1 | 12.6 | 15.6 |
| Canada | 8.5 | 14.8 | 19.8 |

Source: Statistics Canada, 1979b:17

significant role being played by the new CEGEPs there. Alberta and British Columbia have lower rates of attendance at the university level than might normally be expected, for they are prosperous provinces. However, they absorb people, presumably educated people, from other provinces at a high rate. Nova Scotia for example, because of economic factors resulting from underdeveloped and regional disparity, is not able to provide adequate jobs for many in its graduating classes. Many move to the more promising West.

We might note that in that year, 1976-77, there were 335,866 students enrolled full-time in post-secondary institutions in Canada, and this represents 19.8 per cent of the 18-24 age group. There were also 190,957 part-time students, an additional 56.9 per cent, although these were not restricted to that age group (Statistics Canada, 1979b:17,37,38). There continues to be an increase in the rate of attendance each year.

It is instructive to note that among seven selected western industrialized nations in 1973 (Canada, United States, France, West Germany, Italy, Sweden and the United Kingdom), expenditure on education as a percentage of G.N.P. ranged from a low of 4.1 in West Germany to a high of 7.7 in Sweden. For Canada the statistic is 7.1 per cent, ranking next to Sweden. The per capita expenditures that year were highest in Sweden ($450), then the U.S. ($410) and then in Canada ($397). The lowest per capita expenditure was in Italy ($130). These statistics apply to all educational institutions and not only to the post-secondary domain (Statistics Canada, 1979b:24). Nevertheless, it is obvious that Canada ranks high among these nations on the basis of these statistics. About 17 billion dollars was spent on education in Canada in 1977-78. This represents about 17 per cent of total government spending (Statistics Canada, 1980:73). Approximately 5 billion of that was spent on post-secondary education.

## Occupation, Income and Educational Opportunity

We noted earlier that education, occupation and income are the principal components of the operational definition of social class or socioeconomic status, and that there is a high correlation between them. We have presented in some detail the educational background of parents of post-secondary students in Canada and related this to differential educational opportunity. It would be redundant to repeat this detail for the occupational and income background of parents as well, since in general the distributions would show approximately the same relationship. Moreover, Statistics Canada reports both more recent and more detailed information on the educational background of parents. Two of the principal sources for information relative to occupation and income are Porter (1965) and Porter, Porter and Blishen (1979; first edition, 1973). However, the statistics presented there are somewhat dated.

Porter (1965:181) citing Fleming (1957) notes that of the grade 13 students in Ontario in 1956, 39 per cent had fathers who were in the professional, managerial or executive occupational level while this group represented only 16 per cent of the male population 35 years of age and older. Eleven per cent of the fathers were in the sub-professional, minor supervisory and proprietor occupational group (7 per cent of males 35 years of age and older). Thus 50 per cent of the grade 13 students were from occupationally more privileged backgrounds which themselves had a representation of only 23 per cent in the population at large. The offspring of the skilled manual group held their own (28 per cent of the students, 29 per cent of the 35 years and over male population). The fathers in the semi-skilled manual, unskilled, unknown and disabled occupational groups represented fully 48 per cent of the male population 35 years of age and over, but their offspring represented only 22 per cent of the student population. Porter shows the same general type of distribution for university students. Proprietors and managers (8.3 per cent of labour force) represented 25.7 per cent of the parents of the student population. Professionals (7.1 per cent) represented 24.9 per cent of the student population. Clerical and sales (16.5) had a 12.3 per cent representation; skilled and semi-skilled (30.6) a 21.1 per cent representation; agriculture (15.7) and labour (20.5) had 10.9 and 5.1 per cent representation.

Porter (1965) also presents statistics pertaining to family income background of university students. We present these in Table 5-4. As is expected, those in the three higher income brackets are overrepresented in university attendance, and those in the three lower ones, especially the final two, are underrepresented. However, we must be cautious in using family income as a descriptive variable. In some cases it refers to one earner only, in others to more than one.

More recent information on family income and attendance at post-secondary institutions is available for 1974 (Statistics Canada, 1974a, cited by Ross, 1980:72) as presented in Table 5-5. Readers should pay particular attention to columns 1 and 4. Notice that the lowest income group (under $5,000) has 17.5 per cent of their children attending post-secondary institutions but they make up only 9.2 per cent of the student population. Moreover, they are overrepresented in non-university institutions by a proportion of 2 to 1 (compare columns 2 and 3), making up 13.0 per cent of non-university students but only 6.1 per cent of university students. The second lowest income group ($5,000-$9,999) is also underrepresented, but less severely so. The second highest income group ($20,000 to $24,999) and especially the highest ($25,000 and over) are greatly overrepresented in the student body. In 1974 these two top categories together made up only 4.6 per cent of all tax filers (National Council of Welfare, 1976:18). Their children attended post-secondary institutions at the rate of 37.9 and 55.4 per cent respectively, and they made up 11.4 and 21.5 per cent of the university student body.

Table 5-4

Percentage Distribution of University Student Families and
All Canadian Families, by Family Income Groups, 1956

| Family Income ($) | Student families | All Canadian families |
|---|---|---|
| 10,000 and over | 15.2 | 3.3 |
| 7,000 - 9,999 | 12.2 | 8.4 |
| 5,000 - 6,999 | 21.3 | 18.7 |
| 4,000 - 4,999 | 14.8 | 15.7 |
| 3,000 - 3,999 | 17.5 | 22.9 |
| 2,000 - 2,999 | 11.6 | 17.0 |
| Under 2,000 | 7.4* | 14.0 |

*Includes families where persons are on pension or out of work, where father is deceased and mother working, etc.
Source: Porter (1965:184) adapted from D.B.S., University Student Expenditure and Income in Canada, 1956-57.

Breton (1973) and Breton *et al.*, (1972) present similar information pertaining to the aspirations of high school graduating classes for Canada as a whole for 1965-66, and Porter, Porter and Blishen (1979) present similar material for 1971 for Ontario. Aspirations of students generally exceed the results, and this is particularly the case for students from lower socioeconomic status groups. There are massive amounts of statistical material in these sources to demonstrate (relative to aspirations) a relationship similar to that which has already been presented for attendance rates. At the risk of being redundant we present a table (Table 5-6) indicating the aspirations of grade 12 students in Ontario in 1971. Note that 63 and 55 per cent of the two top socioeconomic status groups planned to attend university compared to 38 and 28 per cent of the two lowest groups. Comparing Tables 5-6 and 5-5 shows that in both cases the aspirations were not fully realized, but must less so for the higher as compared to the lower status groups.

Before leaving this section and passing on to some special stratification relationships resulting from sex and race, we would like to repeat that we have used post-secondary attendance rates primarily as an indicator of educational opportunity. It is probably the best statistic readily available for this purpose, but it does overlook the differences in opportunity which exist for the majority of the population which does not attend, or is just now in the 1980's beginning

Table 5-5

Children's Attendance at Post-Secondary School
by Level of Parent's Income, 1974

| Parents' Income Group($) | Percentage Attending | Attended Post-Secondary | | |
| | | Non-University | University | Total |
|---|---|---|---|---|
| Under 5,000 | 17.5 | 13.0 | 6.1 | 9.2 |
| 5,000 to 9,999 | 21.6 | 21.1 | 15.1 | 17.8 |
| 10,000 to 14,999 | 29.0 | 28.6 | 22.8 | 25.4 |
| 15,000 to 19,999 | 35.9 | 18.2 | 23.1 | 20.9 |
| 20,000 to 24,999 | 37.9 | 11.7 | 11.4 | 11.5 |
| 25,000 and over | 55.4 | 7.3 | 21.5 | 15.2 |
| Total | 29.4 | 100.0 | 100.0 | 100.0 |
| Average Income ($) | — | 14,196 | 19,017 | 16,665 |

Source: Statistics Canada, 1974a. Cited by Ross (1980:72). Adapted.

to attend, post-secondary institutions. Nevertheless, virtually every research effort and study points out that the relationship we have demonstrated here exists even at the lower level.

Table 5-7 indicates the monetary return to education in Canada for 1967. Even though these statistics are dated, and almost certainly need adjusting following the more recent changes in attendance patterns, they are a good crude indicator of the returns to education in Canada on the basis of lifetime earnings. This also serves to introduce our next section which deals with sex stratification in the educational domain. As a general rule we can adjust 1967 income to 1981 dollars by multiplying by a factor of four.

## Sex Stratification and Educational Attainment

During the past two decades a great deal of attention has been given to differences, socially determined, between males and females relative to those things that are valued in our society, usually summarized as some form of power, privilege or prestige. Because occupation is such an important component of our stratification system, and because sex discrimination in this area

Table 5-6

Educational Aspirations After High School
by Socioeconomic Status (Grade 12)

| | Socioeconomic Status | | | | | | |
| | (High) | | | | | (Low) | |
| Aspirations | I | II | III | IV | V | VI | Total |
|---|---|---|---|---|---|---|---|
| | (percent) | | | | | | |
| Go to work | 11 | 11 | 15 | 13 | 24 | 26 | 19 |
| Apprenticeship or private training school | 1 | 4 | 6 | 7 | 11 | 13 | 9 |
| Teachers' college or nursing | 5 | 5 | 5 | 7 | 8 | 8 | 7 |
| Community college | 10 | 9 | 12 | 16 | 16 | 14 | 14 |
| University but not graduate | 2 | 1 | 2 | 1 | 1 | 1 | 1 |
| Graduate from university | 51 | 42 | 35 | 36 | 22 | 24 | 31 |
| Post-graduate work | 10 | 12 | 9 | 6 | 5 | 3 | 6 |
| Total university | 63 | 55 | 46 | 43 | 38 | 28 | 38 |
| Other plans (not specified) | 3 | 4 | 6 | 6 | 5 | 4 | 5 |
| Does not know | 7 | 12 | 10 | 8 | 8 | 7 | 8 |
| | 100 | 100 | 100 | 100 | 100 | 100 | 100 |
| N = | 180 | 218 | 300 | 555 | 1042 | 300 | 2595 |

Source: Porter, Porter and Blishen (1979:36).

has for many years been so blatantly obvious, women themselves became concerned with the basis of social inequality as it existed first in the world of work, in most cases the unpaid blue collar level work of feeding families and changing diapers (Huber, 1973). After the concern of many women began to express itself in what many traditionalists considered to be a movement of radical reform, still relatively unsuccessful, sociologists began to investigate the pervasive presence of sex stratification, and this investigation soon spread to the educational domain.

Table 5-7

Adjusted Lifetime Earnings by Sex and Education, 1967
(Full-time and Part-time Workers)

| Education Level | Male | Female |
|---|---|---|
| | dollars | |
| No education | 106,664 | 36,469 |
| Some elementary | 122,348 | 45,092 |
| Elementary | 157,597 | 52,450 |
| Some high school | 173,464 | 66,873 |
| High School | 212,545 | 96,759 |
| Some university | 234,524 | 120,357 |
| University | 351,635 | 169,327 |

Source: Statistics Canada, 1974b:27.

Nielsen (1978:1-63) carefully distinguishes between social position and social role. "Social *position* refers to the place of an individual or social category within a system of relationships" (p.5). A social position which is associated with just one sex is called a *sex-specific social position*, and it is generally static in nature. Every social position brings rights (different kinds of rewards) and responsibilities (expected behaviour in accord with norms). "The behaviours that are attached to or considered part of social positions are called social roles" (p.6). These social *roles*, because they are concerned with behaviour, are dynamic, and when they are related to sex-specific positions they may be referred to as *sex-roles*. Just as the evaluation of social categories is referred to as social stratification, so the hierarchy which results from evaluating sex-specific categories is called *sex-stratification*.

Measurement of sex status is very difficult because it overlaps so much with other categories such as age, race and occupation. It is generally associated with the division of labour where positions may be related to use-value or exchange-value. In horticultural and especially agrarian and industrial societies, where it has become possible to build up wealth or surplus, positions associated with exchange-value tend to be more highly evaluated, and are generally dominated by males. In hunting and gathering societies, where subsistence rather than surplus was the norm, virtually all positions were related to use-value. While there was a sex-specific division of labour, males did not dominate and equality between the sexes was closer to the norm.

That there are differences in sex roles and sex-role stereotyping in our society is beyond doubt. These lead to sex inequality and sex stratification. There are three general groups of theories which attempt to explain the basis of these differences. Instead of looking at what is, or what actually exists, the theories attempt to explain why this is so. There are (1) biological explanations, (2) social learning explanations which attempt to explain cultural differences on an individual basis, and (3) structural explanations. Nielsen (1978:93-142) gives a good summary explanation of the three.

The biological explanations in general posit that there are certain personality and behaviour characteristics, differing in males and females, which are innate. They are the result of some form of genetic transmission with a physiological, hormonal or similar cause. Most researchers see aggression, or some variant such as assertiveness, as the most consistent sex-linked difference.

The social learning theories tend to emphasize culturally different patterns of sex-specific behaviour and attempt to explain them on a cultural or individual basis related to learning theory. As yet there is not a great amount of empirical evidence available to validate such theories.

The structural explanations, contrary to these first two, investigate to a lesser extent individual sex differences and to a greater extent sex stratification. The functionalist explanation holds that sex stratification is, or was, necessary for the ongoing operation and even survival of society. Ideological theories view the value, belief and attitudinal systems of society as the basis of the stratification because they define the appropriate nature of men and women, and the appropriate sex roles. The materialist or Marxist theories view sex status as the result of economic factors, the relations of production, wherein a different and inferior status is imposed on women. These structural explanations appear to be more satisfactory in explaining sex stratification, but there remain a number of theoretical weaknesses.

That sex inequality and stratification shows itself in the educational domain is a demonstrated fact. It is manifested in two particular ways. Because of sex-role stereotyping which is both overt and covert, males are socialized into a different and more dominant set of roles than females. A second aspect of such institutionalized inequality deals directly with educational opportunity. Females attain less education than males, although they are equal or slightly superior, on the basis of grades. Moreover, the education they do attain is worth less in the world of work.

Virtually every study in Canada and the United States which includes a content analysis of school textbooks, especially at the elementary level, shows stereotypical presentation of males and females (boys and girls, sons and daughters, fathers and mothers, brothers and sisters) in a manner which portrays the male as dominant, multidimentional and the one who excels. Females are presented in such literature far less frequently, in a more passive role, and generally as homemaker, nurse or teacher (Women on Words and Images, 1975:38-40). Presuming that there is a social basis to sex inequality and stratification which determines that females are inferior in status to males, this social determination is reinforced in the institution of schooling. It is found not only in textbooks; it exists also in the curriculum, the attitudes of teachers both male and female, and in the occupational inequality existing in our schools among teachers and especially administrators on a sex basis. This is one form of inequality of opportunity. It is not likely that educational institutions cause this stratification. Like other forms of inequality, it exists at a deeper or more basic level in inequality of condition, and is passed on and reinforced in the schools, as in the family and other social institutions, through the process of socialization.

A second form of inequality of opportunity for females to be found in the institution of schooling appears in unequal rates of attendance and attainment especially in the post-secondary or higher educational institutions, particularly at the graduate level.

There is little difference in attendance rates between males and females during the period of compulsory attendance. From that point on the rate of attendance declines more rapidly for females than for males. There are at least two kinds of reasons for this. Females in the secondary level of schooling have a lower mean age relative to the specific grade or level. There are fewer females, proportionately, above the modal student age. As a group, they finish a specific grade at a younger age, on average, than do males (Martin and Macdonell, 1978). As a result, even if both sexes had equal attainment, the age distribution for males would be broader.

We may term this a relative difference. There is also an absolute difference in attendance at the post-secondary level, which we present in Table 5-8. This rate of attendance for females increased proportionately more than for males between 1961 and 1977, but the existing inequality is still very pronounced, especially at the graduate school level. In 1971 females made up 45.9 per cent of the post-secondary student population. The proportions at different institutional levels were: 50.5 per cent of the non-university group; 44.4 and 31.9 per cent respectively at the university undergraduate and graduate level; and 43.0 per cent at the university sub-total level.

There are other statistics which are illuminating even if somewhat confusing when presented in such abundance. Full-time undergraduate post-secondary enrollment in Canada in 1977-78 was 185,437 (55.6%) for males, and 148,063 (44.4%) for females. Women were overrepresented in arts (52.2%), education (65.2%), fine and applied arts (61.5%), miscellaneous health professions (81%), nursing (97.5%), pharmacy (61.9%) and household sciences (97.5%). Males were the majority in science (63.3%), agriculture (68.8%), commerce and business administration (70.5%), engineering and applied sciences (92.5%), environmental studies (67.4%), dentistry (82.9%), medicine

Table 5-8

Female Enrollment as a Percentage of Full-Time
Post-Secondary Enrollment (Canada), by level

| Year | Non-University | University | | | Total |
| | | Sub-Total | Total | | |
| | | Undergraduate | Graduate | Sub-Total | Post-Secondary |
|---|---|---|---|---|---|
| 1961 | 69.1 | 26.2 | 16.4 | 25.7 | 38.4 |
| 1966 | 55.3 | 33.7 | 18.0 | 32.4 | 38.3 |
| 1971 | 45.9 | 37.7 | 22.6 | 36.0 | 39.5 |
| 1976 | 49.8 | 43.7 | 30.6 | 42.3 | 45.1 |
| 1977 | 50.5 | 44.4 | 31.9 | 43.0 | 45.9 |

Source: Statistics Canada, 1980:79

(68.2%), law (67.9%), religion and theology (70.0%), and veterinary medicine (62.0%).

Full-time graduate enrollment that same year was 27,713 (68.1%) for males, 12,972 (31.9%) for females. Males were in the majority in every category except the fine and applied arts (48.0%).

In 1976-77 males earned 82.0 per cent of the doctorates awarded in Canada (Statistics Canada, 1978a:44-46,56). That same year they made up 85.6 per cent of full-time university teachers (Statistics Canada, 1979b:89).

The consequences of this inequality show themselves in many ways, but particularly in employment rates and income. Females have lower participation rates in the labour force. It is difficult to determine how much of this is purely voluntary and how much is determined by structural or other factors. Despite the existing inequality the rate for females continues to rise. This is mostly because of a tremendous increase in the rate for married females, which now stands at approximately 40 per cent (Nett, 1980:368).

The spring unemployment rates in Canada in April 1979, according to level of education, were: elementary, 26.7; secondary, 15.7; some post-secondary, 11.0; and degree, 7.3 (Labour Canada, 1979:84). It is very difficult to compute *real* unemployment rates. The rate as defined by government is based on a number of qualifications which have the effect of reducing it considerably. For that reason it also becomes rather difficult to compute the real differences between the sexes because in times of high unemployment many more women than men, porportionately, drop out of the labour force, or do not enter when, under normal employment circumstances, they would. However, the real unemployment rate is generally higher for females, but this narrows as level of education increases.

Table 5-9 presents the employment-population ratio by educational attainment for males and females in 1978. It is immediately apparent that as educational level increases, the participation rate increases as well, and the gap between males and females narrows proportionately. This is especially onerous for females because it is at the university level where their educational attainment falls behind. More women are concentrated in that area of the distribution where unemployment rates are higher.

There is one area where the inequality between the sexes has been narrowed greatly: income received by full-time workers with some post-secondary education. Statistics Canada (1980a:74) notes that, with similar post-secondary educational qualifications, females are earning 80 to 90 per cent of males' salaries. Males probably have been working longer, on average, and for that reason would command higher salaries, narrowing the gap even more. That is a substantial change from even five years earlier.

Table 5-10 shows the average difference in male-female earnings for those employed full-time with similar post-secondary educational qualifications. Besides the differential in income between the sexes, one striking element is

Table 5-9

Employment-Population Ratio by Educational Age and Sex, 1978 (percent)

| | | | Educational Attainment | | | |
|---|---|---|---|---|---|---|
| | Less than High School | High School | Some Post-Secondary | Post-Secondary Certificate or Diploma | University Degree | Total |
| Males | 58.0 | 73.3 | 74.4 | 85.3 | 88.4 | 72.1 |
| Females | 23.0 | 45.3 | 54.1 | 59.6 | 67.2 | 43.2 |
| Persons 15-24 years | 36.1 | 53.9 | 57.1 | 73.2 | 73.6 | 55.0 |
| Persons 25 years & over | 41.0 | 61.1 | 69.8 | 68.2 | 81.2 | 58.2 |
| Canada | 40.6 | 58.5 | 64.8 | 69.2 | 80.4 | 57.4 |

Source: Statistics Canada, 1980:91. Adapted.

Table 5-10

Median Salaries of 1976 University and College Graduates Working
Full-Time in June, 1978, by Sex[1] and Qualification Level

|  | Males $ | Females $ | Total $ |
|---|---|---|---|
| College Graduates |  |  |  |
| One-year diploma | 13,237 | 9,515 | 10,211 |
| Two-year diploma | 13,638 | 11,348 | 12,261 |
| Three- or four-year diploma | 13,758 | 12,463 | 13,129 |
| University Graduates |  |  |  |
| Bachelor's degree | 15,393 | 14,152 | 14,813 |
| Master's degree | 21,772 | 17,456 | 20,420 |
| Doctorate | 21,742 | 19,875 | 21,565 |

[1]The female-male earnings gap is partly a reflection of different fields of specialization. Moreover, this tabulation does not control for years of experience.
Source: Statistics Canada, 1980:81.

the uniformity in income for males with one, two, three or four year college diplomas rather than degrees. While the gap between the sexes is narrowing for those who have the same education and do the same work, it is well to remember that females with educations equal to that of males tend to be employed in less prestigious occupations.

## Native Canadians and Educational Opportunity

Native people in Canada, both Indian and Eskimo, are among the lowest in educational attainment. There are a number of reasons for this. One is ethnocentrism, the feeling or belief, whether consciously or unconsciously held, that a given culture is superior to another. Opposed to ethnocentrism is cultural relativism, a belief that while cultures are different — sometimes in the extreme — there is no question of inferiority or superiority among them. All are adaptive. Associated with ethnocentrism is discrimination, a process by which a person or group is deprived of equal access to privileges and opportunities available to others. Discrimination is often the result of prejudice, a negative feeling toward a person or group prior to or not based on actual experience (Driedger, 1980).

It is likely that the Native People of Canada experience prejudice and discrimination to an extreme degree. We do not have available empirical data measuring these factors, although employment and educational statistics may be regarded as an indirect measure of discrimination. Responsibility for the education of Native Canadians falls on the federal government, and the response for many years has been highly paternalistic. Most Canadians are unable to control completely ethnocentric feelings and attitudes. Most are unaware of the problems, conflicts and contradictions experienced by Indian and Eskimo people in an educational system which has been essentially alien to their cultures.

Harold Cardinal (1977), one of the principal spokesmen for Canadian Indians, claims that the disparity between the Indian cultures and the dominant Canadian culture is so great that most Canadians do not really understand what it means for them to say they are Indian, nor do they appreciate what we say when we profess to be Canadian. Gue (1971) found highly significant differences in value orientations between Indian and non-Indian samples in northern Alberta. "For the Indian child, achieving high academic goals may mean intellectual, physical and emotional separation from his parents, family and culture. . . . The escape route for the Indian child seems to be to drop out of school and avoid the pressures of individualism" (p.29-30). Presumably these findings apply to other Indian groups, and to the Inuit as well. Social policies which are meant to overcome the low level of educational attainment by native people will have to bear this in mind. To be successful they must provide a truly Indian or truly Inuit education, rather than one for southern white Canadians which may be applied to Native People as well.

Cardinal (1977:81), citing directly from a paper on the Indian Philosophy of Education, which we will discuss subsequently, speaks of the problems experienced by the Indian child when thrust into a new and strange environment such as the one which generally prevails in non-Indian schools. "Inferiority, alienation, rejection, hostility, depression, frustration, are some of the personal adjustment problems which characterize the Indian child's experience with integration. These are also factors in the academic failure of Indian children in integrated schools."

Bowd (1972) discusses the problem of achievement for Indian children who, on the average, are two grades behind white children in Canada, and two and one-half grades behind in the United States. The two best predictors of underachievement are degree of Indian ancestry and the child's preschool language. We cannot overemphasize that underachievement is not the result of inferior ability. We pointed out in chapter three, for example, that the Canadian Eskimo has a measured intelligence (I.Q.) equal to that of the Canadian population. This is before controls for social class are inserted. Class affects intellectual development strongly. Because the social class position of the Inuit is generally lower than it is for all Canadians (although in many respects a comparison is somewhat meaningless because of cultural differences) one might expect their I.Q. to be lower. This is not the case.

Bowd (1972) also notes that, as with white children, social class and verbal achievement have a strong correlation with educational achievement. He found that Indian children whose parents experienced the least unemployment achieved more. The children are not low achievers because they are culturally deprived but rather because the schools require facility in the English language which they are largely unable to attain. Indians have the lowest income of the fourteen principal ethnic groups in Canada (Adams *et al.*, 1971:73). It is variously estimated that as many as 80 per cent of the Indian people live below the poverty line. It is important to understand that there are structural reasons for this poverty, and for the lower-social class position in entails.

The retention rate for native people is extremely low, the dropout rate among the highest in the nation (Hobart, 1970). Adams *et al.*, (1971) report that only 25 per cent of Metis and Indian children get to the grade six level in elementary schools, that of the 7,000 Indian students in Canada in 1962-63, only six per cent were in grades 9 to 12. That year there were only 70 Indian students in the post-secondary educational institutions, most of them in trade schools. Only six were attending university.

Cardinal (1977) reports that the National Indian Brotherhood in 1971 began work on a paper that would reflect a national Indian position on education. Represented on the working committee were people from all across the country who were involved in Indian education. The final draft of the paper was approved in 1972 and adopted by the Department of Indian Affairs the following year. Adoption in this case meant giving official departmental recognition to the document, and a joint announcement formally accepting the principles enunciated there. The paper was entitled "Indian Control of Indian Education." Cardinal's position indicates that this adoption, regardless of intention, was a political move which had little real consequence in fact.

There are a number of important principles contained in that document, cited extensively by Cardinal (1977:56-58). These include the responsibility of the federal (rather than the provincial) government for the financing of Indian education. This responsibility follows from the early treaties between the Government of Canada and the Indian nations, and assumes the provision of facilities which ensure an education which may be somewhat different from but equal to those provided by provincial governments to all Canadians.

A second principle is that the education is to reinforce the children's Indian identity, and in order to do this decisions on specific issues should be made only in the context of local control of education. It is the right of Indian Bands and Indian parents to make the decisions which would provide the best possible education for their children. These are the people who understand the culture and the specific nature of the problems.

One of these responsibilities is the formulation of a curriculum (or a variety of curricula) which is not alien to the Native People as is the case now. "Unless a child learns about the forces which shaped him: the history of his people, their values and customs, their language, he will never really know himself or his potential as a human being" (cited by Cardinal, 1977:66). Other items in the curriculum should include preparation for the occupational world, but not at the expense of Indian culture. All Native People are to be given the right to a variety of educational opportunities.

There is special concern about the language. Classes to Indian children, particularly at the elementary level, should be taught in the native language, and only after this is mastered should they be subjected to instruction given in either English or French. In the extreme case where this is not possible, instruction should be given in the native language as a second language so that it may be mastered. In the interim curriculum is presented, perhaps temporarily, in English or French.

The role of the teacher is especially important. Instruction should be given by Indian teachers who are, in most cases, the only ones prepared to understand and cope with cultural problems. The same thing applies to the use of counsellors who must assist in shaping a positive self-image. The opinion of the Brotherhood is that the present counselling system is not only ineffective but is a contributing factor to the children leaving school so early.

Finally, the document emphasizes the need for homelike accommodations for those who must attend schools off the Reserve. When a student must commute a long distance to school, or live in residence away from home, he has special need for support from Indian people whose culture he shares.

Other important matters are discussed in this paper. The existing system is not working now, nor has it in the past. It is probable that only a positive approach to education based on principles such as these will begin to overcome the problems culminating in the great inequality of opportunity suffered by Canada's Native People.

# 6

# *The Family, Socialization and Educational Achievement*

Throughout this book a distinction is maintained between 'education' and 'schooling'. Schooling is taken to be both the activity which occurs in schools and the results, in the individual and the group, of that activity. Education is a broader term, much more difficult to define adequately, but taken here to refer to all those activities, within or outside the school, which directly advance the individual toward goals chosen by himself or imposed by society. The goals may be further defined as related to mental, aesthetic, physical or moral development. As with schooling, the term 'education' can also be taken to denote the result of those activities.

Education, then, begins in the family, and the family continues to be, for each person living within this social unit, an agent of his education. Although circumstances differ from family to family, it is generally the case that the educational influence of the family relative to that of other agencies is greatest in the preschool years. Readers will undoubtedly be familiar with statements variously attributed to persons as diverse in their outlooks as St. Thomas Aquinas and John B. Watson that the most formative years are the first five of life. For this reason we treat the family in this segment of the book, but we in no way intend to leave the impression that the educational influence of family ceases when schooling begins. Perhaps such an obvious point need not be made, but there is sometimes a tendency to equate education and schooling, and thereby to act as if education no longer occurs in the home once schooling has begun.

## Meaning and Function of the Family

### Family

For our purposes, the family will be defined quite simply as "two or more people related by bonds of marriage or blood who customarily maintain a common residence" (Nye and Berardo, 1973:16). At this point it is not necessary to distinguish between nuclear and extended families, one- or two-parent families, or even, for that matter, legally married and common-law relationships. Without arguing whether or not they constitute a family, we will not deal with the relationship of two married adults with no children living at home. Since our concern is primarily with the educational effect of family on the young, we will assume the presence of one or more non-adult offspring.

Since the members of a family continually interact with one another in a patterned way, they constitute a social system. As the basic unit of a society, the family shares certain common values and beliefs with other members, and contributes in certain ways to the perpetuation of that society. One of the more important ways in which the family fulfills this function is in inculcating in its younger members the very values and beliefs which undergird the society.

**Functions of the Family**

Function is taken here in the sense of "an activity performed for an institution or class of individuals" (Nye and Berardo, 1973:7). In considering the functions of the family, we are simply trying to say what it is that the family does for the society of which it is a part. Though not all agree precisely on this matter, there is sufficient commonality to allow us to present the following as representative of recent writers on sociology of the family (cf. Rodgers, 1973:25-34; Clayton, 1975:20; Leslie, 1976:9):

1) Maintains biological functioning of group members
2) Reproduces and recruits new members
3) Socializes new members
4) Produces and distributes goods and services
5) Maintains order and protects members
6) Maintains meaning and motivation for group activity.

We will concern ourselves primarily with the function of socialization, which Reiss (1965) argues is probably the single function found universally attached to the family system. It is the function most closely related to education. We shall see that even this function of the family is increasingly taken over by other agencies, including the school, as society becomes more complex and technologically developed. As Rodgers (1973:29) says in comparing the process of socialization in the United States with that in Israel, "American society concentrates the socialization function in the roles of parents in the early years of role sequence of the child but divides the responsibility between the family and the school system in later childhood until, finally, the school becomes the primary socialization experience in late adolescence and young adulthood."

## Socialization

But what is socialization? There are almost as many definitions of the term as there are texts in sociology. We will use the one provided by Leslie. He states that "the term *socialization* encompasses the whole process of learning the values, attitudes, knowledge, skills, and techniques which a society possesses — in short, it involves learning the culture. A very important part of the culture is the normative system, including the major social institutions. Socialization moulds the child's biological potential into the pattern of functioning that we call human personality" (Leslie, 1976:11). Perhaps the first thing we should note about socialization so described is how it overlaps with education in general. Socialization is not as comprehensive a process as education, in that education may involve the learning of much that is not valued or even accepted by one's society or culture. To the extent, however, that the goals of education are those imposed by society and not chosen by a person aside from or at cross purposes with those of society, socialization and education are very similar.[1] Perhaps that is what Leslie (1976:11) had in mind when he said that "the organization of the socialization process outside the family is, of course, what we call the educational institution."

When the definition says that an important part of the culture to be learned is its normative system, reference is being made to the learning of what is expected of members of society in different status positions when they are playing different roles. Indeed, this is not only one important aspect of socialization, but the central aspect, at least as seen from the viewpoint of society as a whole. To anticipate a later theme, what seems most important to society is not what individual members know, believe, or value, but that they behave in predictable ways consistent with status. The development of knowledge, beliefs, values, etc., is encouraged to the extent that it makes possible this predictability.

A more involved but perhaps more interesting definition of socialization is the one given by Bernstein (1974:174):

> Now, what about socialization? I shall take the term to refer to the process whereby a child requires a specific cultural identity, *and* to his responses to such an identity. Socialization refers to the process whereby the biological is transformed into a specific cultural being. It follows from this that the process of socialization is a complex process of control, whereby a particular

---

[1]One could dispute this statement from a philosophical point of view, especially if one were to take the position that the pursuit of education is necessarily uplifting for the one being educated. In that case, the goals of society must necessarily be ideally suited to human development.

moral, cognitive and affective awareness is evoked in the child and given a specific form and content. Socialization sensitizes the child to the various orderings of society as these are made substantive in the various roles he is expected to play. In a sense, then, socialization is a process for making people safe. The process acts selectively on the possibilities of man by creating through time a sense of the inevitability of a given social arrangement, and through limiting the areas of permitted change. The basic agencies of socialization in contemporary societies are the family, the peer group, school and work. It is through these agencies, and in particular through their relationship to each other, that the various orderings of society are made manifest.

The earliest socialization takes place within the family. In primitive societies socialization occurs almost entirely there. However, increasing technological sophistication brings with it increasing societal differentiation, with the result that "the socializing role of the family is fragmented among a variety of institutions and agencies — school, peer group, church, police, social workers, economic agency or organization, etc., even though the family probably remains the primary agent of socialization" (Nye and Berardo, 1973:404).

## The Family as the Source of Values, Attitudes and Norms

### Values, Attitudes and Norms

It was stated above that socialization involves the learning of the values, attitudes and norms of the society, and that at least in the early years the family is the primary agent of socialization. It is appropriate at this time to state more precisely what values, attitudes and norms are, and how they are distinguished from one another.

A *value* is a stable belief resulting from a judgement that an object is personally and socially desirable as a good, action, or mode of conduct, and entailing both affect toward the object and intentions consistent with the belief (Mifflen, 1971). It should be noted that a value is primarily cognitive or intellectual, though it may imply or result in feelings about what is valued. The statement that a value entails intentions consistent with it implies that values are dynamic rather than static, influencing if not determining our actual behaviour. Finally, values are stable, which means that they last over significant periods of time and are somewhat resistant to change or loss.

As defined here, a value may be characteristic of an individual or a group; in the case of the group, the value is generally shared by the group's members. Societal values are, therefore, values that characterize the society as a whole (although not necessarily every individual living within that society). Our definition is not much different from that given by Parsons and Shils (1962:395), which is ". . . a conception, explicit or implicit, distinctive of an individual or characteristic of a group, of the desirable which influences the selection from available modes, means and ends of action."

An *attitude* is the affective disposition of a person toward a specific object, based upon one or more beliefs about that object, and influencing the formation of intentions toward the object (Mifflen, 1971). Attitudes have in common with values that they are dynamic, related to and helping to determine actual behaviour. However, attitudes are primarily feelings (affective dispositions) rather than beliefs, though based upon beliefs. As such, they are less stable and less resistant to change, although some attitudes seem to be solidly entrenched, especially when they have resulted from or are associated with feelings of hurt. As with values, attitudes may be said to characterize individuals or groups.

A *norm,* as the term is used here, is a rule prescribing expected behaviour in a given situation. The key word here is 'expected,' for norms are not objective, inflexible or unchangeable in the sense that a standard of linear measure (meter, kilometer) is. Rather, it is a societal expectation of how individuals and groups within the society will behave, given their status in that society. Birenbaum and Sagarin (1976:10), citing Gibbs, say that the term norm, when used in the generic sense, must have three attributes. It must be "(1) a collective evaluation of behaviour in terms of what it ought to be; (2) a collective expectation as to what behaviour will be; and/or (3) particular reactions to behaviour, including attempts to apply sanctions or otherwise induce a particular kind of conduct."

Values, attitudes and norms are all learned. Values and norms particularly, because they more closely reflect the structure of a given society than do attitudes, are more often the product of the socialization process. When a parent, for example, is conveying to a child what should or should not be done, he or she is more apt to relate this to a societal value or norm than to an attitude. Attitudes are not usually deliberately inculcated (though they may be) but are more often the result of some experience, direct or vicarious, with the object of the attitude. For example, a child may dislike school, based on his experience in school or even on the experience of someone significant to him, despite the fact that his parents, reflecting social values, believe schooling to be important and may try to convey this to the child. On the other hand, attitudes can be learned simply through the process of identification, about which more will be said below.

**Learning Within the Family**

Socialization is a learning process which ordinarily begins within the family circle. Here we shall examine some of the social psychological processes which either undergird or partially constitute early socialization. Each of these will be seen to have an effect either on what is learned (e.g., much of what is learned results from identification with one or both parents) or on the ease or difficulty with which it is learned (e.g., the degree of trust or attachment developed within the child determines to some extent how easily he will accept the socialization process). This is of major importance for learning in other social settings later on, especially in the school.

### Trust and Attachment

The words 'trust' and 'attachment' come from two different psychological traditions (psychoanalytic and social learning) and offer different explanations of what is essentially the same observable phenomenon. Within the first year of life, infants usually change in relation to their parents and other caretakers from being dependent on them for physical care alone to establishing a relationship of love or affection. It is in terms of this love and affection that they differentiate these persons from others around them. The relationship develops out of the very fact that the child has been regularly cared for with regard to his physical needs. It now becomes the medium and to some extent the measure of the child's efforts to relate to others. In other words, if the child experiences regular and sufficient care from those in his family, he is more likely than not to *expect* the same from the rest of his 'world' and therefore to trust that world (Erikson, 1963). On the contrary, if physical care has been irregular and insufficient, he may develop a sense of *mistrust* not only in the caretaking persons, but in all with whom he comes in contact. This primitive sense of trust or mistrust, as the case may be, is likely to last, though it is subject to revision as a result of later experiences. The success of efforts to socialize the growing child within the family will be affected by the degree to which the child has acquired a sense of trust.

If we look at this same phenomenon in terms of social learning theory, we can say that the child gradually becomes *attached* to his caretakers (family members) not just for what they can do in meeting his physical needs, but for the persons in themselves. As a result, the child is likely to be comfortable in situations in which those to whom he is attached are at ease and, by extension, disposed to accept their values and imitate their actions.[2] Conversely, the child who forms no close attachments is less likely to be so disposed, but rather more likely to be moderately alienated from what is commonly accepted.

### Identification

Identification is the process by which one person internalizes the attitudes and values of another. It is most commonly manifested in the identification of

---

[2]This disposition is not so much a direct result of the process of attachment as it is mediated by the process of *identification,* to be treated below.

a child with one of its parents, although it may occur at practically any age and in reference to people outside one's family. The process of identification is explained differently by different psychological and sociological theories, but the description of the end result is a matter of fairly common agreement. Our concern here is with the child's identification with parents or older siblings. This is an extremely important part of the learning that occurs within the family, and something very pertinent to the sociology of education.

Most children perceive their parents, and to some extent their older siblings, as the sources of reward and punishment. Parents are apt to reward (reinforce) the behaviour of children which reflects their own values and attitudes, with the result that the children will learn to a certain extent to avoid behaviour which reflects values and attitudes conflicting with those held by their parents. Indeed, to the extent that one or the other parent is seen as the source of rewards and punishments, the child's behaviour will begin to conform more with that parent's manifest will. As the child's consequent behaviour takes on a regular pattern, he or she is said to *identify with* the parent, and it may be inferred that the child's attitudes and values are somewhat similar to those of his parent. Of course, to this point we can speak of the child's values as something *accepted* but not truly formed in the sense of having been the result of rational justification. They are much closer to attitudes than to the values one would expect of a mature adult (cf. below, 'Values and their development'). Nevertheless, to the extent that the child identifies with his parent, and the parent's values reflect those of the larger society, *socialization* has occurred. Included in the process will be the learning of norms, not the least of which is related to *sex-role identification* or what is expected of a male or female person in virtue of that person's status as male or female. Beyond this, the youngster will learn other norms and roles, e.g., the role of parent, the norms of the work-a-day world, etc., depending on his parent's own status or position in society. What the child learns will be more or less well-defined depending on the parent's own value structure and consistency of behaviour, including the consistency with which he or she punishes and rewards the child.

It can be seen that, at the point at which the child identifies with his parent, he may be internalizing values, attitudes and norms which are characteristic of one of the social classes within a stratified society. Thus, the son of a lower-class father may internalize values typical of the lower socioeconomic class, but this is not necessarily the case. It is more than theoretically possible for a lower-class parent to reinforce in his child behaviour which reflects middle-class values, though the child in this case is identifying less with a parental model than with what might be considered an abstract ideal.

Clearly, although we have been using the example of the male child in the family, the same principles hold true for the young girl. It might be noted that in the social learning explanation of identification, the child is not necessarily expected to identify with the parent of the same sex, but rather with the parent who controls the rewards and punishments. This is an important difference between this explanation and that of most psychoanalytic theories.

Language

We have defined socialization in terms of the learning of the values, norms, etc., of a *society*. However, it was strongly suggested in the last section that a child is socialized as much into a *social class* as into a society as a whole. If this is the case, it is appropriate that we examine here the position of those who say that the way in which language is learned is strongly related to his social class and, in the case of members of the lower social classes, may help to limit access to the upper classes.

In what follows we will present as concisely as possible the position identified by Edwards (1979) as *environmentalist-deficit,* that is, the view that the language commonly used by members of the lower social classes is deficient in itself and constrains their social mobility. We will then present briefly the counter-view that the language patterns commonly associated with lower-social class groups are *different* but not deficient in comparison to the language patterns of the middle and upper social classes. We will then suggest some relationships that language has to socialization and to education.

The environmentalist-deficit view of the sociology of language is most closely identified with Basil Bernstein, an English sociologist, despite the fact that in his later work Bernstein eschews this position (Edwards, 1979, chapter 2). Bernstein described two distinct language variants,[3] which he called *public* and *formal.* Public language is typically characterized by short, often unfinished sentences, with poor syntax, repetitive use of conjunctions, rigid and limited use of adjectives and adverbs, frequent use of idiom, low-order symbolism and much implicit meaning. Formal language, in contrast, displays grammatical and syntactic accuracy, frequent use of relational prepositions, a range of adjectives and adverbs, the use of expressive symbolism, and makes its meaning more explicit. (Bernstein, 1959; more characteristics are listed there, and only the principal ones are shown here.) From these variants, Bernstein inferred two deep-structure *codes*, which he named *restricted* (corresponding to public language) and *elaborated* (corresponding to formal

---

[3]Although Bernstein's empirical data results from studies of the English language, his conclusions are of the sort which, if valid for English, would seem to be valid for any language used in a similarly stratified society. We would therefore expect them to apply in francophone as well as anglophone regions of Canada.

language). Eventually, he began to refer to the two variants themselves as restricted and elaborated *speech* (rather than language).

Restricted speech is said by Bernstein (1974) to convey *particularistic* meaning, that is, meaning which is only implicit in the speech and depends greatly on context and the shared experience of the participants. Elaborated speech conveys *universalistic* meaning, which is quite explicit in the speech and relatively context free. The user of elaborated speech clearly differentiates himself from the context and other participants. Elaborated speech is more expressive of abstract thinking, and the person who has access to the elaborated code is, on that account, more likely to engage in abstract thinking and have a greater facility with it. In Bernstein's view, the code that is learned has results so deep that they affect the actual pattern of thinking, giving their users differential ability to deal with essences. In an argument which is too complex to reproduce here, Bernstein (1974) relates the two codes to roles and statuses, and finally to social classes. In general, the restricted code is typical of members of the lower social class (for Bernstein, the working class), while members of the middle class use both the restricted and the elaborated code. Indeed, not only are the classes so differentiated, but *"one of the effects of the class system is to limit access to elaborated codes"* (Bernstein, 1974:176, italics in text).

What Bernstein called restricted code was interpreted by many to be a deficient form of language, even though Bernstein himself offers a disclaimer to the interpretation (Edwards, 1979:36). He concluded that each code has its advantages, and neither is necessarily superior to the other. At any rate, the former position was espoused by some in the United States (e.g., Deutsch, 1965; Bereiter and Engelmann, 1966) who were inclined to identify restricted speech with the language patterns typically found among poor ethnic groups, particularly ghetto Blacks. This was one of the main factors leading to the compensatory education movement. The purpose of compensatory education was to help disadvantaged children 'catch-up' with their (middle class) age mates before starting regular school programs. The main area of school-related disadvantage was felt to be language. Since this alleged language deficit was thought to be a result of deprived environment, it was suggested that an accelerated program in a linguistically enriched environment would compensate for the earlier deprivation. Compensatory education became a highly visible facet of President Johnson's "war on poverty."

A view contrasting with and to some extent countering the environmentalist-deficit view is what is usually called simply the *difference* view. The proponents of this view (e.g., Anastasiow *et al.*, 1969; Anastasiow, 1971; Labov, 1973; Edwards, 1979) suggest that the speech of those often classified as language disadvantaged is as syntactically well structured as middle-class speech. They therefore refer to middle-class speech as *standard* English (SE) and to other systematic variants as *nonstandard* English (NSE), and suggest that it is only as a result of bias that nonstandard English is regarded by some to be substandard or *deficient* in comparison to standard English (Edwards, 1979). Further, it is mistaken to suppose that NSE constrains the user in terms of cognitive functioning (Anastasiow, 1971, 1976; Edwards, 1979).

Though it was Bernstein's work in great part which led to the labeling of nonstandard variants as deficient, there is no demonstrated correspondence between the nonstandard variants studied in the United States and the restricted code studied by Bernstein. While it seems appropriate to regard nonstandard variants as dialects, it would probably be inaccurate so to designate the restricted (or elaborated) code (Edwards, 1979:78).

One might ask why the controversy between the two explanations of the structures of speech variants is important in the sociology of education. In general, as with so many issues, the question must be answered in terms of the potential for social control and equality of educational opportunity implicit in each position. The standard form of the language (whether described as 'standard English' or 'elaborated code') is regarded in schools as the proper form. It is the form to be taught as well as the medium of both teaching and learning. Children who use nonstandard variants or the restricted code alone are required to learn the standard form and elaborated code to be successful in school. They are already disadvantaged on entrance to school compared to those who have been socialized to standard language and elaborated code. Further, if the deficit position is taken, teachers are justified in believing that those who do not possess the elaborated code are less able to think abstractly and consequently less able to benefit from schooling. But these same children are most likely, according to Bernstein and his American followers, to belong to the lower socioeconomic class. On beginning school, they are faced with multiple difficulties not faced by middle- or upper-class children: they must learn a new code and/or speech variant; they must overcome the effects of social status difference, of which their speech is a continual reminder; and they must catch up in their ability to engage in abstract thinking. During their out-of-school hours, however, these children return to the environment in which they were originally socialized and they suffer a discontinuity of experience (between home and school) which seldom exists for middle and upper-class children (Bernstein, 1974:183-184). Conversely, users of elaborated code and standard variants are rewarded in school, in terms of both social continuity and ability to handle the content of schooling.

If the language-difference position is held, it would not be appropriate to say that users of nonstandard variants start school with a disadvantage related to thinking. There may be no significant difference in cognitive development between them and the other school children.[4] The other disadvantages remain, however, and these are likely to affect both their achievement and their educational opportunity.

It was stated above that the environmentalist-deficit position on language variants would imply, in terms of educational intervention, the use of compensatory education programs for the 'language disadvantaged.' The difference position, on the other hand, would imply that the schools themselves should change so as to be able to accommodate without prejudice the users of non-standard English. Perhaps that accommodation means, in practical terms, that the schools should help such children *add* standard English to their nonstandard variant, rather than *replacing* the latter by the former as if nonstandard English were indeed a deficient form of the language (Edwards, 1979).

To return to the theme of this section, language is first learned within the family. Individual families, however, will belong to particular social classes, and often to social groups (ethnic, regional) which are identifiable by the speech variant used. The variant the child learns will be a *sign* of the group into which he has been socialized and, to some extent, may even be a *means* of that particular socialization (Bernstein, 1974). To put it another way, a person's speech variant may be an indicator of his values and norms, and it may at the same time act to keep him from changing those values and norms, even in the further socialization process that is schooling.

Self-concept

Socialization is largely a matter of finding one's place as an individual within a group, whether that group be one's family or the whole of society, or anything in between. "To find one's place" in this context is to discover and to shape one's relationship with others. This leads inevitably to a set of feelings and cognitions about oneself — about one's own worth, abilities, weaknesses, and so on. A stable set of the most central feelings and cognitions about oneself is called a *self-concept*.

Self-concept is, of course, an hypothetical construct; something which serves to explain observable behaviour but is not directly observable itself. In this it is similar to intelligence. Whereas intelligence, typically measured by I.Q. tests, is labeled high, average or low, self-concept, measured by various personality tests, is typed as positive or negative. A person with a positive self-

---

[4]We have not introduced into this discussion the distinction between language *competence* and language *performance*. The user of NSE is normally quite competent to understand SE, but the form he speaks, and therefore his performance, is the nonstandard variant.

concept is usually confident, self-assured, somewhat independent, willing to take moderate risks, and so on.

The self-concept, or more simply the self (in the reflexive sense in which sociologists, following Mead, 1913, 1934, use the term) is a product of the interaction of a person with society. That is to say, one develops his self-concept from perceiving the communications, evaluations, and expectations of others with whom one interacts, and from one's own processing of these perceptions. The self is the *object* of a person's introspection, the 'me' rather than the subjective 'I' which is presupposed (Mead, 1913). Such introspection occurs only with a person's differentiation of himself from others in his environment, and the self becomes more clearly defined to the extent that a person can separate the roles of himself and others in their mutual social interaction. For this reason, the ability to *take on* roles is a good indicator of the degree to which the self has developed (though not a sign of whether the self-concept is positive or negative).

Commentators on Mead refer to three stages in the development of role-playing ability and consequently in the development of self or self-concept (Meltzer, 1978; Mackie, 1980). First there is the *preparatory stage*, in which the very young child simply imitates an adult, usually a parent. Such imitation, e.g., dialing on a telephone, is primitive role-playing but does not imply much reflection or introspection, and is not clearly rule-governed (Piaget, 1951). Next comes the *play* stage, in which role-playing is seen to be deliberate, but where it is limited to a duality: the role of the person other than the actor, and the role of the self in reaction to this other. Thus the child takes on a parent's role in a series of behaviours which display some degree of consistency and life-like quality in an interactive framework. The self is clearly differentiated from the other and is seen to have a particular role. Third is the *game stage*, where the youngster sees himself playing one role in a network of roles, each of which is familiar to him and which he may or does take on at times. Mead's example of the baseball player who, in order to fulfill his own role well, must be aware of the roles of the other team members, is often cited here. The complex role in terms of which the actor now defines his own role, and conceives of his 'self,' is that of the *generalized other*, as Mead (1934) called it. As the actor plays his role in this complex interaction, he will form a clearer (subjective) impression of his own abilities and worth. His self-concept, then, reflects the evaluations he perceives (correctly or not) that others make of him through the social interactions involving him; that is, self-concept is *learned*.

For our purposes, the most important aspect of the child's self-concept is that of his ability to learn. This plays a highly significant role in his decision-making about school learning (Brookover and Erickson, 1975). To the extent that a child is stereotyped by the social class to which he belongs, the language or dialect he speaks, his colour or his religion, and to the extent that his stereotype affects his own family, he may already before entering school have developed a self-concept that tells him he is less able to learn in school than he really is; however, the main stages of development of the self-concept would appear to occur after schooling has begun. There are, indeed, many influences in school which affect the child's perception of his ability to learn, often resulting in a far from realistic self-concept.

## Values and Their Development

Value has already been defined above. We would like to point out here that there seem to be two distinct stages in the development of values. Both relate to learning, though in different ways. Insofar as the first stage is particularly related to learning in the family, we have chosen to place the treatment here.

We shall call the two stages of value development (1) *value acceptance* and (2) *value formation*. The two terms are not entirely satisfactory, especially since their connotation is not mutually exclusive. Value *acceptance* is taken to mean the development of values the justification for which depends on the authority or knowledge of another. For example, a child may defend the value of truthfulness or honesty because his parents have told him it is "good" to tell the truth or it is "bad" to steal. Indeed, he may have internalized these values unconsciously through the process of identification or some similar channel of socialization; the point is that if asked to justify the value in any but the most superficial fashion, he appeals to another who has "told him so." This strategy is not reserved to children, but is only too frequently found in those who have reached the age of adulthood.

Value *formation*, on the other hand, refers to the process of value development which occurs when a person rationally examines the particular value in relation to others, understands the implications of behaving in accord with this value, and freely chooses to espouse it. The value may be the same as one that had previously been accepted on authority, e.g., honesty; or it may be quite different, e.g., tolerance or open-mindedness where stereotypic prejudice had once existed. The process of value formation depends on the ability to engage in formal operations (see chapter 4).

Value acceptance typically occurs in relation to familial authority, although conflict may occur when the child goes to school and begins to accept the authority of the teacher in matters of value. When conflict does occur, it is most likely because of a discontinuity between two value systems, the one learned at home, and the one that is characteristic of school. Since the latter is typically the middle-class value system, the discontinuity is especially likely to occur for children of the lower social class. There is a parallel here with what we have been regarding as standard and nonstandard language forms. Since the "deviant" group is in both cases likely to be composed of the poor and of ethnic minorities (though not all ethnic minorities), the discontinuity is exacerbated rather than neutralized.

Value formation begins to occur generally with adolescence, and the role of the family in this aspect of socialization is a very different one. The process of value formation often involves stages during which a person *appears* to reject the values he had hitherto accepted on authority. Suffice it to say at this point that with the completion of the value formation process a person frequently returns to a value position relatively close to that of his parents, but now he is able to justify those values rationally.

Most people reading this book would probably say that one of the more prominent values of our society is a "good education." Aside from the fact, however, that not all groups in our society value education, it is also the case that education may be valued as an end in itself or as a means to an end. In the latter case, education is usually seen as a means toward future employment, though it may also be viewed instrumentally in relation to social mobility, status, and so on. In this context, it is not difficult to see that there is likely to be a difference between social classes in the value they put on education, and this difference is likely to affect children from the very beginning of their schooling. To cite an example, we in Canada are not at all free of the notion that vocational education is principally for children of working class families while academic education is for children of middle and upper-class families.

## Attitudes and Their Development

Whereas values are predominantly cognitive, attitudes are dominated by emotional content. In relation to socialization, this has various implications. First, attitudes may be learned earlier than values and are probably more likely to result from preschool identification with parents or other family members. Second, attitudes are less susceptible to change through rational discussion than are values. Third, the very feelings that constitute attitudes may restrict the person from gaining the experience that would result in a change of attitude. (For example, the person who "dislikes" a particular ethnic group is not likely to mix with its members sufficiently to disconfirm his attitude. Indeed, the attitude is likely to influence his behaviour so that his experience will confirm the attitude.)

Attitudes may be learned from direct experience, as when a child likes school because the teacher is nice to him; or they may be learned indirectly, as when a child internalizes the attitudes of his parents through the process of identification, or a person internalizes the attitudes of a group in which he takes membership, e.g., the Ku Klux Klan. In sociology we are more interested in the latter, indirect learning of attitudes, not because it is indirect but because it is typically the way that attitudes of social groups are learned. In this way attitudes become part of one's group identity. Several examples come to mind: the contemporary attitude of English and Irish to one another; the middle-class attitude toward recipients of social welfare; the attitudes developing in Canada between westerners and easterners. No matter that the attitudes are stereotypic; if anything, this results in a greater rather than a lesser likelihood that the attitude will be passed on within the group and will serve to keep groups apart.

We have been talking here about negative attitudes, but of course the same principles apply in the case of positive attitudes, except that the likelihood of gaining experience which disconfirms them is greater.

As with values, social groups and classes can sometimes be differentiated in terms of their attitudes to schools and schooling. The objects of attitudes, however, will be more concrete than those of values. Attitudes will be directed toward teachers, "the system," principals, particular schools, school subjects, and so on, rather than the more general category of education or its major subdivisions. This differentiation may have a substantial bearing on achievement.

## The Development of a Normative System

A norm is a rule prescribing expected behaviour in a given situation. Norms may be written, as in law, or unwritten, and they differ widely in the sanctions attached to them. A norm is essentially a social rather than an idiosyncratic reality. A *normative system* is that complex of norms which regulates behaviour within a given society or group. The normative system for a group is learned as one takes on one and more roles within the group, since a role is a complex of behaviours related to a status.

Children very quickly learn within the family the normative system for that family — what is expected of them as children and, eventually, what is expected of parents, siblings, and so on. They also learn the norms of society as these affect members of their family, e.g., that boys and girls go to school, that people dress differently for different occasions, and that there are things like speed limits, jails to punish lawbreakers, etc. They also learn that norms are related to status, so that the norm for behaviour in a given situation may be different for a person of high status than for a person of low status, and indeed the sanction for violation of the norm may be different. Familiar examples in contemporary western society are the norms and sanctions for drug possession, tax evasion, or the more informal norms for social drinking, as these interact with status. Again, norms are the sort of thing that are passed on through the social learning process, rather than through direct experience, though attention to a norm will frequently be stimulated by the effects of its violation.

If the normative system is biased in favour of a subgroup within society, it becomes a medium for social control. To the degree that schools promote the bias, they are also instruments of social control. The dilemma of the disadvantaged subgroup within such a society is that to maintain membership in the society as a whole, and to gain its benefits (e.g., education), it must subscribe to norms which perpetuate its disadvantaged position. Conversely, the bonus for the advantaged (privileged) subgroup is that in subscribing to the same normative system, it maintains its privileged position. In learning the normative system, children learn how people are "kept in their places."

## Psychosocial Development: Erik Erikson

Erik Erikson is a contemporary American psychologist, with strong interests in anthropology, whose views on human development are closely related to the theme of socialization we have been treating here. Differing from many in the Freudian psychoanalytic tradition in which he has his root, Erikson sees the relationship between the individual and society as one of cooperation rather than conflict (Erikson, 1963; 1968). This means, in his view, that society has the responsibility to socialize its members with the aim of providing for each the best opportunity for personal growth. Such a brief statement of his position may appear trite, especially if confused with position statements of recent humanist psychologists; however, Erikson provides a detailed foundation for this position, and it has clear implications for schooling.[5] For each of eight stages of human development, Erikson sees the person acquiring some critical aspect of socialization. These are trust (in those around him and, by extension, in society); autonomy (decision-making); initiative (trying of new things, creative effort); industry (productive effort, goal-directed activity); identity (sameness and continuity of personhood); intimacy (ability to share on a personal level); generativity (responsibility for the young); and ego integrity (wholeness and identification with the culture). The first three of these are acquired during preschool years, the next two by the end of adolescence, and the last three in adulthood.

Because these acquisitions normally build on one another, the foundation for socialization occurs in the family, but for socialization to be complete, there must be continuity between the family and the school. If the climate for healthy development is not present, socialization will result in just the opposite of the acquisitions mentioned above, e.g., mistrust instead of trust, inferiority instead of industry, role confusion instead of identity.

---

[5]One of the best commentaries on Erikson's theory appears in the book *Adolescence and Individuality* by Judith Gallatin (New York: Harper & Row, 1965), devotes five chapters to it, addressing some sociological as well as psychological issues.

This bare outline of Erikson's position makes the stages of socialization appear rigidly sequential and reserved to particular times. He does not in fact view them in this way. One of the major implications of his theory for schooling and the role of teachers is that adolescence (the period for establishing a sense of identity) provides an opportunity for the person, given the appropriate societal environment, to make up for failures in socialization at earlier periods. This can happen only if the extra-familial socializing agents (teachers, coaches, etc.,) provide the required understanding and support. Nevertheless, the ideal situation is that in which socialization for personal growth occurs continuously through childhood, school years and into working life. The process, which combines the complementary facets of psychological development and socialization, is referred to as psychosocial development.

**Extra-familial Influences**

The extra-familial socializing influences we wish to consider here are primarily those of the mass media, especially television, and particularly as these penetrate the home.

The burden of conventional wisdom on the topic of the effect of television and other mass media on the socialization of children was, until recently, that children were being alienated from their parents' generation. The impression was often given that children were addicted to television from their early years; that school children spent so much time before the TV set that they no longer did much homework; that reading was disappearing as a cultural pursuit in favour of the more passive pastime of watching television (McLuhan, 1964); and especially that children were being socialized into violent behaviour as a norm (U.S. Department of Health, Education and Welfare, 1972; LaMarsh *et al.*, 1977; Bandura *et al.*, 1963).

An article by McCormack (1979) reviews the research relating television to the socialization of children and concludes (1) that there is surprisingly little good research available, most of which is relatively old, and (2) that there is much less cause for alarm than conventional wisdom would imply. This latter conclusion rests less on empirical data than on "a theory of human nature, a theory of childhood socialization, and a theory of communication" (p.317). She points out fallacies of both fact and interpretation in reported correlations between (a) heavy television viewing and membership in low income groups, and (b) light television viewing and intelligence. She also argues that television viewing tends to lessen rather than increase the generation gap and assists parents in passing on their values, given that children are found to prefer adult programming to that designed specifically for children. While McCormack's article does not assuage all the concerns about possible ill effects of television viewing on the socialization of children, it is refreshing to find a well reasoned exposition of the current state of knowledge on the topic.

We cannot resist suggesting, however, that whatever socializing influence television does exert directly would tend to emphasize middle-class values and attitudes. This suggestion is based on the fact that most progamming is sponsored and directed at consumers. Advertisers, who generally belong to the middle class, have at least three options in choosing what they will sponsor. They may sponsor programs which deliberately portray values, attitudes and norms consonant with their own ideological commitment; they may remain indifferent to what is portrayed but appeal to the ratings based on surveys of their target audience; or they may sponsor programs which might, objectively and independently of class bias, be considered uplifting and educational in the best sense of the term. In the case of the second option, the values will be those written in by the program authors, who typically have difficulty portraying other than middle-class culture. It seems not overly cynical to say that the third option is seldom exercised in North America, except perhaps by sponsors on the Public Broadcasting System in the U.S. and, to a far lesser extent, in programs directly subsidized by the Canadian Broadcasting Corporation, and even in these cases there is room for skepticism.

One television phenomenon may deserve special mention in the context of the sociology of education: programs such as *Sesame Street* which are directed particularly to preschool children. It is widely assumed that such programs are not only entertaining for children but that they will have some beneficial effect on the effectiveness of formal schooling when that begins.

## Values Particularly Related to Schooling

To this point we have talked about values and attitudes in a general sense, related to their development within the family. We should like to treat more specifically some selected values which may have particular relevance for school success or failure.

### Achievement and Competition

Achievement and achievement motivation have been the focus of a good deal of research since Murray (1938) included need for achievement in his taxonomy of human needs (see above, chapter 4). There is confusion in much of the research literature as to whether the variable under consideration is achievement level, achievement orientation, or achievement motivation. It should be clear that a relatively high level of achievement may be attained by a person who does not have the internalized standard of excellence which is characteristic of achievement motivation. On the one hand, achievement is valued instrumentally, as a means to an end; on the other, it is valued as an end in itself. For our purposes, however, we will consider achievement level, achievement orientation and achievement motivation all under the umbrella of the term 'achievement.'

We have paired competition with achievement because we think that, although it is distinct from achievement as a value, it has a related connection with school success. Whereas achievement is measured by some task-related standard (e.g., correctness of answers, thoroughness of completion of a task), competition implies comparison with the performance of one or more others on the same task. One of the unfortunate things about schooling is that achievement is too often confused with competitive success, e.g., 'coming first' may involve different levels of achievement in two groups of students at the 'same' grade level. We are assuming, however, that their antecedents in terms of early socialization are similar, if not exactly the same.

Zigler and Child (1973) review the research to that time relating to the socialization of achievement, and Vidler (1977) cites fewer studies but nothing related to the origins of achievement motivation that was not mentioned by Zigler and Child. Though the data are not consistent, there seems to be a preponderance of support for the hypothesized relationship between independence training in childhood and later achievement. However, achievement is not the only variable which results from independence training, and it does not always result. There is a much stronger relationship between direct early training for achievement and later achievement motivation. Not unexpectedly, "parents of high- as compared to the low-achievement boys had higher aspirations and expectations and set higher standards for their sons' performances" (Rosen and D'Andrade, 1959, cited by Zigler and Child, 1973:138). Evidence is also cited to the effect that achievement level in the individual is positively related to the general cultural evaluation of achievement. While this data comes from cross cultural studies, it is not inconsistent to suggest that, by extension, it might apply to subcultures found within a given country (e.g., white middle class compared to native people in Canada). The reviewers support this suggestion by citing studies showing that members of the middle class, on average, have received greater independence training and have higher achievement motivation than members of the working class, and that being right has been found to be more rewarding for middle class than for lower class children.

Achievement, however, is still a very general term. Perhaps people can value achievement in one sphere and be indifferent to it in another. In that context, to suggest that the members of one subgroup differ from members of another in their valuing of *academic* achievement is not to say that they differ in the degree of total achievement orientation. It is, however, to introduce another factor bearing on expectations of school success: if academic achievement is valued less by the lower class than by the middle class, and this seems to be the case, their aspirations in this respect will be lower. Again, if they are known by teachers to value academic achievement less, than less will be expected of them as a group. Unfortunately, this often translates into diminished expectations for each individual within the group.

Unlike achievement pure and simple, competition implies and involves comparison with others. No doubt competition can exist among preschool children in the home, but theories of human development (Erikson, 1963) tell us that it is particularly important for children in late childhood (6-11) when, Erikson tells us, it is appropriate for them to acquire a sense of industry. If the forum for competition is the classroom, those who have already been socialized to the value of academic achievement from their early years will have an advantage in this phase of development. Certainly the rewards for academic achievement would lead one to believe that winning in this sphere is most important. The system of grading used in most schools, which is norm-referenced rather than criterion-referenced,[6] is itself subservient to this notion.

## Creativity and Conformity

Whereas achievement and competition appear to be positively related values, creativity and conformity,[7] at least in the context of schooling, seem to be almost inversely related; that is, the most creative students tend to be the least conforming in terms of the patterns of behaviour considered desirable by school authorities (Wallach and Kogan, 1965, cited in Gage and Berliner, 1979). It is interesting that Charles Silberman entitles one of the chapters of his book, *Crisis in the Classroom*, "Education for Docility" (Silberman, 1970).

Creativity is closely associated with independence and intrinsic motivation, while conformity is associated with traits such as rule orientation, consistency, dependability, punctuality, predictability, perserverance, and extrinsic motivation. This is borne out in a study by Bowles, Gintis and Meyer (1975),

---

[6]*Norm-referenced* grading measures performance on a task in relation to the performance of others doing the task. Thus 70% would be a good mark in an exam if most of the class made less than that. *Criterion-referenced* grading measures performance in relation to a pre-established set of objectives to be achieved. Thus 70% indicates that the objectives were met to that level, and the criterion for satisfactory performance would often be higher than that.

[7]By conformity, we mean conformity to authority, rather than acquiescence to majority opinion as it is defined in many experimental studies reported in social psychology texts (cf. Kohn, 1969, p.37).

cited in Bowles and Gintis (1976).[8] This study showed that in a sample of 237 students in one New York high school, the traits associated with conformity correlated positively with grades (as a measure of school success) while creativity, independence and aggression correlated negatively. In this study, being creative was defined as follows: "Inventive; is always coming up with new ideas; sometimes crazy, unrealistic ones; thinks of unusual (often weird) possibilities for solving problems." For 'independent' the definition was "likes to be independent and wants to arrange his or her own activities; dislikes being told what to do." More tellingly, its opposite was "is able to accept directions easily; follows teacher's directions, even if doing things another way seems better" (Bowles and Gintis, 1976:299f.). While caution must always be used in generalizing from a small, narrowly specified sample, this study gives some basis to the view that creativity is not rewarded in school, while conformity is.

Kohn (1969) maintains that the personality traits associated with conformity are more characteristic of the lower than of the middle class, reflecting the values consonant with efficient industrial production. In one study he found that parents of lower-status children value obedience, neatness and honesty in their children, while higher-status parents emphasize curiosity, self-control, consideration and happiness. In summary, he says:

> Middle-class parents are more likely to emphasize children's *self-direction,* and working class parents to emphasize their *conformity to external authority.* . . . The essential difference between the terms, as we use them, is that self-direction focuses on *internal* standards of direction for behaviour; conformity focuses on *externally* imposed rules (Kohn, 1969:34-35)

We shall have more to say about this in chapter 11 in dealing with what has been called the 'correspondence principle.'

There is further evidence (Zigler and Child, 1973:116-143) to associate independence (which is related to creativity) with the middle rather than the lower class. If, then, children of lower-class parents are more likely to be socialized to conform, it might be appropriate to ask whether this wouldn't give them an advantage in schooling. The answer seems to be that it would indeed — in certain levels and streams of schooling. According to Bowles and Gintis (1976, chapter 5), the value structure related to conformity and obedience is especially rewarded up to and including high school, and thence into vocational education and community colleges. Creativity and independence tends to be recognized as virtuous only in the honors academic high school programs and the universities, to which students from lower-class families are

---

[8]A good summary of the data is included as an appendix to Bowles and Gintis (1976).

less likely to have access (see below, Part IV). The dichotomy was popularized in the characters of Archie Bunker and "Meathead" in the TV series *All in the Family*.

## Family Influence and Educational Achievement: Empirical Evidence

To this point we have emphasized that the family is the earliest agent of socialization and, in many respects, primary in importance. Through the mediation of the family, the child is socialized not simply into society in general, but into a social class, with all that that implies in terms of values, attitudes and norms. If we want to know the effect that family background has on educational achievement *for large groups of people*, we will find it convenient to use social class as an intervening variable; indeed, we normally infer the relationship of family background to educational achievement from the social class-educational achievement relationship, assuming the parameters of family background and social class to be similar enough to justify the inference in most cases. Clearly, there are other variables such as ethnicity and religion that can complicate the analysis. For example, the high value a family of low social class places on education because of its ethnic or religious origin may supersede the low value it would be expected to give it on the basis of social class membership. Nonetheless, in most cases for large groups, the inference is justified.

Is there a systematic difference in educational achievement among students from different family backgrounds? If so, is the difference an effect of family background itself or simply of systematic differences in ability to learn (I.Q.)?

Let us respond to the latter question first. It will be shown in chapter 11 that I.Q. makes much less of an independent contribution to the level of educational achievement attained by a particular group than might be expected. We can safely say, anticipating the argument given in chapter 11, that if students from different family backgrounds vary systematically in educational achievement, the variance is not due simply to differences in intellectual ability. Moreover, differences in *measured* intellectual ability can themselves be partly a function of differences in family background and socioeconomic status. We can now concentrate on the first of the two questions posed above.

Brookover and Erickson (1975) demonstrate that self-concept of ability is a crucial variable affecting educational achievement, and that it is positively related to social class background. Moreover, they stress that the instrumental value to self of the decision to learn (i.e., to achieve an education) is also of critical importance. The family background which stresses the utility of schooling as a means to an end will also give an advantage to the student from that family. We have shown in chapter 2 when discussing Bourdieu that the instrumental value of schooling is also related to social class. Many sociologists (Kohn, 1969; Porter, 1965) have demonstrated the relationship between education and parental support, parental background and social class. Rocher (1975:148) states, again in line with the research of others, that "the school is a reflection of the spirit, the culture, the aspirations of the middle class." He takes pains to demonstrate empirically, using data provided by Porter (1965), that students from higher-social class backgrounds have a higher level of achievement.

Forcese (1980) has a good summary of the relationship between family background, schools and educational achievement in Canada. He notes especially ". . . that lower-class children tend not to succeed in school and complete university" (p.87). Laying aside lower I.Q.'s as a cause, he attributes much of the reason to a better supportive environment for the middle-class child. This includes verbal and reading skills, the presence of books and magazines in the home, the use of pens and pencils, the more advanced literacy of the parents and their higher-prestige occupations, all of which act as role models. There is also preferential availability of preschool training such as nursery schools, better nutritional and health care, and even tutoring. Moreover, lower-class parents are more likely to be suspicious of and even hostile to school, and the child from this background who applies more strenuous efforts to succeed in school may meet more opposition and even ridicule from peers, parents and teachers. As a result, non-achievement is reinforced.

Forcese (1980) uses statistics from Information Canada to point out the overrepresentation of students at the post-secondary level from families whose fathers are engaged in occupations at the managerial, professional and technical, and clerical and sales levels, and the underrepresentation of such students from family occupational backgrounds involving crafts, manufacturing, manual labour and service industries. A similar type of presentation showing the child's educational level by the educational level of the parents for 1966 reinforces this data. For families where both parents are university graduates, 51 per cent of the children graduate also, and virtually all of the remainder achieve at the secondary level. For families where both parents have a secondary education, 19 per cent of the children receive a university education and 6 per cent achieve only at the elementary level. But in the case of families where both parents have only an elementary education only 5 per cent of the children achieve at the university level while 52 per cent drop out with only the elementary level completed. Where there are varying levels of education for the parents the levels achieved by the children vary accordingly. Clearly the relationship between family socioeconomic background and the educational attainment of the children is a very strong one.

What is said about family background, social class and educational achievement here complements the conclusions of chapter 5 on the relationship of social class to educational opportunity. Later, in Part IV, we shall examine the issue of whether these relationships are functional or dysfunctional in society. First, however, we will turn our attention to a description of schooling in Canada. In doing so, we shall be looking for those factors that may facilitate or impede the realization of the ideal of equal educational opportunity and the highest possible levels of educational achievement.

This concludes Part II of this text, the section dealing with preschool influences which are particularly important for educational achievement. We have dealt in a special way with a description of how people from various social categories, and more specifically social class, achieve in school. We might say that in a general way or on average it is determined, in the sense of exerting influence and setting limits, that this kind or this degree of achievement will result. It is possible that social policy in the educational domain may change this influence or determination, but we have seen no substantial evidence to indicate that this has come about in a realistic way in the past. In that sense, much of the influence of class has been brought to bear before the child begins school.

The family is the most important intermediate or intervening variable between the macro level structural variables such as class, and educational achievement. Like class, the influence of family and early socialization will continue on during schooling, but much of its influence has stamped the child in a specific way before school is begun.

# Part III

This section of the book is concerned especially with organizational variables which are internal to schooling and the local community. In chapter 7 we investigate the school as a formal organization or bureaucracy, and attempt to point out how there are, or may be, conflicting goals. We try to understand the meaning of the roles which fall to various administrative positions and to teachers. We follow this, in chapter 8, with some coverage of the clients of education: the community, the parents, and especially the students — many of whom graduate, some of whom drop out. In chapter 9 we present material on different ways of organizing schools and classes for teaching. We are concerned especially with ability grouping, tracking, and with different formats such as team teaching, open classrooms and free schools. As we shall see, these factors all have an important bearing on the inequality of educational attainment.

# 7

# The Organization
# and Management of Schooling

This chapter will deal with the way in which the process of formal education (schooling) is organized and controlled in Canada. There are two principal aspects to this organization: the structuring of the *phases* of schooling from kindergarten or earlier to postgraduate programs, along with the tracks involved in the various phases; and the structuring of the *management* of schooling, from the provincial minister to the classroom teacher and support staff. As a preliminary to the consideration of both the phases and management of schooling, we will treat the characteristics of a formal organization with specific reference to education, so as to provide a framework for the understanding of educational organization and the effects that formal organization can have on schooling.

## The School as a Formal Organization

### The Meaning of Complex Organization

Whenever a group of people come together to pursue a common goal, some form of social organization is required. Different actors in this common pursuit play different roles. We refer to the interrelationships between these roles as the structure. Organizations may range from the very simple such as a foursome which regularly comes together to play bridge, to the very complex such as the Canadian Army. All of them have these characteristics: a division of labour, power centres, and substitution of personnel (Spencer, 1979). As the structure becomes more complex so that the people involved become more dependent on one another it is moving in the direction of or has become a formal organization. This element of organization is meant to regularize and make predictable the human interactions involved; otherwise there would be irregularity, non-predictability, even chaos.

Gordon (1975:344) describes complex organizations in terms of four characteristics: they are stable patterns of interaction, among coalitions of people who have a collective identity, pursuing interests and accomplishing given tasks, co-ordinated by power and authority structures. The provincial educational institutions in Canada are complex organizations and have these characteristics. The individual schools are parts or branches of this educational structure. It is unwise to consider any one a complete organization in itself. Schools are interdependent and interrelated and hence form parts of a whole.

Complex organizations have different kinds or sets of goals, and we may regard the organization as ". . . the sum total of the meanings that its members (and certain non-members) apply to it" (Gordon, 1975:344). The point being stressed here is that the organization is not a static entity but rather a dynamic and changing one, the nature of which depends on the meaning given to it by its members and clients and even the external public. So it is with schooling. The meaning which that institution has depends on the meanings, especially the goals, imputed to it by a wide variety of people. It is not accurate to say that an organization such as the formal education system in Nova Scotia or Alberta is what it was established to be. There are other factors which give it meaning, and we must understand these as well. Nor is it accurate to say that the institution is what any individual perceives it to be, important as that is for the individual concerned.

It is the goals of the organization which largely determine the structure, and it is the collective meaning which these goals have for all who interact within it which gives the structure a meaning. Gordon (1975) lists five types of organizational goals. We must understand their meaning if we are to have a good understanding of what this complex organization of schooling really is.

The first is usually referred to as the charter or *formal* goal. This is the formal purpose for which the organization was established. It is usually defined in writing, as in a constitution, even in an act of the legislature, and often imposes legal limits on the organization and indicates a line of authority. Provincial governments do this for the educational institution, usually through an education act.

Organizations do not generally operate fully in accord with these formal or express goals. They are modified in many ways, and such modification gives meaning to what the organization really is rather than what it is supposed to be. The *informal* goals are an interpretation and modification of the formal goals by those who are directly involved, giving a collective interpretation of what the purpose and structure does or is. People routinely act in such informal ways. They see the official purposes as altered or modified in unofficial ways and tend to interact and respond somewhat in accord with this interpretation. Thus the allocative function of schooling, as interpreted by the Marxists, should it be an accurate assessment and shared informally by clients and staff, would represent an informal goal. In this case it would be in conflict with the formal goal, not an altogether unusual occurrence.

There are also *personal* goals held by individuals within the organization. These refer to the intent which an individual has for himself. A particular student may attend school merely to avoid being in the work force, or to find a marriage partner. A teacher could 'teach' simply to earn a salary, or primarily to earn a salary. When the same personal goal is held in common by a significant number of people it will alter the meaning of the organization, and may even become a shared informal goal.

*Ideological* goals, as the name implies, lie in an external or broader value system. These in turn may affect an organization significantly. In Canadian society we have the ideologies of equality of opportunity and meritocracy, even if we lack the reality. External to schooling and founded in a common value system or an imposed value system, they nevertheless modify the structure and purposes which schooling takes. The phenomenon of testing, used to allocate students into specific tracks supposedly on the basis of ability and motivation, exists in relationship to such ideological goals. It would not be required if advancement on the basis of ascription were a generally accepted norm. There are, of course, competing ideologies. The treatment given to females in our schools is substantially the result of stereotypical models imposed by a set of ideological beliefs about the characteristics of women (nurturers, spectators, passive recipients). Thus an ascriptive ideology existing in the broader society makes a substantial mark on the structure and functions of schools.

There are also *inertial* goals. These simply refer to the tendency of an organization to perpetuate itself, even when its formal goals have been fulfilled. It is difficult to assess this goal in relation to the overall institution of schooling. It is easier to view it from the perspective of a subunit or part. The declining enrollment in schools and universities may modify considerably the role of teachers or the organization of the classroom, including teacher-student ratio and specialized classes. If not, then large numbers of teachers would be out of jobs.

Given the nature of these types of goals, and that an organization is a function of what the goals are for the people who interact within it, it should now become more apparent why the meaning of an organization is so difficult to establish precisely. Such meanings change, and sometimes may change rather quickly. However, there is one type of formal organization, the bureaucracy, which is its highest form and which attempts to control in a more specialized way the goals which may be competing with the formal goals. We emphasize that there is an *attempt* at control, for certainly a bureaucracy does not eliminate these other goals.

## Characteristics of a Bureaucracy

A bureaucracy is the highest form of complex organization. Bureaucratic structures are frequently viewed with an element of displeasure, sometimes even alarm. It is well to remember that bureaucracies are among the most efficient organizations which have ever evolved, and frequently the very characteristics which make them displeasing to clients are the same ones which make them efficient for those who exercise formal roles within the structure. One of the principal reasons for criticism of a bureaucracy is its ruthlessness rather than its inefficiency.

A bureaucracy is a type of formal organization designed to accomplish large scale administrative tasks by systematically co-ordinating the work of many individuals (Blau and Meyer, 1971:4). Bureaucracies are based on rational-legal authority relations. The legitimacy of such authority rests on the belief that the rules established are among the better means of achieving the end. The person in authority is presumed to be competent to perform the task on the basis of rational criteria. He holds the office on the basis of impersonal characteristics and the subjects owe obedience to the office rather than the person.

Max Weber was the great pioneer in the study of bureaucracy, and much modern analysis is simply a refinement of insights he provided. Following his analysis, Blau and Meyer (1971) list six main characteristics of bureaucracies:

(1) There is a specialized division of labour in which the regular activities required to achieve the goals are distributed in fixed ways. As a result each person performs specific duties in which he or she is particularly competent. There is detailed co-ordination of all such specialized tasks.

(2) The offices are organized in a hierarchy. Each official is responsible to his superior not only for his duties but for those of his subordinates. There is a chain of command (line) complemented by supportive personnel (staff).

(3) Operations are standardized. They are governed by a consistent system of abstract rules which are to be applied to specific cases.

(4) Officials are to conduct their offices impersonally, with the highest loyalty to the firm rather than to the individual.

(5) Employment is based on technical qualifications related to competency. There is a system of promotion based on achievement and the employee is protected against arbitrary dismissal.

(6) A purely bureaucratic organization is capable of attaining the highest form of efficiency from a technical perspective.

There is a tendency to overemphasize the functions of a bureaucracy and overlook the dysfunctions. These are not only proper to the specific organization as such, but to the *kind* of organization as well. Bureaucratic organization is more appropriate for one type of association than for another. Where considerations of efficiency are especially important in order to produce certain end results, then a bureaucratic structure may be in order. But when people associate in co-ordinated activities where efficiency is less important than the attainment of intrinsic satisfaction, then a bureaucratic structure is less fitting, and may be counter-productive. Where people associate to pursue common goals decided upon in a democratic manner through free expression, a bureaucratic structure is almost always uncalled for. It impedes free expression (Blau and Meyer, 1971). Schooling probably better fits the second of these three types. A concentration on efficiency will tend to impede the goal of intrinsic satisfaction from formal learning. The element of standardization contributes to this in a special way. Instead of being treated as individuals with different interests, students in a bureaucratically organized school system are treated as a group where the pursuit of different interests is impeded.

Despite its efficiency in administrative tasks, perhaps because of it, there are dysfunctions which are proper to bureaucracies. Because of the element of impersonality there is frequently lack of morale and *esprit de corps*. There is less room for individual judgement because of the requirement of standardization. Each case is to be treated in the same way even if individual circumstances might appear to call for an exception to the rule. Moreover, subordinates interested in promotion want to please their superiors. For this reason they tend to conceal defects resulting from the superior's policy. Specialization and the fragmenting of tasks make it difficult for higher level management to make sound decisions. Frequently the specialized subordinate has more knowledge than the superior. Where decision making calls for input from a number of such specialists, co-ordination may become difficult. Moreover, as organizations and individual units become older and more established the inertial goal tends to impede change. Such change may endanger the personal goals of superiors or make them more difficult to attain. Hence it may be and frequently is resisted by those in power. Again, organizations generally have socially integrating myths meant to promote high morale. These tend to distort the perspective of the members. Objective criticism may be interpreted as disloyalty (Blau and Meyer, 1971).

It is because of these kinds of dysfunctions that many recent educational historians like Katz (1971, 1973) are so critical of the bureaucratically organized institution of schooling. The formal goals have supposedly been established in accord with (what is considered) the welfare of the students, the presumption being that this also is in the best interests of society. But as we have already noted, these co-exist with conflicting ideological goals. The very characteristics of the bureaucracy tend to promote informal goals such as tracking which may be opposed to the personal development of the student. The personal goals, especially of those in authority positions such as supervisors, principals, teachers and coaches, again often come in conflict with the formal goals and with the best interest of the student. A coach who wants to win at any cost is perhaps a good example. Inertial goals and the adaptation required by progressive change may cause added conflict.

The situation is complicated by the large numbers of students and other personnel who are in the system. Education is expensive and the taxpayer normally wants a good rate of return on his investment. This is often interpreted as meaning efficiency. A less highly bureaucratized educational system which would better permit the treatment of individual differences is perceived as being more expensive. This is a special problem for the teacher for whom the service motive has traditionally been regarded as highly desirable.

The standardization which is so frequently found in schooling militates against those who do not fit or are opposed to the stereotype on which such standardization is based. This, of course, is generally the middle-class stereotype. The upper classes can afford to pay for different treatment. The lower classes and certain ethnic groups are the ones on whom the price of such standardization falls.

## The Canadian Educational Structure

### The Heritage of the B.N.A. Act

In Canada the responsibility for formal education belongs generally to the provincial governments. Provincial jurisdiction is founded in the British North America Act, section 93, where it is stated that the provincial legislature "may exclusively make laws in relation to education." However, provisos appended to that statement safeguarding the educational rights of religious minorities, together with the fact that the Parliament of Canada was given exclusive legislative authority over Indians, armed forces and penitentiaries, resulted in an actual division of jurisdiction along federal-provincial lines where education is concerned. The federal jurisdiction was augmented by the setting up of the Northwest Territories as a political entity to be governed by Parliament. Today the federal involvement in education is very great, whether directly as in the administration of schools for native peoples, armed forces personnel, Northwest Territories, and penitentiary inmates, or in manpower training programs, or indirectly through transfer payments to provincial governments for post-secondary education, sponsorship of study and research through the Social Sciences and Humanities Research Council and the National Research Council, and so on. Nonetheless, federally run educational agencies have operated alongside rather than in competition with provincially regulated schools, and their organization has generally been similar. There have been many cooperative programs, in most of which federal agencies have been very sensitive to provincial control. It is generally the case, then, that when we speak about the organization of education, we are talking about the way education is structured and managed under provincial legislation.

Since there are ten provinces in Canada, and their entrance into confederation was spread over 82 years, we should not be surprised to find many differences among them in the way that education is organized. There are many differences, of course; what is surprising is to find how much they have in common. We will refer briefly to these commonalities before noting the differences.

## Similarities Among Provinces

All ten provinces structure their schools into three roughly distinct levels, which are traditionally called *elementary, secondary* and *post-secondary.* Secondary schools usually, but not always, comprise junior high schools and senior high schools. Post-secondary educational institutions include universities and community colleges, the latter often include technical institutes. All provinces provide at least twelve years of free schooling. In some cases, kindergarten or primary classes are provided, and in at least two provinces (Ontario and Manitoba) a nursery or junior kindergarten year is provided.

This tri-level structuring is not accidental; it is the remnant of the philosophy mentioned in chapter one which suggested that all children require basic education, and some children should receive advanced education. Advanced education was further divided into high school and post-secondary education and streams were introduced within these levels to meet the need for occupational preparation while preserving the allocative or selective function of schooling. Secondary education was distinguished from elementary education primarily in terms of its emphasis on distinct subject discipline and its teaching methods. It is interesting to note that the introduction of junior high schools as different from senior high schools copied the American effort to move the content and methods of high school teaching to the two upper grades of the elementary school, thus reducing the latter from eight years to six. Currently there is a move to reverse this policy.

In the past fifteen years in Canada the theory of continuous progress has been very prominent. Its main tenet is that students should be allowed to proceed at the rate best suited to each individual in different subject areas and skills from school entrance to graduation. Carried to its logical conclusion, continuous progress in practice would imply the virtual elimination of the traditional lock-step grade system. With few exceptions, this approach has succeeded only in elementary levels, and its practice seems to be diminishing again after reaching a peak in the mid seventies. What is especially relevant here is the difficulty that was encountered by both students and teachers when students from elementary schools where continuous progress was in effect moved on to junior high schools. This difficulty served to make concrete the distinction between the two levels, a distinction which many would like to think is realized only in the fact that the students are served in different buildings.

Now that it is so widely proclaimed that all children should have at least ten to twelve years of schooling, and more is desirable, it is pertinent to question the continued existence of the very real differences between elementary and secondary education. The issue will be dealt with in part later in this chapter when we look at the practice of tracking (or streaming, as it is often called).

Another commonality among provinces with regard to education is that school attendance is compulsory from at least seven to at least 15 years of age, with most provinces requiring attendance from six to 16. It is interesting to note, however, again in relation to the social history of education in Canada, that the Graham Royal Commission in Nova Scotia recommended that the age for compulsory school attendance be lowered from 16 to 14 (Graham, 1974).

We will see that there is a good deal of similarity among provinces in the way that they manage education. All provinces have a cabinet minister of education, though three have two ministers, giving one of them responsibility for post-secondary education.

**Provincial Differences**

Of the differences that exist among the provinces and territories in the way that they structure the phases of formal education, most are of minor importance. The most important, perhaps, from the sociological point of view pertain to (1) the status of denominationally separate schools; (2) entrance requirements for university; and (3) the existence and function of CEGEPs in Quebec.

Separate Schools

As a general rule, the B.N.A. Act gave official standing to the state of affairs regarding separate schools that existed in a given province at the time of its entrance into confederation. For example, when in 1867 the original four provinces joined to form Canada, separate schools for Catholics and Protestants, with separate regulating superstructures, existed in Quebec, but not in Nova Scotia. As a result, separate school systems for these denominations have continued to be supported in Quebec, but have no legal foundation in Nova Scotia, where in fact they have sometimes existed purely by "gentlemen's agreement." (Interestingly, most of Nova Scotia's universities owe their establishment to church denominations, and five of them maintain religious affiliation.)[1] In Ontario, separate elementary schools exist where supporters

---

[1]The five are Acadia (Baptist), King's (Anglican), Mount St. Vincent, St. Francis Xavier and Université Ste. Anne (Roman Catholic). St. Mary's is officially non-denominational but has a history of Catholic affiliation. Regardless of affiliation, all universities are funded equitably by government.

assign their taxes to the system of their choice. A slightly different but quite similar system exists in Alberta, but it includes high schools. There were separate schools in Manitoba originally, but these were legislated out of existence through a series of measures, surrounded by acrimonious dispute, during the 1890's. Publicly supported separate schools do not exist in British Columbia, New Brunswick or Prince Edward Island, though the private denominational schools existing there frequently enjoy some measure of unofficial support, such as the provision of textbooks. Newfoundland presents perhaps the most interesting picture with regard to separate schools: virtually all of their schools are religiously affiliated. At the time Newfoundland joined Canada in 1949 five denominational school systems were recognized and publicly supported: Church of England, Salvation Army, Seventh-Day Adventist, United Church, and Roman Catholic. Shortly thereafter a sixth denominational system was added, for the Pentecostal Assemblies. Since then the first four of these have formed an integrated system, reducing the number of systems to three.

Many of the federally operated schools for native people are also denominational, or at least make provision for religious instruction.

University entrance requirements

The differences among provinces with regard to university entrance requirements are not great, but they are politically and sociologically significant. In general, high school education in the academic track results in junior matriculation (usually Grade XI) or senior matriculation (Grade XII). Senior matriculation is required for admission to three-year degree programs and to most four-year degree programs, though it frequently happens that a student with junior matriculation will be admitted to a four-year program in some provinces (e.g., Nova Scotia). In Ontario, the university preparatory stream terminates in Grade XIII, which is treated as the equivalent of Grade XII in most other provinces. Grade XII in New Brunswick and Prince Edward Island is, in some respects related to university admission, equated to Grade XI. Newfoundland high schools terminate at Grade XI, from which students are admitted to university without further ado. (However, a new program was begun in September, 1981, which will result in the addition of Grade XII by 1983.) We repeat that it is not at all surprising that these differences exist, given that education comes under provincial jurisdiction. The interesting thing is that the regulations affecting the way in which these differences are dealt with have little if anything to do with education in its pure sense, and much more to do with schooling. Little if any effort is made to determine if the requirements for senior matriculation (Grade XII) in Nova Scotia, for example, are *educationally* equivalent to those of Grade XII in Alberta or Grade XIII in Ontario, or are superior to those of Grade XII in New Brunswick or Prince Edward Island. An effort to establish standardized university admission tests[2] in the early seventies died in infancy, principally from the reluctance of individual provinces to be subject to its results. The consequence of the inconsistencies among the provinces is a good deal of unnecessary and unjustified discrimination among students applying for university.

### Quebec

Following the Parent Commission Report (1963-66), the structure of education in Quebec was significantly altered. There was a consolidation of degree-granting universities, involving some amalgamation, but the most important change was the establishment of CEGEPs (colleges of general and professional education). These institutions, which require Grade XI for admission, offer both academic (university preparatory) programs and technical education. The two-year academic program is required for admission to university, where a further three-years' study is followed toward a degree. The technical program is of three years' duration and is terminal. The CEGEP is very similar to a community college except that (1) tuition is free, and (2) it is virtually the only route for Quebec students to reach university, at least within that province.[3] In many cases, CEGEPs were established by taking over preexisting classical colleges, which have no place beyond high school in the new order.

To the extent that CEGEPs are like community colleges, they give Quebec another step in the selection process for both academic advancement and 'cooling out.' In the other provinces there are community colleges and post-secondary technical institutes also, but they serve mainly as an alternative to university education, which is most often begun after high school.

## Levels of Schooling

The basic tri-level structure of Canadian schooling has been alluded to above in dealing with the similarities among provinces with regard to educational organization. A little further detail seems appropriate here, emphasiz-

---

[2]The tests were administered through the Service for Admission to Colleges and Universities (SACU) which was sponsored by the Association of Universities and Colleges of Canada.

[3]Some students, wishing to eliminate a year of study towards a baccalaureate, have been admitted from Quebec Grade XI into universities in other provinces.

ing differences in this basic structure both among provinces and within individual provinces.

Up until mid-century, there had been obvious differences between urban and rural school systems in terms of levels. In most rural areas, children went from grade one to eleven or twelve in the same school, and might have had as few as two or three teachers along the way. (Many older teachers smiled at hearing of the educational "innovation"called non-graded schools; they felt they had, of necessity, implemented this system in the older rural schools.) However, the phenomena of school consolidation and amalgamation of school systems resulted in the elimination of most of these small schools, though some continue to exist. Nonetheless, in what follows it must be kept in mind that the structures found in urban school systems and the resources available there are often quite different from those found in many rural systems.

Structured, if not formal, education in Canada now begins as early as age three in nursery schools. Most nursery schools provide more of a day-care function than an educational one, though there are some where the organizers are very committed to accelerating the children's intellectual development. (Not surprisingly, these are most frequently found in areas where professional people live.) Nursery schools are rarely publicly supported, though Manitoba and Ontario support education for four-year-olds. Most of the appeals for public support for nursery schools are coupled with requests for day-care centres and come from groups of working mothers and single parents. All provinces except Prince Edward Island and New Brunswick[4] provide kindergarten for five-year-olds, though Nova Scotia calls it Grade Primary. Originally, this was a year of social adjustment, but it has taken on more and more of an academic flavour. As a result, what was originally optional has now become virtually compulsory and the child who does not go to school until age six, the earliest age for compulsory attendance, will still start with kindergarten. In 1978-79, slightly over seven per cent of the elementary-secondary school population was in pre-Grade I classes (Statistics Canada, 1980b).

The elementary level of schooling lasts for six years in most provinces, for seven years in British Columbia, and for eight in Prince Edward Island and Ontario. Ontario follows this with five years of high school for those preparing for university and four for those who want a terminal diploma or admission to a technical institute or similar community college. P.E.I. provides four years of high school for both groups. All other provinces divide secondary education into junior and senior high school, though they do not always call them by those names.

---

[4]It is partly because these provinces don't have a kindergarten that their Grade XII is not equated to that of Nova Scotia, even though the age of graduates would be the same.

In some provinces, individual school systems have established what they call "middle schools" in place of junior high schools. These usually incorporate the sixth to eighth grades, and the purpose is to emphasize the transition from elementary to high school as one which parallels early adolescent development. Here we have an instance of a change in school structure which originates more from an educational than from a political rationale and seems consistent with the formal goals of the institution.

Frequently vocational high schools are established as entities separate from the other schools. These normally range over four grades, though not all the programs offered in them take that long to complete.

Though we have been dealing principally with publicly supported schools, most private schools are structured along the same lines, probably to facilitate transfer in and out. There is one notable exception: Montessori schools. They are structured on the basis of what Maria Montessori regarded as good educational principles, and they have little grade structure at all. They receive children as early as age three. Most children transfer to the public schools at five or six, but the Montessori school is designed to keep them at least to age eight; indeed, there are private schools where the Montessori method is used through to adolescence. Relatively few Montessori schools exist in Canada.

On the other hand, while they maintain basically the same structures as public schools in terms of grade levels, private schools are able to make far more allowance for individual differences among students, and in that way they overcome some of the constraints that bureaucratic organization imposes on schooling. It is generally the children of the elite who attend private schools, and who are thus exempted from those constraints.

In the academic year 1978-79, the elementary-secondary school population in Canada was distributed as shown in Table 7-1. Several facts might be worth noting, based on these figures: (1) Direct federal involvement affects less than one per cent of students at these levels. More than nine-tenths of those so affected are elementary children. (2) Private schools involve almost four per cent of students, but whereas in the total distribution the ratio of elementary to secondary is two to one, in private schools it is almost even. In other words, a higher proportion of private school students is at the secondary level than is normal for the general population. (3) With compulsory education and a decrease in the dropouts of students 16 and over, the average enrollment per grade level is not very different for secondary schooling than for elementary. Interpretation here, however, is complicated by the pattern of declining enrollments which affected elementary schools more than secondary schools in the seventies, and by the fact that the table does not present per capita enrollments.

Table 7-1

Distribution of Elementary-Secondary Students in Canada, 1978-79
(Based on Statistics Canada, 1980-81)

|  | Public (Provincial) | | Federal | | Private | | Total | |
|---|---|---|---|---|---|---|---|---|
|  | No. | %* | No. | % | No. | % | No.** | % |
| Pre-Grade I | 360,752 | 6.9 | 6,724 | .1 | 9,549 | .2 | 377,025 | 7.1 |
| Grades I-VIII | 3,084,825 | 58.4 | 28,341 | .5 | 91,635 | 1.7 | 3,204,801 | 60.6 |
| Grade IX and up | 1,607,292 | 30.4 | 3,296 | .1 | 90,350 | 1.7 | 1,700,938 | 32.2 |
| Total | 5,052,869 | 95.7 | 38,361 | .7 | 191,534 | 3.6 | 5,282,764 | |

*Percentage of grand total, rounded.
**There were also 3,253 blind and deaf students distributed throughout these grade levels but counted separately by Statistics Canada.

## The Comprehensive School

With the growth of urban centres, and later with the consolidation of rural schools, the possibility arose of having enrollments as high as 2,500 students in one school. Since it could not be assumed, on the one hand, that all students would profit by the same type of education or, on the other hand, that society would be best served in this way, it became an aim of public education to provide within the one school as many options as possible. These options took the form of streams or *tracks,* into which students were channelled on the basis of previous performance, achievement and aptitude tests, and the less formal consultation process involving teacher, principal and guidance counselor (and sometimes, but not always, parent and student). At present, although the tracks vary from system to system, they typically involve (1) the *academic* or university preparatory track, within which is included an *honours* program; (2) the *general* track, which usually provides instruction in most of the basic academic subjects but at a more fundamental level than in the academic track, and frequently is split into two or three levels, the lowest of which is called the *adjusted* program; and (3) the *vocational* track, in which students take a minimum in the academic subject areas but get specialized instruction in one of a wide variety of trades; and (4) a *special education* track, for the education of the mentally and emotionally handicapped. Actual student programs may comprise elements from more than one of these tracks, and sometimes students in the general track take courses leading to specific occupations (e.g., typing and bookkeeping). All but the academic track are regarded as terminal; that is, they do not of themselves prepare the student for further schooling and completion of these programs does not normally qualify a student for admission to a post-secondary institution.

Tracks in comprehensive schools differ in more than curriculum content. In line with what has been alluded to when dealing with conformity, and will be referred to again in chapter 11 in treating the correspondence principle, there is evidence that the values inculcated in students in the terminal tracks are different from those encouraged in the academic students. As stated by Bowles and Gintis (1976:132), "Even within a single school, the social relationships of different tracks tend to conform to different behavioural norms. Thus in high school, vocational and general tracks emphasize rule-following and close supervision, while the college tracks tend toward a more open atmosphere emphasizing the internalization of norms." There is no reason to believe the situation is different in Canadian schools.

The crucial matter within the comprehensive school is the way in which decisions are made that particular students will follow particular tracks. Taking into consideration what has already been said about I.Q. and social policy and about the relation of social class to educational aspirations, the potential for social control within the comprehensive school is enormous. The insidious aspect of this is that mechanisms for social control are frequently exercised precisely by those people (teachers, principals, and guidance counselors) who believe they have the best interests of the student at heart and are acting on the basis of good educational principles. Brookover and Erickson (1975:333-334), citing studies by Kariger (1962) and Brookover, Lere and Kariger (1965), demonstrate that in the school system they studied "there were significant differences in the student's track placements associated with the socioeconomic level of his or her family and (the data) clearly indicate that one of the likely outcomes of the tracking system is the perpetuation of the social class differentiation." Controlling for achievement test scores, it was found that 80 per cent of the upper-class students who qualified for placement in the academic track were actually placed there, compared to only 47 per cent for lower-class students; and that only two per cent of the upper-class students whose test scores qualified them for the lower track were placed in that track, while 85 per cent of the lower-class students with similar test scores were placed there. Again, while we have no data from comparable Canadian studies, we have reason to believe the conclusions would be similar. It would also be interesting to compare the data cited by Brookover and Erickson with the perceptions of teachers, principals and guidance counselors on the matter; we suggest that there would be a significant disparity between the perceptions and the reality and that most of the professionals concerned are simply not aware of sending a proportionately large number of lower socioeconomic status students into terminal programs.

One rather interesting consequence of the implementation of tracking is the confusion that results among prospective employers about the meaning of a high school diploma. Given the variations among programs, graduation from Grade XII means different things for different students, and requires interpretation in order that the allocative function of schooling be fulfilled. This confusion has sometimes led business groups like the Chamber of Commerce to seek the reinstatement of standard departmental examinations.

## Post-secondary Education: A Comprehensive Model

While the examination of post-secondary education receives less attention in this book than earlier school programs do, it is important to see how this level is structured. We will see again that its structure reflects certain social relations as well as the intention to fill various educational needs.

Post-secondary education in Canada, from having originated as a replica of European university education (the Collège des Jèsuites was established on this model in Quebec in 1633), has evolved especially in the last 30 years to the point where it can be called *comprehensive* in the sense in which that term is used for secondary education. Until about 1950, a large majority of post-secondary institutions of any significant size[5] offered almost exclusively academic programs or professional programs with a high degree of academic content (e.g., medicine, law, theology). Today a student graduating from a high school academic program has a wide variety of choices for education at the post-secondary level, from the traditional university academic and pre-professional degree programs, through two-year academic diploma programs, to occupation-oriented technical programs of rapidly increasing variety. The main difference between the 'comprehensiveness' of post-secondary education and that of secondary education is that there is seldom a case where a proportionately large number of the 'tracks' are housed in the same institution. Rather, the institutions are themselves distinguished largely in terms of the particular set of options they provide.

Post-secondary education is structured in two main divisions, *degree-granting* and *non-degree-granting* institutions. Each is further subdivided. Degree-granting institutions, usually called universities but in some instances colleges, have undergraduate and graduate levels (the professional programs, such as medicine, are included on the graduate level). Non-degree-granting institutions are generally of a type called *community colleges*, though there

---

[5]We exlude here business colleges, nursing schools and small, privately operated educational enterprises serving fewer than 100 students.

are also others such as teachers' colleges (only one remains in Canada) and institutions catering to one particular occupation (e.g., fisheries schools in Newfoundland). Community colleges may be academic and provide for university transfer, or technical/vocational, or they may combine both. An interesting example is the College of Cape Breton in Nova Scotia, which resulted from the amalgamation of Xavier College, a two-year academic affiliate of St. Francis Xavier University, and the Eastern Technical Institute of Nova Scotia, a provincially sponsored school.

Community colleges are most numerous in Quebec and Ontario. In Quebec, they are principally the CEGEPs, which were described briefly earlier in this chapter. The academic (university preparatory) and technical programs are distinct in the CEGEP, but are coordinated within the one institution. Virtually all Quebec students who take post-secondary education in Quebec attend such community colleges, of which there were 58 in 1978 (Statistics Canada, 1980b).[6] By contrast, in Ontario the community colleges are principally technical institutes, referred to as Colleges of Applied Arts and Technology (CAAT). University preparation continues to be made through Grade XIII in the high schools, while admission to the CAAT is from Grade XII. In 1978 there were 30 CAATs (Statistics Canada, 1980b).

The community colleges in the other provinces are more varied in nature, although Alberta and British Columbia have established systems similar to those of Quebec and Ontario. In 1978, these two provinces had a total of 41 non-university post-secondary institutions. The remaining six provinces had a total of 42. Yukon and the Northwest Territories had none (Statistics Canada, 1980b).

Community colleges are provided partly so that students in a given locality will have access to post-secondary education without having to leave home, as is often the case when one attends university. This is one of the reasons for the relative proliferation of community colleges while the number of residential universities remains rather stable.

There are other non-degree-granting post-secondary institutions which do not fit the community college model, whether because they draw from outside the community where they are located or because they offer only one main program. Included here are nursing schools attached to hospitals rather than universities or colleges, one teachers' college, private business colleges, and such specialized institutions as forest ranger schools, police academies, marine navigation schools, fisheries schools, surveying schools, etc. There are also two

---

[6]This includes 48 institutions with both academic and technical programs, the CEGEP as we have described it, plus 10 other colleges with university (academic) transfer programs. There were also 15 colleges with technical programs only, for a total of 73.

military colleges, one in Victoria and one in St. Jean, Quebec, which are affiliated with the degree-granting Royal Military College in Kingston, Ontario.

Most of Canada's early institutions of higher education had been established by the churches and were religiously affiliated. Church influence has declined rapidly in the last three decades with the need for substantial government support for the private universities, and with the proliferation of community colleges which are government financed and run. Only in Nova Scotia and, to a lesser extent, New Brunswick is there still a significant degree of religious affiliation in the universities, preserving through government non-interference a firmly rooted tradition. Also, from a point where policy was set largely by the academic community, change occurred to the extent that by 1970 non-academics formed the majority on university boards of governors in 49 of the 59 boards (Martin and Macdonell, 1978). The latter half of this century, then, is seeing post-secondary education pass from private to public financing and from academic to lay (government and business) policy control.

Prior to the expansion of post-secondary education that has recently occurred, the allocative function of schooling (see chapter 10) was served largely by the selection process restricting admission to universities. Now, in a society grown much more technological, it is aided by the process that determines who goes to university and who goes to technical institutes and other community colleges, though this is somewhat complicated in Quebec with its CEGEPs. At the same time, technical education in itself, especially in fields like computer programming and electronics, provides a potential base for a rising technocracy. Here there is a new avenue of social mobility to positions of relative power and wealth. Altogether, the comprehensive model of post-secondary education appears to serve a function similar to the parallel system at the secondary level, and students continue to be differentiated on the basis of social class as much as, if not more than on intelligence and aptitude.

## Continuing Education

The second half of this century, in comparison to the earlier period of Canada's history, has seen (1) a considerable reduction in the work week for most people; (2) increasing urbanization; (3) a rise in the average number of years of basic schooling; (4) a tremendous expansion in the awareness of the number of areas of potential education for the individual; (5) the increase in the tendency to change one's occupation during his working life; and (6) the proclivity for spending one's leisure hours outside the home (despite the presence of a television set therein). All of these phenomena, together with others that have had an influence, have led to a booming expansion of more or less formal education of adults. Both the philosophical emphasis and the empirical fact that it involves adults of all ages is captured in the new catchword: lifelong learning, though professional adult educators feel that the term is being used before the philosophy has caught on. They see in lifelong learning not only the tendency of adults to go back to school, but the acquisition of the disposition for and skills of autonomous learning. For this reason, they prefer to maintain for now the more familiar term, *continuing education.*[7]

Since at this point we are concerned principally with the structures of education in Canada, we will not take the space to recount the history of the evolution of the adult education — continuing education — lifelong learning movement. Suffice it to say that from a time earlier in this century when it was rare for a person to re-enter a classroom after he had terminated his basic schooling, it is fast approaching the norm that people will go back to school as adults at least once if not more often. Their studies may be leisure-oriented (arts and crafts, etc.) or occupation-oriented. The teaching and administration of continuing education opportunities constitutes a very significant segment of what can properly be called the education industry.

Whereas the three more formally structured levels of education generally fall under the jurisdiction of the provinces, responsibility is less clear-cut in practice when it comes to continuing education. Programs are sponsored by a variety of agencies.

### Colleges and universities

Whether it is because the formal educational institutions see themselves as having an expanded role in the community, as is certainly the case with many, or in order to retain faculty at a time of declining enrollments, their offerings designed to attract adult part-time students have greatly increased in this decade. They have also allocated significantly more in staffing and resources for extension and continuing education courses, utilizing modern technology to facilitate distance education and establishing a great many off-campus centres for part-time study. The courses offered range from formal, degree-credit academic courses through professional development courses (e.g., certification courses for teachers) to non-credit courses of varying duration offered principally for interest and enjoyment. The market has changed from a seller's to a buyer's, courses are widely advertised, and there is strong competition among institutions serving the same constituency to attract adult learners.

### Provincial Programs

---

[7]Summary of a brief discussion with Dr. Teresa MacNeil, Head of the Department of Adult Education, St. Francis Xavier University.

All provinces have adult education courses and programs that are administered either directly out of the central office or indirectly through the local school board. These courses are divided mainly between academic upgrading programs and general interest programs (art, crafts, music, carpentry, etc.), with a proportion of career-oriented courses included, higher or lower depending on the province. Saskatchewan even has a Department of Continuing Education with its own deputy minister, but its responsibilities overlap a good deal with those related to the administration of post-secondary education. Provinces also run a number of career-oriented programs, trade schools and educational rehabilitation centres through their departments of labour.

Federal Programs

It is perhaps more at the level of adult and continuing education then at any other that the federal government becomes involved in education. This has been the case especially since the passage of the Occupational Training Act of 1967. Much federal activity is focussed on manpower retraining programs designed for the unemployed and those whose present occupational skills are becoming redundant. This includes educational rehabilitation or upgrading such as what was provided through the Basic Training and Skills Development program as well as on-the-job training programs. In most cases the federal government funds such programs but they are carried out through provincially employed educators. The federal mediating agency is Canada Employment, which also provides much of the counseling involved and helps supervise the programs.

When adult learners are enrolled in these programs they are paid either directly by government, which thus provides an alternative to the payment of unemployment insurance; or indirectly by government through the employer, in that on-the-job training programs are subsidized and the employer gets relatively cheap labour. In either case, while there is little doubt that the adult learner benefits in some cases, the program is most certainly focussed on industry and the employer is the big winner.

Privately Sponsored Programs

Business, industry, labour unions, etc., frequently contract with educational institutions or hire instructors to conduct courses for employees or members. Much of this is directly related to the person's responsibilities within the sponsor's organization and may be referred to as professional or career development education (e.g., courses in investment, accounting, etc., sponsored by the Institute of Canadian Bankers; courses in public speaking, economics and social leadership sponsored by the Atlantic Regional Labour Education Council). However, a growing number of businesses support the continued education of their employees in less obviously job-related areas, and the idea of paid educational leave has spread from the educational institutions to many segments of society.

In 1978-79 there were more than one and three quarter million enrollments in continuing education courses, not counting community college credit courses or privately administered programs (Statistics Canada, 1980b). This number includes many instances where a given person took more than one course. Our estimate is that about twelve to fifteen per cent of the adult population was involved in continuing education, and the trend has been to rapidly increasing numbers of participants.

### Conclusion

From the preceding it can be seen that Canadian education is at present highly structured and highly diversified. Not all of the educational options available have been mentioned, for fear of losing sight of the forest for the trees. It is perhaps more difficult to see clearly how this vast complex can be an instrument for social control than it was to arrive at that conclusion concerning the educational structure of fifty or a hundred years ago. Nevertheless, when it comes to the question of repressing social mobility, of putting the education structure at the service of the power elite and of reproducing in the lower socioeconomic class (which may be relatively better off than its earlier counterpart but is still poor in relation to society as a whole) the values and attitudes which tend to 'keep them in place,' the changes that have taken place in that time are far from revolutionary. Indeed, the structure has simply become that in which a bureaucracy typically operates to achieve the variety of goals of an organization that were described in the first section of this chapter. We will now move on to discuss the positions in that bureaucracy and how the process of education is managed or controlled.

## The Managers of Education

### Management Function in Education

As long as colonial status was maintained in what was to become Canada, schools were largely under the control of church bodies or, perhaps less frequently, local school committees; many were simply the private enterprises of itinerant teachers. Whatever secondary schools existed were most often private and catered to the upper and middle classes. As the colonies became more stable and permanent, and government within them became more centralized, the desire arose of having more uniformity among the schools. Government financing of education in Upper Canada began in Ontario when the District

Public Schools Act of 1807 authorized the granting of one hundred pounds toward the salaries of teachers in eight Grammar Schools. In 1816 the Common School Act granted twenty-five pounds per teacher to local school boards for the setting up of schools at the elementary level. Until 1822 there was no established supervisory control of the schools, but then the General Board of Education was set up and John Strachan became the chairman and, in effect, the first Superintendent of Schools for Upper Canada (Johnson, 1968). Lower Canada (Quebec) got its first permanent Commission on Education in 1829. Development toward a centralized provincial department of education was similar in most of Canada's ten provinces, the main differences being in the dates of occurrence and in the allowances that were made for denominational systems. P.E.I. was the first province to have widespread free education (1852). The provinces which joined confederation in the twentieth century already had centrally administered systems at the time of union. The evolution of school boards with authority to levy taxes followed a fairly common pattern; in Quebec, however, the French common schools were for a long time administered by the local parishes. When Newfoundland joined Canada in 1949, it had five denominational school systems, soon to be six, with Denominational School Committees at the provincial level.

The control of education evolved to the point where it was divided between provincial departments and local school boards, with various degrees of input from religious bodies. Local boards, which were originally small committees with jurisdiction over one school, eventually took on a variety of forms known as urban, municipal, or regional school boards. These have jurisdiction respectively over towns and cities, counties or municipal districts, and combinations of towns and/or municipal districts. Different names are used in different provinces, but virtually all types of boards are represented by these three levels. Smaller units such as school sections, with their three-member boards of trustees, still exist in some places but most of their functions have been absorbed by the larger units. Provinces which allow for publicly supported denominational schools have parallel boards for each school denomination, usually with overlapping territories. In all provinces except Newfoundland at least some of the school board members are elected. In Newfoundland the board members are appointed by the government on the recommendation of the appropriate denominational committee.

## Organizational Charts

Figure 7-1 provides a chart of the organization of the Department of Education of Manitoba as of 1980 (Annual Report, Manitoba Department of Education, 1980). It provides a reasonably typical picture of the way in which provincial education departments are organized. Where other provinces differ in major ways, we will point out the differences, but basically the Manitoba chart will serve to enable us to comment on departmental structures.

All provinces now have a minister of education who speaks for the department in cabinet. British Columbia, Alberta and Ontario have two ministers dealing with education, dividing responsibilities roughly between elementary-secondary education under one minister, and post-secondary under the other. The minister frequently has a staff that reports directly to him, sometimes even by-passing the deputy minister; in the chart for Manitoba it can be seen, for example, that the University Grants Commission occupies such a position. Next in line to the minister is the deputy minister. Saskatchewan actually has two deputies, effectively dividing the ministry in two and giving some autonomy to the department of continuing education, operating mainly at the post-secondary level. New Brunswick has a francophone deputy and an anglophone deputy. Under the deputy minister there may also be staff responsibilities, as in Manitoba dealing with Frontier Schools and Research. In line with the deputy minister will be officers variously called assistant or associate deputies, chief directors or directors, each usually in charge of a division of the department (in Manitoba, there are four of these). Quebec has two associate deputies, one Catholic and the other Protestant, as staff for the deputy minister. Finally, divisional responsibilities are shared by assistant directors and, in line with them, supervisors. For example, a curriculum supervisor would serve under an assistant director for program development, who in turn reports to the director (or perhaps assistant deputy minister) for program development and support services. Lines of authority and division of responsibilities are presumably clearly established, and so the department is organized along the lines of the bureaucratic structure described earlier in this chapter.

In Figure 7-2 the typical local school system is charted. Obviously there will be many variations from this typical structure in the thousands of school systems within the country. The chart is presented here to call attention to the relationship between the local system and the provincial department; other comments about the local structure will be withheld until a later section.

The position that is labeled "Inspector" in Figure 7-2 is a provincial, not a local position. The inspector (or a person with a different title but fulfilling similar functions, depending on the province)[8] is the principal link between the local school boards and the provincial department insofar as implementation of educational legislation is concerned. His or her office may also serve as a local base of operations for provincial consultants, committees, etc., that are at the moment providing service to the local system, and the inspector frequently assists in the coordination of inter-system professional development programs and so on. In earlier times the inspector's authority was quite com-

---

[8]Ontario provides for this function through Regional Offices of the Provincial Department of Education.

THE DEPARTMENT OF EDUCATION

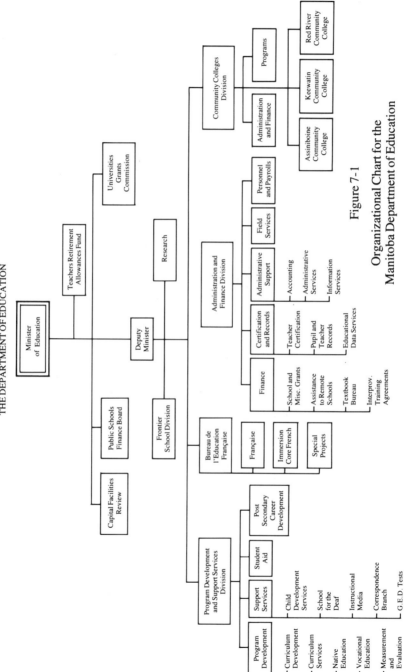

Figure 7-1

Organizational Chart for the
Manitoba Department of Education

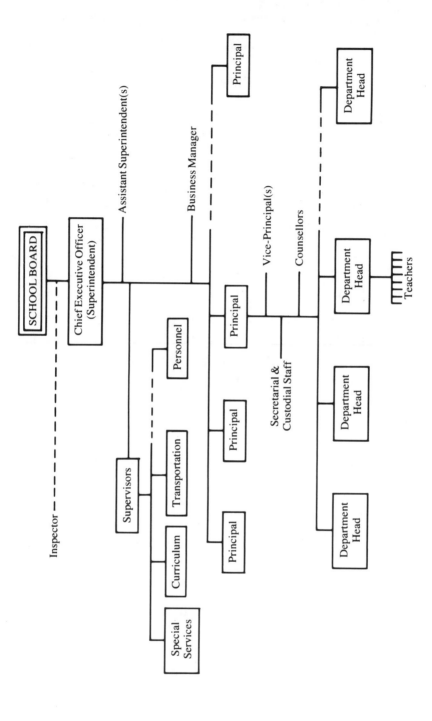

Figure 7-2: Organizational Chart of a Typical Medium-sized School System

prehensive. Increased ease of communication has led many system officers to by-pass the inspector and deal more directly with the central provincial office.

In the case of schools that come under jurisdiction other than that of the provincial education department, the superstructure is normally less complex. When trades schools are operated by the provincial department of labour, or any other provincial department; when federal schools for native peoples are operated on reserves; when schools for children of Canadian servicemen overseas are operated by the Department of National Defence; or when trades training schools, adult vocational training programs, and on-the-job training programs are sponsored by the Department of Manpower and Immigration, then the appropriate central office is usually a relatively small division of the department involved, and there is rarely an intermediate body serving functions like those of school boards.

What has been shown in this section is the organizational framework within which the managers of education operate. It remains to see what the persons in each level of the organization do, and how the structure of the organization affects the manner in which schooling occurs in Canada.

## The Provincial Managers

### The Minister of Education

The Minister of Education is seldom a professional educator; he is a government leader and a politician. It is his role to report to cabinet and the legislature on educational matters; to promote within government the policy which he, in consultation with his professional advisors, considers beneficial to education in the province; and to implement government policy as it affects education. Since his function is largely political, in the good sense of that term, what he obtains in terms of policy is frequently the result of compromise and often is more or less beneficial depending on his skill as a bargainer in the political game. At this point the educational system, like most things under governmental jurisdiction, is particularly vulnerable both to external lobbying and to the individual value commitments of the particular minister. Often these commitments are at odds with the views of professionals in the field, and the minister seldom has the time, opportunity or desire to acquaint himself thoroughly with the professional literature. This might be seen as a breakdown within the bureaucratic organization, for within an ideal bureaucracy the persons in higher positions are assumed to have greater expertise than their subordinates.

In recent years, in some provinces, the minister has taken on a new role — that of chief negotiator for the government (in this case, the employer) in contract talks with teachers' association negotiators (acting for the employees). In Nova Scotia, for example, the main issues in teachers' contracts are settled at the provincial level between the minister acting for the government and the negotiating team from the Nova Scotia Teachers Union. Only the more minor issues are left for negotiation at the local level. There is danger in this situation, at least at times when negotiations become bitter or break down completely. The minister then finds himself either taking a political position against those whom he considers professional educators with the good of students at heart; or he may consider himself the champion of students and parents, and then necessarily he sees the teachers' organization, which otherwise he must consider his ally, as being less than professional in its concerns.

## The Deputy Minister

The deputy minister will normally, if not invariably, be a professional educator with previous experience as a school teacher and administrator. He is relatively permanent in the sense that he normally retains his position when ministers or governing parties change. Nevertheless, he must be politically skilful, for he is the link between all the other professionals in the system and the non-professionals who establish provincial educational policy. In that role he must translate professional advice into terms that can be handled by the non-professional, and be able to justify recommendations in ways that make sense both educationally and politically. However, he does not make decisions on policy, and herein lies the possibility of role conflict for him. Often he will be the first to see that the policy established by government is harmful or at least not the best for the system. It is his responsibility, under the minister, to see that the policy is carried out. His role as a professional educator conflicts then with his role as a civil servant. We will see the same kind of potential for role conflict in the position of the school superintendent.

What ways does the deputy minister have open to him to reduce this role conflict, other than resigning his position? He may (1) anticipate the political arguments that the minster will have to overcome in order to promote good policy, and help him counter these arguments; (2) make available to the minister and cabinet more information related to the professional argument for the desired policy, in the hope that this will help counter political expediency; or (3) work directly on the political factors involved, trying to influence the people concerned and becoming involved in the related bargaining. The last step is one that can seldom be handled by a deputy minister without endangering his own position, so he must rely on one or both of the other steps. It can be seen that, although he is in a less conspicuous position than the minister, the educational system is still very vulnerable at the level of the deputy minister.

## Provincial Officers

Most of the people on line and staff below the level of deputy minister of education, excluding clerical help and data analysts, are professional educators. Whatever decisions they make are supposedly constrained by established policy, though in fact this is not always the case. However, the input they might have at any time to potential policy decisions is channeled through superiors who are professionals. Their recommendations, then, need be justified only on professional grounds; they need not take much account of political realities (we are not referring here to intra-organizational politics governing promotion and privilege). In the ideal organization, each person in these intermediate positions functions with the right balance of freedom and organizational support to enable him to use his expertise without becoming either frustrated or insecure. As in most organizations, however, and especially government departments where the criteria for decision-making at the top are not the same as those at other levels, departments of education frequently contain many bureaucratic functionaries. It is a situation in which it is apparently very difficult for an educator to maintain concurrently both his idealism and a pleasant disposition, not to say his sanity. Unfortunately, therefore, many good educators lose themselves or are lost within provincial departments of education. On the other hand, exceptional leadership is frequently noticed and rewarded by promotion, and most of Canada's provinces have been blessed at times with fine educational leadership in key positions.

## Local Control

The provincial departments of education provide the superstructure of legislated policy, broad curriculum directives, and resources for education. The day-to-day control of education occurs in the schools, and these are usually combined in organizational units headed by school boards. The organization of schooling at the local system level is shown in Figure 7-2, presented earlier.

### The School Board

With school consolidation that has taken place in Canada since World War II, the number of local school boards has been reduced considerably. For example, the number of school boards in Ontario was reduced from 3,200 to about 200 by 1974; in New Brunswick, from 422 to 33; in P.E.I. from 216 boards to five administrative units (Council of Ministers of Education, 1975). From having jurisdiction over only one or two schools, as was the case in the former school sections, these boards now administer systems sometimes including more than 100 schools (although there are still some small-town school boards with fewer than five schools).

School board members are generally not professional educators, though they are frequently members of other professions. Most occupational levels, however, are represented on school boards. Because they are not professional educators, school board members as a group present another focus of vulnerability to external influence on the educational system. To the extent that they are elected, or appointed by elected bodies, they are political entities and subject to political pressures. Moreover, school boards increasingly find themselves in a counter-advocacy position with teachers as the latter become increasingly organized and militant, though often teacher organizations bargain now at the provincial level. This can result in their taking stands on educational issues which are grounded in budgetary considerations more than anything else. Out of all this arises the potential for major role conflict and confusion of goals.

A major function of school boards has traditionally been the financing of education. Although they have for a long time received provincial grants, a significant portion of educational monies was derived from local tax levies. This provided the boards with a power base. However, the basis of educational financing is shifting more and more to direct provincial funding, with allocations being made to school boards on the basis of decisions made at the provincial level. There has been a corresponding shift of power, so that the provincial department directly or indirectly controls many matters which had been under school board control. Thus a board will submit an inventory of its needs to a provincial committee (e.g., in Nova Scotia, the Education Assistance Committee) which, in consultation with the minister and senior department officials, will either be funded or cut back. In effect, this means that the total educational budget is determined at the cabinet level and then the pie is cut up among all the school boards in the province.[9]

Lane (1981), commenting on the implementation of the recommendations of the Walker Commission Report in Nova Scotia, has indicated the dilemma school boards find themselves in when proposals are made for centralized control and global financing. The Report recommends amalgamation of school boards into fewer but larger units, and virtually total provincial funding. On the one hand, larger administrative units are said to operate more efficiently. On the other hand, this efficiency is purchased at the cost of dimin-

---

[9]This also allows for the possibility that a powerful politician who happens to be Minister of Education will have a tremendous influence on the state of education in a province. Thus, under William Davis, education in Ontario underwent awesome expansion until, with a change in public sentiment, Davis decided to shut the tap. See Lind, 1974, chapters 7 and 10.

ished local autonomy. Lane points out that, in Nova Scotia, school boards are being given the option of amalgamating or not, but those that choose not to do so will suffer a loss of 10 per cent of funding relative to the funding of amalgamated boards.

It still remains the school board's function to supervise expenditures on those things that come under its jurisdiction: school buildings and equipment, professional and non-professional staffing, textbooks and curriculum (to a modified extent), transportation of students, and a host of smaller items. However, it hires a professional educator as its chief executive officer, and, depending on the size of the school system, a staff to assist him or her. The chief executive officer may be known as the Director or as the Superintendent. He is the board's delegate in matters under its jurisdiction and he advises the board in matters requiring professional expertise.

Examination reveals two ways in which the power of the local school board has been eroded in recent years. Provincial departments of education, by taking control of educational funding (and thereby appearing to befriend the tax-paying property owner), have undermined the board's power base. But besides that, in large systems the administrative staff can reduce the board's control by the simple process of withholding or obfuscating information (Lind, 1974, chapter 8). Indeed, some school systems have grown so large that their administrative structures have become huge bureaucracies, and the school boards themselves, made up principally of elected part-time members, are isolated from the central decision-making process. Thus, they find themselves either legitimating decisions made by administrators or struggling with them to get more information and retain their authority.

An analysis (Holdaway, 1970) of the topics dealt with over a three month period by 13 rural and urban school boards in Alberta showed that of 11 topics discussed at meetings, 70 per cent of the discussion concerned five of these: plant (24%), educational staff (16%), community-school relations (10%), transportation (10%) and salary negotiations (10%). Curriculum took up only 3% of the discussion.

School board members are often thought to have a conservative as opposed to a liberal political orientation. The evidence is not at all one-sided, however. American studies indicate considerable interaction of political orientation with social class, education, and the issue involved in discussion (Brookover and Erickson, 1975:180-181). Board members with higher occupational status and education tend to be more liberal on educational issues and more open to innovation. A review of Canadian educational journals revealed no research done in the last decade precisely on the political orientation of school board members, though one article by Konrad (1977) reported on the self-perceptions of community college trustees on several dimensions, including political orientation. Forty-seven per cent of those surveyed in a nation-wide study identified themselves as liberal, 43 per cent as moderate, and 11 per cent as conservative. The distribution in terms of political party affiliation showed 36 per cent as NDP, 29 per cent as Liberals, 21 per cent as Conservatives, six per cent as Social Credit, and eight per cent as 'other'. There was a clear interaction between political identification and province of residence. Disproportionate numbers of those claiming liberal orientation came from Quebec, Ontario and British Columbia, while conservatives were overrepresented in Alberta.

## The Superintendent

We shall refer to the chief executive officer of the local system as the *superintendent,* though occasionally he is called the *director.* His position is similar to that of the deputy minister at the provincial level: he is a career educator but he is directly responsible to a political body. The line and staff positions under his direction are supposedly politically neutral. He becomes, therefore, a filter whereby the board's decisions and goals are passed on for implementation, and the information upon which decisions are to be made is passed on to the board. To the extent that educational policy is determined locally, the superintendent's position is another vulnerable spot in the system and one which can vary greatly in its effect depending on the personality and orientation of the incumbent. The superintendent will be perceived differently, on the one hand, as the agent of the board, and therefore as a manager, or on the other hand as a professional staff member, and therefore as an employee. The ambiguity of his role is reflected in the controversy in some provinces as to whether the superintendent can legitimately belong to the teachers' professional association. (As we shall see, the existence of this controversy points up the question of whether such associations are really professional or are better characterized as labour unions.)

The superintendent's power in relation to the system itself and to the school board will vary greatly depending on the size of the system and the complexity of the bureaucracy which he directs. In a small system he will likely remain subordinate to the board; in the large system he may be able to use confidentiality and complexity to enhance his authority and dominate the board, in which case he will more often deal directly with the provincial ministry. In Ontario, a superintendent (or director) can not be hired or fired without the approval of the Minister (Lind, 1974:166).

Commenting on the school board/administrator relationship, Cistone (1977:97) says:

> . . . (A)s is often the case in the relationship between elected officials and their administrative employees, the school board typically under-utilizes its resources and the administrator typically maximizes his. In this way, the legal power of the board is blunted and the actual influence of the administrator expands. Indeed, the predominant fact of educational policy making today seems to be the inordinate influence of the chief school administrator, who, typically, enjoys a much greater latitude of discretion-

ary authority than any other professional public administrator in the community.

Cistone goes on to say that this can give rise to a situation where the school board legitimates the administration to the community rather than democratically representing the community. In such a situation, the administrator has effectively taken over the directive role of the board. Of course, it is much easier for this to happen in a large system than in a small one, where the administrator is more likely to try to reflect community values and politics.

## The Principal

Insofar as the principal of a school occupies a management position, he has relatively little input into decision making but tends to enforce decisions which have been passed down, or make rules for behaviour in the school. On the other hand, the principal has another role, that of instructional leadership. In this role he acts as head teacher, and with his staff makes decisions that directly affect the education of the students in his school. If his superiors are sensitive to his efforts, those decisions may be filtered upward and have some general effect on the system; otherwise his effectiveness will be constrained by his school boundaries. Although the principal occupies an important educational position, it is not one that is especially sensitive to the kinds of external influence that bring about educational change. However, if he is the principal of a large school, he may be instrumental in initiating policies such as team-teaching, school-wide I.Q. testing, and so forth, even when these are not general throughout the system.

## The Teacher

Interaction between the professional educator and the client happens principally in the classroom. No matter what goals have been set for the system, no matter what the policy might be, it is the classroom teacher who determines to a large extent, consciously or unconsciously, whether those goals and policy will be achieved or have their intended effect on students. However, the achievement of the goals of education is less affected by any one teacher, in the way that it might be by one superintendent or by one deputy minister, then it is by the group of teachers as a whole. It is therefore appropriate that we examine the characteristics of teachers as a group.

Background: Social Class and Sex

The upper working class and the lower middle class are generally overrepresented among teacher applicants. At least, this is the case in the United

States (Scimecca, 1980) and in England (Banks, 1976), and there seems to be no reason to suppose it is different in Canada. The career they have entered is a typically middle class one, and so it is for a major portion of teachers a means of upward mobility (Scimecca, 1980). This may result for the occupants of such a group in a degree of *status anxiety*, the fear of appearing too different from the members of the class to which one aspires, and a reluctance to rock the boat. Teachers may not, therefore, express openly their disagreement with policy set down by the authorities; that is not to say that they will willingly adhere to that policy within the classroom, which they may consider their sanctuary.

Female teachers outnumber male teachers in elementary schools, while the reverse is true in high schools. For Canada, in 1978-79, 70 per cent of the teachers up to and including Grade VIII were women; in high schools, the proportions were exactly reversed and 70 per cent of the teachers were men (Statistics Canada, 1980). Men were extremely overrepresented in administrative positions.

There is still a relatively high proportion of teachers in Canada who do not possess a university degree, but this is changing rapidly as the provinces raise the requirements for teacher certification. All but three provinces (Newfoundland, Nova Scotia and British Columbia) normally require a degree for certification, but in most cases these regulations were only recently established and did not affect already certified teachers.[10] There is a higher percentage of teachers without degrees in elementary schools than in secondary.

Teacher Education

At one time most teachers got their professional education in Normal Schools or Teachers Colleges, apart from universities. This could consist of as little as one year after Grade XI to as much as three years after Grade XII, and resulted in a diploma which would qualify the holder for a particular level of certification. Teachers Colleges were usually run directly by the provincial departments of education.

Nova Scotia is the only province which still maintains a Teachers College. An affiliation agreement has recently been worked out whereby its graduates may qualify for a Bachelor of Education degree by successful completion of one further year of study. This was a political compromise designed to keep the Teachers College in place but provide its students with the opportunity to acquire the minimum degree recognized in the rest of Canada.

---

[10]Vocational teachers generally are not required to possess a degree in order to be certified.

Elsewhere, and to a substantial extent in Nova Scotia as well, teachers receive their general and professional preparation at universities with faculties or departments of education. They may do this by taking the so-called *integrated* program, during which their professional courses and practice teaching are interspersed throughout a four-year program, constituting about half of it; or by taking a one-year Bachelor of Education program after having acquired a degree in Arts, Science or Business. In the latter case, their professional course work constitutes only about one-quarter of their university program, but is concentrated in one year. Many universities offer both options, while some offer only the consecutive (one year B.Ed.) program. Again, there are variations from province to province related to certification requirements (e.g., New Brunswick requires a ten-month program rather than the conventional seven-and-a-half month academic year). Practice teaching requirements vary from eight to thirteen weeks in the consecutive program and up to eighteen weeks in the integrated program.

A good deal of formal teacher education occurs *after* rather than before teachers are employed. Most teachers continue to take summer school and winter courses to improve their qualifications; many take graduate degrees, especially at the master's level, to qualify for positions as department heads, curriculum consultants or administrators. In some of our smaller universities over half of the enrollment in degree-credit part-time courses is made up of teachers. Perhaps no other professional group obtains certification with so little pre-service education, or acquires as much after entrance. Besides regular course work, teachers customarily spend several days a year attending professional development days.

Provincial Control

Of all professional groups, teachers are most closely bound by provincial regulations. Most professional groups are self-regulating and control the certification of their members. Teachers, on the other hand, are certified by the provincial governments through their departments of education and are regulated to a great extent by the Education Act in each province.

In practical terms, control of certification by the departments of education has meant the gradual raising of the educational requirements for entrance to the profession and for advancement to the higher salaried levels. There appears to have been no concerted effort to limit the number of those entering the profession, as is sometimes alleged to occur among some other professions, by setting quotas as such. Rather, periods of surplus of teachers have been taken advantage of to raise the entrance standards a step at a time. This occurred throughout most of Canada, for example, in the seventies, counteracting the period of expansion in the sixties when the provincial governments funded recruitment and education of teachers as never before.

Most provinces have at least two or three levels of teacher certification; Nova Scotia has five active levels, plus three levels that still exist in the teacher population but to which entrance is no longer permitted. At present, the general situation is that initial entrance to the profession is through certification that requires a university degree including at least one year of professional education, and the certified teacher may thenceforth qualify for one or two higher certificate levels. Most often these require the teacher to take graduate programs, though a provincial department of education may offer certification courses independently of the universities.

The biggest problem connected with this system arises from the fact that salary levels are usually tied in to certification levels. For that reason alone, if not for professional zeal, teachers' associations aspire for the highest level of certification for their members. This results in pressure on universities to make courses available in numerous off-campus centres; pressure on department officials to be lenient in the interpretation of certification regulations in individual cases; and a good deal of frustration that might not exist if teacher certification were controlled by the teachers' associations. In this case, however, it might simply give rise to new sources of dissatisfaction. It remains the case that when teacher groups are advocating changes in regulations governing certification, they are suspected of being concerned less with professional development than with salary-related welfare issues. It may be worth noting here, however, that the evils of credentialism that are social-class-related are less prevalent within the teaching profession than in many others.

Professionalism

With one exception, the provincial organizations of teachers in Canada are known as either associations or federations. The exception is the Nova Scotia Teachers Union. This name sticks out as a reminder that teacher organizations are characterized less by the marks of professionalism than perhaps any other recognized professional group.

From a review of the literature on the topic, Scimecca (1980:58-59) has provided a summary list of the most important characteristics of professionalism:

1. A unique, definite, and essential social service.
2. A long period of specialized training.
3. A broad range of autonomy for both the individual practitioners and the occupation as a whole.
4. An esoteric body of knowledge to be used in performing the service.
5. A comprehensive, self-governing organization of practitioners.
6. Control over entry to the profession.

To this list, most would add "a code of ethics for professional practice" (McGrath, 1980).

It is not appropriate here to argue the degree to which each of these dimensions or marks is found among organized school teachers in Canada. It can be said, however, that the control of admission to the profession is lacking, and that this lack affects at least the third and the fifth of the listed characteristics. Neither do teachers evidently possess an esoteric body of knowledge. Therefore, though teachers share some of the essential characteristics of professional groups, and though they often refer to themselves as professionals, they do not fully qualify for this designation. Nevertheless, within a narrower definition of professionalism which emphasizes social service, code of ethics and encouragement of professional development, most teacher groups qualify.

Even recognized professional groups such as the Canadian Medical Association have come close to the use of confrontation politics in recent years, so it is perhaps not surprising to see an increased militancy within teacher organizations, and the use of union-related strategies such as collective bargaining and strikes. Teachers' associations have called strikes in at least five provinces (Alberta, Ontario, Quebec, New Brunswick and Nova Scotia) since 1972. Moreover, with the establishment of collective bargaining at the provincial level, between teacher organizations and provincial government departments, contract negotiations have achieved dimensions resulting in significantly increased power for teachers. The splintering that could occur from the need to negotiate with individual school boards has been replaced by the solidarity of a single negotiating stance.[11]

Thus teacher organizations present a rather ambivalent and schizophrenic image both to themselves and to the public. On the one hand, they aspire to professional status and call their members professionals. On the other hand, they use methods most closely associated with labour unions, at least when it comes to salary and other benefit considerations. We do not wish to suggest that their methods are in any way unethical or unsuitable in themselves, but only to say that in a society which so dichotomizes professional associations and labour unions, and marks them off in terms of social class characteristics, teachers find themselves with a foot in each camp and not clearly identified with either one.

Although many individual teachers are held in the highest respect by both teachers and parents, as a group they enjoy a prestige below that of traditional professions and near the mid point on a range of occupations graded according to prestige in which they are held (Banks, 1976). Indeed, in the universities in

---

[11]Alberta is one province where salaries are still negotiated primarily at the local level. It can happen that teachers in the same community, working for the public board on the one hand and the separate board on the other, have different salary agreements.

which teachers are prepared, the education departments command below average respect as a general rule.

## Informal Influences: Support Staff

While the actual decision-making affecting education may be done at the various levels mentioned above, there is another set of internal factors which influence the decisions that are made. These are the constraints placed on the school managers by various members of the support staff of the school: coaches, secretaries, janitors, bus drivers, librarians, and so on. There is first the all-too-common situation where a particular secretary, janitor, or whatever acquires either by default or by force of personality an authority far exceeding the degree of responsibility accorded the position, and gains a positive share in decision-making. There is also the situation in which decisions that might seem to be most beneficial from an educational point of view are evaded, or a contrary decision is made, so as not to offend or inconvenience a member of the support staff who has gained an inordinate degree of power. The fact that the power structure in this case is informal makes it no less effective; in fact, it frequently gives it more than ordinary permanence because of the difficulty of dealing with it through normal channels. The person whose authority has been pre-empted or subverted is often unwilling to admit the existence of a problem.

Examples of the kinds of situations referred to here might be: decisions affecting school policy being made by secretaries who have been allowed to become buffers between the principal and the school staff; program rearrangement to coincide with the maintenance schedule; allowances being made for student athletes in terms of absences and grade requirements, at the coach's insistence; subservience of the school program to the librarian's will for neatness and efficiency. There is no intention here to stereotype any of the positions mentioned, but the examples are familiar enough to justify thinking of the informal power structure within the school as both real and influential.

## Conclusion

In this chapter, the educational institution in Canada has been described in the framework of a formal organization. The complexities of the organization have been made apparent in two ways. First, the structure through which the student passes has been shown to consist of three phases, elementary, secondary and post-secondary, with their various tracks. While one might assume from the expression of belief in the ideal of equal educational opportunity that these three phases would be structured to facilitate the passage of as many as possible through the total structure, we have seen that they are not. This is an example of the conflict of ideological goals with informal goals in an organization.

Second, the management structure of formal education has been described, concentrating on the elementary-secondary phases. This has been shown to exemplify a bureaucracy, with the Minister of Education presiding. The foci of vulnerability within the system, that is, the points at which the system is most likely to exhibit goal conflict and system dysfunction, have been emphasized. Much more could have been said to make explicit the ways in which personal and informal goals interfere with the achievement of the formal goals of education. Space prohibits this expansion, though the topic will be touched on lightly in another chapter. Meanwhile, the student is urged to examine the organization of schooling in his own community and province to discover where such interference exists in the concrete.

Ostensibly, the institution of formal education exists for the student, and to assist the student's family in facilitating his or her personal development and occupational training. We turn now to a consideration of the client in the educational organization.

# 8

## The Clients
## of Educational Institutions

### Introduction: The Clients of Schooling

In this chapter it is our intention to deal in a particular way with some of the characteristics of the principal clients of schooling, the students. We will enquire into the nature and importance of adolescent culture and of student social culture, look at some of the social factors affecting students as a result of the relationship with their peers, and enquire into causes and consequences of the termination of schooling, specifically graduation and dropping out.

Before we begin this discussion we should point out that in the broad meaning of the term the clients of education include more than the students, although we will not go into that matter thoroughly here. Durkheim, as we frequently pointed out, saw the school as an agent of moral socialization for the state, that is for society in general and for the specific community. One indicator of the community's routine involvement in the educational institution as a client is the frequency of articles in the popular press about the importance of stressing the basics, the so-called back-to-the-basics movement. A similar indicator is the ongoing debate about the success or failure of schools in developing the character of the students.

Understanding that society and the community has a vested interest in the institution of schooling, and is concerned with both curriculum and results, we must view the school as an agent of political socialization. The whole of society, or a significant part of it, may be regarded as the recipient of this service or imposition. Political socialization, not restricted to schooling but partially accomplished there, refers to the inculcation of the value and normative system which is supportive of the prevailing structure of society. It is concerned with the origin of political ideology and outlook, and socialization into that which is considered appropriate. Canada varies somewhat in political socialization from other nations, as might be expected. Pike and Zureik (1975:VIII-IX) point out that Canadians have a weak sense of national identity with strong regional identification; a hierarchical system of stratification with class-based inequalities in educational and occupational achievement; an ethnic stratification system and an official ideology espousing pluralism rather than assimilation. Socialization into this national identity is one of the functions or goals of schooling in Canada.

The specific socialization into the prevailing value and normative system may appear quite proper, routine and normal. However, this system, which includes role expectations and is itself a cause of much social inequality, is an arbitrary one. There is nothing absolute about it, and there is really no objective, empirical way of determining that one system is better or more proper than another. Moreover, all of this must be learned. The school has an important role to play in the existing system, and in this learning process, and the community itself — both national and regional — may be regarded as client. It is in recognition of this fact that the government is primarily responsible for establishing educational policy, and all citizens are expected to contribute to the cost which this entails.

There are differences between societies in the way such values, norms and attitudes are passed on to children in the schools. In some cases, such as the Soviet Union, this political socialization is very open. In others, such as Canada, it is much more covert. The United States probably falls somewhere in between. The fact that this socialization is more overt or covert has little to do with equality *per se*. In either case there is a hidden curriculum involved which is restricted to latent aspects of the prevailing value system, one that supports inequality in a generally accepted way.

A study in the United States (Haller and Thorson, 1970) has shown that the social structure of the elementary school makes it particularly adept at conservative political socialization. The communal nature of the class leads to the development of a sense of community, stressing co-operation rather than functional conflict. There is considerable stress on the importance of peers and on integration, with the inculcation of norms which are basic to the functioning of the political machine and which give it legitimacy.

Hurn (1978:188) claims ". . . that both the functional and the radical models are misleading in their accounts of what schools teach and in their accounts of the relationship between what schools teach and the demands of the wider society." Schools do teach the cognitive skills which are required for future adult roles. They also are agents of moral education for society as a whole. There is never unanimity in any assessment of this, and radicals are accurate when pointing out that there is repression involved. Claiming that these are two sides of the same coin, Hurn's argument is not a particularly persuasive one, but the point he raises is important just the same.

Rather than thoroughly discuss political socialization as a function of schooling, however, we merely wish to emphasize here that the goals of schooling are directed beyond the children or the parents involved. For that reason there is always the likelihood of some degree of conflict between the students, the parents and the wider society.

Parents may also be viewed as clients of education in this broad sense, perhaps a little more proximately. They do have, or at least those who can afford it have some discretion in choosing the school to which they send their children. Their choice is based not only or not especially on the quality of the teaching involved but also on the value and normative system which is peculiar to the school, generally referred to as the social climate. Schools vary not only on a social class basis but along ethnic and religious lines as well. Frequently there are alternate formats available. In one case parents may choose open or even free schools, in another they may opt for more of the traditional approach.

An interesting suggestion for social policy which acknowledges as a right the option of parents to enroll their children in competing schools is the *voucher* plan. This has been discussed for many years in the United States. While there are variations in the suggestions made, in general parents would receive a voucher for each child which could be turned in at any school for admission. This would create competition between schools, and it is presumed that this would increase their efficiency.

In most provinces in Canada there is much less discretion in the public school system, but there are many exceptions. Several provinces allow choice along religious lines. Quebec and many communities in the other provinces provide an ethnic choice, at least between French and English, and isolated communities in Canada provide public schooling in still another language. Even in communities where no alternate system is available, parents use influence to gain admission for their children to elementary public schools which they are not normally eligible to attend, perhaps in another area of the community. Nevertheless, in the sense that they are clients, many are captive groups. The alternatives are far more restricted than is the case for many other types of service. Moreover, parents are required by law to make use of schooling in some acceptable form until the children reach a certain age, usually 15 or 16.

Another indication of their involvement is participation in voluntary associations such as parent-teacher or home and school associations. Middle-class parents have a much stronger record of such involvement, indicating an interest which is frequently translated into higher achievement by their children even when other variables are controlled.

Society in general, the community, the parents — these are the remote clients of the institution of schooling and the socialization process it entails. The proximate clients are the students. It is they who must do the study and work, and be the subjects of the socialization process, from the first days of kindergarten to the highest graduate level. For most of that period they are a captive group, and it is to more specific matters pertaining to this aggregate that we turn now.

## The Adolescent Culture

In an interesting study which is rather dated now but whose conclusions almost certainly continue to apply, Brittain (1963) determined that adolescents look to parents and peers as guides for different aspects of their lives, indicating that in many respects the generation gap is not as wide as it is frequently made to appear. Brembeck (1971) and Brookover and Erickson (1975) both indicate that the adolescent subculture or the solidarity of adolescent values is not as cohesive and uniform as it would appear, nor is adolescent isolation from the family the norm. Friesen (1972) makes this point strongly for Canada.

Young people have a need for both family and peers. The family provides stability during what may be a very difficult period in life. The peers on the other hand bring the opportunity for experimentation and even some functional rebellion in that stage of development leading to maturity. Parents rank very high among the significant others in adolescents' lives. Brittain's (1963) study found that the adult society provides for status needs. Adolescents looked for advice from parents in such matters as occupational choice and part-time work, and in many elements of the normative system as well. On the other hand, relative to peers, there is a strong element of conformity involved. The youth did not want to stand out or be noticeably different. They were concerned with being separated from their friends who had much more influence on certain common aspects of their lives such as choosing a particular course in school or the kind of clothing to wear (Brembeck, 1971).

Coleman's (1961) *The Adolescent Society* is probably the most significant work that has been done on the social structure of the high school and on adolescent subculture. We will attempt to present a summary of his principal thesis now.

In modern industrial society students are forced or required by law to spend much of their lives in schools. The prevailing system of norms and expectations ensures that they remain in that setting for a longer period of time than in earlier ages, in most cases exceeding twelve years. In that school setting they are instructed in more sophisticated technological knowledge. In addition to this responsibility in the cognitive domain, schools are responsible for affective learning and for psychomotor skills as well.

In practice, these processes occur in schools to and for virtually all young people, almost by a process of immersion. These students are a captive group. As these functional requirements of schooling were broadened over the years, accompanying other changes in society as it advanced so thoroughly into the period of industrialism, the functions of the family tended to decrease or become more specialized. Earlier the family setting had been the major source of emotional support and involvement for youth. In a time when people lived to a much greater extent in a rural setting, without the quick and easy communication we have today, it was not an easy or routine practice for young people to come together in the group or communal format which appears so routine now.

Industrialism, the accompanying new emphasis on schooling, more convenient modes of communication and travel, all of this implied a new style of living in which young people were required to turn more toward their own age group. Social life for them became, to a much greater extent, restricted to the peer group and divided or separated from adult society. The connection with family and other adults was not severed, but was less extensive. As a result, the younger group came much more to constitute a community within itself, a society in microcosm Coleman, 1961; Boocock, 1980). This is what Coleman refers to as the adolescent society.

Coleman's assessment of social influences increasing the importance of peer groups for young people was not at all new, and his major contribution was in applying this to the high school setting. Earlier Eisenstadt (1956) had published a study which demonstrated that youth had always congregated and socialized in groups. He compared modern society with earlier or less developed types of society, noting that this practice fulfilled an important function within them all. However, that function was changed, and became more extensive in modern industrial society where achievement is reputedly more important and where people are judged more on the basis of universalistic criteria. Parsons (1962) analysed this phenomenon for American society and arrived at similar conclusions. He noted a kind of duality of orientation among youth. There was an almost compulsive independence relative to certain adult expectations and demands, and also compulsive conformity and loyalty to peers (Boocock, 1980). This should be interpreted in the light of the statement made earlier, that adolescents tend to look to their families for status needs but to their peers for identity.

Brookover and Erickson (1975) do not agree completely with the terminology used by Coleman, the 'adolescent society' or 'adolescent subculture.' The adolescent stage is a transitory one, whereas 'subculture' is more accurately used to indicate a social group with a more enduring value and normative system into which one has been socialized on a more or less permanent basis. Their point is a good one. In order to understand the basis of concern we must stress the transitory nature of adolescence. It is the last of a series of intermediate developmental stages or periods of maturation before adulthood. One is socialized into adolescence with its insecurities and peculiar style of life as a part of the overall developmental process leading to adult socialization. The latter should be viewed as the stage of more or less full integration into society. It is less than precise to view adolescents as detached from the mainstream culture, even though by its very nature that stage points to a period of less than full integration. It is an integrating period. The attempt to resolve the problems and conflicts which are experienced therein is a part of the maturation process and serves an important function. To designate this period as a subcultural one is inaccurate if it means or refers to any more than a peculiar style of life leading to this potentially full integration in adult life. A certain amount of independence is required for adulthood, and the resolution of conflicts helps the individual to achieve that independence. As Eisenstadt (1956) has indicated, this process exists in every society even though each one gives it its own peculiar stamp. It is this particular imprint, itself the result of peculiar social influences, which may broadly be referred to as a 'subculture,' but only in this transitory, functional and socially determined way.

In chapter 9 we shall discuss the nature and importance of groups in the organization of schooling. It may be useful to anticipate a little of that here. Predictable co-operation is an essential characteristic of social life. One must learn the rules of co-operation and the values and beliefs on which they are based. Each individual in the social group must have standards on which to model his behaviour and to use as a basis of judgement about the propriety of that behaviour. But given the importance of co-operative and predictable behaviour, some element of conflict is also functional. Conflict leads to change. There is generally both co-operation and conflict within and among social groups, and within society as an integrated structure. Society is never perfectly integrated and probably would be less exciting if it were.

Robert Merton (1968) uses the concept of reference group in two ways. In one case it designates those who provide us with our values and beliefs which eventually we may or may not internalize on the basis of rational thought and choice. We discussed this in chapter 6 when dealing with value acceptance, a more immature stage, as opposed to value formation. In the other case reference group is used to designate those who provide us with standards for comparison.

A reference group is not necessarily a group in the strict membership sense, although frequently it is. It may be somewhat abstract, as in the case of Mead's generalized other, and this is more generally the case in the relationship between adolescents and that segment of adult society from which values and beliefs are accepted. While the young person may not belong to this group in any strict sense, he or she is still integrated with it in the sense of drawing therefrom values and beliefs and certain other models of behaviour. A reference group may also be concrete and specific, and this is more generally the case when it is used as a standard for judgement or evaluation (Brookover and Erickson, 1975). An adolescent *belongs* to the peer group in this latter sense, or at least this is generally the objective. In the former case he may *refer* to it rather than be a member. Both types of groups are important, and serve important functions, even though the young person is associated with each in different ways and for somewhat different purposes. It is for this reason that authors such as Brittain (1963) and Brembeck (1971) insist, on the basis of research, that adolescents look to both parents and peers as guides, but as guides to somewhat different aspects of their lives — in the one case status needs, in the other identity. Studies have tended to show that the influence of adults has not diminished greatly (Friesen, 1972). Brookover and Erickson make an important point when they insist that the solidarity of adolescent values is not as uniform as it would appear, nor is their isolation from parents and the adult world.

The significant other always refers to a singular relationship. It designates a person who serves as a model or standard of belief or behaviour. A significant other may be a member of a wider reference group but is not being considered in terms of group involvement. Either parent, a best friend, and other individuals with whom one has established an important relationship frequently are important significant others for adolescents.

Adolescents may be influenced to a considerable extent by different individuals and groups on both the adult and peer level. Moreover, there is substantial diversity from the point of view of values, belief and behaviour among them. It is for this reason that researchers question the use of the word 'subcultural' in this context. Having this important relationship with both adults and peers, young people may experience a good deal of role conflict, and such conflict may be widely different for different individuals. Presumably attempts at the resolution of this conflict are an important part of the maturing process.

Friesen (1972) conducted an interesting Canadian study which has an important bearing on the reality or meaning of the adolescent 'subculture' concept. After reviewing the literature, he postulated three specific models which potentially explain the value orientations of Canadian youth. One he refers to as cultural discontinuity, and this corresponds to Coleman's adolescent subculture in the strict sense. A second postulates cultural continuity, where value differences come from the adult culture, and are passed on to children. The third model, with which we are less concerned in this particular context, regards social class rather than any adolescent 'subculture' as the determinant of different value orientations. Friesen studied students in three different high schools, each having a different ethno-cultural background. He found a number of similarities among the groups and, as might be expected, he found dissimilarities as well. "Considerable evidence derives from this study in support of the cultural continuity theory. . . . The current popular line of reasoning that youth culture is separate and distinct from the parent culture gains very little support from these data" (Friesen, 1972:271). Clearly, this Canadian position is not in accord with any strict subcultural model such as Coleman proposes.

Eve (1975) also offers support for the continuity position. "Taken as a whole, this study has provided evidence that although students do maintain a statistically distinct value system, this system is primarily conventional in its orientation and differs only to a relatively small degree from the value system of the adult world" (p.265).

In the sociology of education we are very interested in the influence of these individuals and groups, both adult and peer. It has a strong bearing on both aspiration and achievement. We have already discussed much of this influence where family and parents are concerned.

Coleman's (1961) statements about adolescents coming to constitute a small society in microcosm must be interpreted with these thoughts in mind. Other studies have shown that they have extensive interaction with parents and other aspects of adult society. Indeed the peer group serves the function of assisting in adult socialization rather than detracting from it. In the cultural system of succeeding adult generations, especially where values and beliefs are concerned, there is more continuity than there is change. Modern industrial society is not so much characterized by less contact between adolescents and adults, as it is by more heterogeneous contact, with the youth being exposed to a greater variety of views and expectations. Studies have not tended to show that the influence of adults has diminished greatly, and as Brookover and Erickson (1975:304) state, that aggregate ". . . may have influence equal to or greater than the peer group."

Martin and Macdonell (1978) briefly summarize the conclusions of a number of Canadian studies which tend to support the position we have taken. We will discuss some of these findings subsequently. At this point we wish merely to use this assessment as support for the point that parental and adult influence is not disappearing. Westley (1955), in a study of students near Montreal, concluded that there are few sharp conflicts between students and parents, and no serious problems about occupational choice or, presumably because it is a means to this end, about educational achievement.

We would not want to be interpreted as denying the importance or the general applicability of this major work by Coleman, some more specific findings of which we are about to present. However, we do feel that it is unwise to carry the concept of subculture too far or to take a stand that the adolescent or peer group has overriding influence in the lives of young people today. Moreover, the general conclusions are based on statistical averages, the normal procedure. There is a great deal of variance relative to specific groups or aggregates on the basis of ethnicity, social class, even gender, and it is important for the student to bear this in mind. A particular study at the micro level, when dealing with an individual school or community, should not be interpreted as indicative of the general situation in Canadian or American society.

## Adolescent Values and Academic Achievement

Coleman's data, as interpreted by Boocock (1980) show six principal components of the high school culture which have a direct effect on academic achievement. These are, in order of remoteness or causal priority: (1) family background and values; (2) individual abilities, sex and age; (3) individual attitudes, values and aspirations; (4) the social context of the school; (5) the social climate of the school; and (6) the organization of the peer group, including friendship groups and popularity status. All of these have direct influence on academic achievement. In a causal model, which we will explain in chapter

12, there would be a direct path going from each of these components to the dependent variable, academic achievement.[1]

As indicated in Figure 8-1, some of these components have indirect paths as well. Thus family background and values, and individual abilities, sex and age both influence individual attitudes, values and aspirations. The reader should readily understand the relationships. Family values vary with social class, and also with other factors such as ethnicity, and these may be broadly referred to as family background (Jencks, 1972). Individual abilities, especially measured intelligence but not restricted to this, affect the individual's attitudes, values and aspirations, as do sex and age. The individual attitudes, values and aspirations would include the self-concept which is influenced by significant others, here to be understood as part of the family background. Thus the influence of family background and of individual abilities, sex and age has an important indirect path to or influence on academic achievement through individual attitudes, values and aspirations.

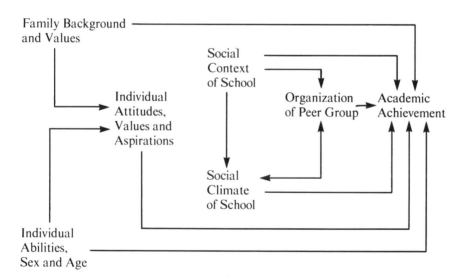

Figure 8-1

Source: Adapted and Modified from Boococck (1980:215).

---

[1]We present an explanation of path analysis in chapter 12. The reader may wish to consult that passage now.

Family background has a direct effect on the social context of the school. Individual attitudes, values and aspirations have a direct influence on the social climate of the school, and this relationship goes both ways. The social climate is also directly influenced by the social context. Social context refers to the characteristics of the student body, global or structural variables such as social class, race, sex and ethnicity. Social climate refers to the normative system, the system of expectations, which is held by the members of the school body, especially the students but including teachers and others as well (Brookover and Erickson, 1975). Social climate is a particularly important variable. It largely defines the student role in a given school. While influenced by the social context, it is also dependent on the individual's attitudes, values and aspirations, being partially the aggregate expectations for the students as held by them and communicated to one another. Thus the social climate, while influenced by individual aspirations, also influences them in a reciprocal manner.

Social context and social climate both have direct paths to academic achievement. This is as expected. Community characteristics have been shown to have a strong bearing on achievement (see chapter 5). However, they may be modified through the social climate; or much of their influence is indirect, going through the social climate. The system of expectations which is characteristic of a particular social context may be altered by changing the climate of the school, the expectations about the student role.

Both context and climate have a direct influence on the organization of the peer group, the final intervening variable leading to academic achievement. This again should be readily apparent. The nature of peer group expectations varies according to the nature of the community (context). It also depends on the system of expectations in the school (climate) on which it has a reciprocal influence. The social climate in a sense defines the student or adolescent role, partly according to the global characteristics of the community, and this system of expectations affects the structure or organization of the peer group. Included in the organization of the peer group are those factors or variables which determine the adolescent's popularity.

In summary, Coleman identified six sets of variables which directly affect academic achievement. Most of these have an indirect affect as well, through the social climate or value system of the school and (especially) through the organization of the peer group. While this latter is the final intervening variable, having a strong direct influence on achievement, it in turn is influenced directly by the social context and, especially, the social climate of the school.

After determining the influences on academic achievement which we have outlined above, Coleman next attempted to determine the attributes most valued by the students. As Boocock (1980:216) notes, these ". . . are discrepant with the central goals of the school as a formal learning system."

Activities which were particularly important to the students included being an athletic star (for boys) or a leader in activities such as cheerleading (for girls). Students valued intellectual ability (brilliance) but not studiousness. While there was variance among schools, on the average or in general the students valued most being a brilliant nonstudious athlete, or leader in activities. The most important element was the athletic prowess or involvement in related activities, then came intellectual ability but with the provision that this did not depend on apparent studiousness. As Tannenbaum (1969) has shown, the attribute of studiousness was negatively rewarded.

Being accepted by the peers was very important for the students. The principal mechanisms of association were dating, talking on the telephone and freely associating with one another. The students perceived their parents as feeling it to be important that they be accepted by their peers even at the expense of some academic achievement. Brilliant students, even without being studious, were somewhat penalized. They were not popular choices for dating, and this was especially so for the girls.

Being popular was regarded as the result of having a good personality, good looks and the right clothes. Academic success is not a prerequisite, while athletic success or leadership activities is. At the same time being brilliant was helpful, provided that the student was not a bookworm, wearing academic interests and success on his or her sleeve. When controls were introduced for the social climate, the elite or most popular students had higher grades than others in schools where the value system included higher evaluation of ability. Elite students were not very interested in pleasing teachers — even less so than other students (Boocock, 1980).

Tannenbaum (1969) as cited by Brookover and Erickson (1975: 318-319) reported on student ratings of eight different types of students. Each category was a combination of some form of Coleman's variables (brilliant or average student, athletic star or not, studious or nonstudious). The results confirmed Coleman's findings. They were, in order of importance:
1. Brilliant, nonstudious athlete
2. Average, nonstudious athlete
3. Average, studious athlete
4. Brilliant, nonstudious, nonathlete
5. Brilliant, studious athlete
6. Average, nonstudious, nonathlete
7. Average, studious, nonathlete
8. Brilliant, studious, nonathlete

The nonstudious student is always rated above the studious one when brilliance and athletics are held constant. The brilliant student is rated higher than the average student provided he is not studious, and athletes are rated higher than nonathletes. Of the eight categories, the highest rating goes to the brilliant, nonstudious athlete and the lowest to the brilliant studious nonathlete. The brilliant, nonstudious, nonathlete is held in slightly higher regard than the brilliant, studious athlete. Being studious is negatively evaluated to such an extent that in this case it counteracts the positive evaluation of being an athlete. (We should emphasize that these ratings are for high school, not university.)

In attempting to determine the relative influence of parents, teachers and peers, Coleman (1961) found the students slightly more concerned about parental disapproval than about peers' reaction. This tends to support the point that they want to be a part of both the adult and adolescent world, but for different reasons. They find it almost equally difficult to be rejected by either.

Returning to the model of Coleman's findings presented in Figure 8-1, we would like to elaborate a little on the social context and social climate of the school and their relative importance. While Coleman isolates the organization of the peer group as a final intervening variable, it also may be considered a part of the social climate of the school.

As we indicated earlier, the social context refers to the aggregate or structural characteristics of the student body. These include especially social class, sex, race and ethnicity, but also other characteristics of lesser importance such as region and specific economic structure. We are aware that social class, as an aggregate characteristic, has a stronger relationship with academic achievement than virtually any other variable. Sex also has an important relationship. Girls are better academic achievers than boys through the high school years. Race also has strong effects, as does ethnicity. The native people in Canada are low achievers. Certain ethnic groups such as the Chinese or Jewish people stress the importance of education and are generally high achievers.

While these social context variables do have an important direct effect on academic achievement, (as when climate and peer group organization are controlled), they are mediated by the social climate and the organization of peers. According to Brookover and Erickson (1975) who did much original research in this matter, ". . . the school social climate encompasses a composite of variables as defined and perceived by the members of the group. These factors may be broadly conceived as the norms of the social system and the expectations held for various members as perceived by the members of the group and communicated to members of the group" (p.364). The norms refer especially to those that are of an evaluating type and which make explicit the forms of behaviour which are expected (Johnson, 1970). There are a number of processes such as surveillance and sanctions which have an influence on the effective application of this normative system. The point we want to emphasize now is that the students themselves have substantial input on what these expectations are, as Coleman has demonstrated; and also that others directly involved in the school, such as teachers, the principal, even coaches, secretaries or janitors who are less closely involved in academic pursuits, are in a position to influence or alter them (McDill and Rigsby, 1973; Brookover *et al*, 1973). For schools of similar social context, the social climate explains much of the variance in achievement. Presumably it does for schools of different social contexts as well. A study in six Ontario high schools by Pavalko and Bishop (1966) demonstrated that the post-secondary plans of students are influenced by their friends. This is the case even when social class, sex and ability are controlled. However, Zentner (1964) has shown that the influence of friends as well as teachers and relatives varies over time and according to the issues involved.

In summary, the role of the students as defined by themselves (and in which they perceived parental support) included a good relationship with parents, and especially a high degree of popularity, acceptance and identification with their peers. Popularity was based on dating, having mutual telephone conversations, and generally spending time together even if it was not directed at a specific activity. Having a pleasing personality, good looks and the proper style of clothing was also important. The life style was such that high academic attainment was not a principal goal, and overt efforts to achieve in this way (a studious life style) were not acceptable. The most important activity was athletic participation and success, or, for the girls, leadership in associated activities. The ability to achieve well intellectually was also valued positively, but less so than athletic success. For the students the life style was such that studying to achieve well in school was little more than a necessary means to an end — graduation. Either active participation in athletics or support of such activities was an important component of high school life.

## The Termination of Schooling

Schooling is terminated in two ways: either by graduating or by dropping out. It has become the accepted practice or norm for young people to continue on in school at least until high school graduation. By 1971 approximately 56 per cent of Canadian youth leaving school had completed high school. This trend increased during the decade of the seventies. Although the descriptive material is not yet available, it has been predicted that two-thirds of Canadians leaving school will have completed high school by 1980, and that this will approach 70 per cent by 1985. Moreover, about 45 per cent of the age group 18-24 were attending university in 1980, and it is projected that this will be well past the 50 per cent mark by 1985 (Hunter, 1981). There has been not only an increase in the numbers gaining a high school diploma and at least some post-secondary education, but an increase in the rate of attendance as well. Attendance rates are even greater in the United States but considerably lower in England. They appear to be increasing in every developed nation in the western world.

We must keep these statistics in mind when we are discussing the meaning of 'dropping out'. Earlier discussions on dropouts restricted the term to those who failed to complete high school. Unless we note otherwise, we will follow that practice here. However, we should point out that because of the increase in the retention rate even at the post-secondary level, we now hear the term applied sometimes to those who fail to achieve a college or university diploma or the equivalent.

The retention rate ". . . compares the enrollment in grade eleven to the enrollment of the same age group in grade two, nine years earlier" (Rocher, 1975:141). This latter boundary (grade eleven) is usually either two or three years away from high school graduation, and for that reason the retention rate and the dropout rate are not complementary. The retention rate for Canada was almost exactly 50 per cent in 1960-61, but jumped to 66.6 per cent within a decade, and to 80 per cent by 1970-71. There was much variation between regions and provinces. Rates in the Atlantic Provinces in 1970-71 were about 13 per cent lower than the national average, from a low of 64.2 per cent for Prince Edward Island to a high of 69.7 per cent for Nova Scotia. The highest rate for the other six provinces was 84.2 per cent for Alberta. Saskatchewan (78.4), was the only one of those with a rate below 80 per cent (Rocher, 1975:142-143). As we noted, these rates are not the complement of the dropout rate, but they do serve as a useful basis of comparison.

There are a number of important predictors of dropping out, including failure or excessive absences in elementary school, frequent school changes, early recorded delinquency and drinking patterns, race, and social class. Also related are truancy, I.Q., father being absent from the home, mother's education, and family size.

There are many studies which attempt to analyse this phenomenon of dropping out. As far back as 1963, Miller suggested that they are both too broad and too narrow: too broad because they assume the category to be a homogeneous one, and too narrow because they do not regard the problems of dropouts as being economic and political issues. There is much variation between regions and communities and, contrary to popular belief, a large proportion of dropouts in certain areas have parents who are engaged in white collar occupations.

Miller (1963) subdivides middle-class dropouts into three categories: those with school-related emotional difficulties; the emotionally disturbed whose difficulties are not directly related to school; and (the largest category) those whose families are economically or educationally marginal to the middle class. He presents four types of low-income dropouts. The first is the school inadequate dropout, referring to those who have difficulty achieving because of low intellectual functioning or disturbed emotional functioning. This category is smaller than is generally assumed. The second is the dropout who experiences a push away from school which he finds boring, confining, of little use, and ego-destructive. In many cases teachers and principals are not sorry to see this person leave. Like the school inadequate, this is not a large category.

The third category, also not large, Miller characterizes as the school-perplexed dropout. These people hold to family or subcultural values about the importance of education, but find schools and school people perplexing. They become lost and sometimes react against the school experience, but there is no real rejection of schooling as such.

The fourth category is the school-irrelevant dropout. Such people never really intended to graduate; they have low aspirations. Viewing education instrumentally, they see the value of high school graduation as being strongly related to social class. Being of relatively low social class origin, they do not feel the diploma will help them much unless they attend college, and they do not plan on this. They think, often correctly, that they can get a job which compares well with the high school graduate of the same social class of origin. They seem to understand that it is the college or university degree which gives the large advantage as far as lifetime earnings is concerned.

The group studied by Miller was in a large American city in the early sixties. A similar study in a large Canadian city for 1973-74 was conducted by Reich and Young (1975). Those researchers interviewed some 544 dropouts of both sexes. Having reviewed the literature on dropouts, they found the classical pattern reported there to be the student who had difficulties in school learning from the first grade, was frequently a disciplinary problem, and only rarely was involved in school activities. Usually this person was from a lower social class background, and often from a large or broken home. They questioned the accuracy of this global description.

Reich and Young found that members of their sample were, on average, 17 years old when they left school, had a longstanding pattern of poor academic achievement, and averaged a year behind regular students in their credits. Only about 25 per cent of the parents supported them in their decision to leave, but about 33 per cent took no position. For those who stayed in school, about 90 per cent had supportive parents. Some 80 per cent of the dropouts were currently working or homemakers, and a small number planned to continue their education in some other setting.

These researchers were able to identify six main patterns. The first was the *classic dropout*, comprising 23 per cent of the sample. Hostile and troublesome in school, their withdrawal was merely a retreat from an institution which they did not like. Having fewer credits and a lower average than the rest of the sample, these were almost entirely male. Because this category made up less than a quarter of the sample, it would appear that the classical description of the dropout in the literature was not an accurate one.

By far the largest category and making up 53 per cent of the sample was the *work-oriented dropout*. These left school for positive reasons, having chosen a life style of the typical blue collar worker. They were usually borderline passes in school.

The other four categories together made up less than one-fifth of the sample. There was the female *homemaker* (6 per cent) who chose homemaking and a family as the desired position in life, corresponding largely to the work-oriented dropout. There was also a small category (3 per cent) referred to as the *intellectual elite*. Most of these are female and many plan to further their education later in a different setting. They can do well in school, are the oldest and closest to graduation and virtually all are in the academic rather than in a vocational track. They have simply rejected the system.

The final two groups, the authors suggest, were unique to this city. There was the *family supporter* (7 per cent), first generation immigrants whose families wanted them to help out financially. There was also the *cultural isolate* (2 per cent). Mostly immigrants, disproportionately female, these had a language problem but despite this they were fairly good students. They were not happy in leaving school and gave education a positive value.

Reich and Young compared their dropouts to a control group of similar background who remained in school. They divided these into four categories. There was the *career-oriented* student, some 42 per cent of their sample. Similar to the work-oriented dropout, they wanted a working career but viewed education as a means to that end. Nearly half had considered leaving but had decided to remain until graduation. There was also an *academically-oriented* category (20 per cent). These planned to attend university, were generally happy with school and had not seriously considered leaving. They had high aspirations, but their averages and number of credits were no higher than normal. There was also the *discontented reformer* (19 per cent). These were generally unhappy with school and most had considered leaving. Similar to the intellectual-elite dropout, about two-thirds were female, they had a higher than normal average and were a little younger. The final category was the *future dropout*, about 10 per cent of the sample. These were similar to the classic dropout and most planned to leave school soon.

For the majority the decision to leave school was not made overnight. With the exception of the work-oriented dropout, and the intellectual elite who sought resources outside of the school, most did not use school or community sources in making their decision. About half left in response to a precipitating incident, although this was not generally the case for the classic dropout.

Reich and Young tried to isolate a causal variable which would be a good predictor of dropping out rather than merely a descriptive indicator such as social class, and they chose alienation. They distinguished between psychological alienation, from self and others, and sociological alienation, from society and its institutions. They suggested that the school may be associated with both. Early failure may lead to psychological alienation and this in turn may lead to sociological alienation with hostility towards authority figures.

Martin and Macdonell (1978) appear to confirm this relationship between alienation and dropping out. Writing within a symbolic interactionist framework, they note the importance of students and teachers co-operating or together working out a collective definition of the situation. In such a process, which is based on negotiation, each person would have a sense of contributing to the input. If the process is denied to the student, a sense of powerlessness will likely be the result, and this is a principal component of alienation. From this point of view it is essential for the student to see his role as a participating one. If so, alienation will be reduced and presumably this will result in lower dropout rates.

Eysenck (1979) found a very strong correlation in a variety of studies, between measured intelligence and dropping out. He reported on a study by Bienstock (1967) of over a million and a half American high school students. The group had been divided into quartiles on the basis of I.Q. range. The dropout rate within one year for the lowest quartile was 20 per cent, but lowered to 12 to 6 to 5 per cent for the succeeding quartiles.

When we have been discussing dropouts the assumption has been that such people have reached the legal age when schooling is no longer compulsory, either 15 or 16 in the various provinces of Canada. There is another case where students may be asked voluntarily to withdraw before attaining this legal age, or failing such a voluntary move they may be expelled. This may also happen to the student who has attained the legal age, but here the position is less complex. In such cases the students are perceived as being some kind of a serious behavioural problem. Analysis of this type of practice, if there really is a serious problem, properly belongs to the field of special education. Care should be taken to insure that the subject's human or civil rights are not violated. While there has been little direct research on suspension and expulsion, there is a correlation with social class and with minority racial and ethnic groups (Parelius and Parelius, 1978).

One of the principal results of being a high school dropout is lower lifetime earnings. Despite the point already made that a college degree is the principal credential for higher earnings today, and that each year below that level including high school graduation is less important than is the degree, there is nevertheless a strong positive correlation between education and earnings. Moreover, in industrial society in general, and in Canada in particular, there is considerable geographical mobility. Dropouts have higher unemployment rates, and when they move to another area to find a job their expectations or aspirations are frequently unrealistic. They are disproportionately represented among the poor and in other social problem areas such as alcoholism and broken homes.

To this point we have been discussing a kind of termination which is generally viewed in a negative manner by society, perhaps with a relatively small number of specific exceptions. There is also the termination which is viewed positively, and here we refer to graduation. There is usually a hierarchy of prestige in the kind of diploma which is granted, depending on whether it is academic, general or vocational. Yet regardless of this, the event is seen as a positive accomplishment, is accompanied with formal ceremonial rites, the most important of the school year, and is generally viewed today as a *rite de passage*, marking the transition to adulthood at least for those who do not plan to continue schooling beyond this point (Parelius and Parelius,1978). This adult status is more easily attributed to those who are about to enter the permanent labour force, self-support being one of the requirements of normal adult life.

In a sense it may appear ironic that those who will continue on in the post-secondary area of schooling, who are pursuing a goal which is more highly valued by society, have full adult status somewhat withheld. This is primarily because they are not earning full-time, even though the serious university student may be spending more effort in his studies than companions of his age who are in the labour force. It is probably for this reason that college pranks are more generally tolerated in our society than is the equivalent type of behaviour by those who have left school. However, the post-secondary student is the recipient of greater accolades when the next graduation stage arrives, and the adult status then imputed has greater prestige.

In this chapter we have been concerned with the clients of education, perceived in the broad sense as including society in general, the community and the parents, and in a more restricted sense as the students themselves. We have generally stated that the adolescent role is not wholly discontinuous with the values of adult society, and that high school students with some parental and community support define their role in such a way that it gives greater emphasis to popularity with peers and athletic endeavours than it does to high academic achievement. We will move on in the coming chapter to certain organizational variables in schooling which also have important effects on student's achievement.

# 9

# *Organization for Teaching*

We have seen that the goal of efficiency and increased productivity in administration often results in the standardization of procedures within an institution according to specific formal rules and procedures. Earlier in this century, Taylorism or scientific management brought with it great emphasis on specialization. To a limited extent this practice found its way into schooling, especially in grouping procedures.

From very early times children in schools have been age graded where numbers made this convenient, and they were usually segregated on the basis of sex. We noted in chapter one that there were attempts to introduce the Lancastrian system in schools in Canada, especially in Ontario or Canada West. As adopted by Dr. Gordon Bell this procedure began in Halifax as early as 1814, although it never really amounted to much in Canada.

As the nation moved more rapidly toward industrialization schools began holding the students for more years and for a longer period each year. The cost to the taxpayer gradually became a heavy burden. The organizational chart became more complex and greater emphasis on efficiency in administration resulted. The traditional independence of the teacher in the classroom impeded such procedures to some extent. The goals of provincial education departments were such that mass production was self-defeating. One of the principal responses was an added emphasis on certain new forms of grouping where students were segregated more and more on the basis of ability and curriculum.

## Formal Grouping

### Groups

There is an important distinction between an aggregate, a collectivity and a group. These are not strictly technical terms and they are frequently used interchangeably, usually with the loss of precision. An *aggregate* is simply a category of people who share some common characteristic. All males form an aggregate, as do all women in the labour force, or the Smiths in a phone book. A *collectivity* is an aggregate of people who are together in the same place, for whatever reason. All of the people in the school yard would form a collectivity. The first of these is a statistical aggregate and the second is a physical aggregate (Spencer, 1979). A *group* consists of ". . . a number of individuals who are aware of one or more significant commonalities" (Martin and Macdonell, 1978:47). The commonalities are such that the people involved have a collective name and share an identity. They have some goal in common and this requires that the members have ongoing interaction in the pursuit of the goal.

This distinction between a collectivity or physical aggregate and a group is an important one for those who are interested in schooling. The fact that a number of individuals attend the same school or even are assigned to the same classroom does not in itself make them a group, or mean that they have a common goal. There may be some who could hardly care less about the curriculum or even about passing exams and advancing to the next level. However, it is likely that over a period of time a collectivity of individuals in the same class will become a group even if this is not essential.

There are several different kinds of groups, the identification of which is quite important. *Primary* groups such as a family share personal face-to-face interaction, being involved with one another in a personal, intimate and emotional way. Opposed to this are *secondary* groups which are generally though not necessarily larger. The members interact and share some common goal, but usually in a less personal and intimate manner. A class is usually a secondary group although there may be a number of primary groups within it, and in some cases it may become a primary group.

It is very helpful if the students in a class participate in a primary group which is directly related to attaining the cognitive and affective goals. They then tend to care much more about one another and to engage in co-operative pursuits. Secondary groups have more impersonal relations, usually caring less about one another (though not necessarily not caring). Their relations tend more to be impersonal and contractual (Martin and Macdonell, 1978).

Another important type is a *peer* group, generally people of approximately the same age sharing a similar status and style of life. A peer group in the broad sense is likely to be a secondary group but within it there are usually several primary groups. Peer groups are very important especially for adolescents, and have great influence in life. Peer group pressure may lead to higher educational attainment, for example, by influencing or encouraging college plans. It may also have a negative influence.

Still another type of group which is important is the *reference* group, those with whom a person identifies psychologically. The identification may be positive (I want to be like these people) or negative (I do not want to be like these people). Reference groups usually include more than one's peers and provide a frame of reference for self-identity. In a sense the members of reference groups may be regarded as models. We either expect to or want to be like them. This in turn may be most important for fostering educational aspirations.

Somewhat akin to reference groups are *significant others*. These people exercise unusual influence, sometimes a very profound influence, on our lives. Significant others usually include parents, perhaps older brothers or sisters, best friends and other important members of peer groups. Also included may be others regarded as important models such as teachers, and some people whom we view as having made significant contributions in society. The recent death of Terry Fox and the adulation offered by so many following the Marathon of Hope points to his being a significant other for many Canadians. We will see in chapter twelve that significant others exercise an unusually strong influence, both direct and indirect, on educational aspirations (Sewell *et al.*, 1970). However, it may be misleading to regard reference groups and significant others as groups in the strict sociological sense. They do not share a common identity or have the interaction which may be expected of those who share a common goal.

Many of the recent studies in the sociology of education, especially in Canada, are concerned with the interaction which takes place in the school setting, with the dynamics of group processes. These studies necessarily are on the micro level, dealing with individual units such as the peer group, the class or the school. We would like to acknowledge the great importance of this work. Ultimately, with sufficient replications, commonalities in group dynamics in the school may be identified and explained. However, in a text such as this it is beyond our goal to deal with or even report on these individual micro level group dynamic studies, except occasionally in an isolated case. We would like to impress upon the reader the point that this is not because they are unimportant. Indeed we would hope that some students now using this general text will progress to more specialized areas in the sociology of education and significantly add to this body of knowledge. We will not understand the influences on educational attainment well until we understand the basis of interaction between, especially, teachers and pupils, and pupils and pupils. The cooperation and conflict that occurs in such group settings are most important relative to aspiration and attainment. We tried to point this out in a general way in chapter four which dealt with interaction and learning. The problem we must face in attempting to bring this material to a common denominator is that interaction within groups and the influence of significant others varies according to personality characteristics, age and stage of maturation, and many other variables. The influence of the teacher or the other students on a pupil in one classroom setting may be very different from that of another teacher or set of pupils in another classroom setting, or in another school setting outside the classroom, or even outside of the school. It is very dangerous to generalize to the macro level from such studies because of the subjective elements of the people involved. It is to be expected that the results of one such study in a particular setting would differ from and perhaps even be in conflict with the results of a similar study in another setting. This is because of *interaction* which brings with it a special or additional effect due to the peculiar combinations of variables (Blalock, 1960).

The participation of students in group activities affects their self-concepts, has an important influence on social control, and has substantial pedagogical relevance directly affecting cognitive and affective learning. Every member of society must learn to function as a social person within the group. This entire process of socialization which is so important, and which helps to build a social awareness and a social identity, also provides the individual with learned interaction techniques which are to be used in a variety of social situations in society (Martin and Macdonell, 1978:64). We must emphasize that the results of group processes in school are important not only in their pedagogical consequences but also, perhaps even especially, in their broader social consequences. It is for reasons such as this that there is so much interest in recent years in the hidden curriculum, which deals with these broad social factors such as personality development, self-concept, social control, and stereotyping. we will investigate in chapter eleven the assertion made by Bowles and Gintis (1976) that such issues as these are much more relevant to occupational success and lifetime earnings than are the cognitive or substantive elements of the curriculum. Yet this social awareness and identity and these interaction techniques which are so important for life are learned, to a substantial extent, within the social setting of the school.

There is a tendency for students in the larger centers and especially at the elementary level to be rather homogeneous in terms of social class. This is because the schools are community-based, and people of similar social status tend to live in the same or similar areas. As one progresses to the secondary level, especially in the larger comprehensive schools, a greater element of heterogeneity is present because secondary schools have a greater tendency to cross community boundaries. We must not carry this observation too far though, for no community is completely homogeneous.

In the remainder of this section we will concentrate on two types of formal grouping which have a profound effect on educational attainment and also on the broader social issues we have been discussing. These are ability grouping and tracking.

## Ability Grouping

In education circles in recent years there has been much interest shown in grouping students on the basis of ability or achievement. The suggested rationale for this practice, usually referred to as *ability grouping*, is that it will let the better or more able students achieve faster and with less boredom from being held to a slower pace required for others, and also that the slower student will be more comfortable and make better progress when working exclusively with those who have comparable ability or achievement levels (Brembeck, 1971).

Several years ago one of us was teaching a regular university course in the sociology of eduction to continuing education students. These were generally mature students, married and in the labour force for a number of years. About half of them were teachers. The setting was a small university town of about 6,000 people. In addition to the university which had several hundred highly educated employees, the town was also the medical and legal center for the surrounding rural area in which about twice as many people lived.

When it came to a discussion of ability grouping the class was asked if there were any primary teachers present. There was one. This lady was asked in turn if the children in her class were divided in groups, at least informally. Responding affirmatively, she explained that there were three such groups. The 'top' group included the fast learners, the 'lower' group included the 'slower' learners, and the third included students of the intermediate range. The teacher explained that this arrangement was made within the first week of school. When she was asked what families from within the community the students from the 'top' group came from she volunteered without hesitation that they were the children of the college professors and doctors and lawyers. One of the most important of the criteria used for sorting was the greater familiarity at the beginning of the year with the instruments being used in the class, a better vocabulary, and greater familiarity with colours, letters and numbers. Moreover, all of the teachers in the class agreed that this was a normal procedure, and while there might be an individual exception, the members would remain in their respective groups in the coming years. We do not suggest generalizing from this one case but use it merely as an illustration of what these teachers considered normal.

We do not mean at this point to question the propriety of this practice, which Rist (1970) also found in the ghetto schools of St. Louis. Our point here is to indicate that ability grouping, at least on an informal level, begins in some cases in the first *days* of schooling. Its effects appear to begin immediately and to persevere on through the school years, and there is usually a strong correlation with social class background. Moreover, the sorting appears to be done on the basis of earlier achievement within the family rather than on the potential to learn. Since the results of this sorting which is initiated at approximately age five will include higher educational attainment some fifteen and twenty years later for a select group, and since this higher attainment will lead to greater occupational success and lifetime earnings, we may say generally that this sorting into ability groups within the first week or month of school either causes or is associated with superior adult success as measured by more prestigous occupations and higher earnings. Nor do we intend to make the assessment solely on the basis of this one experience we have indicated. There are many empirical studies to demonstrate the timing of ability grouping and its relationship with social class, the classical one being the Rist (1970) study.

Banks (1976) refers to ability grouping as streaming and distinguishes it from setting. However, we must not confuse streaming with the practice of tracking. The distinguishing aspect in ability grouping is the degree of homogeneity involved. At one extreme the entire class, which presumably is somewhat hetereogeneous as far as ability and achievement are concerned, is treated in a similar manner. There is no grouping. At the other extreme the students are permanently separated into groups on the basis of some measure of ability. These groups then become the teaching unit. The speed of learning, even the curriculum varies according to the group which continues to be homogeneous in nature. We shall refer to this as universal ability grouping. Between these extremes is the system Banks refers to as setting, where students are grouped on the basis of ability for individual subjects, but are brought together again for other purposes or other subjects. There may be homogeneous groups for one subject, other homogeneous groups with different cross-sectional members for another subject, and still no grouping for a third. Thus the same student may be in a slow setting for mathematics, an advanced setting for English literature, and in a heterogeneous setting for geography. We may regard setting as one kind of ability grouping, and oppose it to universal ability grouping. It is likely that the harmful results to self-concept which are so frequently attributed to universal ability grouping are diminished or will not occur at all in setting. We will subsequently discuss this matter further.

We should clearly distinguish between ability grouping and tracking, although the distinction is frequently blurred in many texts. Fundamentally, ability grouping is an organizational process wherein students are separated into groups as a mechanism for achieving a common goal or a common curriculum. It includes the idea of the same, or similar, goals for different groups. The division is usually made on the basis of ability or achievement, and the segregation is more or less permanent. There is considerable room, theoretically, for mobility. Tracking, which we shall examine in the next subsection, includes different goals for different groups (Brookover and Erickson, 1975). It is frequently justified in terms of *aptitude,* a construct even more difficult to measure than ability. We are familiar with the academic, general and vocational tracks. There is a hierarchy of prestige involved, with little room for mobility, unless downward, between the tracks. Moreover, there may be and frequently is ability grouping within the various tracks.

We mentioned earlier the distinction between informal and formal grouping. It is likely that at one time or another, given the opportunity, the well-motivated teacher will separate out or call together certain students who have special needs or interests. This is a temporary or transient process and may be highly informal. Opposed to this would be a more highly structured classification which, even for setting, would be more permanent. This is much more formal.

Richer and Breton (1968) conducted a national survey of public secondary schools in Canada for the year 1965-66. They found that most schools administered mental ability tests, but that only a minority had ability grouping, at least in the formal sense. At that time, then, ability grouping was far from being universally used in Canadian secondary schooling. The experience of one of the authors, who has spent a great deal of time in various elementary schools, indicates it is much more common at that level.

Another important matter to investigate is the *reason* for grouping. Presumably it is to enhance the learning experience, but this is not necessarily the case either for some or all students or teachers. It is quite possible to segregate students into those who will achieve well and those who will not, with much concern for the former group (relative to achievement) and little for the latter, or vice versa. Groups may also be segregated for the convenience of the teacher, regardless of results. Again they may be separated on the basis of behaviour, and not necessarily thoroughly disruptive behaviour. Those students regarded as having a relatively short attention span may be segregated and dealt with differently. Rist (1970) found students in the black ghetto of St. Louis separated on the basis of such criteria as darkness of skin colour, hair characteristics, dress style and smell. Obviously a thorough evaluation of ability grouping must take such matters into consideration, yet this is very difficult. It is little wonder that there are so many conflicting reports. In any assessment it is vital to understand if teachers like and want grouping, or have it imposed on them by school policy. Almost certainly the results will vary. The same question must be asked about the pupils. Just from the point of view of these criteria alone we may arrive at a fourfold typology: students and teachers both favouring grouping; students and teachers both opposed; students favouring and teacher opposed; and finally students opposed and teacher favouring the grouping. Obviously we may expect the results to vary for each setting.

Bearing these restrictions in mind, the literature on ability grouping, while having somewhat conflicting reports, tends to indicate a balance of undesirable effects. Hurn (1978), in assessing the practice, notes that there is little conclusive evidence that such grouping has favourable results on learning, on affective development or on self-concept. However, there are many indications of the opposite and negative results, especially for students in the lower level groups. Brookover and Erickson (1975) suggest that where there are special benefits, this usually involves a modification of the materials and methods used, and that this modification rather than the grouping itself may be the causal variable. Hurn (1978) cites a study by Borg (1964) on ability grouping in schools in Utah which found neither an increase nor decrease in achievement, a finding similar to that of Banks (1976) for England. Douglas (1964) found positive gains for the higher groups in England but noted that these effects were greater there than in 11 other nations which were used as a basis of comparison.

The strongest criticism of ability grouping pertains to its effect on self-concept. Brookover and Erickson (1975) report that there is no evidence that it is helpful, but plenty of evidence to the contrary. Borg (1966), in surveying the practice in the United States, found that it was generally associated with less favorable self-concept scores for all samples at all levels. Finley and Bryan (1971) noted that members of average and low ability groups tend to feel stigmatized, and Mann (1960) goes so far as to say it is cruel for all but the top level group. However, Torrance and Arson (1963) found just the opposite. Banks and Finlayson (1973) showed in England that the only positive effects on aspirations were for the gifted student.

Brookover and Erickson (1975) report on two surveys of the research done on ability grouping in the United States. The first (Eash, 1967) summarized the work done prior to 1960. In general it showed that there was no improved achievement for children, and that it does not improve college achievement. It may damage the student's perception of self, and this is particularly the case for the members of the average and lower level groups. The second survey, conducted by Finley and Bryan (1971) covered the additional research done up to 1970. It showed no consistent positive value for students generally or for particular groups. The balance of findings shows no strong effects either way in the overall pattern, although there is some slight evidence of positive effects on the learning of high ability students and negative effects on other students.

The findings on part-time grouping or setting are less unfavourable. Brembeck (1971) reports that this tends to enhance the emotional security of some bright students but that some other students did not like the limitations of contacts and were offended by teachers' attitudes.

Hutcheon (1975) notes that students learn a great deal from one another and suggests a policy of organizing classes on the basis of heterogeneity of ability but homogeneity of interest. This precludes ability grouping but allows different subjects or curricula for different groups of students on the basis of their own choice.

Martin and Macdonell (1978) emphasize that conflicting results may be expected in the assessment of ability grouping. This is because of the tremendous variation in the characteristics of both teachers and students, and because of interaction. However, our general assessment is that there are few positive results for the students, and in some cases at least there are strong negative effects on some students.

## Tracking and Community Colleges

*Tracking* is an organizational element of schooling by which students are separated into groups which then attempt to achieve different goals. It usually includes different curricula for each track, and generally leads to different life chances. Tracking may be thorough with virtually a completely different curriculum in each track; or it may be partial and incomplete with different content made available in the one subject leading to the same or a similar certificate.

Canadians are quite familiar with tracking. It is found in comprehensive high schools, most of which offer certificates in an academic, general and vocational track, sometimes including special vocational tracks such as secretarial. It may be found in the junior high or elementary school, although less frequently, and is found in community colleges as well.

One of the characteristics of tracking is that there is a hierarchy of prestige involved. Once a student begins in a given track there is little or no opportunity to move to a higher prestige level such as from the general to the academic.

Tracking is highly correlated with social class, even when ability and achievement are controlled. The more prestigious the track the greater the proportion of students from the 'better' social class backgrounds. This is almost certainly inequitable. However, we would like to point out that tracking is not necessarily inequitable or unjust. Provided the track selected by a given student is the result of a freely exercised mature choice, and provided students in different tracks receive equal even if different inputs, then injustice need not be involved. This seems more apparent at the post-secondary level where the selection of a vocational track such as dental hygiene may appear quite normal. Unfortunately, especially at the earlier level because of its relationship with social class, students are placed into tracks without a full knowledge of the ramifications. The process of counseling may serve merely to legitimate a selection which is being imposed.

This applies to community college allocation as well (Clark, 1960; Pincus, 1978). It is generally possible to gain entry into a four-year college or university only if the applicant has a high school academic (college preparatory) certificate. There are, especially in the United States, universities which have an open enrollment policy but this is the exception rather than the rule. Community colleges tend to accept high school graduates from any track, but not for admission into any program. As a result, if a student selects or is allocated to a track at the beginning of junior or senior high school this really means that the decision relative to university entrance is being made then. We shall see in chapter eleven that, relative to occupational prestige and lifetime earnings, this may be an expensive choice. These variables (economic success, lifetime earnings) are not necessarily the most important in life, but in our society they are valued highly. There are fairly strong correlations between occupation and/or earnings and variables such as health, alienation, alcoholism and the education of one's children.

The tracking which occurs in community colleges presents a special problem in the sense that it appears to be more covert. It is also related strongly to social class (Pincus, 1978). Clark (1960) has shown that, at least in one such college, fully half the students who want or intend to pursue an academic course leading to transfer to a university are allocated to a terminal vocational track. Karabel (1972) describes the community college as a peculiar response to opening up the educational system to all without sacrificing achievement which tends to have an ascriptive base. This gives the appearance of a meritocracy without sacrificing the influence of ascriptive variables.

Karabel (1972), reviewing the literature, presents detailed data on the social class and occupation and income variables of community college students. It is needless to pursue this thoroughly. Virtually every study in Canada and the United States shows the same negative relationship in type of college attended.

Still a better predictor of type of college attended, however, is measured ability. Community college students are more like non-college students in measured ability, but more like college students in family background. The modal community college student does not receive an associate of arts diploma or a college degree. Most drop out of college or receive some vocational training.

Clark (1960) described the process by which the community college student of high aspirations is counseled down and away from the academic non-terminal track as the 'cooling out' function. There is a series of steps involved, but fundamentally the student is switched from the transfer to a terminal track in such a way that it appears as if the change is made because of lack of ability. In this way the student regards himself rather than the system as the reason for the failure. Thus higher education appears to be democratized when in fact it is not. Community colleges provide "the chance to try" concept of equality of opportunity, but they are largely unconcerned with equality of results (Pincus, 1978).

Pincus refers to two sets of goals of community colleges. There are public goals with which parents and teachers are quite familiar. These are: comprehensive curriculum, open door principle, convenient location, provision of a second chance to succeed, and community orientation. Fundamentally this means that these colleges are established for all who have a high school certificate, or for mature students even without the certificate. They provide on a selective basis academic and vocational tracks, are meant to be within commuting distance and their personnel are to provide community services. The non-public goals are less overt. They include the training of a para-professional work force, the screening out of students who lack motivation, cooling out as described by Clark (1960), and custodial care.

Studies on the effects of tracking at the elementary and secondary level give conflicting reports, as they do for ability grouping. However, as a general rule they do not consistently show positive results. There is virtually unanimous agreement that tracking is related to social class, although Coleman's (1966) study is an exception. Yet academic ability is the best predictor of track assignment (Alexander and McDill, 1976), although these authors also note that achievement is related to track assignment when ability and social class are held constant. Hurn (1978) notes that teachers' expectations are affected by tracking; they expect less of students in lower tracks. Moreover, in assignment to tracks, even when objective evidence such as ability and achievement tests are used, teachers still make subjective evaluations based on such factors as deportment, dress and attitudes (Cicourel and Kitsuse, 1963). Alexander and McDill (1976) have shown that students' academic confidence is consistently related to track even after aspiration of peers and academic performance are controlled. Students in lower tracks are more likely to drop out even when ability and social class are controlled (Schafer and Olexa, 1971). Jencks (1973) reports that track assignment has only trivial effects on test scores three years later, with only one point difference in the change for college preparatory as compared to terminal tracks. Brookover and Erickson (1975) in assessing Coleman's (1966) findings note that schools which have a high proportion of students in higher tracks had higher rates of achievement in either track than did schools with a lower proportion of students in the higher tracks. Tracking then almost certainly affects the social climate of the school, the expectations of parents, peers and teachers.

## Teacher Expectations

One of the major contributions of early sociological pioneers such as Cooley, Mead and W. I. Thomas was the body of theory pertaining to the formation of the self, or self-concept. This has been enlarged and modified in recent years by the school of sociologists and social psychologists known as symbolic interactionists.

Basically, symbolic interactionism is concerned with the subjective definition or perception of a situation. This definition is the result of social interaction. The classic statement relative to the importance of this subjective interpretation was made by W. I. Thomas (1928:527). "If men define situations as real, they are real in their consequences." This 'definition of the situation' is assuming an increasingly important place in the sociology of education, and nowhere is it applied more than in the study of teacher expectations.

Cooley (1964) had earlier proposed his theory on 'the looking glass' self. Here the self or self-concept is seen as a mirror image of the perceptions of significant others with whom the subject interacts. A person would tend to view himself, his abilities and potential in accord with the way he perceived others viewing him, or them. It is not the actual assessments of these others which is so important but rather the perception (whether accurate or not) held by the subject. It is as a result of this theory that Thomas formulated his classic statement.

G. H. Mead (1962) probably had the greatest influence on symbolic interactionism and the theory on the formation of the self. Mead was a very influential professor at the University of Chicago, but was not one to publish his work. Many of his lectures were published subsequently by his students, one of the most influential being Herbert Blumer (1969). One of Mead's most important contributions was in describing the stages in the development of the self. He pointed out that the infant was socialized through role playing, first in a simple way by taking the role of one person at a time (the particular other), then in a more complex manner by taking the role of many others at the one time. This latter Mead referred to as the *generalized other*. When the maturing child reached this stage he was able to organize his perceptions of the views and expectations of others. The way he viewed himself (the definition of the situation) Mead presented as the result of the perceptions and expectations of others. He then tended to behave in accord with this definition (the reality of the consequences). Mead distinguished between the 'I' and the 'Me,' the 'I' being the active, unique self more or less unfettered by social interaction, and the 'Me' representing the self with the internalized social attitudes and expectations (Mackie, 1980).

Many authors have since theorized on how the expectations of one person influence another. One Canadian scholar who has made a notable contribution relative to teachers and how the interaction of teacher and student leads to the definition of the situation in the classroom setting is Wilfred Martin (1975, 1976). A particularly important point Martin makes is that there is a process of negotiating involved, something already discussed in chapter two. The student may regard some of the teacher's expectations as he perceives them as being inaccurate, and not fully change in accord with that assessment. Nevertheless, there tends to be some modification of the perception of self and subsequent behaviour, and a modification of teacher expectations as well.

Teacher expectations viewed from this perspective have been regarded as representing a self-fulfilling prophecy. This may be both positive and negative. If the expectations are high the student tends to view himself in this manner and behave accordingly. If they are low the opposite result occurs. Robert Merton (1957:423) explains that ". . . the self-fulfilling prophecy is, in the beginning, a 'false' definition of the situation evoking a new behaviour which makes the originally false conception come 'true.'" As he states it this prophecy perpetuates a reign of error. "For the prophet will cite the actual course of events as proof that he was right from the very beginning." The nature of such expectations or prophecy then is a critical matter because people respond to situations in a different way than if the expectations did not exist.

There are two categories of student behaviour which are held to influence teachers. One is ascribed factors such as sex and physical appearance that are virtually irrelevant for performance. The other is the characteristics students take on as a result of their achievements, including performance, aspiration and attitudes. The first of these categories is often cited as the major variable transmitting inequality (Williams, 1976). It includes especially social class or family background. Sex does not appear to be an important variable relative to ability, but it is of major importance in regard to allocation to adult roles.

The study which raised teacher expectations and the self-fulfilling prophecy to the point of being a major issue in the sociology of education was *Pygmalion in the Classroom* by Rosenthal and Jacobson (1968). It caused a great deal of controversy at the time, alarming many, including teachers, about potential inequities. The book dealt with a controlled experiment in a Mexican-American elementary school setting near San Francisco. The team involved in the experiment first tested the children's ability. They then selected randomly some whom they designated as 'bloomers,' informing the teachers accordingly. Claiming they were able to determine from a specific test that the children designated would show a rapid spurt in intellectual development and achievement, they again tested the entire group at the end of the experiment and found that there had been in fact a significant increase in the I.Q. of the designated children during the course of the year.

As we noted, there was much controversy about this study. There have been a number of replications (e.g., Mendels and Flanders, 1973) which failed to produce the same results. Even if the experiment were methodologically sound, which is questionable, there are several possible ways of explaining the results. Rosenthal and Jacobson were not able to determine this in the study, but they assumed that the change in the behaviour of the children designated as 'bloomers' was the result of changed expectations on the part of the teachers, and thus a self-fulfilling prophecy.

Other studies have been conducted on the importance of ascribed characteristics relative to teacher expectations. Clifford and Walster (1973) designed an experiment using report cards accompanied by photographs of children, arranged so that some would appear physically attractive, some not. The target group included 504 fifth grade teachers in Missouri. The results showed that the attractive children received a sizeable advantage over the unattractive ones. The teachers expected them to have higher I.Q.'s, to have parents especially interested in academic achievement, and to attain a higher level of education. The experiment, of course, could not demonstrate if these results actually did occur, or if teacher expectations were the cause.

In a Canadian study, La Voie and Adams (1974) studying teachers in grades one to six were able to show that their expectations were significantly related to conduct. Those students rated higher in good conduct measures consistently were rated higher relative to ability measures, aspirations, and leadership potential. There were no significant findings relative to physical attractiveness, and the sex of either teacher or child was not an important variable. It is interesting to note that the teachers' lower ratings for children scoring low in good conduct pertained not only to aspirations, which is understandable because the conduct problem could reflect lower motivation, but to ability as well. The study indicated that it is interpersonal factors such as warmth, conduct and personality which are the influential determinants of teacher assessments. These were much more influential than physical attractiveness.

Another Canadian study (Adams and Cohen, 1976) did find that level of attractiveness had substantial effects on teachers' expectations though it was not the most influential variable. Some 490 elementary teachers in two mid-western settings were provided with folders containing report card material and other information pertaining to academic and social behaviour for children for the period from kindergarten through grade two. While level of attractiveness did have an influence, statements about the child's home life had by far the greatest impact. Children described as being middle class received more favourable assessments than those living in a lower-class home climate. Sex related differences were not important.

The classic study on the formation of teacher expectations is that of Rist (1970). Noting that expectations are based primarily on subjectively interpreted attributes, Rist proposed a number of steps. In the first place the teacher had in mind a kind of ideal type image for the achiever, and this was related to social class. At the beginning of the first year the teacher evaluated each student relative to this image, and the students were divided into groups on the basis of this subjective evaluation. The group of fast learners received most of the teaching time, attention and reinforcement. This interaction pattern became increasingly rigid and the gap widened as the school year progressed. Finally, the process was repeated in subsequent years, except that no new subjective evaluation was required, the groups having already been formed. Rist's study is a longitudinal one of a school in the black ghetto in St. Louis from kindergarten through grade two. It is, of course, impossible to generalize accurately from it.

Grieger (1971) suggests extreme caution in interpreting these studies on teachers' expectations and the self-fulfilling prophecy. Having reviewed the principal studies up to 1971, he notes that there are many methodological problems and the results are primarily non-significant. Experiments such as the Rosenthal and Jacobson one hardly make sense because the teacher already has so much raw data available. It would seem ludicrous that teachers would be swayed so much by external evidence. Again it comes down to the interaction factor. Variables such as personality type (for both teacher and child), socioeconomic background, sex and actual level of achievement have different interactive effects. Grieger (1971) found considerable evidence in individual cases to support all the points made in the literature, and reminds his readers that teachers have been proven quite accurate time after time in identifying the more intelligent children and in predicting academic achievement years in advance. While such a statement does not alter the importance of expectations or defeat the self-fulfilling prophecy hypothesis it does suggest that more uniform evidence is required before coming to hard conclusions.

Long and Henderson (1974) found that the strongest effects on teacher expectations came from achieved rather than ascribed variables, particularly test scores. Teachers agreed that such scores were mediated by other variables, and held that attention had the second strongest effect. While these kinds of variables are related to ascribed characteristics such as social class background, it is important to note that the ascribed characteristics are prior (and perhaps causal) to intellectual development and achievement. We should be aware that individual teachers may behave inequitably, but at the same time it is wise to be able to demonstrate systematic and intended discrimination before making hard and fast accusations made.

## Teaching-Learning Situations

A teacher may be called upon to be virtually all things to his pupils. Most spend some time in presenting new material, are available as resource persons, are leaders for both class and extracurricular activities such as athletics or drama, or at least are expected to offer support for such activities. Teachers are also called upon to settle disputes, to enforce rules and to administer punishment. In addition, they frequently become friends and lifetime models for the students.

There is a variety of organizational settings in which teacher-student interaction occurs. There are traditional classrooms and open-area classrooms; there are self-contained and departmentalized arrangements; there is the single versus team teaching approach; there are so-called free schools. Any option may be more or less effective for a given teacher and a particular set of pupils. Again there may be a substantial degree of interaction involved. However, despite the protestations frequently heard from those who are 'on a bandwagon,' there is no hard evidence that any one organizational format consistently has higher rates of achievement than that of the traditional classroom setting. There are studies which show superior results in a particular instance but they have been unable to control for interaction effects. There are also studies which result in opposing conclusions. For that reason we will not devote a lot of attention to sociological implications of these different types of organizational formats. They have not really been proven (or disproven) in most cases. Brookover and Erickson (1975) refer to them as fads, not really in a pejorative sense but simply because schools find it fashionable to try new approaches even though there is no consistent demonstration of superior results.

The teaching-learning situation may vary in accord with both shape and size of a classroom. We are all familiar with the traditional classroom. Rectangular in shape, it usually was built to accommodate 30 or more students with desks arranged in rows, the teacher's desk in the front, and aisles between the desks to permit mobility. In the primary and lower elementary grades it is desirable to have a little more room for mobility.

There is nothing magic about this shape and size. Classrooms have been designed and used effectively in a variety of shapes including the hexagon and 'L' shape, and size may vary from the very small to quite large. In a school where the teacher-pupil ratio is approximately 1 to 20 there is often considerable variation. Coleman (1966), Jencks (1972) and many others have demonstrated that the quality of schools including teacher-pupil ratios and class size has little bearing on achievement. The size of the class may be an important variable for teacher satisfaction. Problems of discipline may be expected to increase once a teacher is called upon to supervise more than about 22 pupils, which is often regarded as the ideal. Today classrooms are sometimes designed with flexible walls so that both size and shape may be altered depending on the situation.

A flexible physical design of a classroom makes it more suitable for *open education* or the open learning situation. Martin and Macdonell (1978) point out that open physical space is only one characteristic of open education, and not an essential one. There is no single plan for an open classroom. Students are allowed their own method of learning, at least to a greater extent, and to learn at their own rate of speed. The teacher generally sets the ultimate goal, and most encourage a discovery form of learning and are non-graded (Cockerham and Blevins, 1976). The social boundaries tend to be more open. Students and teachers have considerable freedom in making choices, though the element of openness may be considerably more apparent to teachers and administrators than it is to students (Friesen, 1972).

Ahlgren and Germann (1977) studied the perceptions of 160 educators who participated in a conference on open schooling. Enthusiastic supporters of the concept, for them the defining characteristic of an open school lies primarily in the area of the nature of the interpersonal interactions. Walberg and Thomas (1972:198) note that "(i)t is not a theory or system of education, but a related set of ideas and methods." Wright (1975) in a study of open-area and traditional classrom children in the fifth grade found the open-area classroom children conspicuously deficient in academic achievement in each of nine achievement tests. Only one non-achievement variable showed any noticeable difference. That was school anxiety, and it was higher in the open-area schools. However, as we indicated earlier, other studies show different and conflicting results.

A similar and related concept to that of open education is the *free school*. Made famous by A. S. Neill and the school in England named Summerhill, more than anything else it emphasizes freedom and a minimal amount of institutionalized authority. There is much greater emphasis on emotional and expressive aspects of the personality than there is on formal curriculum (Graubard, 1972). Most such schools are middle class, residential, expensive and have a short life span, Summerhill being an exception as far as permanence is concerned.

Novak (1974,1975) provides a very interesting account of the development of a free school in a large Canadian metropolis. The work is actually a phenomenological study illustrating how this particular social organization came to be an organization with social, and therefore predictable, meaning for its members.

Established in 1970 at the request of a number of parents, the school was at first to provide an environment of complete freedom for the students, providing this did not infringe on the rights of others. In the beginning the parents, teachers and administrators were totally inexperienced, and there was no tangible moral ground or normative system on which a social order could be based. There was almost no real dialogue among those involved for this reason. After some months the introduction of a curriculum and spatial and temporal order allowed more meaningful communication, but to some extent restricted freedom. The curriculum then was more than just an organizer of time and space and became an organized center around which thought and language and evaluation could be based.

The school had major problems in its initial stages because of the lack of systematic organization. Half of the children were withdrawn by the end of the first year and all of the teachers had been replaced. Three years later Novak found dissention and stagnation among the teachers, apathy among the parents and discontent among the students. The only new recruits were the brothers and sisters of children already enrolled (Murphy, 1979).

The problems experienced in this school are not atypical of the free school movement. They probably originate from or are compounded by the minimal social organization and system of norms. The lack of accepted and required means-to-an-end makes it very difficult for people to share in and communicate about a final organizational goal. Without mutually agreed upon expectations, organizational evaluation becomes both difficult and controversial.

Another organizational format which is more frequently being used in Canadian schools is *team teaching.* It involves staff utilization where there is co-operative planning and evaluation, with two or more teachers sharing the responsibilities of instructing the same students in a given content area (Martin, 1975). There is more by way of continuous interaction among these teachers who pursue their common goal through mutual planning, instructing and evaluating. Patterns may vary. Teachers may work as a team within a given subject area or across related areas of learning. Team teaching is really a pedagogical approach. It will only be as effective as the co-operative planning and practice of those involved, and there is no consistent evidence of this practice resulting in superior achievement.

Before concluding this section it is appropriate to mention the suggestion of Ivan Illich (1971) to deschool society. Illich's major point is that schooling contributes to social inequality in both developed and developing nations because it educates children to accept an alienating system of consumerism. His suggestion is to remove the link between schools and occupational opportunity. That opportunity should be based on demonstrated competence which is acquired outside of the educational system. A nation would have a system of resource centers freely available (but without compulsion) to young people where they could pursue their interests. Reimer (1971) gives an appraisal of the wasteful resources of our public education system, which he considers to be very large. Fundamentally, he suggests putting public funds in the hands of the learners rather than the teachers. Bereiter (1971) is less radical, favouring schooling for skill learning purposes and putting the rest of the funds into other cultural resources available to children during their free time.

Illich and the deschoolers are regarded as radicals. Gintis (1972), also known as a radical, is very critical of the deschooling proposal. Stating that it is basically a rejection of progressive liberalism, Gintis holds that reform or abolition of the system of schooling would not overcome the systematic inequality. Taking exception to Illich's locating social problems in the area of consumption, Gintis, a neo-Marxist, holds that their root is in the productive system of capitalism and state socialism. It is the relational aspect of class which is at the root of social problems. Schooling is but one institution in the superstructure which is supportive of institutionalized inequality. Abolish it and it will be replaced by another. All such institutions including schools and occupations are structured by the way people structure their productive relations. Only the abolition of such basic relations will overcome the problem. To claim that reform of schooling, including deschooling, will eliminate or reduce existing inequalities is not getting at the root of the problem and is not radical at all. Gintis faults Illich severely for being strong on description but weak on analysis.

## Grading and Evaluation

Teachers have many roles, and one of them is that of judge of the student's performance and progress in relation to the goals of education. It is the teacher who marks the student's exams and assignments, reports to parents either directly or through the medium of the report card, and recommends to the principal that the student be advanced to the next level. This role carries with it the potential for much confusion. It can also give the teacher a good deal of power in relation to particular students. This is especially important in a society where educational achievement, measured in terms of levels of schooling completed, is a principal gateway to economic success and privilege. we shall see that in our present system, social class status has more to do with educational achievement than do differences in intellectual ability. We believe this is due partly to weaknesses inherent in grading practices which allow for the kind of misrepresentation that appears to legitimate inequitable selection and allocation procedures.

The potential for confusion arising from the teacher's role as evaluator is twofold. First, it is very difficult for the teacher to keep in mind that he is grading some objective manifestation of a student's performance such as an

exam paper and not the worth of the student himself. This is doubly complicated if one is attempting to individualize instruction and therefore know as
much as possible that is relevant about each student. The need to keep this
distinction in mind is especially great when the mark achieved is low or below
passing. If the teacher is confused in this matter, it will not be unusual for the
student to fall victim to the same confusion and develop a low self-concept.

The second potential source of confusion pertains to the *meaning* of a
mark or grade. Both teacher and student may regard it as simply a point of
information, so that they know something of where they stand in a co-operative process the object of which is the achievement of some educational goal.
In this case, a low mark can mean that either the student or the teacher, or
both, have performed inadequately and there is need for improvement. On the
other hand, they can regard it as a reward provided to the student who has
met the standards set by the teacher. This is a quasi-adversary position and
assumes basically that any failure in the attainment of the goal is the student's
fault. One frequently hears a teacher say that he has "given" a student a
particular mark. He may not intend to be taking an adversary position, but
the language betrays him. There is a serious potential for manipulation inherent in this position.

## Formal Grading

By formal grading we refer to the process whereby the teacher assigns a
mark to a piece of work submitted by a student who knows that his work is to
be evaluated and has at least some idea of the standard on which it will be
marked. We will restrict our comments to what teachers call summative evaluation, the mark given upon termination of a project, course or level of study.
(The other kind is formative evaluation, which involves interim assessment of
progress intended to let the student know if he is moving in the right direction.)

There are two major approaches to grading, and they have distinct implications for schooling and its results. The first, and the one more familiar to
most people, is called *norm-referenced grading*. The assumption underlying
this approach is that the population of students being tested is distributed
throughout a range of ability with reference to what is being tested more or
less according to the normal distribution. In other words, if a teacher is testing
a group of 25 students on the material in a history course, he would expect to
find the students' knowledge ranging from low to high, with most clustered
around the middle of the range. Perhaps the lowest mark would be 38, the
highest 92 and most would be in the range between 55 and 80. The practical
result of this is that students end up being evaluated on the basis of comparison
with one another rather than in relation to an objective standard. Take the
example of the case when the range of marks is below the teacher's expecta-

tions, say a range of 23-71 with an average around 47. The teacher committed to norm-referenced grading may simply move the marks upward to give him the range and average he expected while preserving the rank order of the students. This practice serves to hide inadequacies that might have occurred in (a) the teaching, (b) the setting of the exam, or (c) the marking.

There are three main criticisms of norm-referenced grading. One was mentioned above, that it results in comparisons between and among students rather than the comparison of the student's performance with an objective standard. It is quite possible in such a situation for a student to be in the top quartile of his group and yet have performed less well objectively than a student in the third quartile of another group, simply because the average performance in the two groups was different. The second criticism flows from the scaling process described above. The mark that results from norm-referenced grading loses some of its information value, since it can be adjusted to hide faults for which the teacher is responsible. It can at the same time confuse the student, who knows he did poorly on the particular exam and yet ends up with a passing mark (or vice versa). The third criticism is one which points toward the invalidity of the process. The conditions for the assumption of normal distribution of a characteristic are seldom if ever met in a student population being tested for knowledge in a particular area. The sample is rarely sufficiently large, and it is not a random sample. The fact that norm-referenced grading continues to be used in the face of these criticisms supports the contention that two principal functions of schooling are selection and allocation.

The second major approach is *criterion-referenced grading*. For this to be used, the student must be made aware of the objectives to be achieved in the particular course or course segment, and the items used to test his learning must be clearly related to those objectives. The teacher must have a clear notion of what constitutes an acceptable response to a test item, and this should have nothing to do with whether or not one student's response is as good or better than another's. The basic assumption is that most if not all the students in a class have sufficient ability to learn what is set forth in the objectives. In such a situation, the theoretical ideal is not that marks will find themselves normally distributed, but rather that all marks will be 100 per cent. Though the ideal is theoretical, the practical result is that the teacher expects most of the marks to be quite high and does not take it as the normal state of affairs that some students will fail. Low marks provide a signal for the teacher and students to look for the cause, and if the marks are lower than expected for the majority of students, the teacher will look first for inadequacies in his own performance, whether in teaching or testing.

The use of criterion-referenced grading implies the willingness to correct whatever faults, on the part of student or teacher, result in lower than acceptable marks; in other words, to take the time for more teaching, learning and testing so that all students with basic capability will achieve the required standard of performance with regard to the stated objectives. The standard, in this case, is likely to be higher than in the case where norm-referenced grading is used. In a system where all students are exposed to virtually the same degree of instruction, and particularly in secondary schools where instruction is departmentalized and rigidly scheduled, criterion-referenced grading is often felt to be impractical. It is more often used in elementary schools or where continuous progress and subject promotion rather than grade promotion is practiced; but even then it is relatively rare. It is especially rare in post-secondary education, except in teacher education programs.

Whether teachers use norm-referenced or criterion-referenced grading practices, they do like to be able to justify a particular mark in reference to what a student has written. It is easier to do this when a question requires a response that is clearly correct or incorrect. Such a question is more likely to be one which elicits basic information rather than higher-order thinking. As a result, the preponderance of items on examinations will be of this type. Consequently, students will pay more attention to basic information that can be remembered and repeated than to the skills of understanding, analysing and synthesizing. The point is that it is the way students are tested that determines the content of the course, rather than the reverse. This is another way in which the attainment of the formal goals of schooling is impeded in actual practice.

The Minister's Advisory Countil on Student Achievement in Alberta called attention to this problem (MACOSA, 1979:83-85). It noted that "assessment programs . . . can unduly influence the instructional emphasis of school programs because educators tend to concentrate on those objectives which are tested and place less stress on areas that are not tested." It recommended that "the proposed assessment program test curricular objectives selected from all domains (knowledge, attitudes and skills) and thought levels, and not only from the most easily tested areas."

**Informal Grading**

By *informal grading* we refer to the less objective ways in which teachers make judgements which result in differentiating students from one another in terms of school progress or performance. These include grouping of students at different levels within the class, the rating of attitudes, conduct, and so on that is done especially at the elementary level, and the rating of students in terms of class participation. These are especially open to bias, which may result from social class consideration, teacher expectations based on previous testing or achievement, or confusion of categories such as when poor handwriting or sloppiness is taken as an indication of low intelligence. Some of this has already been explained earlier in this chapter. We will deal explicitly now with the rating of attitudes, and of class participation.

The two approaches of formal grading involve primarily the evaluation of cognitive learning. However, the goals of education include affective learning as well; students are expected to learn certain attitudes and work habits. Evaluation in this area is generally less systematic and less well related to an objective standard. Students in elementary school especially are commonly rated on habits, attitudes and personal conduct, usually in terms of categories such as 'satisfactory' or 'needs improvement.' It is the teacher who does the rating, and the standard of reference is almost necessarily subjective. However, there is a certain consistency in the overall system whereby different attitude-value clusters are judged appropriate for different levels and types of schooling, as will be shown in chapter 11. This results, according to Bowles and Gintis (1976), in the reproduction of the social relations of the workplace, and the rating procedure is thus a means of social control and allocation, informal as it may be.

Another questionable practice is that of grading on class participation. Ostensibly, when a teacher says that a certain percentage of the course grade will be based on class participation, he is encouraging active learning — questioning, probing, discussion and similar behaviour. The signs of participation must be observable. Yet it is common to have in a class students who understand the material presented very well and feel no need of questioning or further discussion, as well as students who are shy or dislike the limelight, or have been previously intimidated. It turns out that to use class participation as a basis for grading is really to attempt to control attention and observable behaviour, and the grade given is the sanction. Because the category includes so many intangibles, it gives the teacher some latitude for manipulating the student's mark on the basis of other subjective judgements. That is not to say that a given teacher is insincere in using class participation as a basis for grading, or conscious of its inappropriateness, but it does indicate the potential that this procedure has for behaviour control.

Teachers who grade on class participation know that some of their students are adept at 'playing the game' to get good marks. Indeed, playing the game, that is, taking advantage of the weaknesses in the evaluation system to get good grades without necessarily gaining the corresponding learning, is a long-established part of schooling (Hughes *et al.*, 1977). This includes cheating on exams, playing up to the teacher's biases, and the elaborate processes students engage in to guess what questions will be asked on the exams. All of this nourishes a kind of adversary relationship between teacher and student, which in turn seems to legitimate the teacher's use of marks as a sanction. The sanction is differentially effective with different groups, depending on educational aspirations. We are continually reminded that one of the categories separating groups on this criterion is social class.

## Results of Grading

If it could be assumed that the great majority of those who enter the school system are capable of attaining a level of education sufficient to qualify them for virtually all except the most specialized of the work positions current in our society, it would logically follow that marks or grades should serve mainly to inform the student how he is progressing toward that goal, and any of the other formal goals of education. Bowles and Gintis (1976) have shown that this assumption is valid. Yet it seems clear that grading is used not primarily as information in this way, but as the medium of a system of rewards and punishment, that is, of selection to or exclusion from higher-status positions in society. This practice is legitimated by stressing the differences among people rather than their basic abilities. It is aided by the setting of convenient entrance standards for the higher educational levels, measured in terms of grade averages. Given that norm-referenced grading is the rule, and that this is subject to manipulation, the result is the use of somewhat flexible cut-off points as admission standards. These cut-off points may be varied depending on demand. It was interesting to see, in the late seventies when there was a surplus of teachers, how often teacher education faculties considered or were advised to raise the minimum average for admission to their programs.

It is part of conventional wisdom that some other professions customarily exercise a raising or lowering of the cut-off mark in their admission exams to give them the predetermined quota of entrants for a given year. An informal investigation by one of the authors, who thought that this was true of chartered accountants in Canada, revealed that such was not the case in this instance. However, it is interesting to note that the success ratio of those writing the chartered accountancy exams at the national level is fairly stable at about 55-60 per cent, and this in spite of the provision of special training for candidates and a high attrition rate between beginning work as an accountant trainee and reaching candidacy.

It is our view that grading practices in our formal educational system do not have to be as they are; that there is a viable alternative which is more in keeping with the formal goals of education, but that norm-referenced grading is retained principally because it supports informal goals and the functions of selection and allocation. It also serves to give the teacher more power in what is essentially a bureaucratic organization.

This concludes our presentation on the organization of schools for teaching. The reader may conclude that our selection of topics has been somewhat arbitrary. We feel that they are sufficiently representative to indicate that such factors may have strong selective influence on achievement. We have now concluded Part III of this Book. It dealt primarily with organizational variables within the school and with some characteristics of the clients, particularly of students. We turn now to several issues which are more directly concerned with schooling in its relationship with broader aspects of society.

# Part IV

# Education
# and the Broader Society

In this section of the text we are concerned with two kinds of issues. The first of these, covered in chapter 10, deals with the functions of schooling, both manifest and latent. As we shall see, these may not be identical with those sought by students, parents or even the community at large. The second issue looks at the results of schooling. In chapter 11 we investigate the model presented by Bowles and Gintis which deals with the relationship between economic success or lifetime earnings and three causal variables: measured intelligence, social class, and educational attainment. We shall see that of the three, I.Q. has the least unique importance and years of schooling has the greatest.

In chapter 12 we look at two models of the status attainment process. Here we are trying to understand the importance of education for occupational success, and the way that differences in educational attainment, so strongly related to family background, come about.

# 10

## *The Functions*
## *of Education*

Education is but one institution which is meant to perform services for the broader society or for some significant part of it. We have already seen that there is an unsettled element, an area of dispute, between the functionalist and conflict models on the question of what groups benefit from the institution of schooling. For the former these benefits go to society in general even if some individuals benefit in a particular way. For the latter they go to privileged groups which we have been frequently designating as an elite; the majority does not really benefit at all, or at least much less so than if the social organization of schooling were not supportive of existing inequities.

## A Note on Theory

### Manifest and Latent Functions

Robert Merton (1968) is perhaps the best known contemporary sociologist to have successfully clarified the meaning of the concept *function*. In his widely respected essay "Manifest and Latent Functions" Merton pointed out that one of the problems in sociology, and particularly in the functionalist school, is that the same term has been used to refer to different concepts, resulting in great confusion. Moreover, the same concept has been symbolized by different terms, with similar results.

We pointed out in chapter two that society is made up of a number of constellations of roles, called structures, which are interrelated in performing a certain responsibility, in fulfilling a societal need, or the need of specific subgroups. The family is perhaps the best example. Within it there are a number of interrelated roles: father, mother, husband, wife, son, daughter, brother, sister. Sociologists generally agree that the institution of the family fulfills at least one universal societal need: the socialization of children. The provision of that need or service by the structure is referred to as its *function*. Merton (1968:78) notes that ". . . the concept of function involves the stand-

281

point of *the observer*, not necessarily that of the participant. Social function refers to *observable objective consequences*, and not to subjective dispositions (aims, motives, purposes)." From this it should be apparent that the consequences which result from a function being fulfilled are not necessarily dependent upon or a result of the intention of the social actors involved. Perhaps the example of crime is a good illustration. Despite the undesirable consequences it may have for society at large it may fulfill the function of integration, uniting the members of the social order in their common goal. It is not likely that the criminal element either foresees or intends this integrative aspect.

Merton is careful to point out that society is not generally so thoroughly or perfectly integrated that every culturally standardized or institutionalized activity is functional. Some may be dysfunctional as well. It is essential then, in functional analysis, to specify the units or collectivities for whom some social institution is functional. There may be a plurality involved, and different functions or dysfunctions may be provided for one group or another. Thus the institution of schooling may provide universal literacy, fulfilling a goal for society at large, and at the same time it may legitimate the prevailing system of intergenerational inequality, fulfilling a function more specifically for the elites. It should be obvious that there are functions which are positive for some, or all, and others which are negative.

Merton (1968:105) introduces the very useful distinction between manifest and latent functions. "*Manifest* functions are those objective consequences contributing to the adjustment or adaptation of the system which are intended and recognized by participants in the system." They are then overt, intended, known, recognized and accepted and, in functional analysis, are held to contribute to societal equilibrium. *Latent* functions are ". . . those which are neither intended nor recognized." These are more covert, unintended by the entire institutional complex though not necessarily by each of its parts. They are less widely acknowledged or recognized, in a sense appearing as a by-product of other manifest intentions. They also may be positive or negative. The same structure or institution may produce both manifest and latent functions at the same time.

Merton is a middle range functional analyst, giving special emphasis in much of his work to latent functions and pointing out subgroups for whom a particular cultural complex may be dysfunctional. Analysts in the conflict school have not developed the concept of function in the same thorough manner because they do not generally regard society as an integrated whole. Since society lacks this integration or equilibrium, these theorists are more inclined to regard the objective consequences of institutional complexes as fulfilling particular needs of special groups, usually an elite. However, the distinction between manifest and latent functions may be useful from this perspective as well, providing one is conscious of these restrictions. Marxists look to the elimination of the private ownership of the means of production as something which would fulfill a function for society at large. On the other hand, the prevailing ideologies in a given social system such as Canada are regarded as serving a legitimating function for the capitalist but are dysfunctional for the workers, preventing them from attaining the appropriate level of class consciousness and overthrowing the system.

**Functional For Whom?**

In any analysis of the functions of a social structure, then, it is critical to ask: functional for whom? A particular institution may provide a service or fulfill needs for society in general and at the same time be dysfunctional for specific subgroups. The control of crime may be taken as an appropriate example, professional criminals being the subgroup suffering the dysfunction. Another institution may have just the opposite effect. Tobacco smoking causes pollution and presumably health problems for society at large but serves a positive function for the farmers and entrepreneurs who grow and manufacture the product. Finally, one and the same institution such as the burning of fossil fuels may provide both functions and dysfunctions for the entire society. Merton (1968:94) has pointed out that for the functional school it is ". . . the net balance of the aggregate of consequences . . ." that largely determines societal efforts towards change. For the conflict school and particularly the Marxists the existing social structure is dysfunctional for society except as an evolutionary stage or as a means to an end. Weberians would not share this enthusiasm.

It is necessary to emphasize the importance of the idea of the net balance of the aggregate of consequences, some of which may be positive, others negative. If the net balance is positive for society at large the institution is regarded as functional, even if other undesirable consequences occur. Liberal reformers tend to recognize many institutions, on balance, as functional. Rather than change the system they then concentrate on strategies meant to reduce or eliminate the negative aspects.

Disregarding for a moment such matters as technological advances, we may say as a general rule that institutions which are perceived as being largely functional for the entire society tend to promote stability. Those which have a higher level of perceived dysfunctions tend to promote change. Of course, society is always dynamic to some degree. Change in even the smallest cultural trait tends to have repercussions which may go far beyond even that cultural complex.

We have presented here only a brief and rather superficial analysis of the theory of functions. There are still vast areas of disagreement among social scientists on this matter. Our intent is simply to present background information to be used in understanding the functions and dysfunctions of the formal institution of education for society in general and also for specific groups.

There are virtually as many different listings of the functions of schooling as there are authors who write on the subject, with advantages and disadvantages to each, as there is to our arrangement. Using Merton's distinction, we present them in two groups: those which are primarily manifest, and those which are more latent. The designation sometimes may appear arbitrary, especially for sociologists who are not sympathetic to the functional paradigm. As an example, under the function of cultural reproduction we have included the teaching of legitimating ideologies. Such ideologies, from the functionalist perspective, provide an important positive service, the promotion of integration and group solidarity. At the same time there are negative consequences for some groups. Ideologies tend to stress the ideal and overlook the inequities or injustices which may exist in reality. If one regards the positive function of integration, on balance, as being more important than the negative function of legitimating inequities for certain groups, then the teaching of such ideologies would have a positive consequence. If this is acknowledged and overt then the function is manifest. If one regards the negative aspective as paramount then the function is negative, it is dysfunctional. If this is covert and not generally recognized then the function is latent.

We present a convenient classification of the functions of schooling which, from this perspective, is somewhat arbitrary. Frequently, perhaps always, there is overlap involved. As one proceeds to finer and more specialized levels of analysis in such a taxonomy the problem becomes aggravated. At this level we would not advise the student to be too concerned with that. As we discuss each of the functions we will try to point out both positive and negative aspects.

Under the heading of the manifest function of schooling we present cognitive learning, cultural reproduction, selection and allocation, cultural production, cultural diffusion and social mobility. Each may have aspects which are both positive and negative. We consider them manifest because the consequences are generally recognized more than they are covert. Under the category of latent functions we present social control, the custodial function, the maintenance of subgroup traditions, and the promotion of critical analysis of society. Again, each may have positive and negative aspects. We consider them latent because they are more covert and unrecognized.

## The Manifest Functions of Schooling

### Cognitive Learning

General and Specialized Knowledge

It is widely recognized that one principal function of schooling is the provision of literacy, and of general and specialized knowledge beyond the level of literacy. Literacy is widely regarded as the ability to read and write in one's native language with moderate ease, and to perform basic arithmetic computations. A phrase which is becoming more commonly used today is *functional literacy*. Usually regarded as approximately the level of a good grade eight, functional literacy enables its possessor to perform or function independently in the ordinary, universally available structures of our society, particularly in accord with the demands of formal organizations and bureaucracies. One who is functionally literate can fill out bureaucratic forms such as a job application or a census questionnaire and in general perform occupational tasks, either at home or in the paid work force, at the basic level.

As we have pointed out in chapter one, basic literacy was not always provided in a school setting. In the less specialized Canadian society of a century or more ago many people learned basic literacy in the home and seldom, if ever, attended school. This still goes on in very exceptional cases today, especially for the severely handicapped. In many homes, particularly in the middle and upper classes, children begin to learn to count, to recite the alphabet, even to print before they begin school, this being one of the advantages they possess at the time of entry. However, virtually all Canadian children attend school now and it is the norm for them to continue at least through high school. It is through schooling that children learn literacy today.

There are several reasons why we use the term functional literacy. One is to attest to the fact that individuals can still attain this goal outside of the school setting. There are still many Canadians of the older generation who have done that. Another is to indicate that not all students who go on in high school, especially in the lower tracks, achieve at this level. From the point of view of mastering even the basic curriculum, schooling in Canada does not always attain its goal. Some students remain functional illiterates.

Cognitive learning in the school setting is not restricted to basic or functional literacy. In the intermediate and higher levels it is the goal of formal education to provide increasingly higher levels of both general and specialized knowledge. The high school graduate is expected to be reasonably well informed, to possess a wide variety of knowledge pertaining to many matters in our own culture and at the international level. The undergraduate university degree still largely conforms to a broad level of learning but at that point the specialized curriculum is beginning to make itself felt more strongly. The post-graduate degree, whether at the masters or doctoral level or in the various professional schools, is highly specialized.

Formal Education and Occupation

People generally regard the institution of schooling as having the responsibility of providing the student with the formal knowledge required for the occupational world. There is good reason to question the relationship between schooling and job performance (Bowles and Gintis, 1976). In fact, Berg (1970) has demonstrated that there is a slight though non significant negative correlation between educational achievement and occupational performance. Collins (1979) has an entire book which explodes the myth of the importance of more advanced formal education for job performance.

Most of the specialized functions which are performed in an occupation are learned in the early weeks and months on the job, providing the applicant brings the requisite background characteristics such as motivation. In still another article which included a broad review of the American literature on the subject, Collins (1974:420) states that ". . . most education, beyond the provision of literacy, . . . contributes little to individual productivity and . . . vocational skills are learned primarily on the job and not in school."

This is not to denigrate the substantive learning which occurs in school. It may be very valuable for any number of reasons, including one's own personal development. The point at issue is that as specialized knowledge it is not very relevant for job performance, a fact of which many Canadians are unaware. There is another important point to be made as well. Neither Collins, nor anyone else to our knowledge, has been able to demonstrate that the better educated person, the higher achiever, is not in a position to learn the skills required for job performance more quickly or more easily. It is quite possible that such workers are not more productive than their less educated co-workers for other reasons which do not pertain directly to the substantive knowledge they receive from schooling.

Overeducation-underemployment

Thurow (1972) has shown that the principal advantage of formal education in occupational selection is to open up the job ladder at a higher level. More advanced schooling, because of credentialism, allows one to enter the work force at a more prestigious level even if proficiency on the job is no greater than it is for those with a lower level of educational attainment (Berg, 1970). We have seen in chapter two that it is primarily as a result of status requirements that higher educational certification has been demanded for job acquisition in recent years (Collins, 1971).

Harvey (1974) and Harvey and Charner (1975) have been able to show that occupational opportunities for university degree holders have been deteriorating in Canada. Substitution or underemployment is the result; there is a slippage to jobs not requiring the education which has been achieved. These are lower status jobs; the more prestigious ones require higher levels of education at least for status (boundary) reasons. Canadian educational institutions are turning out so many graduates with higher credentials that the economy is simply not able to absorb them at what is considered the appropriate level. Harvey (1974) reports that his examination of university graduates in Ontario for the 1960 decade revealed that fully one-third reported their university education as not important for their occupation, with just over half reporting it as important. He also hypothesized that the occupational prestige for first jobs would show a decline during that decade. Using the Porter-Pineo Occupational Prestige Scale he found that 64.3 per cent of the 1960 graduates took first jobs which registered 60 or above on that scale. The statistic decreased to 53.9 per cent for 1968 graduates — a very substantial change.

### Education and Personal Development

The theory of the relationship between education and personal development falls within the field of the philosophy of education. It was one of the principal concerns of liberal reformer John Dewey and the Progressive Movement which was so popular early in this century. Bowles and Gintis (1976) point out that this goal — personal development — is incompatible with the integrative function of progressive liberalism.

It is largely beyond the scope of sociology to determine what personal development means, and especially what it should be. Hurn (1978) points out emphatically that there is no evidence to suggest that schools are less successful now than they have been in the past in this regard. The crisis which exists relative to the results of schooling is due to expectations which may go unfulfilled. Objectively, one of the principal functions of schooling is to pass on our culture to the young. It is assumed that a more advanced education leads to greater maturity and psychic health, but this assumption has not been demonstrated. If the cultural heritage includes a value system which is incompatible with personal development it is difficult to place the blame for this on schools. Critics of the educational establishment claim that it so frequently stifles creativity and independence (Hurn, 1978). The major problem, however, is not within the schools. If we are unable to decide among ourselves at the broader societal level what values should be passed on to the young or what the nature of our cultural values should be, then it is unwise to blame the schools for the broader societal confusion.

One of the goals of schooling, especially at the higher level, is the attainment of a capacity for critical thinking. Presumably this ability will enable the recipient to establish a personal set of values leading in the direction of self-actualization. With limited exceptions, there is little evidence that formal education has been successful in achieving this goal (Bowles and Gintis, 1976; Reich, 1976).

## Cultural Reproduction

This discussion leads quite naturally into a second manifest function of schooling: cultural reproduction. This is the socialization or enculturalization function. As Parsons (1959) has pointed out, schooling is the principal secondary socialization agency of industrial society. We are not dealing here with the responsibility of the formal education system to enlarge our cultural heritage through the development of new knowledge, but rather to pass on that value and normative system which presently exists. We live in a society which includes great inequality, perhaps much injustice due to various forms of discrimination which appear to be the norm rather than the exception. Schooling assists in passing on this value and normative system to the young.

Durkheim regarded the school as an agent of moral socialization. As such it acts on behalf of the state to instill in the student population the idealized version of society's values. The contradiction between the ideal and the pragmatic is the concern of Bowles and Gintis (1976) when they discuss the incompatibility of liberal educational goals: the integrative, eqalitarian and personal development goals.

Loyalty to Society

One of the traditional functions of schooling is to promote among the students a loyalty and respect for the existing social order (Parelius and Parelius, 1978). We have already discussed in chapter one the importance of this function in the minds of leaders involved in the evolution of schooling in Canada. It is essential for any existing society to promote integration, a uniform feeling of satisfaction and belonging held by the majority of members. Without such integration the existing society will cease to function. People will not agree on the means to achieve common goals, assuming that such goals exist. Social order would tend to disappear and anarchy would be the result until some new social arrangement promoting order came about. The functionalists view the production or reproduction of loyalty to existing society as serving this integrative function and hold that some institution or complex must fill this role. Conflict theorists tend to view the promotion of loyalty to society's major institutions as a process of legitimation. This succeeds in masking the pervasive injustice and making the existing social arrangements appear, despite their imperfections, as just and proper when in fact they are not. To promote such loyalty is to do a disservice to the majority of the people.

This function of schooling promotes the *status quo*. Liberal reformers tend to concentrate on overcoming the abuses within the existing system. At least indirectly schooling would encourage that route. Radical reformers are more interested in overthrowing the existing social order. Schooling tends to impede that. One of the principal criticisms of Bowles and Gintis (1976) is directed at their emphasis on the failures of the existing social order in the United States without indicating how a new decentralized order could exist without similar abuses.

Nevertheless, in line with this function there can be little doubt that the major institutions of society are presented, especially in the early years of schooling, in a highly idealized form (Parelius and Parelius, 1978). Haller and Thorson (1970) in the United States have shown that the social structure of the elementary school has made it quite adept at political socialization which emphasizes integration and cooperation rather than conflict. Canada is more of a mosaic than a melting pot and tends to give greater emphasis to pluralism and regionalism, but still within a spirit of cooperation (Sullivan *et al.*, 1970).

Traditional Culture: The Mazeway

The structures of society are composed of a tremendous variety of inter-related roles. These roles in turn include a stable system of responsibilities and, in the accompanying status domain, of rights. One of the functions of socialization is to instill in the newer members of society at least a general knowledge of this very large number of positions and the relationships between them, which Wallace (1956) refers to as the mazeway. Schooling is one of the principal institutions to do this, although more and more in modern times it is complemented by the media. Studies of occupational prestige such as Pineo and Porter (1973) in Canada or Hodge *et al.* (1966) on the international level demonstrate that by the time they are in their teens the younger members of society have a well-founded grasp of the occupational mazeway. They under-stand in general terms the rights and responsibilities of each of these positions, and it is not particularly difficult for them to take up one of these positions and fit easily into the entire complex of interrelationships which they have and which is required for smooth operation of the entire culture.

Assimilation of Subgroups

Canadian society is regarded as being a pluralistic one with a general acceptance of and respect for a variety of subcultures. It is commonly held that cultural differences enrich our heritage rather than detract from it. This position is somewhat different from the melting pot theme which is more generally accepted in the United States.

Society does have a basic culture which promotes a common identity. One of the functions which schooling performs is to promote this cultural identity among the children of immigrant families. As a result of this, second and especially third generation Canadians become socialized through the schools in a way which largely makes them conscious of their common identity rather than their differences. All of this is a matter of degree. The various ethnic groups such as the Scots in Nova Scotia or the Ukranians of Manitoba do hold on to many elements of their traditional ethnic heritage, but they tend to share a common Canadian identity which is more basic. We have seen in chapter one that this kind of assimilation, relative to the immigrant Irish, was one of the express goals of the early school promoters in Ontario. Whether intended or not, it continues to be a function of schooling today as it has been during the intervening years.

There is a special problem in this regard in Canada. The native Cana-dians, the Indian and Inuit people (Parry, 1977; Brant, 1977), have their own cultures which are qualitatively different from that of most Canadians. As

Brant (1977:176) has noted, schooling for Eskimo people has certain basic features which include ". . . (1) almost exclusive use of non-native teachers; (2) instruction given almost wholly in English; (3) heavy utilization of residential schools, with recent emphasis on large units; (4) curriculum very heavily oriented to the southern Canadian culture and value system." With the exception of the emphasis on residential schools the problem is similar for our Indian people. It is not difficult to appreciate the problem of marginality which such a system brings to these students. Partly as a result of this their retention rate is extremely low. As a result the Indian and Inuit population generally lack the credentials so necessary for assuming many of the more prestigious roles in the occupational structure at the same time that problems of encroachment continue to deprive them of the hunting, fishing and trapping lands required for their traditional occupational pursuits. Schooling tends to promote assimilation into a broader Canadian value system which is hardly compatible with native culture.

### Teaching Legitimating Ideologies

In a stratified society those who find themselves in a position to receive benefits which are greater than the norm have an opportunity to pass this form of privilege on to their children. As a result the rewards are not distributed solely on the basis of achievement, and there is wide disparity between them. We have already mentioned the necessity of legitimation, a process which makes this unequal distribution of rewards on an ascriptive basis appear as just and inevitable, like death and taxation. One of the most important and most successful mechanisms of legitimation is ideology. Marxists give it special emphasis, although consideration of ideologies is not restricted to them alone. We are generally familiar with and perhaps critical of the role of ideology in schools in some communist nations such as Russia (Dobson, 1977; Parelius and Parelius, 1978). This is one aspect of political socialization, and it is found in the institution of schooling in Canada as well (Rocher, 1975; Marchak, 1981).

It is in matters pertaining to legitimation and the role of ideology that we find one of the wider gaps between the functionalist and the conflict perspectives. Marxists especially see Canadian society as fundamentally unjust because of its class nature. Ideologies such as liberalism, the meritocratic perspective, equality of opportunity and democracy they regard merely as unfounded myths which support the *status quo* but perform no positive function for the workers. The functionalists regard stratification as inevitable. At most they recognize abuses and as a result generally do not call for radical reform. Liberalism tends to regard our social order as good but not too good; democracy stresses that we are free, politically and, economically. The egalitarian ideology, which is very complex, proposes equality of opportunity in our schools although many scholars such as Rocher (1975) have demonstrated that this is not so. Canadians tend to believe that ability and hard work is like the rainbow, with a rich reward at the end. While there is some truth to this for individuals, it hardly applies to groups.

Our schools promote these ideologies. They are as much a part of our culture as are the Montreal Canadiens or the Toronto Maple Leafs. Perhaps the greatest danger is that they are, to some extent, accurate. We do have civil rights to a substantial extent, even if they are frequently violated. Females are making some small progress up the occupational ladder, even if in this and many other ways they are routinely treated unequally. The child of the lower-class background can attain a Ph.D. or become a great surgeon or corporation president, even though this is the exception rather than the rule. But the routine acceptance of liberalism, democracy, egalitarianism, a meritocracy — these and other ideologies — overlooks the fact that a large number of Canadians are denied the rewards of our society on an ascriptive basis. Canada is a racist and sexist society practicing many other forms of institutionalized discrimination as well. Ideologies such as those mentioned not only overlook but deny the existence of many inequities. Schooling tends to legitimate such discrimination.

## The Selection or Allocation Function

We have already discussed the selection and allocative function of education to a substantial extent in chapter two. It would be well for the reader to review the positions of the various theorists which were presented there.

### Selection: The Functionalist View

Parsons (1959) is probably the leading spokesman for the functionalist perspective. In that view one of the principal functions of education is to prepare students for the occupational world. Schooling is an important process of socialization which bridges the gap between the particularistic and ascriptive roles of childhood and the more universalistic and achieved roles of the adult world.

Occupations, in the functionalist perspective, are ranked along a continuum of prestige. The order of ranking is rather universally shared in society. It is based on a number of factors including the importance of the role to the social network, the abundance or scarcity of alternate roles fulfilling approximately the same function, the degree of difficulty involved, and the ability and motivation demanded of the one who occupies the position (Davis and Moore, 1945).

Society socializes its newer members for occupational performance. There must be a process of selection involved because not all members are equally suited to a given occupational task. Presumably some would be quite inept. Schooling is the principal institution in industrial society to perform this selection function. Ideally, children begin school with equal internal or institutional opportunity; they are treated fairly and different rates of achievement are the result of different abilities and motivation. Some do better or advance farther in the system than others, although the schools themselves reputedly offer equal opportunity to all. Those who achieve at a higher rate are selected to advance to a higher level and eventually to transfer to the more prestigious occupations in the world of work (Parsons, 1959).

It is in the area of equality of opportunity that this presentation tends to break down. Most social scientists will agree that when they begin school children have different abilities and even that there is a genetic basis to some of these differences. There is a social basis to the differences as well. On the other hand, a large number of sociologists, probably the majority, hold that children of equal ability and motivation are not treated equally in school. Ascriptive factors such as social class, race, ethnicity, sex and even physical characteristics and appearance are the basis of differential treatment. The theme of equality of opportunity breaks down and is replaced by inequality, the result of preferential treatment given on an ascribed basis.

This unequal treatment, critics claim, is institutionalized. It is systemic and not necessarily based on conscious or intended discrimination on the part of teachers and other school officials. Whatever the case, the school is not a meritocracy as functionalists claim. The ideal of equality of opportunity has not been achieved.

Allocation: The Conflict Perspective

Adult roles in the occupational world command different ranges of power, privilege and prestige. There is inequality of condition (Clement, 1975) among those exercising these roles with some individuals possessing greater and different kinds of power than others. United in groups on the basis of communal action — classes in Marxist theory, status groups for Weberians — these groups impose on society's institutions restrictions which result in special privileges for themselves. As a result of this, inequality of opportunity is the normal condition in the institution of schooling.

Educational institutions allocate students on the basis of this inequality of condition to different levels of the occupational world. The schools are institutions which systematically favor the more privileged groups. This preference is hidden by a variety of mechanisms, especially I.Q. testing and tracking. Those who are destined for lower level and primarily dead-end roles in the world of work are taught, through the hidden curriculum, a set of personality characteristics which ensure that they fulfill the roles without causing undue strain. Principal among these characteristics are a respect for authority and de-emphasis on creative thinking and action. The students who are allocated to positions in this level do not do well in school, not usually because of lack of ability but for other systematic social reasons. These include a diminished respect for schooling, alienation and discrimination.

Other students are allocated to intermediate levels of the work force where a different set of personality characteristics is required. This includes ". . . dependability and the capacity to operate without direct and continuous supervision . . " (Bowles and Gintis, 1976:132). They are passed on in the intermediate range of schooling, especially community colleges and most undergraduate universities, and include a respect for the existing system of social relations with the appropriate class or status distinctions.

The third level of schooling at the elite private schools and universities and in graduate schools teaches students to internalize the goals of the capitalist system. In the work force at the higher level, these graduates do not work only for external rewards such as salary but also because as individuals they identify with and share in the goals of the firm, especially profit maximization and preservation of the existing class system.

The allocation system does not work perfectly but instead in a rather universal but general way. There are individual exceptions. The small number who become substantially upwardly mobile, reaching the top managerial or owner levels, have nevertheless internalized the appropriate personality characteristics. A limited amount of such mobility is required because the upper classes do not fully reproduce themselves.

This entire process, which Bowles and Gintis (1976) refer to as the correspondence principle, is well hidden. There are screening devices such as testing, counseling and tracking which make the systematic discrimination appear as if it were a meritocracy based on ability and motivation.

**Cultural Production**

The function of cultural production refers to the fact that much of the *new* knowledge which is produced in an organized way in our society comes from the institutions of higher education. We are perhaps more conscious of technological innovation when we think of this new body of knowledge, but our consideration here goes far beyond that, including the social sciences and humanities, business techniques and the arts.

University professors have as one part of their responsibilities the development of new knowledge through research. There were 32,600 teachers in 65 universities in Canada in 1978-79 (Statistics Canada, 1980a). A significant proportion of these men and women are involved in original research on either a full-time or part-time basis. Frequently, engagement in such work is one criterion for tenure and for promotion in rank.

There is, of course, much research done in private industry as well, especially in the area of the physical sciences. The engineers and scientists who are occupied in this way have usually been trained in graduate schools and participated in research there earlier. One of the requirements for the Ph.D. degree is the dissertation, supposedly an original piece of research through which the candidate demonstrates his professional ability to the satisfaction of his peers.

Much university research is paid for or sponsored by one level of government or another. This may be done in a number of ways. The state, through one of its agencies, may contract out a research project to a university professor or department. Alternatively, individual projects may be submitted to government sponsoring agencies such as the National Research Council or the Social Sciences and Humanities Research Council for approval and financial support.

There may be a problem of bias in the selection of such projects. Governments are usually conservative institutions and it is likely that they will approve or fund projects primarily when they are supportive of the *status quo* or prevailing system of power relations. As a result they have an important influence on the selective process through which one kind of new knowledge, as opposed to another, is developed. However, recent research in the United States (Useem, 1976) indicates the government's principal purpose in funding such studies, at least in the social sciences, is to acquire policy-relevant research. Its purpose is not to enhance the legitimacy of the government. Policy-relevant research may be expected to be partially restricted to specific areas in which the government has a special interest.

There have been tremendous breakthroughs in technology in the past generation, particularly since the beginning of the space race. University researchers, whether hired by government or industry, have been responsible for much of the scientific discoveries which have led to this great technological growth.

### Cultural Diffusion

Much of the new knowledge which is developed through research is disseminated to the public through schools and universities. Professors write up their research projects in learned journals and, less frequently, in books. These articles are usually technical in nature and are interpreted and simplified for students and the public. This second level presentation is frequently made by other university professors. We have gone through literally thousands of articles and books in the preparation of this text, most of them published in journals quite recently.

Again there is the possibility of control being exercised in the dissemination of such knowledge. Universities themselves are frequently somewhat conservative. This is so for a proportion of the professors as well. There is the possibility that a textbook is more likely to be adopted in the schools and colleges if it tends to avoid controversial topics, especially those that may appear threatening to the *status quo.*

## Social Mobility

When dealing with the selection or allocation function of schooling it was pointed out that the mobility which occurs through schooling is generally, though not always, restricted to a narrow range. It is important to make a distinction between *individual* mobility and *group* mobility. We may see, or have pointed out to us, rather sensational cases of individual mobility. This would be the case when the son of a working-class family becomes a major executive in a large corporation, or a daughter comes to hold a cabinet post or, is as yet to happen in Canada, becomes the Prime Minister. Most of the individual mobility which occurs in our society is within a rather narrow range such as from working class to lower middle or middle-class level (Hurst, 1979). Moreover, at least in the United States, there has been no significant increase in mobility in the past 50 years (Vanfossen, 1979), and there is no indication that the situation is different in Canada despite the prevalence of educational inflation. There is very little group mobility, on a class basis, provided through the educational system. There may be such mobility for certain minorities or ethnic groups and there usually is when some ethnic groups become assimilated (Richmond, 1973). There has been no substantial collective mobility for Blacks in Canada, for our native people, or for females. In these cases the exception usually 'proves' the rule.

In industrial society there is also a measure of *structural* mobility. This is due to the upgrading of the occupational structure as more and more lower level jobs are dropped off the job ladder and replaced by more technically sophisticated roles. Education almost certainly contributes to this mobility by assisting in developing the higher levels of technology which upgrade the occupational structure. There is also *circulation* mobility, that which exists and is independent of structural mobility (Jackson and Crocket, 1964), and is more generally individual in character.

Over the past several generations there has been substantial mobility within the Canadian occupational structure with the result that the overall average level of prestige is greater now than it had been 40 years ago. This is the result primarily of structured mobility, an upgrading of the entire occupational force. There is no evidence of a lessening of the inequality gap.

Individual mobility may be intergenerational or intragenerational. Intergenerational mobility refers to the position of a person of one generation relative to the preceding one, usually a son relative to the father. Intragenerational mobility refers to the mobility within the career of one individual, from the time of his entering the work force until he reaches his highest peak.

Most intergenerational mobility is between neighbouring status positions; rarely does it include a large jump. Despite the tremendous educational inflation which has occurred in the past 30 years in Canada, the occupation of the father is still the best predictor of the status of the son. This is because educational attainment has increased proportionately for all classes or status groups. The less prestigious groups have, at most, kept pace. They have not really narrowed the gap.

Mobility studies have traditionally concentrated on males, comparing the position of a son to that of his father. There has been little integrated research done on mobility of females or the role that education plays. With the increasing emphasis being given to studies about women in the recent past, more studies on female mobility may be expected. The class position of women in Canadian society is more complicated than it is for men. Our normative system assigns females to a greater extent than males a class position which is partially determined by the position of their spouses. Moreover, partly because they are considered second earners, females are paid substantially less than males even within the same occupation and with the same education (Chekki and Hofley, 1980). Women tend to have higher education than men, up to but not including the graduate level where they are greatly underrepresented (Boocock, 1980).

Despite these restrictions, we will see in the next chapter that education is the single most important factor contributing to intergenerational circulation mobility. While the position of groups, especially classes or status groups, is not generally improving, the position of many individuals is; education is the principal contributing factor.

## The Latent Functions of Schooling

It has already been mentioned that the distinction between manifest and latent functions is somewhat a matter of degree or emphasis, and there is frequently overlap. In our discussion of the manifest functions of schooling we chose to include those which were more generally recognized by the state itself, by the educational institution and by the clients.

The latent functions, with which we shall deal briefly now, are less fully recognized by the entire network or group involved. They may be very useful, at least for certain groups, but they are not really the functions for which the institution of schooling was openly and consciously established and/or accepted by the general population. They are frequently fulfilled through what is often referred to as the *hidden curriculum*, a term which points to their latent characteristic.

**Social Control**

We have already referred to this function frequently, especially in the first two chapters. Social control refers to the practice of imposing on less privileged groups (classes, status groups, gender groups) the type of restrictions and life styles which smoothly and easily ratifies the prevailing stratification system. It is not merely a question of preventing or controlling deviant behaviour in some sense in which that may be objectively defined. It includes the idea that the criterion for deviance is *imposed*. The value system supports the *status quo*, and social control ratifies that system of values. It controls the behaviour of subgroups in the established system, forcing or determining that they act in accord with an imposed set of values.

The Learning of Appropriate Behaviour

Schooling, through the hidden curriculum, teaches and imposes on different classes or status groups and on minority groups the kind of behaviour and aspirations which are deemed appropriate, as defined by elites, to continue or replicate the prevailing system of privilege. The correspondence principle, suggested by Bowles and Gintis and discussed earlier in the section dealing with the allocative function, is an example of social control. Those destined to lower level occupational slots and therefore to lower or intermediate status groups or classes are covertly taught or trained in the appropriate life style and behaviour. The same holds true for sex-stereotyping. Females are covertly taught to follow a life style which is regarded as being naturally sex-related when in fact it is not. This serves the function of preserving male dominance.

Programming for Failure

We have already discussed most of what is generally understood by this subheading. We saw, when presenting the selection or allocative function, that some students are 'set back' or impeded from attaining adequate grades on the basis of insufficient ability. These become dropouts or are directed into less prestigious terminal tracks which do not give the credential necessary for advancing at the post-secondary or university level.

The same phenomenon occurs at the community college level (Clark, 1960; Pincus, 1978). About two-thirds of the students in American community colleges, half of them against their will, are counseled out of the academic track and so are unable to transfer to a regular university. Such selection also takes place in Canada.

At the lower level of schooling some students are held back, or let through but with a record that tends to reduce the expectations of subsequent teachers, and alienates the student or gives him a lower self-concept of ability. At the secondary level and also in community colleges many students are relegated to tracks which exclude them from many occupations, especially those in the top half of the prestige continuum. All of this occurs despite the assertion of Bowles and Gintis (1976) that intelligence is not a scarce commodity, and the demonstration by Berg (1970) that there is no correlation between educational achievement and occupational performance. By virtue of being denied more advanced academic attainment, these students who have been programmed for failure are denied the credentials required for mobility.

## Custodial Institutions

There were approximately 5.9 million students in elementary and secondary schools in Canada in 1978-79. Most of these are under the age of 16. The 1981 census will probably show a decrease in number because of changes in the population pyramid.

Both parents of a substantial number of these children are in the labour force. Almost 40 per cent of married women in Canada work outside the home today (Nett, 1980). The care of the school children is taken out of their hands five days a week for ten months of the year, leaving them more free to engage in their work or other pursuits and saving them from making arrangements (frequently with pay) for a baby sitter.

This, of course, is very convenient for the parents. One event which only occasionally takes place in our society and which helps us to understand the magnitude of this convenience is a teachers' strike. We can observe, in our own homes or among our neighbours, the frantic arrangements being made to replace this custodial service at such a time.

The more advanced level of schooling, particularly at the post-secondary level, serves another function which we have not set aside in a separate way. It is a forum for the selection of marriage partners. In a stratified society young people tend to marry within their own class or status group. Colleges and universities provide an appropriate and large sample of potential marriage partners with similar social class backgrounds. These are mostly in the middle-class range relative to family of origin and especially family of destination. The children of elite families encounter this marriage mart at the private schools and elite universities.

## Maintaining Subgroup Traditions

At the elementary level in the larger communities the student body tends to be homogeneous in nature because of the common neighbourhood background. Here, and also in schools which have a particular religious or ethnic affiliation, it is possible to give more emphasis to subcultural characteristics. This is more the case when such characteristics are regarded as being in addition to rather than in opposition to the national culture. Thus Catholic schools stress the Catholic identity. In Nova Scotia the Acadian population is scattered in many geographically dispersed areas. Through the schools the Acadian subculture may be strengthened, as the francophone subculture is emphasized in isolated areas in other parts of Canada, or the anglophone culture in many areas of Quebec. Eastern European cultures are often reflected in the schools of the prairie provinces.

Canada is regarded as being a pluralist society. We must be careful in carrying this assessment too far. We saw, when dealing with the function of cultural reproduction, that our schools stress loyalty to society and that they have an assimilation function. The element of pluralism only goes so far. Native people in Canada, both Indian and Inuit, are one example of a subgroup which has had considerable difficulty in maintaining its subgroup traditions and schooling is responsible to a considerable extent (Brant, 1977). As a general rule we may say that pluralism is tolerated, perhaps even encouraged, in Canada up to a degree. But there is also an attempt to identify a national culture, and the schools assist in this.

**Promotion of Critical Analysis**

Inevitability of Change

Change is an ongoing phenomenon in every society. It comes about in many ways: advances in technology, a different value emphasis — even an imposition by external groups. We hardly need to give examples of the tremendous changes wrought in Canadian society as a result of technological advances during this century. A recent emphasis on the companionship characteristic has changed our marriage pattern considerably, delaying or preventing births, and increasing the number of divorces (Nett, 1980). The Second Vatican Council of the Catholic Church has caused tremendous change in that organization and much of it has found its way into Canada. Ecumenism and religious tolerance is but one example. Change is often difficult for those who live through it, particularly those who as adults see its initiation.

Challenging the Establishment

Those who are in control of major institutions are frequently reluctant to change. One of the functions performed by higher education is that of providing a critical analysis of existing institutions (Parelius and Parelius, 1978). Academics, as we indicated earlier, do much research and some of this explodes existing myths and ideologies. When the results become public the existing institutions must re-examine themselves in the light of public demand. Two examples which come to mind immediately are social policies dealing with the rights of the poor and of women. Much of this is the result of challenges which were issued by academics, especially women in the latter case.

Change, of course, may be real, or it may be cosmetic. While most Canadians are much more conscious today of the rights of women and the inequality they traditionally have borne, except in isolated cases the changes which have taken place to date are more token than real. Males are still the great majority in graduate schools, and females in the Canadian work force remain greatly underrepresented in the more prestigious occupations, and underpaid in virtually all occupational positions.

## Promotion of Centers for Ferment

A function which schooling sometimes fulfills, especially at the college and university level, is often referred to as student unrest. Young people tend to be idealists and frequently become organized at a rudimentary level to promote reform. Occasionally such organization may take on national proportions. Post-secondary students in the United States played an important role in bringing to an end the Viet Nam War, and also in the promotion of civil rights for minority groups, especially Blacks (Miles, 1977).

This concludes our presentation on the functions of the institution of schooling. Again, we ask the reader to bear in mind that the arrangement is somewhat arbitrary. There is considerable overlap not only between the major categories, the manifest and latent functions, but also between the more specialized functions indicated within each of these categories. The distinctions sometimes are as much analytical as real. The presentation necessarily has been general and brief. There is a great deal of literature available on any one of these functions, and scholars are far from being unanimous in their presentations concerning specific details.

# 11

# *Educational Achievement and Economic Success*

## Controlling The Results Of Schooling

In this chapter we are concerned primarily with the relationship between education and earnings. There is a vast spread in the income distribution in Canada and other industrialized nations. The lowest 20 per cent of income recipients in this nation received 4.1 per cent of total income in 1976, only one-fifth of the share they would receive if it were distributed evenly. The highest quintile received 43.4 per cent of income, a little more than ten times the average share of those in that lower group (Caskie, 1979). There is much variance in lifetime earnings among adults. Here we are interested in investigating two questions: (1) What are the principal causes of the variance in earnings (frequently referred to as economic success), and (2) What unique contribution does education make to this variance? Education in this case is treated as an independent variable.

### Schooling: An Open or Closed System

Brookover and Erickson (1975) speak of the boundaries of an institution, and specifically of the institution of schooling. Boundaries refer to the barriers to interaction and control which exist between a given institution — in this case the school — and its environment, especially the social environment. Boundaries may fall along a continuum that goes from being relatively closed to extremely open. In a closed system there is very little interaction with external social forces. The institution is rather autonomous and tends to control itself. Obviously no system is completely closed. Each one is dependent to some extent on external cultural factors. It is a matter of degree. An open system is one in which the institution is dependent to a high degree on external factors. It has less autonomy, less control and so is not in a strong position to formulate its own policies, or even to carry out policies without some outside input.

It is apparent that the formal education system in Canada is a relatively open one. Schooling is influenced considerably by such external factors as family value systems, religion, sex stratification, social class and the economy. Much of this comes about indirectly. One institution which is particularly influential in a more direct way is the state. In Canada, to a very large degree, even in the case of higher education, it builds the schools, pays the employers from the highest level down, decides the curriculum, determines the specific organization and the tracks, makes the laws and in general determines the nature of the structure. The state includes the government but is not restricted to it. Also included are the civil service, the administrative offices, the judiciary, the police and military forces and the subcentral governments, both provincial and municipal (Kopinak, 1980).

### The Influence of the State

It is important to be aware of this pervasive influence of the state which establishes the social policy relative to schooling. But there remains the important consideration of understanding whether the state itself is an open or closed system. The functionalist perspective, while viewing all the parts of a social system as interdependent, would nevertheless see the state as relatively autonomous. Marxists, on the other hand, regard the state as being very much dependent on the economy and subservient to it. Those who own the means of production control the state. In practical terms the state is an institution which engenders an environment which is favorable to the capitalist or bourgeois class. The principal interests of that class are the security of their class position, and profit maximization. Security of class position is ensured by the process of legitimation which calls for respect for the prevailing invidious distinctions, by the perpetuation of supportive ideologies, and by legal, police and military institutions which control any attempt to overthrow the system by force or other illegal means. Profit maximization calls for a number of supportive strategies within the society such as a favorable tax system, the absorption of surplus, an emphasis on consumption and similar factors.

One function which the state fulfills relative to schooling, and which is particularly important from this point of view, is allocation. This refers not only to the placement of individuals in specific categories of the occupational system but to the allocation of people on a collective basis (see chapter 10). In this way there is balance within the work force. A sufficient number of people are designated or allocated to the appropriate level of the occupational system so that the manpower needs of the economy may be met. We have already pointed out that this is done largely through mechanisms such as tracking and community colleges. If there is an oversupply of people for one area of the economy or one occupation the state gradually withdraws support from the branch of the education system dealing with that group. In recent years in Canada there has been a surplus of teachers. Some provincial governments have placed a quota system on teacher training institutions as a result. Any students accepted in provincial institutions beyond the quota do not qualify for the supportive grant. The important factor here is not so much that the number of teachers is controlled but that the potential surplus is shuttled to some other area of the occupational structure, in many cases a less prestigious one. Thus the manpower needs of the capitalist system are maintained.[1]

In meeting this allocative function schooling is very much influenced by the economy: in Canada, the capitalist system. This influence is, or appears to be, largely indirect. This is the case for many other external social forces as well. When we are investigating the relationship between education and earnings we must bear this in mind. Though an independent or causal variable in this particular relationship, schooling as an open system is itself dependent on many other institutional forces. They affect not only the organization of schooling but the results in later life as well.

## Educational Attainment and Economic Success

Education is generally regarded as a desirable or valued commodity in Canadian life. The human capital theory which, as we noted earlier, has fallen into disrepute, stresses that formal education provides the skills and training which enhance one's earning ability. Most Canadians probably accept this statement as being generally accurate. They hold that higher educational attainment, on its own merit, will substantially increase one's lifetime earnings. In this case schooling is an instrumental goal, a means to an end, leading supposedly to higher economic success. Recent empirical findings in the United States have seriously challenged this position (Berg, 1970). They indicate little or no relationship between education and job performance or productivity. What this is saying really is that when people with different educational levels have the same job those with the lower education perform just as well as or a little bit better than those who have a higher level of schooling or who at the same level have higher grades.

Samuel Bowles and Herbert Gintis (1973, 1976) have shed considerable light on the nature of the variables which are important for economic success or lifetime earnings. Their main concern was in establishing the relative unimportance of measured intelligence. The Bowles and Gintis data are for white

---

[1]Such quota imposition can turn out to be dysfunctional. Alberta universities cut back on acceptances of teacher education applicants in 1977. In 1981, there were fewer than 500 graduates of teacher education programs, whereas the province needed more than 1900 teachers, due to both employment shifts and policy change regarding teacher-student ratio.

males in the United States between the ages of 25 to 34 who are in the experienced labour force. The reader should bear this in mind when considering the results of their analysis. While the sample is restricted to this group, from our point of view generalization to the entire adult white male population is not unreasonable, although it will almost certainly include some inaccuracies. The 25 to 34 age group has one advantage. It includes and is restricted to that segment of the population which was exposed to the period of educational inflation of the past several decades. Christopher Jencks (1972, 1979) and his colleagues in research have to a considerable extent corroborated these findings. We will discuss these studies now. In keeping with the format presented earlier we shall first provide a brief, low level and general explanation of the statistical reasoning on which this research is based, for the sake of the reader who has little or no background in statistics.

## The Bowles and Gintis Equation

### The Meaning of Correlation

We noted briefly in chapter three that a correlation indicates the strength of relationship between two variables. The best way to understand this relationship is to view it as having a mutual influence or overlapping factor so that change in one variable (for a group) will produce change in the other. There are many kinds, but we will restrict our discussion to the Pearson correlation coefficient, symbolized r. This in turn may be of two types, either a simple or zero order correlation, or a partial correlation.

A *zero order* correlation establishes the strength of relationship between two variables without any controls. It examines the relationship of two variables to determine if they vary systematically. Bowles and Gintis (1973) report a correlation of .55 between social class background and economic success (earnings). Remember: a correlation varies from zero (no relationship) to one (a perfect relationship). The sign (positive or negative) has no meaning as far as the strength of the relationship is concerned. The sign is concerned only with the direction. If the sign is positive then as one variable increases so does the other; or as one decreases so does the other. If the sign is negative then as one variable increases the other decreases, or vice versa. Remember too that we deal with a group, not with an individual. For a group, as you raise the level of social class background you would also have an increase in the lifetime earnings. This does not necessarily follow for a given individual within the collectivity.

The zero order correlation does not give any indication of how important the independent variable, in this case social class background, is all by itself. Much of its influence may be because it is an intervening variable; the effect of some other variable may be working through this one. Social class background contributes to higher earnings partly because people of the higher classes get more education. Part of the influence of social class background is because of education, but the zero order correlation, in this case .55, does not tell us that. It includes the influence of education, and of other important variables as well.

For that reason a simple correlation may be quite deceiving. It indicates a relationship but does not single out other variables which may cause the relationship. In fact, when these other causal relationships are separated out the unique relationship may virtually disappear (because the other causal variables explain most of the variance).

One way to separate out the influence of other variables is by using partial correlations. A *partial* correlation is a kind of residual relationship. It indicates the relationship (which is left, which remains) between two variables after other designated variables have explained all the variance in the relationship which they can. Bowles and Gintis (1973) note that economic success (ES) is some function of or is dependent upon measured intelligence (I.Q.), social class background (SES), and years of schooling (YoS). We could write a simple equation:

$$ES = I.Q. + SES + YoS$$

where it is understood that the influence of each independent variable (on the right hand side) may not be the same. The partial correlation between ES and any one of the three independent variables is the strength of relationship which remains after the other two independent variables have explained all they can. For the sake of clarity let us number these variables: ES(1), I.Q.(2), SES(3) and YoS(4). Now when we are talking about the partial correlation between economic success (ES) and social class background (SES) (variables 1 and 3) we mean the strength of relationship which *remains* after I.Q. and YoS (variables 2 and 4) have explained all of the variance they can. This is valuable information. The partial correlation reduces to .45 which is somewhat smaller than the zero order correlation of .55. "The partial correlation is a measure of the amount of variation explained by one independent variable after the others have explained all they could" (Blalock, 1960:345).

We write the partial correlation by using numerical subscripts separated by a dot or period. The subscripts to the left of the dot point out the variables about which we are indicating the relationship. The subscripts to the right point out the variables which we control or hold constant. The partial correlation for ES(1) and SES(3) when controlling for I.Q. (2) and YoS(4) would thus be written $r_{13.24}$. It tells us the strength of relationship between economic success and social class background which remains when intelligence and education have explained all they can. If there is one control variable (thus one numerical subscript to the right of the dot) we refer to it as a first order partial correlation. If there are two control numbers it is called a second order correlation, and so on.

If we square the value of the correlation the result indicates the percentage of the variance explained by this variable. It is not always immediately apparent which is the independent variable. Only the theory with which we are dealing can tell us that. If we square the zero order correlation ($r = .55$) between social class background and economic success the result (.30) indicates that 30 per cent of the variance in lifetime earnings is the result of or explained by social class background either as an independent or intervening variable. If we square the value of the partial correlation ($r_{13.24} = .45$) the result (.20) tells us that 20 per cent of the variance in lifetime earnings is explained by social class background as an independent or intervening variable after the effects of measured intelligence and years of schooling (but only these) have been eliminated.

The Meaning of Regression

Regression analysis is very similar to the use of partial correlations. Returning to the Bowles and Gintis equation used above (ES = I.Q. + SES + YoS) we could determine partial correlations for each of the three independent variables. Each partial correlation would indicate the strength of relationship between economic success and one of the independent variables after the effect of the other two independent variables had been eliminated. While the mathematics (with which we are not concerned) and the terminology are somewhat different, that is part of what regression analysis does. Actually it gives us two very useful pieces of information. It will give us a multiple correlation (symbolized R) which indicates the strength of relationship between the dependent variable (economic success) and the three independent variables (I.Q., SES, YoS) taken together. If we square the multiple correlation (R) the result ($R^2$) indicates that of the total variance (100 per cent) which is explained by the independent variables in our equation. It is very useful to know that. It is not likely that these three independent variables explain all the variance so we want to know, by use of the $R^2$, how much they do explain. Let us say that for our equation $R^2$ equals .40. this would mean that 40 per cent of the variance in lifetime earnings would be explained by these three variables (I.Q., SES and YoS). The remainder, 60 per cent, would be explained by other independent variables not included in our equation (such as luck), and by measurement error.

The first thing that regression analysis does, then, is to indicate how much of the variance in the dependent variable is caused or explained by all of the independent variables in the equation taken together. Regression analysis is used a great deal in sociology. Whenever we encounter it the first thing we should do is determine the value of $R^2$ so we will know what percentage of the variance we are dealing with. If it is very small then that informs us that these are not very important variables.

The second thing that regression does is indicate the *unique* contribution which is made by each independent variable in the equation. We refer to the statistic which gives us this information as the *beta weight* or standardized regression coefficient. The beta weight is not quite the same but very similar to the partial correlation. Remember that the partial correlation we used earlier in our example eliminated the influence of the other independent variables and indicated the unique influence of this one independent variable. The beta weight does the same thing.

Let us return to the Bowles and Gintis equation: ES = I.Q. + SES + YoS. Actually that equation is a little bit of an oversimplification. It tells us that economic success (ES) is some function of each of the three independent variables. We can rewrite the equation using f to indicate function.

$$ES = f_2(I.Q.) + f_3(SES) = f_4(YoS)$$

Since each f has a different value, we used the numerical subscripts to avoid confusion. When regression analysis was being developed, instead of using f (which already had a special meaning: function) the originators used B which stands for the nonstandardized coefficient. Substituting B for f our equation now becomes

$$ES = B_2 IQ + B_3 SES + B_4 YoS$$

Each B has a subscript because each one is different. But each one is simply a constant (such as 1.42 or 0.39) which is used to multiply the scores of the independent variables so that they will cumulatively equal the value of the dependent variable, and each will have its appropriate weight. Thus we often refer to a coefficient as a weight; a different weight is given to each variable.

Let us take a practical example. Suppose we administered a questionnaire to the fathers of all the students in a college or university. In the questionnaire we asked for information on all the variables we could think of which would help to explain why these men had differences (variance) in lifetime earnings. We put all of the results on the computer. After some preliminary analysis we were able to determine that the most influential variables were measured intelligence (I.Q.), social class background (SES) and educational attainment or years of schooling (YoS).

We now have information (in dollars) on the different earnings of all of these men. We also have information (in I.Q. points) on the measured intelligence of each, on the social class background (in units of class from 1 to 5) and on the number of years of schooling (in units of years). Comparing them is like comparing apples, oranges, lemons and grapes. Because they are not the same (they are nonstandardized) it is difficult or impossible to compare them. That is a problem in our equation with the B coefficients. They are not standardized or comparable. In our equation we have dollar units, I.Q. units, SES units and YoS units, all of which are different. So if the B coefficient for SES ($B_3$) were the same size as the B coefficients for YoS ($B_4$) it would not have the same meaning. It would only have the same meaning if they were standardized. Fortunately there is a mathematical formula for doing this. We will not be concerned with the formula. The computer does the standardizing for us. But it is very important for us to understand what the meaning of standardization is: these coefficients are now expressed in the same units, no longer dollars, I.Q. units, SES units or years, but standard deviation units, and they are comparable. We write them using the Greek letter *beta,* written and again we use the subscripts. Our equation[2] now becomes:

$$ES = B_2IQ + B_3SES + B_4YoS$$

Each of these beta weights indicates ". . . how much change in the dependent variable is produced by a standardized change in one of the independent variables when the others are controlled" (Blalock, 1960:345). The difference in the size of the beta weights indicates the different importance of each independent variable. If the beta is small the variable is relatively unimportant.

In summary, the second very useful information regression analysis offers is an indication of the unique importance of each independent variable in causing change or variance in the dependent variable, i.e., when the other independent variables are controlled. This is similar to but not identical with the partial correlation.

This description of correlation and regression analysis should suffice to enable the reader to make sense out of the remainder of this chapter and related literature. We have concentrated on what these statistics do, rather than on the underlying mathematics. Further study would be necessary for one who wishes to use them as research tools.

Empirical Findings

In their 1973 article "I.Q. in the U.S. Class Structure" Bowles and Gintis present the simple or zero order correlations between the dependent variable, economic success, and each of the three independent variables of the equation. These correlations are: .52 for I.Q.; .55 for SES; and .63 for YoS. They construct probability tables in deciles for each of the three relationships with the dependent variable. They then present similar probability tables for the beta weights of the variables taken from the standardized regression equation:[3]

$$ES = .13I.Q. + .46SES + .56YoS$$

The first thing to note is the difference in the size of the zero order correlations and the beta weights. I.Q. drops from r = .52 to Beta = .13; SES

---

[2]We have deliberately omitted discussion of the intercept, holding that it is not important at this level.

[3]Again we have omitted the intercept for simplicity. We simply construct this equation from the betas presented in the tables.

drops from r = .55 to Beta = .46; and YoS drops from r = .63 to Beta = .56.

The Independent Contribution of I.Q.

The beta weight .13 for I.Q. is quite small, almost but not quite insignificant, and very much smaller than the correlation of .52. The beta indicates the unique contribution of I.Q.. A change of one standard deviation in I.Q. will produce a change of .13 standard deviation in earnings if SES and YoS are held constant. The correlation includes some of the contribution of the two other variables; it is deceiving, for that reason. Based on this correlation, a person who was in the lowest 10 per cent (decile) in adult I.Q. would have 6 chances out of 1000 of being in the highest decile in lifetime earnings, not a very high probability. Conversely, the person in the highest decile in adult I.Q. would have 309 chances out of 1000 of being in the highest 10 per cent in lifetime earnings, a very high chance indeed.

When these authors construct a similar probability table based on the I.Q. beta weight (.13) these probabilities are changed tremendously. Now it becomes apparent that for people who have the same social class background and the same education, adult I.Q. becomes much less important. In that case a person who is in the lowest 10 per cent in I.Q. would have 66 chances out of 1000 of being in the highest decile of earnings. (If I.Q. had no relationship, each person in a decile would have one chance out of 10, or 100 out of 1000). A person in the highest decile of I.Q. would have 141 chances out of 1000 of being in the top 10 per cent of earnings. This informs us that adult I.Q. in itself is relatively unimportant for economic success, although it has some importance, especially at the extreme levels. But we also know (from the zero order correlation or the probability table based on it) that those who have high I.Q.'s have a much higher chance than normal of being very successful financially, *but mostly for some reason other than intelligence.* One does not have to be smart to be rich!

It is for this reason that Bowles and Gintis are so severely critical of liberals and environmentalists in the heredity-environment I.Q. debate. These people, they claim, miss the point that I.Q. in itself is relatively unimportant and that the high degree of importance it is generally assigned because of the simple correlation is deceiving. For the same reason they are critical of policies favoring ability grouping, tracking, assignments to community colleges and anything else which determines (without the individual freely or maturely choosing it) that educational achievement will not be high or necessarily will be terminated at a specific level. As we pointed out in chapter two, these authors demonstrate with data such as this that the principal function of education is allocation along class lines. It provides credentials (Collins, 1979) which open up the job market selectively (Thurow, 1977) even though the people with those credentials do not produce more effectively on the job (Berg,

1970). Moreover, the intelligence required to master the curriculum in the system of formal education is not scarce (Bowles and Gintis, 1976). It is the influence of other variables such as motivation, self-concept and aspirations, which are related to social class, which make it difficult for the person of lower I.Q. (within the normal range) to succeed in school. It is other variables such as credentials, personality characteristics and access to career ladders which make it difficult for that same person to succeed in the world of work.

### The Independent Contribution of Social Class

Family background or social class of origin is the second most important variable in the equation. Its zero order correlation with economic success is relatively high, .55 and the beta weight drops only to .46, still rather high. A change of one standard deviation in social class will produce a change of .46 standard deviation in earnings if I.Q. and YoS remain constant. This tells us that regardless of adult I.Q. and no matter what level of schooling is attained, a person of favorable class background has a much higher chance than average of having high lifetime earnings. Bowles and Gintis (1973) present similar probability tables for the correlation and beta relationships between this variable and economic success. The table based on the beta weight of .46 indicates that a person in the lowest decile in social class background has 11 chances out of 1000 of being in the top 10 per cent in earnings, while a person in the top decile has 277 chances out of 1000. These probabilities apply independently of I.Q. and educational level. Social class background is an ascriptive variable, but it brings tremendous advantages relative to financial success in life which are different from or over and above ability (as measured by I.Q.) and education. There are many such advantages depending on social class, including health, aspirations, teacher expectations, exposure to printed material such as magazines at an early age, self-concept and money — to mention but a few. The important point where equality of opportunity is concerned is that they are partially denied to people of lesser class origins.

### The Independent Contribution of Education

Of the three independent variables in the equation, the number of years of education (YoS) has the greatest unique influence on lifetime earnings, with a beta weight of .56. The zero order correlation is .63. This means that educational attainment explains 40 per cent of the variance in lifetime earnings, either because of the education itself including the credential, or because of the influence of other variables which work through it. This latter or indirect influence is relatively small as far as I.Q. and family background are concerned because the beta weight is nearly as large as the correlation. No matter what ability (I.Q.) a person has and regardless of class of origin, the single most important variable influencing lifetime earnings is educational attainment. Stated in another way, an increase of one standard unit (not one year) of education will result in an increase of .56 standard units of lifetime earnings for people of the same measured intelligence and family background.

When Bowles and Gintis (1973) convert this relationship into a probability table based on the appropriate beta weight, then we are informed that a person in the top decile of education has 332 chances out of 1000 of being in the top decile in lifetime earnings. A person in the lowest 10 per cent of educational attainment has only 4 chances out of 1000 of being in the top decile of earnings. When we consider that this is for people of similar ability and background then the importance of education is truly remarkable.

At this point we should repeat the findings of Berg (1970) that people with higher education do not perform better on the job than those with lower education who have the same occupation. This leads to the conclusion, or at least the assumption, that economic success or future earnings is not the result of the cognitive content of advanced schooling, but of some other aspect included in educational attainment. Long before these empirical findings were published sociologists were investigating important related matters such as the hidden curriculum, credentialism, modes of self-presentation and personality characteristics. These were associated with schooling or educational attainment and it was felt that they were important factors in explaining the success of the more highly educated.

Perhaps it would be useful for the reader here to conduct a little experiment based on memory and self-examination. Try to recall for the elementary and secondary levels of schooling whom you consider to be the better teachers. In all probability those with the highest licenses (the most years of schooling) are not disproportionately represented in the results. Yet they certainly make the most money. Repeat this experiment in groups for a number of other occupations.

Reproducing Consciousness

Bowles and Gintis (1973, 1976) continue with their presentation and affirm that the principle function of IQism is legitimation of the hierarchical division of labour, a social phenomenon which is essential if the stratification system is to reproduce itself. This reproduction allows those who are already in a privileged position to pass on these benefits to their children. It ensures that the working class and lower middle class of this generation will largely be recruited from young people whose parents occupy similar class positions.

Legitimation is based on the reproduction of consciousness or what is referred to as the social relations of production. These social relations include what people sometimes refer to as the 'system'; in Canada and the United States, the advanced capitalist system. It has a number of characteristics including bureaucratic organization, hierarchical lines of authority, job fragmentation and unequal rewards. Bureaucratic organization, which is also found in state socialist societies, is not at all essential for a productive economy.

Neither are the authority relations which exist in the world of production. The assumption is that non-bureaucratic organization and decentralized authority could be equally productive. At the same time they would be less alienating and more humane. Job fragmentation refers to specialization. Generally the work of production is split up among many workers in such a way that no one individual or group below management understands or is able to manage or give direction to the entire operation. Moreover, the specialized workers are in competition with one another. Such competition leads to conflict among groups of workers instead of promoting class consciousness. The unequal rewards increase this conflict and encourage a climate in which profit maximization is regarded as normal.

The legitimation of these social relations of production is brought about through ideologies, especially the technocratic-meritocratic perspective. The technocratic aspect entails the belief that production increasingly requires more advanced technical skills which are brought about through education. The meritocratic perspective holds that the more able people, especially those with the higher measured intelligences, are in a better position to attain these technological skills because of superior ability, and for this reason they merit higher rewards. It is assumed that these skills are difficult to attain, an assumption which has not been demonstrated. The I.Q. myth supports this perspective despite the demonstration that I.Q., is relatively unimportant for economic success.

The social relations of production include all these ordinary traits: the ideologies and beliefs, rules and customs which are associated with the capitalist system. They are taken for granted. It is assumed that such a system of relations is necessary when in fact they are not required at all. The capitalist class encourages this position, thus ensuring the perpetuation of its own privileged position.

The social relations found in the institution of schooling mirror those which are found in the productive world, including bureaucratization, hierarchical authority relations, job fragmentation and unequal rewards. The young child is exposed to this from the first day of school. It is the only system he sees or understands. Thus the assumption of its inevitability and propriety is strengthened. When the student, either as a dropout or upon graduation, prepares to enter the work force, this is the only set of social relations he is familiar with.

The Correspondence Principle

Bowles and Gintis (1976:131-141) give special emphasis to what they refer to as the correspondence principle. They use this to demonstrate how the allocative function of schooling is fulfilled. This is one of the most important aspects of their theory, and we already outlined it briefly in chapter two.

The allocative function directs students to the occupational world along class lines. Depending on the nature of the family background from which a student comes, the educational system directs him to the higher, intermediate or lower level of the work force. This is not an inviolate rule. If it were, the process of legitimation would be more difficult. Moreover, some mobility is essential because the capitalist class does not fully reproduce itself. It must recruit partially from lower classes. But such allocation is a general rule. Remember: the beta weight for social class is rather high (.46), and the zero order correlation (.55) indicates that social class either directly or indirectly explains 30 per cent of the variance in lifetime earnings. Other important explanatory variables leading to success in the worlds of school and of work are also strongly related to social class and would explain part of the variance.

Since intellectual ability (I.Q.) is hardly responsible for the fact that the children of economically successful parents have a much higher than normal chance of being successful themselves, what is it that brings this about? A large part of the answer is schooling. But what aspect of schooling causes such differential success rates? Obviously it is not the cognitive aspect (Berg, 1970). For Bowles and Gintis the answer lies in the correspondence principle.

According to these authors "(d)ifferent levels of education feed workers into different levels within the occupational structure and, correspondingly, tend toward an internal organization comparable to levels in the hierarchical division of labour" (1976:132). Those organizational characteristics in the occupational structure stress rule-following at the lowest level, dependability and the capacity to operate with restricted supervision at the intermediate level, and the internalization of norms at the highest level. This last characteristic refers to working for the goals of the organization without special external rewards. Wanting what the enterprise desires would bring with it a willingness to work overtime or in the evenings and weekends at home without extra pay, and characteristics of this kind.

It is precisely these characteristics which are emphasized in the corresponding levels of schooling. The lower level, including high school, stresses rule-following. The intermediate level including community colleges and many four-year undergraduate colleges or universities emphasize dependability with a minimum of direct supervision. The elite four-year universities and graduate schools emphasize the internalization of norms. Thus the student who leaves the educational system at one of these three levels has been prepared, has been trained in the social relations which enable him to fit in the corresponding level of the work force, and expects to acquire work in that level. To work at a lower level would be to be underemployed; to work at a higher level would be difficult because of a lack of preparation in general role requirements.

Bowles and Gintis (1976) report on a number of studies conducted by themselves and others which demonstrate this correspondence principle. In a sense these studies are only indirect evidence for their position. They were not generally initiated to demonstrate the correspondence principle. Taken cumulatively, however, they succeed in demonstrating it rather well.

In closing this section we must again remind the reader that we are dealing with groups. Despite the overall importance of social class, for a group the single most important variable for lifetime earnings, at least for this large sample of American males, is education. While there are extraneous variables such as ethnicity which may be very important, it appears that for white males education is the most important variable of all. We are not aware of any comparable study for females, and we would not expect the same results. The same vacuum exists for Blacks and the Native People of Canada and the United States.

## Jencks and Inequality

### The Quality of Schooling

Christopher Jencks (1972, 1975, 1979) and a number of his colleagues became very interested in determining why there was so much inequality in the results of schooling. *The Equality of Educational Opportunity* (Coleman et al., 1966), earlier had tentatively indicated that, contrary to popular opinion, the reason some groups such as Blacks or inner-city lower SES groups in the United States did not do well in school was not because of lower financial input. A number of replications, including Jencks', had indicated the same thing. The so-called quality-of-a-school variable included such items as financial input, the availability of libraries and equipment, the student-teacher ratio, the experience of teachers, and recreational facilities. These did not significantly effect student achievement.

In trying to understand and explain this surprising finding, Brookover and Erickson (1975) make an important distinction between the social context and the social climate of the school. The social context refers to the global characteristics of the majority of students who make up the student body: gender, social class, race, age and similar variables. These are attributes of the students, often ascribed attributes. There is a relationship between these variables and educational achievement but it is not entirely a direct one. On the other hand, the social climate of the school ". . . refers to the attitudes, beliefs, values and norms that characterize the social system of the school" (Brookover and Erickson, 1975:360). It is a cultural characteristic. Frequently it is systematically related to the composition of the student body but in many cases it is not. Coleman (1966) had demonstrated that context variables such as race and socioeconomic status are strongly related to school achievement, but it had not been demonstrated that they were causal. Brookover and Erickson (1975) report on a number of subsequent studies which indicate that social climate variables are the more direct or causal significant predictors of academic success. These climate variables include the student norms and expectations, and appropriate surveillance and sanctions by the parental, peer and school personnel. Thus, in a school where the system of expectations is such that all students are meant to progress in an academic track, achievement will be generally high regardless of the social context of the student body. In a school where a significant proportion of the student body such as the working-class group is expected to be in the lower tracks and do poorly, that is generally what actually occurs. It is important to emphasize that these climate variables or system of expectations are not created by the teachers or school personnel, although they may share them. They reflect the expectations of the community, of the homes and of peers as well. Cumulatively they establish role requirements for the students, and given the appropriate surveillance and sanctions the students tend to live up to these expectations.

In his study Coleman (1966) had shown that there is more variance in achievement within schools even of the same social context than there is between schools of different social contexts. To characterize a school as poor disregards the fact that there are good students within it. The difference between the average achievement of students in schools characterized as good and poor is not usually as great as the average difference between good and poor students within the same school. Jencks' studies produced the same results.

Background of Jencks' Analysis

Coleman's (1966) study was concerned primarily with the equality or inequality of educational opportunity. What are the more important variables which lead to educational achievement? Jencks (1972, 1979) carried this investigation one step farther. Like Bowles and Gintis he and his colleagues tried to isolate the variables leading to economic success. In doing so he confirmed many of Coleman's findings. The data he used in his first study came from a number of surveys conducted in the United States primarily in the 1960 decade. The second study used even more secondary survey material, the results not always being strictly comparable. Moreover, the type of statistical analysis used is so complex that it becomes very difficult for all but the trained statistician to follow the procedures.

Jencks attempted to isolate the variables, mostly social but to some extent biological (genetic) which explained the variance in earnings or economic success. Education is one of these variables; cognitive ability or intelligence is another, as are non-cognitive traits such as personality variables. Family background is also very influential. The study, however, was meant to explain economic rather than educational inequality, as was the Bowles and Gintis work.

The principal results of the 1972 study were that family background (which we may take as a stand-in for socioeconomic status although they are not exactly the same), cognitive abilities, non-cognitive traits and educational achievement explain from one-third to one-half of the variance in earnings. This means that $R^2$ in the equation using these variables would be between .33 and .50, certainly an important finding. The remainder of the variance was explained by factors which the researchers were not able to isolate from their data base, but which they referred to as contingency or luck. These included such things as switching careers, fluctuations in the economy, technological breakthroughs and lucky or unlucky breaks. While these explained more than half the variance in earnings they could account for less than a third of the variance in occupational status (Yankelovich, 1979), indicating that the 'contingencies' were more explanatory for how much one earned than they were for what work one did. The 1979 study was a replication produced with a broader data base covering a longer time span. The results were not substantially different.

## The Effects of Family Background

Family background includes ". . . all the environmental factors that make brothers and sisters more alike than random individuals" (1972:77). These include, as specified in the 1979 work, economic factors and some thirteen demographic characteristics including race, ethnicity, religion, parental occupation and education, geographical or regional background, and family size. As reported by Yankelovich (1979), Jencks estimates that these explain from 15 to 35 per cent of the variance in earnings and from 45 to 50 per cent of the variance in occupational status. One reason for the percentage gap is the overlap existing between these and other factors. The demographic factors explain more than half their effects through cognitive skills and educational attainment.

## The Effects of Academic Ability

In discussing academic ability, which is strongly associated with family background, Jencks (1979) notes that tests of this ability predict economic success better than other tests, and that such tests are efficient predictors as early as the sixth grade. The predictive power of the tests is not due merely to their assessment of cognitive skill or ability but is also related to the presence of motives and attitudes that lead to the development of cognitive skill. The economic benefits of cognitive ability occur to a considerable extent because of family advantages which affect both ability and adult success, and some of these advantages are genetic. Moreover, young people with higher academic ability succeed economically substantially because they are encouraged more than others to have high aspirations and remain in school longer. The academic ability factor explains 34 per cent of the variance in education; yet there is a great deal of inequality among those with the same test scores. About 60 per cent of the observed correlation between test scores and education is independent of family background.

When Jencks discusses *how* ability affects schooling he notes a number of very interesting points. Those with higher test scores are treated differently from lower scoring individuals. They are more likely to be in a college preparatory track, to receive higher grades, to have parents who want them to attend college, to have friends who plan to attend college, to discuss their college plans with teachers, and they are more likely to have ambitious educational (and occupational) plans. These factors fall into the category of what Brookover and Erickson (1975) referred to as social climate variables. Young people with higher academic ability as measured by appropriate test scores as early as the sixth grade tend to fall into or to be disproportionately represented in those groups which have favorable social climate variables.

About 20 per cent of the advantage received by those with high test scores is the result of their coming from families that are smaller, more stable, more successful economically and more educated. Another 20 per cent is the result of unmeasured family characteristics such as type of socialization and genetic differences. But when family background is controlled more than 50 per cent of the correlation between academic ability and education remains. This means that for people of the same family background academic ability explains 25 per cent of the variance in educational attainment, and 75 per cent is explained by something else including aspiration and motivation.

When Jencks (1979) discusses the relationship between academic ability and occupational status he notes that it comes about mostly through greater educational achievement. Without education those with higher ability lose most of their advantage. Moreover, there is almost as much difference in occupational status between individuals with identical test scores as there is between those with different abilities as measured in this way.

When the relationship between academic ability and earnings is studied it appears to be a substantial one, but mostly because of family background and education. Nevertheless, when these two are controlled those with higher test scores still have slightly higher earnings, even within the same occupation. This may be because of attitudes and personality characteristics or because they search more diligently for better jobs. There is no evidence that they are more productive.

At the conclusion of their study on the relationship between cognitive ability and both occupation and income Jencks and his associates discuss the importance of non-cognitive traits. They could find no single such trait that was of critical importance and overall they explained only a moderate portion of the variance in occupational achievement and earnings. These did not appear to be related to family background or cognitive ability. Their conclusions are tentative but they suggest that non-cognitive traits constitute an important area and taken together they may contribute more to achievement than the literature suggests.

The Effects of Education

When Jencks (1979) analyzed the effects of education on both occupation and earnings he determined that a year of college education contributed more than a year of secondary education, at least as far as initial job is concerned. He found that four years of high school are associated with a 5 point advantage in initial job status (on a 100 point scale) while four years of college are associated with a 23 point advantage. That is a large difference.

When controls for family background and test performance were introduced the effect of elementary and secondary education was lowered by more than 50 per cent but the effect of college education was lowered by only about 7 per cent. This tends to confirm the findings of Bowles and Gintis (1973), at least as far as college is concerned. High school education makes its contribution mostly through family background and ability. A college education makes most of its contribution 'on its own'. It is much more important than either background or ability. There are several potential explanations for this. One may be, as suggested by Bowles and Gintis (1976), that college helps students acquire non-cognitive characteristics which employers value. Or it may be because employers are not concerned with the differences among college graduates but are concerned with the difference between college and non-college employees. Alternatively it may be that the degree is a convenient mechanism for distributing higher status jobs.

This kind of relationship between education and initial job status tends to remain for current occupational status as well. The importance of secondary education drops substantially when background and ability are controlled, but that decrease hardly takes place for college graduates. If education is merely a credential which employers use in the beginning, for lack of better information, its importance could be expected to decrease as one continues in a career and other more important information becomes available on which to base judgement for promotion. But for those with college education this does not occur.

The effects of education on earnings is substantial, as one might expect from its relationship with current occupational status. If one wants to measure the effects of each additional year of education on earnings, then an extra year at the elementary and secondary level seems to provide a greater percentage increase than does a year at the post-secondary level. However, as with occupational status, this decreases substantially when controls are introduced for family background. The percentage increase for each year of post-secondary education, and especially for the degree, is maintained to a large extent when controls for family background are introduced, but the percentage increase for earlier school years drops dramatically. When test scores are controlled, the effects of elementary and secondary education are lowered by a third, less so and closer to a sixth for college education.

When controls are introduced simultaneously for family background and ability the value of education at the elementary and secondary level is small, but this is not the case for college. The effects of elementary and secondary education tend to come about because people with more education tend to be already advantaged. Again, this does not hold for college education. Moreover, the value of college education relative to income does not appear to be greater for graduates of higher ability, as measured by test scores. Getting the college degree, no matter where, seems to be the most important variable.

By way of conclusion we should again mention a number of the characteristics of this work. It is based on very complicated statistical analysis, too difficult in many cases even for the experienced social scientist to understand. The 1979 study had a broader sample base than did the 1972 analysis, and for that reason may be presumed to be more valid. However, in many cases the survey data (there were 11 surveys in the 1979 study) are not comparable, and there was considerable variation in the findings for each. Despite statistical attempts to control for this and for measurement error the results must be interpreted with caution. We are not attempting to downplay the importance of the study, which is great. We simply want to point out its limitations.

The principal results of the 1979 study were that family background makes a very important contribution to economic success. It accounts for 45 to 50 per cent of the variance in occupational status, either directly or indirectly. Much of this comes about through its relationship with educational achievement. That achievement is extremely important at the college level but not at the elementary or secondary level when one controls for family background. Thus the two most important contributors to adult earnings and status are college attendance and (even without this) being born in the right family environment. Test scores as a proxy for ability are far less important in themselves. Having high scores, at least 15 points above the average, even for those of the same family background and the same education mean a real but lesser increase in earnings. High ability without college is not worth much extra in income (Yankelovitch, 1979).

In general terms the results of the 1979 study are comparable to the earlier findings of Bowles and Gintis (1973, 1976). Both show that intellectual ability as measured through test scores has a relatively low unique or independent relationship with economic success. Its overall relationship with earnings comes about through family background and educational attainment, both of which make strong independent or unique contributions. In the analysis of Jencks' data these three variables together with non-cognitive characteristics account for a little less than one-half of the variance in earnings, a substantial contribution. Bowles and Gintis seem to attribute slightly more independent influence to education, probably because their socioeconomic status variable is more narrowly defined than is the family background variable used in Jencks' analysis.

## Conclusion

This concludes our discussion of education and its relationship with economic success. While emphasizing how important this is, we would like to repeat that over two-thirds of the variance in earnings is to be attributed to other variables, some of which have not been isolated. Moreover, we have not indicated other dependent variables which, potentially, may be very important. These include such things as job satisfaction, family stability, marriage patterns, and overall enjoyment of life. Earning a lot of money is not necessarily the most important thing in life, or the aspect of life to which people attribute the greatest priority.

# 12

# *The Results of Schooling*

## Social Class Revisited

In the preceding chapter we investigated the impact of formal education on lifetime earnings and, to a lesser extent, on occupation. We saw that the relationship is a strong one. This is because education is now required to a substantial extent as a credential granting entry to the 'appropriate' rung in the job ladder, without having much influence on the level of performance or productivity once the occupation is undertaken and earnings are begun. Occupation is most influential in determining earnings although there are other important causal factors as well. If society were based solely on achievement, the causes of educational and occupational attainment might be presumed to be somewhat different, but we could anticipate strong similarities with ability ranking high in both. As it is societies are not based solely on achievement. There are many vestiges of ascription remaining and in some cases these are particularly strong. Because of this the direct importance of education is modified to the extent that these ascriptive factors remain. A person's occupational attainment does not depend solely on causal factors such as ability. It also depends on indirect ascriptive factors such as the occupation and education of one's father or mother, on sex, on race and a number of other such factors. The same holds true for an individual's educational attainment.

In further considerations of the results of schooling we will disregard the income variable and concentrate on occupation. We do not do this for purely arbitrary reasons. The class or stratum one assumes in adult life is the effect of a number of variables, but principal among them are occupation, education and income. Occupation, however, is the best predictor of income. In effect the two are measuring somewhat the same thing, although as Jencks (1972) has pointed out, contingencies play an important role as well. In a path analysis, which we are to discuss subsequently, and in a multiple regression equation we would have undesirable multicollinearity if we included both occupation and income. Because the two are measuring to a substantial extent the same thing we would get more valid results if we were to drop one or the other. Hence, as most researchers do in their analysis at this stage, we will drop the income variable.

A person's class of destination, then, i,e., the class he will end up in as an adult, is largely determined by occupation and education. Persons of different educations and different occupations may have similar incomes, such as in the hypothetical case of a plumber and a teacher. However, plumbers do not usually have as high an education as school teachers. Moreover, the occupational prestige of a public school teacher as measured by the National Opinion Research Center in 1963 is 81 while for a plumber it is 65, a substantial difference (Hodge, Siegel and Rossi, 1966). Teachers are considered to occupy a higher class position even though income is approximately the same. One of the principal factors determining occupational prestige is education. And we have seen that education is the result of a number of factors, principal among them being the ascriptive variable, social class of origin, i.e., the social class of one's parents. Social class of destination (one's class position as an adult) is dependent upon education more than anything else, as Bowles and Gintis (1973) have shown. However, education is very much dependent on one's social class of origin, the class position of one's parents. In this sense education is an intervening variable. Children from collectivities of lower-class origin may 'beat' this relationship by getting a superior education. However, as a group they do not do so, as indicated by the high correlation between eduation and social class of origin, and also because of the high correlation between measured ability (I.Q.) and social class where ability is seen as an excellent predictor of educational attainment.

At the risk of appearing repetitious we want to emphasize that education is the best unique and independent predictor of social class of destination. This tells us that, regardless of the class position of one's parents, those who achieve higher levels of education will also have higher class positions, on average. However, on average, it is the children of the intermediate and higher class parents who attain the better education. One's family background as measured by the social class of one's parents makes an important independent contribution to one's social class of destination. People tend to occupy a social class position which is very similar to that of their parents. Father's occupation is the best predictor of the occupation of his son. One's family background as measured by parental social class is the most important factor influencing educational attainment even though *whatever* education is attained, on average, is the most important direct influence on one's occupation (and income). To state the relationship as succinctly as possible and at the risk of oversimplification, we can say that one's educational attainment is influenced more than any other factor we are aware of by the occupation and education of one's parents. One's adult occupation is influenced more than anything else we are aware of by that educational attainment.

Thus the relationship between social class and education is a vital one. We cannot emphasize too strongly that we are dealing with groups and averages. An average, in this case the mean, is a statistic which summarizes information and makes it more easily handled and categorized. In the process of doing this it also loses or sacrifices information. It is analytical. In reality the individual cases are different from the average, although where the dispersion or standard deviation is reasonably close to normal then most cases are close to the average, within one standard deviation. If we concentrate on the exception we tend to overlook the point that we are leaving out of consideration most of the cases involved in the relationship. Most people would probably find it desirable to lessen this ascriptive relationship between social class and educational achievement. We must remember that social policy which has been designed to do so may have affected individuals and produced desirable results. It has not altered the relationship. It has not significantly changed the average (mean) or the standard deviation. As Jencks (1979) has indicated, equalizing educational attainment would not go really far in eliminating inequality.

Boocock (1980:40-48) gives an excellent summary of the importance of socioeconomic status. Noting that the higher the socioeconomic status the higher the academic achievement, she points out that this relationship holds no matter what measure of status is used:

> It holds with a variety of achievement/aspiration variables, including grades, achievement test scores, retentions at grade level, course failures, truancy, suspension from school, dropout rates, college plans, and total amount of formal schooling. It also predicts academic honors and awards, elective school offices, extent of participation in extracurricular activities, and other indicators of 'success' in the informal structure of the student society (p.40).

The *way* in which social status affects educational and occupational attainment is not completely clear. This is because different aspects of status affect different educational variables in different ways or, as Boocock (1980:40) puts it ". . . the indicator that most affects one kind of educational success . . . may not be the one that most affects another. . .."

Recent stratification research has given a great deal of attention to explaining the processes by which both educational and occupational positions are attained. What are the causal variables which explain such attainment, and how important are they in their direct and indirect influence? These investigations usually take the form of path analysis, and are generally referred to as the status attainment processes (Haller and Portes, 1973).

There are two principal theoretical models of this status attainment process. They are the Blau-Duncan model which concentrates on the structure of status attainment, investigating particularly (for males only) the influence of the father's education and occupation working through the son's education, his first job and his present occupation, which is the best indicator of current socioeconomic status. This model is really trying to explain the extent to which inherited status, an ascriptive variable, accounts for educational attainment, and in turn how much educational attainment explains current occupational status. This model explains 31 per cent of the variance.

The second is the so-called Wisconsin model developed later by William H. Sewell and his associates. It focuses on social psychological variables including mental ability, the influence of peers and the level of educational and occupational aspiration on educational attainment and subsequent occupational attainment. This model explains 39 per cent of the variance. In both cases educational attainment is a relatively strong predictor of occupational attainment, and it mediates other variables which have a strong ascriptive character (Haller and Portes, 1973). We will briefly look at both, but first we will try to explain in simple terms the meaning of path analysis.

## Education and Occupation: The Status Attainment Process

### The Meaning of Path Analysis

Path analysis is a statistical technique based on multiple regression which, using explanatory variables arranged in the priority of causality, through path coefficients allows the computation of the direct and indirect influence of a prior variable on a given dependent variable. It does not discover the order of causality but rather, where this is known or assumed, it gives a quantitative interpretation of the influence of the variables included in the model on a given dependent variable. The causal or temporal ordering of the model is a basic assumption. The regression technique does not make this temporal order apparent. Hence, it must come about in some other way or through some other procedure.

Figure 12-1 presents the basic model of the Blau and Duncan Status Attainment Process. It is a relatively simple diagram, and it should be apparent from the first glance that four independent variables which are causally prior are explaining some part of the variance in the 1962 occupation of the respondents in the sample. These variables are: father's education, father's occupation, the respondent's education and the respondent's first job. The two variables U and W (respondent's education and first job) are intervening between the dependent variable Y (occupation in 1962) and the more remote independent variables V and X (father's education and father's occupation). Hence, the dependent variable Y is explained or influenced directly by U and W and indirectly through U by V and through W by X, the latter also having some direct influence.

Notice that the arrows, with the exception of those on the curved line, all go in one direction: from left to right. This is to indicate that the influence of the variables, with the exception noted, all goes in the direction indicated by the arrows. They are recursive. That means that the influence of the first variable in a specific relationship does not go to another whose influence in turn goes back to this first one. This is an important and basic assumption.

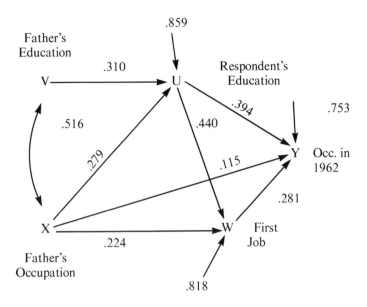

Figure 12-1

Basic Model of Blau and Duncan for the Status
Attainment Process (Blau and Duncan, 1967:170

The causality goes one way, with the exception noted. The numbers on these straight line arrows are path coefficients. They are very similar to standardized regression coefficients or beta weights and are proportional to one another. Thus the path coefficient from U to W (.440) would indicate that it has approximately twice the influence of the path coefficient from X to W (.224). Again we need not be concerned with the mathematical basis or formula for the computation of these coefficients so long as we understand what they are doing.

The curved line between V and X which has arrow heads on both ends is meant to distinguish it from the other lines. The coefficient there (.516) is a simple correlation (Pearson's r) rather than a path coefficient. This is to indicate that the variables V (father's education) and X (father's occupation) not only are related and could be nonrecursive in a general model, but that there are probably common causes behind both which have not been measured or included in the model (Blau and Duncan, 1967). These common causes are called exogenous variables. Variables U and W are called endogenous variables because they act as both independent (intervening) and dependent variables. Variable Y is the dependent variable, neither exogenous or endogenous.

At this point we would suggest that the reader make a special effort to differentiate between exogenous and endogenous variables. These are new terms, technical terms with which the reader is perhaps unfamiliar. The prefixes (ex and en) are the keys. Exogamy refers to from without, *ex* being the Latin root for outside. Endogamy refers to from within, *en* being the root for within. Exogenous variables contain influences not indicated in or outside of the model. Endogenous variables have their sources indicated, including the residuals. This is not a 'big thing' but we will be using these technical terms frequently so one must become familiar with their meanings.

Notice also that the variables U, W and Y have short lines with arrowheads with no source, coming from outside the model. These are called *residuals* and are meant to represent causes of the unexplained variance and indicate their explanatory strength. Only so much of the variance in the endogenous and dependent variables has been explained by the prior variables in the model. In multiple regression analysis that would be $R^2$. The rest of the variance $(1 - R^2)$ is that which is left over or unexplained by the variables in the model, and the path coefficients from the external sources (the residuals) are meant to indicate the strength of those other unexplained influences. The square of the residual for a given variable indicates how much of the variance is explained by variables outside the model and by the error terms. In our example the residual for Y = .753. The square of this is .567 telling us that 56.7 per cent of the variance in 1962 occupation is not explained by the model. Conversely, 1 - .567 = .433 is the amount of variance in Y explained by the four variables in the model. Again, since the coefficients are proportional, the residual for U (.859) is approximately three times the strength of the path coefficient (.279) for variable X (father's occupation) and about two and three-quarters times the strength of the path coefficient (.310) for variable V (father's education). This unexplained variance is the result of causes not measured or indicated in the model, measurement error and other potential errors which we will not be concerned with here (Blau and Duncan, 1967). The residuals are comparatively strong or high relative to the strength of the other path coefficients. In the example we just used the residual of .859 is the largest coefficient in the model. It is roughly three times as strong as the path coefficient V on U (.310) and also X on U (.279). However, the cumulative strength of these two coefficients would be greater than either one of them taken singly against which the residual may be taken as a comparative statistic. "The fact is that the size of the residual (or, if one prefers, the proportion of the variation 'explained') is *no* guide whatever to the validity of a causal interpretation" (Blau and Duncan, 1967:175). It is not an index of the adequacy of an explanation. The important thing about the residual is that the factors it represents be uncorrelated with the measured antecedent variables. If there were such a correlation then that factor should be included in the model and be represented with the appropriate path coefficients.

In summary, path analysis uses a model which includes a number of variables arranged in order of causality or priority. This order is determined on the basis of theory and also from the way the information is gathered in the collecting instrument. Like regression analysis, and based on a correlation matrix, it indicates the direct net effect of a given prior variable on the independent variable, and it also makes possible the computation of indirect net effects which go through other intervening variables. This process will be explained subsequently. Returning to our example in Figure 12-1 the path coefficient (.115) from X to Y indicates the direct net effect of father's occupation on the son's occupation in 1962. But it also makes possible the computation of the indirect net effect of X on Y through U and also through W. These are additive, and we can then determine the total or gross effect of father's occupation on son's first job.

Before discussing the computation of these indirect effects we should remind ourselves that we are dealing in general and rather simple terms the technique or process of path analysis. The observations we are making will apply to any other model as well, such as the Wisconsin model we will be investigating subsequently. A second important point for readers of this text is to recall that we are interested in this particular analysis because of the education variables. We will have a good understanding of how important they are relative to occupation.

We will not discuss here how the path coefficients are determined. Fundamentally, they are computed algebraically from a number of equations based on the correlation matrix. The computer will do this for the nonspecialist. Our principal concern here is the computation of the direct and indirect effects of variables in the model. The general rule is that the correlation between two variables, say U and W in Figure 12-1 (which is equal to .538) is equal to the direct effect (the path coefficient WU, which is .440) plus the product of all the indirect influences.[1] Remember that the path coefficient (direct effect) is given for the straight line arrows and the correlation coefficient is given for the curved line, the so-called exogenous variables. In this particular example

$$r_{WU} = P_{WU} + P_{WX}P_{UX} + P_{WX} \, r_{XV}P_{UV}$$

---

[1]The accepted terminology is to indicate either the correlation (r) or the path coefficient (P) with subscripts designating the appropriate variables. When using the subscripts the dependent variable is placed first. Thus the path coefficient U to W is written $P_{WU}$; the correlation $r_{WU}$.

where the item on the left represents the gross effect, the first item on the right is the direct effect and the rest are the indirect effects. Thus gross influence = direct influence + indirect influence

$$.538 = .440 + (.224)(.279) + (.224)(.516)(310)$$
$$= .440 + .062 + .036$$
$$= .440 + .098$$

The gross influence of respondent's education (U) on his first job (W) equals the direct effect which is the path coefficient (.440) plus the indirect effect of the other variables (.098) (Blau and Duncan, 1967:176).

This statistical procedure, path analysis, is frequently encountered in stratification studies and in the sociology of education. Again we remind our readers that while it may appear complicated mathematically — and we are not concerned here in understanding this — it is very simple to understand what it is doing. That is our principal concern at this level. We know the gross effect of one variable on another through the correlation coefficient. That gross effect is composed of the direct effect of the first variable on the second plus the effect of the first variable working indirectly through other variables. This kind of information may be very useful. The reader who is not particularly interested in doing so would probably be wise to avoid the exercise of computing the gross and indirect effects. The important point is to know that this may be done and to understand its meaning. We would hope that once our readers become familiar with causal models they will intuitively understand the relative importance of each factor in the model without directly computing the indirect effects, a process which may be onerous for some.

**The Status Attainment Process**

Haller and Portes (1973) have an excellent presentation on the status attainment process. They define this process as ". . . sets of events by which individuals come to occupy their positions in the social hierarchies of wealth, power and prestige" (p.54). These latter three variables, wealth power and prestige may be taken as both the sign and the result of status attainment. Status, which is frequently used interchangeably with social class and socio-economic status, refers to one's position in a hierarchy which is manifested by wealth, power and prestige. The process by which this comes about is similar to or identical with the mobility process, but the use of the term mobility may be confusing.

Status may be determined in a number of ways. The processes which are included may be either ascriptive or achievement processes, usually some combination of both (Davis, 1972). In modern industrial societies the achievement characteristic is regarded as having a greater emphasis or importance. This suggests that one's status in modern society is increasingly being determined by what one does and that there is more opportunity for any member of society to do any of a variety of things. Ascription, which is usually determined at birth, is becoming less influential. However, we must be careful not to take the position that it is not influential at all. We are talking about a diminishing influence rather than a disappearing one. There are still vestiges of ascription remaining and in certain cases such as sex stratification these are substantial (Haller and Portes, 1973).

There are different variables from which status variations result. Typically the three which have been given the greatest consideration are occupation, education and income. Of these occupation is the most representative summary measure. Education is more a determinant of occupation and income more a result. Occupational prestige is itself often used as an index or indicator of socioeconomic status.

In Canadian and American societies individuals have considerable latitude in choosing an occupation, or in gaining a high level of educational attainment which in turn leads to high occupational prestige. At the same time on an aggregate basis the occupation of fathers is still the best predictor of the occupational prestige of the sons. So despite the choice of alternatives which are available this ascriptive feature, father's occupation, is still very important. Moreover, the education of the father is again one of the strongest predictors of the education of the son. These structural variables then are of major importance and despite such characteristics as motivation and aspiration we may say that there is a strong element of ascriptive determination involved, on the average.

Nevertheless, the influence of such background ascriptive variables as father's occupation or socioeconomic status works through a number of social psychological variables which are particularly important relative to educational attainment, which in turn is the best intragenerational predictor of occupational attainment. These variables include earlier academic performance, the influence of significant others and level of educational aspiration. Beyond the educational realm, level of occupational aspiration also has some though a lesser degree of influence.

The two principal status attainment models with which we are concerned use these different sets of variables in establishing causal models which attempt to describe the status attainment process and indicate the strength or degree of influence of the explanatory variables. The Blau and Duncan model uses the structural variables. The Wisconsin model includes social psychological variables. Education holds a major position in both.

**The Blau and Duncan and Wisconsin Models**

Blau and Duncan (1967) are concerned primarily with the process by which the fathers' occupational statuses are transmitted to the sons'. Their model ". . . seeks to identify those basic factors describing the persons and their situations which account for whatever status locations they come to occupy" (Haller and Portes, 1973:55). Since it is a causal model it allows prediction of status outcomes for any group of people similar to the population from which their data is taken, in this case white males in the United States on the basis of census data. The empirical data lead to the conclusion that the effect of father's education and occupation are transmitted to the son through the son's educational attainment, and this in turn largely determines the son's occupation. The path coefficients from these two exogenous variables are reasonably strong, indicating that they will have a relatively strong indirect effect on the dependent variable, occupation in 1962. This indirect effect works through the endogenous variables, respondent's education and first job.

The Wisconsin model adds to the objective or structural variables several important social psychological variables. In effect it is concerned with the dynamics of status attainment. It investigated a number of models containing variables not included in this final one and determined that this is the best model available from the data. It interjects (earlier) academic performance, significant other's influence, educational aspiration and occupational aspiration as intervening or endogenous variables between the parental background variable and mental ability (the exogenous variables) and educational and occupational attainment. Figure 12-2 presents the causal model and path coefficients.

The Wisconsin data were collected from a large sample of Wisconsin male high school seniors in 1957. A second set of data was collected in 1964 from a follow-up sample, giving more information on educational attainment and early occupational attainment (Sewell, Haller and Portes, 1969). These data then are longitudinal while the Blau and Duncan data are cross-sectional.

The variables in the two studies are not strictly comparable. The exogenous variables for Blau and Duncan are father's education and father's occupation; for the Wisconsin model they are parental socioeconomic status and mental ability. The dependent variable for Blau and Duncan is (mature) occupational attainment with first job as an intervening variable. The dependent variable in the Wisconsin model, occupational attainment, more closely approximates the intervening first job variable of the other model because it is measured only seven years after high school graduation. Many of the respondents attended college in the meantime. Moreover, in the Wisconsin model there may be some problems in the way significant others' influence has been operationalized, for it includes only parents, teachers and best friends.

In their article Haller and Portes (1973) deal with these problems of comparability and operationalization satisfactorily. Since we are not interested in the methodology for its own sake we will not complicate our presentation by including these discussions here. Having run a series of tests with comparisons and correlations they conclude that even though some variables are operationalized differently there is no real problem in making comparisons.

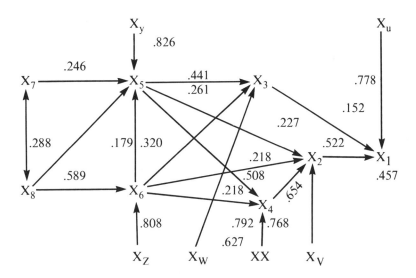

X₁ - Occupational Attainment
X₂ - Educational Attainment
X₃ - Level of Occupational Aspiration
X₄ - Level of Educational Aspiration
X₅ - Significant Other's Influence
X₆ - Academic Performance
X₇ - Socioeconomic Status
X₈ - Mental Ability

Figure 12-2

The Wisconsin Model
Source: adopted from Haller and Portes, 1973:59

Haller and Portes (1973) present a good comparison. The purpose is not a critical assessment of either study. We will indicate their major findings relative to the educational variables, our principal interest. Table 12-1 presents the correlations between key common variables contained in each.

The Blau and Duncan model, using simple averages of the correlations of father's education and father's occupation for the SES variable, explains 31 per cent of the variance of early occupational attainment, which in this model is not the principal dependent variable. It is not surprising that the Wisconsin model explains slightly more (39 per cent) because the variables are a little more comprehensive.

Table 12-1

Correlations of Key Common Variables, Both Models

|  | Blau-Duncan | Wisconsin |
|---|---|---|
| Early occ. attainment/education | .538 | .618 |
| Early occ. attainment/SES | .374 | .331 |
| Education/SES | .445 | .417 |
| $R_{1.23}$ | .560 | .623 |

Source: Adapted from Haller and Portes, 1973:63

If we consider the total effect ($r^2$) of parental status on early occupational attainment then the Blau-Duncan model explains a little more, as indicated in Table 12-2. However, the difference is relatively small, 14 per cent compared to 11 per cent. But in this case the additional educational effect for the Wisconsin model is much greater, 28 per cent compared to 17 per cent. If we consider the gross educational effect ($r^2$) as indicated in Table 12-2 it is greater in the Wisconsin model, 38 per cent compared to 29 per cent. This is based on a three variable causal model and is not readily apparent from Figures 12-1 and 12-2. At this point we should warn the reader against holding that the Wisconsin model is a better one.

It is more accurate to say it is different, and while its greater complexity explains more variance it also presents more theoretical problems. It is adding to the Blau-Duncan model an explanation of how the effect of parental status is mediated by social psychological variables. The Blau-Duncan model shows the importance of parental status in explaining occupational attainment. The Wisconsin model shows how this is mediated by certain additional variables, especially the influence of significant others and the level of both occupational and educational aspiration. As Haller and Portes (1973) point out, this has important implications for social policy. The negative aspect of low parental status may be reduced or eliminated by social policies which enhance the positive influence of significant others and of educational and occupational aspirations.

Fundamentally the Wisconsin model shows the direct influence of significant others to be quite strong on educational aspirations, occupational aspirations, and educational attainment. It also has substantial indirect effects on

Table 12-2

Variance Explained
on Basis of Gross Parental Status, Both Models

|  | Blau-Duncan | Wisconsin |
|---|---|---|
| Gross Parental Status Effect(1) | .14 | .11 |
| Additional Education Effect(2) | .17 | .28 |
| Total Variation Explained ($R^2 = 1 + 2$) | .31 | .39 |

Source: Haller and Portes, 1973:64

Table 12-3

Variance Explained on Basis
of Gross Education Effect, Both Models

|  | Blau-Duncan | Wisconsin |
|---|---|---|
| Gross Education Effect(1) | .29 | .38 |
| Additional Parental Status Effect(2) | .02 | .01 |
| Total Variation Explained ($R^2 = 1 + 2$) | .31 | .39 |

Source: Haller and Portes, 1973:64

occupational attainment. The aspiration variables, especially educational aspiration, are very important and they depend on or mediate the influence of significant others. Haller and Portes (1973) indicate that as attitudes these aspiration variables include or are based on the possibilities indicated by significant others, plus self-reflexive or self-evaluative conclusions based to a considerable extent on earlier academic performance. This latter variable is probably also an important one in helping the significant others assess the aspirations of the subject which they in turn pass on to him. However, it is his *perception* rather than their objective assessment which is of critical importance. They hypothesize that mental ability is not so important directly as a determinant of aspirations. Rather the perception of the assessment made by significant others, and the assessment made by the subject himself, based to a substantial extent on academic performance, is more critical. However, the path (direct influence) from mental ability to academic performance is a strong one (.589).

Many sociologists have emphasized the importance of significant others in determining self-concept. Brookover and Erickson (1975) point out how behaviour (e.g., educational attainment) is so strongly influenced in this way, based on self-concept of ability which is determined by the perceptions the subject makes of the views of significant others, and also self-reflexive perceptions. The decision to engage in certain kinds of behaviour or not, which is roughly equivalent to aspirations, is based on an assessment of one's ability to perform or complete the actions and the degree of difficulty and rewards involved. There is very close correspondence between the theory presented by these authors and the Wisconsin model derived from empirical data. Aspirations reflect the mirror image of self which is perceived in the interaction with significant others. They also reflect an assessment of one's ability based on earlier behaviour, which behaviour may in turn have influenced the expectations of the significant others. The educational aspiration has a very strong direct effect ($p = .457$) on educational attainment which in turn has an unusually strong ($p = .522$) direct effect on occupational attainment. Occupational aspirations are formed in the same way. However, their direct effect on occupational attainment is less strong ($p = .152$) principally because educational attainment as a credential is so important for occupational attainment.

Haller and Portes (1973:62) note that the impact of significant others ". . . includes, but is not exhausted by, direct parental influence on the formation of status aspirations. The family's socioeconomic position also sets limits on the pool of potential significant others confronted by the individual and the nature of their orientations." The social class background of the family tends to set limits on the class backgrounds of friends who, as significant others, may be so influential.

The Wisconsin model explains 39 per cent of the variance in (early) occupational attainment, principally through the mediating social psychological variables. The Blau-Duncan model explains 43 per cent of mature occupational attainment, although that statistic is somewhat inflated because many in the sample were yet to experience intragenerational mobility. That model explains 33 per cent of the variance in first job, i.e., early occupational attainment. Educational attainment explains most of the variance in both first job and mature occupational attainment. The Wisconsin variable adds to this the strong influence of significant others working through educational aspirations which in turn lead to level of educational and occupational attainment. Both models support the conclusions of Bowles and Gintis (1973, 1976) and Jencks

(1972, 1979) which indicate that educational attainment is the most important variable in explaining occupational inequality.

## Canadian and American Comparison

Gilbert (1977) has an excellent article comparing the formation of educational and occupational aspirations in Canada and the United States. Holding that both are stratified societies with high levels of inequality of condition and low levels of equality of opportunity, he notes, based on a review of the literature, that ". . . Canada is more elitist, ascriptively oriented and particularistic than the United States" (p.284). Income inequality is the major form of inequality of condition in both nations, and the distribution of income in quintiles is almost identical. While condition may be superior in the United States, with its higher standard of living, the inequality of condition is virtually the same in the two nations. However, in Canada equality of opportunity is lower, or inequality of opportunity is higher. The level of educational attainment is lower in Canada; the Americans are less elitist in this regard, stressing more the equality of educational opportunity. Moreover, there is a more elitist content to Canadian education, with less vocationalism. Greater emphasis is given to ethnicity in Canada. Canadians tend to make judgements more on particularistic grounds. Gender also makes more of a difference in Canada than in the United States, at least as far as labour force participation is concerned.

Gilbert (1977) summarizes by stating that Canada and the United States have about the same level of material inequalities. However, equality of opportunity, and especially of educational opportunity is lower here. While still a stratified society the U.S. is closer to the meritocratic typology than Canada. As a result, he hypothesizes ". . . that SES would play a greater role in determining the formation of educational and occupational aspirations of high school students in Canada then in the U.S.A." (p.285). He then presents the Wisconsin model leading up to occupational and educational aspirations (Figure 12-3) and a duplication of this model based on data gathered from grade 12 students in English speaking schools in Ontario (Figure 12-4).

Both models begin with mental ability (MA) and SES as exogenous variables. The effects of these go through academic achievement (AA) and the influence of significant others (SOI) to the dependent variables, level of occupational aspirations (LOA) and level of educational aspirations (LEA). The Wisconsin model explains 37 per cent of the variance in LOA while the Canadian model explains only 32 per cent.

More important for our interest and concern, both models explain 41 per cent of the variance in level of educational aspirations (LEA). We should recall from the full Wisconsin model (Figure 12-2) that it is LEA which has the strongest influence on both educational and occupational attainment.

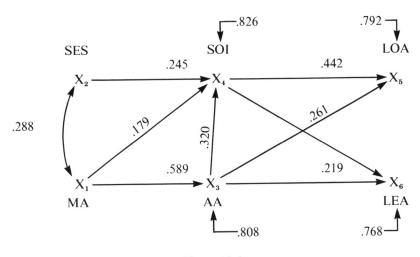

Figure 12-3

Path Coefficients for Antecedents of Educational
and Occupational Aspirations for Wisconsin Boys

Source: Sewell, Haller and Ohlendorf, 1970:1023

The author interprets these models to conclude that the effect of SES is relatively greater in Canada. This is based on the fact that while performance variables (MA and AA) are more strongly related to LOA and LEA than is SES, ". . . the gap between their relative effects has narrowed substantially" (p.288). The path coefficient for the relationship between academic achievement and mental ability is much stronger in the Wisconsin (.589) than in the Ontario (.297) model. Even though the path coefficient from SES to SOI is moderately stronger in the Wisconsin model (.245) than in Ontario (.196) the gap is much smaller and the difference in the explained variance almost negligible. As a result, the effect of SES, an ascribed characteristic, is relatively greater in Canada.

Gilbert (1977:281-284) presents a theoretical framework which is meant to locate ". . . the formation of educational and occupational aspirations among the more general social processes pertaining to industrial societies" (p.281). The technological level of a society affects the range of occupational positions which require different levels of skill or training, generally broadening the range. The population of every society must be motivated to perform at various levels within the existing range. The ideology which the individual learns as part of his socialization creates within that individual the educational

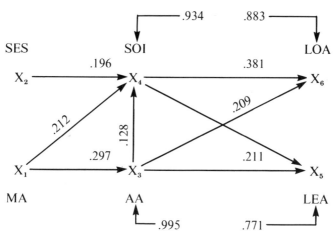

Figure 12-4

Path Coefficients for Antecedents of Educational and Occupational
Aspirations for Ontario Grade 12 Boys in English Schools

Source: Gilbert, 1977:287

and occupational aspirations which has such a strong influence on the objective position he will occupy within the existing range.

Gilbert presents a fourfold typology of societies based on the relationship between inequality of condition (minimal or maximal) and equality of opportunity (high or low). Two of these are egalitarian and communal societies, where inequality of condition is low and equality of opportunity is either high or low. We are not particularly concerned with these now because we have high inequality of condition. The other two types both have maximal inequality of condition. In the meritocratic society equality of opportunity is high; in the stratified society it is low. Canada and the United States, like most industrial societies in the western world, are stratified. They have high or maximal inequality of condition and low equality of opportunity (or high inequality of opportunity).

It is instructive to compare the meritocratic and stratified societies as far as motivation leading to educational and occupational aspirations is concerned. In a meritocracy the existing inequalities of condition are held out as inducements for motivation to achieve, and the achievement itself is based on ability (which includes a genetic component). Thus educational and occupational aspirations ". . . should be strongly related to variables that attempt to measure differences in innate ability or motivational drive" (Gilbert, 1977:283). One can expect high correlations and path coefficients between mental ability and educational and occupational aspirations, and also between mental ability and educational attainment. A student would be located in a high school track primarily on the basis of ability. Ascribed variables such as SES, gender and ethnicity would be only weakly related to aspiration.

In a stratified society there is a much greater likelihood of privilege being passed on from one generation to another even when ability is controlled. Hence material rewards are held out as inducements, but the particularistic system of attainment to a substantial extent prevents their acquisition by those originating in less privileged class backgrounds. Thus motivation and aspiration would be less strongly related to ability but more strongly associated with SES, gender, religion and ethnicity (Gilbert, 1977).

## Conclusion

This concludes our presentation on the results of schooling. In chapter 11 we indicated how very important educational attainment is for occupational attainment, and for lifetime earnings. In this chapter we indicated how this attainment is largely the result of ascriptive variables summarized as social class of origin, mediated by social psychological variables, particularly the influence of significant others and educational and occupational aspirations. Thus the strong correlation between social class background and occupational attainment is largely the result of that background determining the nature of significant others' expectations in one's life, and this in turn determining educational aspiration and achievement.

# Part V

# Conclusion

This concluding section, restricted to chapter 13, points out that one of the problems of schooling results from competing interest groups looking for different results. Here we look at the meaning of inequality in a more detailed way and investigate several important distinctions which pertain to that concept. It should come as no surprise that groups do not agree on the amount of inequality which is to be regarded as acceptable in schooling if there is disagreement on the meaning of the concept.

We conclude the chapter, and the book, with a consideration of the meaning and role played by ideology and hegemony in the beliefs held about schooling as an institution, and about society at large. It is our contention that these beliefs, which have no objectively valid position, have as their major function the support and the legitimation of institutionalized inequality which is beyond the school and prior to it.

# 13

# *The Problem*
# *of Competing Interests*

In this concluding chapter we would like to elaborate on certain important issues which have a special bearing on social policy in the education domain. By now it should be apparent even to the casual reader that there are special problems in the Canadian educational system when viewed from almost any perspective, as there are with schooling throughout the western world. We refer to the content of this presentation as the problem of competing interests, in order to emphasize that one reason for the pervasiveness of these problems is a lack of agreement among Canadians on just what schooling is to do. We would like here to identify the various meanings of inequality and, from a class perspective, to point out the determining influence that ideology has on the institution of schooling.

We mentioned that this has a special bearing on social policy. It is not our intention to recommend specific social policies as some recent authors such as Jencks (1972) or Bowles and Gintis (1976) have done. We do not hold that the formulation of social policy as such falls within the scope of sociology strictly defined, although the influences leading to specific policy and its consequences certainly do. We take a personal stand, sometimes a very firm one, on most of the issues which appear problematic to us. The knowledge and understanding we have of the problems of schooling in Canada, their causes and consequences, are peculiar to ourselves and certainly have a grounding in our own ideological perspectives. We will not here impose these on others except perhaps in an indirect way related to the format we have followed. It is our hope that the reader, indeed the majority of Canadians, will become suitably informed on educational issues and their own ideological perspectives from this and other sources so that, relative to social policy, we may have a more rational debate. However, that will not be easy. As we hope to show in the body of this chapter, very complex issues are involved.

Students who are using this text are likely to become involved in educational policy in the near future, for several reasons. Most will become parents, and because of that issues pertaining to schooling will be of vital interest to them. It is likely that, on an average, their children will be ranked among the more privileged as far as educational achievement is concerned. A smaller but significant number of readers will probably become more directly involved as educators, both administrators and teachers. Others will be concerned as politicians and government bureaucrats, in some cases being responsible for the formulation of educational policy. For most readers the content of this course is not restricted to academic interest or intellectual enquiry. There are very practical issues involved. It is our hope that the issues presented will stimulate special interest in this entire domain, and assist in promoting the kind of analysis which is critical for the formulation of social policy based on serious consideration of these issues. That policy will not exist in a vacuum. It is itself influenced by broader social issues. There are no closed boundaries, no such thing as an autonomous institution of schooling.

At this point we would like to emphasize several issues which we feel are basic in making such an analysis. We can distinguish between two types: those that are connected with the organizational aspect of schooling, and others such as inequality and ideology which pertain to the broader value system. It is this latter set which is our special concern here.

## Organizational Issues

In various places throughout this text, and in particular in chapters seven and nine, we pointed out how organizational variables affect the outcomes of schooling. These include not only aims and objectives but the various kinds of organizational structures. They are internal or intrinsic to the organization. While not completely independent of outside influences they come more directly under control of professional educators. On the local level, administrators and teachers usually have it within their sphere of authority to initiate one or another format such as ability grouping, team teaching or open education. Clearly when making this decision they should not do so lightly if the well-being of the students is their goal. They should be precise in formulating the goals they wish to achieve through any such special format, and be aware of potential undesirable effects. Any new format might best be initiated on an experimental and, where feasible, a voluntary basis. It is critical to have periodic objective assessments on both cognitive and affective achievement. These may serve as the basis of comparison with other formats. A special attempt should be made to identify the groups which appear to benefit in a special way, and to identify others who appear to do less well. The educator may well be faced with the problem of economies of scale. Where one or another format has strengths and weaknesses which vary for different groups it may not be possible to implement each one accordingly. One should clearly understand that the format chosen may result in advantage to some at the expense of others.

## Class and Inequality

The reader by now should be quite familiar with the competing theories of social stratification, and with a Marxist analysis of class which is not precisely the same thing. One, the functionalist model, holds that inequality is required for social organization. The other, the conflict model, states that it is not, that it is imposed. Marxists hold that class is a necessary consequence of the private ownership of the means of production which itself is a social and political imposition. Class for the Marxists has a meaning different than the distributive one, but inequality inevitably results from these class relations. It is not our intention here to suggest a solution to this enduring debate although we would point out that the functionalist model has fallen into disrepute. Each perspective has important contributions to make, and we do not feel that it is beneficial to regard them as an 'either-or' dichotomy. Marxist principles of analysis have not traditionally been well accepted in Canada except among a minority of intellectuals. We make a distinction between these principles of analysis and Marxist political thought. In our opinion the principles may be very useful. We have problems with the political thought, although certainly not with this kind alone, because even with the abolition of class in the relational sense inequality may remain.

It is impossible to deal with inequality without relating it to this entire institution of stratification, and this includes the problem of inequality as found in schooling. Social class differences have existed in every known society, including primarily egalitarian ones. The dilemma is not resolved by accepting a Marxist definition, class in the relational sense. Hofley (1980) has pointed out that the abolition of the private ownership of the means of production does not bring with it the abolition of inequality on an intergenerational basis, that is, class in the distributive sense.

It is apparent from this that the issue of inequality cannot be separated from an analysis of class. This applies to the inequality which exists in schooling. As Clement (1975) has indicated, inequality of condition leads to inequality of opportunity and is almost certainly causal. As we shall see in the following section on ideology and hegemony, the basic assumptions of one's value system are reflected in the organization and meaning of knowledge. They have a bearing on the stance one takes not only on the propriety of inequality, the justice or injustice involved, but go so far as to determine the meaning of both inequality and justice.

The effects of schooling on equality and equality of opportunity rank very highly among the most controversial issues in the sociology of education. However, if the problem is to be solved, and we do not suggest that a solution is imminent, then it is in an area beyond this sub-discipline that the solution will be found. We are really dealing with a political question, and the nature of the institution of schooling will be determined by the collective stance we take. To date there is no indication that members of Canadian society generally are deeply concerned about this problem, although there certainly are individual exceptions. It is not just a matter of not knowing the answers. We do not even know the appropriate questions to ask. As Apple (1979) points out so well, the nature of these questions, and therefore the structure of the analysis itself, is dependent on ideological perspectives which are so deeply entrenched that we hardly understand that there is anything questionable about them at all. Hurn (1978) notes that equality of opportunity already exists in the perspective of those who are on the political right. Here talent and effort and motivation coupled with equality of input are the proper determinants of one's life chances, and it is claimed, although not convincingly, that our liberal society allows these variables full sway. Those who take this stand necessarily overlook or are deliberately blind to the point that for specific groups all the talent and effort and motivation in the world will not overcome the barriers to equality which are imposed by other social institutions, even if schooling were neutral (and it is not). On the other hand, those on the political left are convinced that schools are institutions which reinforce the inequality of condition which already exists. The weight of empirical evidence is on their side, but if schooling is not seen purely as an intervening variable through which rather than because of which intergenerational inequality is (partially) passed on, then the major difficulties in analysis which remain are compounded to a serious degree. Schools should not be regarded as major causes of inequality except in an intervening sense.

## Types of Inequality

There are many different kinds of inequality, or stated in another way, inequality may be viewed from a number of perspectives. To begin with, there are *natural* differences of kind such as differences in strength or in intelligence. Without reopening a major debate, there are or may be biological or genetic bases to such differences. However, the situation is compounded by the fact that we frequently add to this a *social* base as well. We should be quite familiar with this problem relative to intelligence. A little thought will point out that there is frequently a strong social basis even to the causes and the importance of differences in strength. We may have two individuals who, because of the nature of their genetic endowment, will have normally developed physiques such that one is vastly stronger than another. We may also have two individuals who, with similar genetic endowment, if normally developed, would be of approximately the same strength. However, in this second case, because of conditions over which no one has any real control, such as a case of polio in childhood, one could end up being much weaker physically than another. There is also the case where, because of the lack of proper food and nutrition, one also ends up as an adult with a much weaker physique. In this case there are predominantly social reasons for the difference in strength. It results from unequal conditions in early life, and these differences could have profound effects on schooling. The one might have the stamina to work hard, the other might not.

There is also the *equal but different* concept such as that which exists between races, or between the sexes. This difference also has a purely genetic base, but society has added a social meaning to it. Sometimes this social construction is very deeply hidden, but it is there and its effects are no less real because of this. The way the members of the two sexes have been treated in traditional schooling is a good example. No one seriously posits that one is superior to the other intellectually. They are regarded as being equal in this way. Yet in Canadian schooling females have not been allowed to achieve to the same degree as males, as any analysis of higher education statistics will show. It is ludicrous to claim that one holds women to be different but equal when such unequal treatment is imposed upon them. Our social definition is such that women are not defined as equals with men, and the persistence of this definition is partly the responsibility of women themselves. Yet it is an arbitrary and social definition just the same.

Opposed to these various kinds of inequalities which at least partially result from genetic differences are the *purely social* inequalities. Sometimes they begin with natural differences, such as in the case of the differences between sexes, sometimes not. The critical point is that thay are founded in some aspect of a shared value system whether imposed or not. This is the result of social interaction and is learned. These social inequalities themselves are of different kinds, or may be viewed from different perspectives. There is *inequality of condition* which results from unequal possession of those things which are of value in our society, some form of power, privilege and prestige. Social class inequalities are of this kind. They result from things that are possessed to a greater or lesser degree and in that sense are external to the person, although it is the person who in the final analysis is ranked unequally. Opposed to inequality of condition, and usually though not necessarily following it, is *inequality of opportunity*. This concept is particularly important in the sociology of education because generally in the functionalist tradition it is the inverse face of the kind of equality which should exist in the institution of schooling. This in itself is a most important concept because it assumes that schooling is not responsible for, or for overcoming, differences among students which are the result of inequality of condition. Theoretically, equality of opportunity refers to the condition that each person has an equal opportunity to succeed at a given task. This, however, is meaningless because of the existence of natural differences of kind, even those which do not have a social base. An example would be differences in intelligence, when the individuals have been exposed to similar or equal environmental influences, something which is difficult to measure accurately. For that reason the concept equality of opportunity has been modified to refer to *equality of input*. When applied to the school this means that all students are exposed to similar or equal school conditions; they receive the same or similar inputs. In this case it is assumed that any degree of inequality which exists in school is not the result of other than school influences, something else which is difficult to substantiate, as our discussion of teacher expectations and the self-fulfilling prophecy should have made clear. Traditionally, equality of opportunity, when restricted to school input, meant that students started out at the same age, were exposed to the same curriculum and were treated in a similar and equitable, even if different, manner by school personnel. In our opinion, equality of opportunity viewed from this perspective will never exist pragmatically, as long as inequality of condition is present, because the same input has different meanings for different students, or for students who are exposed to different levels of inequality of condition prior to and co-terminous with the school years. Equality of opportunity in this sense is opposed to *equality of results*. Going beyond the concept of an equal chance to try, equality of results recognizes the presence of unequal conditions, whether genetic or social and usually a combination of both, and it attempts by applying unequal inputs to bring students to the point of equal educational achievement. It is here that compensatory education enters the picture, being an attempt to overcome earlier deficiencies.

Up to this point, then, we may view inequality from the perspective of its origin as being purely genetic, as purely social, or as biosocial which is a combination of both. In either case the inequality exists at least partially because of social evaluation. When we view inequality as existing, regardless of its source, we are talking about inequality of condition. This refers to one's position on a continuum composed of degrees of power, privilege and prestige. However, if we regard inequality as potential rather than as existing, that is, related to the future achievement of some goal, we are discussing inequality of opportunity, which may or may not be restricted to inequality of input. And finally, when we view it from the point of view of the achievement attained, as a matter of degree, we are discussing inequality of results. We have now returned to an existing inequality and once more are concerned with inequality of condition.

Inequality may also be regarded in a number of other ways which are important in the sociology of education. There is *individual* inequality and *group* inequality. In this latter case we are talking about an average, and between groups averages may and frequently do vary significantly, usually for social reasons. Somewhat related to this and also of considerable importance is *regional* inequality, that which may exist between different areas of the one nation, or between different nations of the world. There are usually structural reasons for regional inequality. Atlantic Canada falls considerably below the national average in per capita income primarily because of the structural underdevelopment which is peculiar to a capitalist economy (Sacouman, 1979). It also falls considerably below the national average in educational achievement (Rocher, 1975), even in measured intelligence (Williams, 1977), because of the inequality of condition resulting from the low per capita income. On the other hand, Canada, including the Atlantic Provinces, falls considerably above the world average in per capita income and educational achievement, also primarily because of structural causes.

There is also *political* inequality, which refers to unequal degrees of power in the pursuit of collective goals. Frequently found between social classes, occupational groups and ethnic and racial groups, this also may have a bearing on educational achievement, as the position of native people makes clear. And we have already mentioned *sexual* inequality which has a political base.

The meaning of inequality, then, is a very complex matter. Because its existence is so pervasive, it is difficult to envision its elimination in the educational system, particularly when, as Hurn (1978) points out, people do not even agree on the ideal.

### The Egalitarian and Democratic Ideology

Rocher notes that the institution of schooling is built on values and value judgements. This means it holds a specific ideological stance. Holding that in the western world, and in Canadian society in particular, the ideology of a democratic and egalitarian educational system has become dominant, he presents three of the principal traits of that ideology (Rocher, 1975:139). The first is that ". . . democratizing the system of education means making education not the privilege of the few, but bringing it to every citizen as his right, a right which is guaranteed by official public declarations and documents, such as a constitution or a law." This trait guarantees the right to try, but not necessarily to succeed, and the state uses its authority to enforce compulsory education up to a certain point.

The second trait is that ". . . each citizen is now called upon to share in the public financial support of the educational system." The education is free, at least to the end of secondary schooling, and because it is regarded as an asset for the nation each citizen is expected to help pay the expenses through general taxation.[1]

The third trait, which Rocher considers the most important 'is . . . the equality of opportunities for all." Rocher understands very well, of course, that equality of opportunity is an ambiguous term. He points out that this is the official ideology, the image that society creates for itself, but that it is far from being realized. Presumably because Canada is a liberal society, it will

---

[1]There is a special problem of inequality here because it is generally agreed that taxation in Canada is itself inequitable. Cf. Gillespie, 1980. Those who receive the least from schooling pay the highest rate of taxation.

continue to work for this goal insofar as it is not incompatible with another goal or ideology such as the capitalist one.

In addition to these three traits, Rocher (1975:156) gives two principles pertaining to the democratization of education and educational reform. The first is that ". . . each student should have the opportunity to benefit by an education which corresponds to his capacities, his tastes, and his interests, and he should be able to pursue his studies in the field or fields in which he is interested as far as he can or will go." As a principle for reform, this suggests making schooling more flexible so that it may provide adequate service to any potential set of academic interests. It is, of course, an ideal. The second principle, claimed to be the more important, imposes on schooling the responsibility '. . . to develop to their utmost all the capacities and aptitudes of each student." Of special concern here are the non-cognitive capacities such as creativity and spontaneity. This also is an ideal. As we have seen, the structures of the organization and the degree of openness of boundaries to other institutions and particularly to the economy make this ideal very difficult to realize.

While these principles have the appearance or the rhetoric of liberal reform which does not attack a problem at the level of basic institutions wherein the problem lies, Rocher points out that there has been a greater effort in the recent past to reform schooling than there has been for any other major institution in our society. However, there are many who claim that such reform is not really possible, or that no radical reform is possible within the framework of a liberal ideology.

Manley-Casimir and Housego (1970) make several interesting points pertaining to the historical development of the meaning of equality of opportunity. 'Equality' has played a central role in the evolution of democratic political theory. The Anglo-American tradition has stressed liberty primarily while the French, following Rousseau, has given greater emphasis to equality. In French Canada, especially Quebec, the people were insulated from the ideas of Rousseau and the French Revolution by the Catholic Church. Democratic innovations were largely imposed from without and were used by the French Canadians only as values which helped to maintain and promote their own culture. So the people of Quebec did not develop a strong democratic tradition, and this was reflected in their schooling.

In English Canada there was a strong pro-monarchist tradition, especially after the arrival of the loyalists, and values of elitism and ascription were more influential in shaping the political heritage than were values of equality and liberty. So neither founding culture in Canada had strong historical traditions of equality or liberty. This became apparent in the evolution of provincial educational institutions, which are committed to differential educational opportunities, especially on the bases of class and culture. This inequality remains, as indicated by regional differences in achievement and per capita expenditure. It is also apparent in cultural differences as seen not only in the curriculum but in the locus of responsibility for the education of Canada's native people (Manley-Casimir and Housego, 1970).

These same authors examine the stages in the development of educational opportunity in the United States as presented by Coleman (1968). These are: (1) a common curriculum in the same kind of school; (2) differentiated curricula which matched the students to a projected career; (3) the 'separate but equal' concept of schooling for minorities, similar to apartheid; (4) the 1954 denial of this 'separate but equal' concept; and (5) the recent stress on equality of results.

"The contemporary development of educational opportunity in Canada appears to be broadly congruent with stage two of the United States experience" (Manley-Casimir and Housego, 1970:84). Provincial systems adopt different curricula matching the child to future expectations. This results in two additional inequalities, accepting as a given the educational and occupational future of a child on an ascribed basis, and matching the curriculum to this expectation, thereby denying opportunities for mobility.

Historically, the Canadian education system followed the European, and especially the British model, at least from the point of view of goals. These were: to provide an educated work force, where education stressed social control; to serve middle-class interests for more advanced cognitive learning; and to maintain the existing social order and system of stratification. The concept of equality was relatively unimportant, or at least had a qualitatively different meaning than it had in the United States. There, despite the presence of immense problems, the 'separate but equal' policy and its subsequent reversal indicated a greater concern with equality of results. However, the qualifying phrase "despite the presence of immense problems" is very important because even in the United States conflicting ideological positions made the realization of equality of results virtually impossible. Reimer notes that equalizing educational opportunity was a public goal in the U.S., but that the pattern of expenditure on an income distribution basis points out how far the reality was from the ideal implicit in that goal. "The children of the poorest one-tenth of the United States population attend school for an average of less than five years. The schools they attend, at this grade level, spend no more than $500 per pupil per year. These children cost the public, in schooling, less than $2,500 over a lifetime. The children of the richest one-tenth of the population finish college and a year of graduate school — their schooling costs about $50,000" (Reimer, 1971:26). The important point here, of course, is not that there is inequality of input, interesting as that is but the conclusion derived from these data relative to inequality of results.

This calls for emphasis on one final problem. Earlier in this century, especially in Canada, the concern with equality in the educational domain was largely restricted to differences between individuals. Today (especially in the United States) the focus is more on diminishing the differences between groups. There, in the United States, the major concern has been with racial groups, but this is inextricably interwoven with social class. Entwistle (1977:VIII) makes the point, an important one, that "(t)aken together with the concept of equality, that of social class raises two important questions: (1) if we are committed to equality are we then committed to a classless society; (11) if not, if we accept the inevitability of merited differences in status, power or economic reward, what do we have to say about those who remain underprivileged or deprived within any of these three categories?" The answer to such questions involves an examination of our deepest beliefs. It is a matter of ideology, a particularly important issue to which we turn now.

## Ideology and Hegemony

When we discuss the ideological role of schools, or for that matter of other major institutions of society, we are dealing essentially with a process of legitimation (Esland, G., 1977). Schools teach knowledge, selective knowledge, and they also teach this knowledge selectively. The dominant culture in every society is characterized by an ideology, or a series of ideologies, which are built on generally unquestioned assumptions so basic that we hardly appreciate that they are there. It is traditional Marxist teaching that the role of the school (as an element of the superstructure) is to support the dominant ideologies of society which themselves owe their existence to the base and have the function of supporting it. It is because of the characteristics of these ideologies that certain kinds of knowledge are selected as appropriate for the curriculum, and other kinds are ignored or avoided. We shall examine this meaning and role of ideology, but we feel it is important to emphasize here that the process of legitimation is not something peculiar to Marxist thought. While it has been developed as a coherent theory almost exclusively in the Marxist tradition, legitimation and the role of ideology also have their place in other schools of thought. This should be apparent for the Weberian conflict theory with its emphasis on the legitimation of power. It also has its place in functionalism. The common value system (Parsons, 1953), the system of evaluation whereby social positions are ranked (Davis and Moore, 1945) may be reduced to an ideological position and a process of legitimation. Durkheim's position on the role of the school as an agent of moral socialization for the state may be regarded in the same way. However, a radical analysis of the role of ideology is peculiar to the Marxist position, something we consider to be one of its strengths.

R. Williams (1976) has an excellent article analysing the meaning of ideology and hegemony, explaining its role in supporting the dominant culture. Apple (1976, 1979), building on Williams, relates this in a more particular way to schooling. Both rely heavily on the theory of the Italian Marxist Antonio Gramsci whose work on hegemony has recently been interpreted by Bates (1975). We shall rely heavily on Williams (1976) and Apple (1976,

1979) in the following presentation, and also but a lesser extent on Esland (1977). This is not an easy process to understand. The meaning of ideology and hegemony is relatively straightforward, but the basic and widespread pervasiveness of their influence is difficult to perceive and its implications hard to appreciate.

"In general terms, 'legitimacy' refers to those rules, beliefs and practices in a society or community which together constitute its basis of order and authority" (Esland, 1977:7). Legitimating beliefs and practices depend on the support of a dominant group. A group may become dominant on the basis of force, or in other ways, but it will not remain in that position unless it gains control over a culture in the sense that it may define from among alternatives such rules and beliefs. While the use of force (armies, police, etc.) does not usually remain overt, the mere availability of force reinforces the prevailing beliefs and practices which became enshrined or embedded in law, custom, education, church. Esland (1977) refers to force as the hard basis of legitimation. The inculcation of the beliefs on a supposedly rational basis in consciousness he refers to as the soft base. It is with this latter form that we are primarily concerned.

An ideology is a system of belief. This belief is concerned with the way things are, the way they should be and the reason something should be done to equate the two (Dolbeare and Dolbeare, 1971). Ideologies embody the interests of the groups who promote them and in this special sense are distortions of reality. When we speak of belief we oppose it to knowledge in the sense that it is not substantiated. It is critical to understand that there is no necessary connection between events, actions, facts and the system of beliefs which is meant to legitimate them. Typically, these systems of belief which are not demonstrable appeal to some 'higher' kind of evidence in the form of logic or 'revelation.' Yet they are built on basic assumptions to which logic does not speak or to which 'revelation' does not address itself. These assumptions are so basic that without serious reflection and analysis we do not even recognize that they are there. Typically, the man-in-the-street response to the questioning of such assumptions is that "everybody knows" or "it has always been that way." Such responses rather ineffectively hide our inability to substantiate the assumption, the existence of which is so basic that it hardly appears to our conscious mind.

It is Marxist teaching that these ideologies or systems of belief which are so basic that they define reality for us serve a political function, and it is the task of sociology to bring out or demonstrate what this political function is and to relate it to the wider structures of power in society (Esland, 1977). The institution of schooling is one of these other structures, and the sociology of education attempts to demonstrate how the processes of schooling, which are determined or limited by this political force, fulfill this ideological or legitimating function. In the study of the social aspects of knowledge as it is disbursed in schools, sociologists try to point out the social structure which is supported or regenerated, and the way this is done. In doing that, sociology attempts to show that the nature of societal institutions such as schools is determined by the prevailing ideologies which in turn are controlled by the dominant group. This dominant group is defined on the basis of its relationship to the means of production, and Marxists refer to it as the dominant class. This is the meaning of class in the relational sense. While it lacks gradations in the distributive sense that another definition of class might have, it is nevertheless a very useful analytical concept. In this line of thinking, ideologies are systems of rules and beliefs which are controlled by the dominant class and serve the function of legitimating the existing reality which gives rise to the prevailing class system. Thus their political function.

Williams (1976:202) notes that an approach to the theory of culture, which is really what we are concerned with, should begin with the proposition that ". . . social being determines consciousness." This, he holds, is preferable to beginning with a proposition about a determining base and a determined superstructure which is a specialized application of the former. He goes on to point out that there are two ways in which the connective 'determines' may be interpreted. One includes the concept of an external cause which totally predicts and prefigures or totally controls the subsequent activity. The other is restricted to a matter of influence which exerts pressures and sets limits. It is this latter meaning which is appropriate for understanding the proposition that social being determines consciousness or, for that matter, that the base determines the superstructure. The determining is to be understood less strictly in the individual case than in relation to the group, although it does apply to individuals as well.

In discussing the base as a prerequisite of what he means by social being, Williams emphasizes the importance of understanding it in a dynamic rather than a static sense. It is not so much an object, a static social existence or mode of production as it is these things in being and in becoming. Marx emphasized that productive *activities*, in particular structural relations, provide the foundation of all other activities (Williams, 1976:203). Relative to the superstructure which is composed of the institutions which are supportive of the kind of activities performed within this particular dynamic set of structural relations, there may be a time lag (the one is more basic than, is prior to the other), and there may be a relationship which is akin to a process of mediation. The social being of man is basically dependent on productive activities within a particular set of structural relations, and the character or nature of the supportive institutions, themselves dynamic, is mediated by this more basic process. Thus social being determines (exerts pressures, sets limits) consciousness. The base determines the superstructure, which moves towards a structural arrangement which is at the same time supportive, dynamic and becoming.

> We have to revalue 'determination' towards the setting of limits and the exertion of pressure, and away from a predicted, prefigured and controlled

content. We have to revalue 'superstructure' towards a related range of cultural practices, and away from a reflected, reproduced or specifically dependent content. And, crucially, we have to revalue 'the base' away from the notion of a fixed economic or technological abstraction, and towards the specific activities of men in real social and economic relationships, containing fundamental contradictions and variations and therefore always in a state of dynamic process (Williams, 1976:203).

"The most important thing a worker ever produces is himself, himself in the fact of that kind of labour . . ." (p.203). Thus the relationship between base and social being.

We must point out that not all Marxists agree with the specifics on the details which we have presented. One may interpret the relationship between the base and the superstructure in a very mechanistic way while another is much more fluid and dynamic. The nature of that relationship is such that the superstructure is remotely dependent on the base but proximately may be quite independent. The superstructure may independently give rise to activities of its own which, in the short run, may be opposed to rather than supportive of the base. But in the long run the effect of hegemony will be to incorporate these into the supporting ideology and institutional framework, unless a new historical epoch results. There is always the dialectic involved.

This brings us back to ideology, which is part of social activity. Although claimed to be natural or have universal validity, ideologies are shown by Williams, following Marx, to be 'determined' by the nature of social being which in turn is dependent on productive activities within a specific set of structural relations. Ideology is part of consciousness, part of the superstructure.

Gramsci uses the term *hegemony*. It refers to a component of ideology, ". . . to an organized assemblage of meanings and practices, the central, effective and dominant system of meanings, values and actions which are *lived*" (Apple, 1979:5). These are so basic, so taken for granted, so much a part of our consciousness that they are beyond opinion and manipulation. They *saturate* consciousness, which is more than a simple reflection of an economic structure, and sees or makes allowance for no other serious possibilities. Hence, they are not something which is held as one from a range of alternatives on the basis of a rational choice. This, then, is not something which is secondary, or superstructural in that sense, but constitutes the limit of common sense for people who come under its influence. Rather than being some kind of training it corresponds more to a process of absorption and for that reason is much more difficult to examine let along change.

Williams (1976), again following Gramsci, goes on to discuss selection and incorporation. Hegemony, or better still, hegemonies refer to a central system of practices which include and are based upon core meanings and values ". . . which we can properly call dominant and effective . . . which are not merely abstract but which are organized and lived" (p.205). This dominant culture requires the incorporation of these hegemonic elements within it. This process of incorporation in turn is based on what is referred to as *selective tradition*, a process of selecting what may be referred to or regarded as *the* tradition, *the* significant past. It is the selectivity which is so important, not the tradition itself, '. . . the way in which from a whole possible area of past and present, certain meanings and practices are chosen for emphasis, certain other meanings and practices are excluded" (p.205). There is even a process of reinterpreting and diluting involved. This entire process of selecting the 'proper' tradition leads to its incorporation into a dominant culture which then supports the dominant class or system of social relations on which the dominance is based. The resulting hegemony is so basic that it saturates our consciousness and effectively precludes alternative opinions and attitudes.

In an interesting article, Gramsci (1976) looks to the role of intellectuals. Noting that they are not really an autonomous and independent social group because they are changed in nature with the emergence of a new dominant group, Gramsci holds that it is an error in method to distinguish them from other groups on the basis of their intellectual activities. They should be distinguished rather because of their function within the complex system of social relations. Every group has intellectuals in the sense of intellectual activity and every social action or practice involves an intellectual element. "All men are intellectuals, one could therefore say: but not all men have in society the function of intellectuals" (Gramsci, 1976:219). It is the function of intellectuals of an emerging dominant group to be specialists in assimilating, or conquering ideologically, the traditional intellectuals who, in virtue of this process, are to be left behind. The intellectuals who emerge in the new system of social relations are specialists in organizing the selective tradition which is incorporated in the now prevailing ideology which gives support to the new dominant group. Thus they have a special function in the new system of relations, and they are not autonomous or independent because of this relationship to the dominant group.

Apple (1979) relates this general theory on ideology and hegemony to the process of schooling. He attempts to point out the way the prevailing structural arrangements of society come to dominate cultural life, and more specifically the process of schooling. Knowledge is structured in a specific way in schools so that some matters are deemed important, some peripheral and some are totally overlooked or ignored. The process of selection and organization is at work, and we must emphasize that this is not a conscious process or a form of manipulation in the minds of educators whom we are quite willing and anxious to identify as people who intend to be of service to all. But "one of our basic problems as educators and as political beings, then, is to grapple with ways of understanding how the kinds of cultural resources and symbols schools select and organize are dialectically related to the kinds of normative and conceptual consciousness 'required' by a stratified society" (Apple, 1979:2). It is beyond the scope of this general presentation to indicate how this is done, although we have repeatedly made reference to isolated ways at many earlier points in the text. Our intent here is to point out the fact that it is a process which *is* performed in schooling. Frequently referred to as the hidden curriculum, this organized but covert process is more appropriately analysed in a specialized course. Within that more specialized area it is critical to understand how the prevailing ideologies ". . . are reflected in the fundamental perspectives educators themselves employ to order, guide, and give meaning to their own activity" (Apple, 1979:15). Through educators schools become agents of cultural and ideological hegemony. They ". . . help create people who see no other serious possibility to the economic and cultural assemblage now extant" (Apple, 1979:6).

It is for reasons such as these that recent analysts of schooling, especially in the United States and England, are so critical of liberal educational reforms. They interpret liberalism as a supportive ideology based on selective belief. The priority of the individual is a good example. We have not been concerned with a sociological definition of man, but any such definition would have to include social interaction and a community setting. Does it make sense, is it demonstrable, that priority should be given to individual rights? This belief is so basic that most Canadians and all liberals hold it strongly. But the other side of the coin is that, because the community is the condition of man, the individual does not have rights which are prior to it. But what a difference this perspective makes in structuring schools on the basis of a meritocracy where the person who is superior in any one or a group of special abilities has as his or her right a greater reward!

# References

Abrahamson, M. 1981. *Sociological Theory*. Englewood Cliffs N.J.: Prentice-Hall.

Adams, G. R., and A. S. Cohen. 1976. "An Examination of Cumulative Folder Information Used By Teachers in Making Differential Judgments of Children's Abilities." *The Alberta Journal of Educational Research* 22 (3).

Adams, H. 1968. *The Education of Canadians 1800-1867*. Montreal: Harvest House.

Adams, I., W. Cameron, B. Hill, and P. Penz. 1971. *The Real Poverty Report*. Edmonton: Hurtig.

Alexander, K. L., and B. K. Eckland. 1974. "Sex Differences in the Educational Attainment Process." *American Sociological Review* 39 (October).

Alexander, K. L., and B. K. Eckland. 1975. "Basic Attainment Processes: A Replication and Extension." *Sociology of Education* 48 (Fall).

_____. 1975. "Contextual Effects in the High School Attainment Process." *American Sociological Review* 40 (Fall).

Alexander, K., and E. McDill. 1976. "Selection and Allocation within Schools." *American Sociological Review* 41 (June).

Ahlgren, A., and P. R. Germann. 1977. "Perceptions of Open Schooling." *American Educational Research Journal* 14 (3).

Allen, D. I. 1974. "Student Performance, Attitude and Self-Esteem in Open-Area and Self-Contained Classrooms." *The Alberta Journal of Educational Research* 20 (1).

Alschuler, A. S. 1973. *Developing Achievement Motivation in Adolescents*. Englewood Cliffs, N.J.: Educational Technology Publications.

Alwin, D. F., and L. D. Otto. 1977. "High School Context Effects On Aspirations." *Sociology of Education* 50.

Anastasiow, N. J. 1971. "Language Reconstruction Patterns of Kindergarten, First and Second Grades as Indicators of the Development of Cognitive Processes: A Study Exploring the Difference-Deficit Explanations of Language Behaviour." Bloomington, Ind.: Institute for Child Study, Indiana University.

_____. 1976 *Language Patterns of Poverty Children*. Springfield, Ill.: C. C. Thomas.

Anastasiow, N. J., L. Shapiro, J. D. Hoban, and D. A. Hunter. 1969. *An Exploratory Study of the Language of Black Inner-City Elementary School Children*. Bloomington, Ind.: Institute for Child Study, Indiana University.

Anderson, B. D. 1973. "School Bureaucratization and Alienation from High School." *Sociology of Education* 46 (Summer).

Anderson, G. J., and J. P. Hanrahan. 1972. "Effects of age of School Entrance on Intelligence." *The Alberta Journal of Educational Research* 17 (1).

Andrews, J. H. M. 1965. "School Organizational Climate: Some Validity Studies." *Canadian Education and Research Digest* 5 (4).

357

Apple, M. W. 1976. "Common Sense Categories and Curriculum Thought." In R. Dale, G. Esland and M. MacDonald (eds.), *Schooling and Capitalism*. London: Routledge and Kegan Paul.

_____. 1979. *Ideology and Curriculum*. London: Routledge and Kegan Paul.

Armstrong, D. 1970. *Education and Economic Achievement*. Documents of the Royal Commission on Bilingualism and Biculturalism No. 7. Ottawa: Queen's Printer.

Ashworth, Mary. 1975. *Immigrant Children and Canadian Schools*. Toronto: McClelland and Stewart Limited.

Assheton-Smith, M. 1979. "John Porter's Sociology: A Theoretical Basis for Canadian Education." *Canadian Journal of Education* 4 (2).

Atkinson, J. W. 1965. "The Mainsprings of Achievement-Oriented Activity." In J. D. Krunboltz (ed.), *Learning and the Educational Process*. Chicago: Rand McNally.

Atkinson, J. W., and N. T. Feather, (eds.). 1966. *A Theory of Achievement Motivation*. New York: Wiley.

Audet, L. P. 1970. "The French Heritage." In J. D. Wilson, R. M. Stamp, and L. P. Audet (eds.), *Canadian Education: A History*. Scarborough, Ont.: Prentice-Hall of Canada.

Bair, M., and R. G. Woodward. 1965. *Team-Teaching in Action*. Boston, Houghton Mifflen.

Baldwin, A. L. 1967. *Theories of Child Development*. New York: Wiley.

Ball, S. (ed.). 1977. *Motivation in Education*. New York: Academic Press.

Baltzell, E. D. 1958. *Philadelphia Gentleman*. Chicago: Quadrangle.

Bandura, A. 1965. "Influence of a Models Reinforcement Contingencies on the Acquisition of Imitative Responses." *Journal of Personality and Social Psychology* 11.

_____. 1969. *Principles of Behaviour Modification*. New York: Holt, Rinehart and Winston.

_____. 1971. *Social Learning Theory*. New York: General Learning Press.

_____. 1973. *Aggression: A Social Learning Analysis*. Englewood Cliffs, N.J.: Prentice-Hall.

_____. 1977. *Social Learning Theory*. Englewood Cliffs, N.J.: Prentice-Hall.

Bandura, A., D. Ross, and S. A. Ross. 1963. "Imitation of Film Mediated Aggressive Models." *Journal of Abnormal and Social Psychology* 66.

Bandura, A., and R. H. Walters. 1963. *Social Learning and Personality Development*. New York: Holt, Rinehart and Winston.

Banks, Olive. 1976. *The Sociology of Education*. 3rd ed. London: B. I. Batsford.

Banks, O., and D. Finlayson. 1973. *Success and Failure in the Elementary School*. London: Methuen.

Bany, M. A., and L. V. Johnson. 1975. *Educational Social Psychology*. New York: Macmillan.

Bates, T. R. 1975. "Gramsci and the Theory of Hegemony." *Journal of the History of Ideas* 36 (June).

Baudelot, C., and R. Establet. 1971. *L'ecole Capitaliste en France*. Paris.

Becker, H. S. 1961. "Schools and Systems of Stratification." In A. H. Halsey, J. Floud, and C. A. Anderson (eds.), *Education, Economy, and Society*. New York: Free Press.

Beggs, David W. 1968. *Team Teaching — Bold New Venture*. London: Indiana University Press.

Belanger, P. W., and G. Rocher (eds.). 1975. *Ecole et Societé au Quebec. Montreal: Hurtubise HMH*.

*Bennett, N. 1976. Teaching Styles and Pupil Progress*. Cambridge, Massachusetts: Harvard University Press.

Bereiter, C. 1969. "The Future of Individual Differences." *Harvard Educational Review* 39 (2).

_____. 1971. "Education and the Presence of Reality." *Interchange* 2 (1).

_____. 1972. "Schools Without Education." *Harvard Educational Review* 42 (3).

Bereiter, C., and S. Engelmann. 1966. *Teaching Disadvantaged Children in the Preschool*. Englewood Cliffs, N.J.: Prentice-Hall.

Berg, Ivan. 1970. *Education and Jobs: The Great Training Robbery*. New York: Praeger.

Bergen, J. J., and D. Deiseach. 1972. "Dimensions of the High School Student's Role." *Alberta Journal of Educational Research* 18 (1).

Berger, A. 1973. "The Education of Canadian Indians: An In-depth Study of Nine Families." *The Alberta Journal of Educational Research* 19 (4).

Berlyne, D. E. 1960. *Conflict, Arousal and Curiosity*. New York: McGraw-Hill.

_____. 1965. "Curiosity and Education." In J. D. Krumboltz (ed.), *Learning and the Educational Process*. Chicago: Rand McNally.

Bernstein, B. 1958. "Linguistic Codes, Hesitation Phenomena and Intelligence." *Language and Speech* 5.

_____. 1959. "A Public Language: Some Sociological Implications of a Linguistic Form." *British Journal of Sociology* 9.

_____. 1960. "Language and Social Class." *British Journal of Sociology* 11 (3).

_____. 1961a. "Aspects of Language and Learning in the Genesis of the Social Process." *Journal of Child Psychology and Psychiatry* 1.

_____. 1961b. "Social Class and Linguistic Development: A Theory of social Learning." In A. H. Halsey et al. (eds.), *Education, Economy and Society*. New York: Free Press.

_____. 1961c. "Social Structure, Language and Learning." *Educational Research* 3.

_____. 1962. "Social Class, Linguistic Codes and Grammatical Elements." *Language and Speech* 5.

_____. 1964. "Elaborated and Restricted Codes: Their Social Origin and Some Consequences." *American Anthropologist* 66 (6).

_____. 1974. *Class, Codes and Control* Vol. 1. *Theoretical Studies Towards a Sociology of Language*. London: Routledge and Kegan Paul.

Bezeau, L. M. 1977. "Equality of Educational Opportunity and Inequality of Per Pupil Expenditures." *The Alberta Journal of Educational Research* 23 (3).

Bidwell, C. E. 1965. "The School as a Formal Organization." In J. G. March (ed.), *Handbook of Organizations.* Chicago: Rand McNally.

Bienstock, H. 1967. "Realities of the Job Market for the High School Dropout." In D. Schreiber (ed.), *Profile of the School Dropout.* New York: Vintage Books.

Biesheuvel, S. 1975. "An Examination of Jensen's Theory Concerning Educability, Heritability and Population Differences." In A. Montagu (ed.), *Race and IQ.* New York: Oxford.

Bigge, M. L., and M. P. Hunt. 1980. *Psychological Foundations of Education.* 3rd ed. New York: Harper and Row.

Bindman, A. 1966. "The Dropout." *Arbos* 2 (5).

Bingay, James, 1919. *Public Education in Nova Scotia: A History and Commentary.* Kingston: Jackson Press.

Bird, F. (Chairman). 1970. *Report of the Royal Commission on the Status of Women in Canada.* Ottawa: Information Canada.

Birenbaum, A., and E. Sagarin. 1976. *Norms and Human Behaviour.* New York: Praeger.

Blackstone, W. T. 1969. "Human Rights, Equality, and Education." *Educational Theory* 19 (Summer).

Blalock, H. M. 1960. *Social Statistics.* New York: McGraw Hill.

Blau, P. 1955. *The Dynamics of Bureaucracy.* Chicago: University of Chicago Press.

_____. 1973. *The Organization of Academic Work.* New York: John Wiley and Sons.

Blau, P. M., and O. D. Duncan. 1967. *The American Occupational Structure.* New York: Wiley.

Blau, P. M., and M. E. Meyer. 1971. *Bureaucracy in Modern Society.* 2nd ed. New York: Random House.

Bleasdale, G. 1978. "Towards a Political Economy of Capitalist Educational Values." In R. W. Nelsen and D. A. Nock (eds.), *Reading, Writing and Riches.* Kitchener, Ontario: Between the Lines.

Bloom, B. S. (ed.). 1956. *Taxonomy of Educational Objectives: The Classification of Educational Goals. Handbook I. Cognitive Domain.* New York.

Blowers, E. A. 1972. "Barriers to Education of Children from Low-income Families." *The Alberta Journal of Educational Research* 18 (1).

Blumer, H. 1969. *Symbolic Interactionism.* Englewood Cliffs,, N.J.: Prentice-Hall.

Blyth, Jack. 1972. *The Canadian Social Inheritance.* Toronto.

Bodner, W. F. 1975. "Race and IQ: The Genetic Background." In A. Montagu (ed.), *Race and IQ.* New York: Oxford.

Bonnell, J. S. (Chairman). 1965. *Report of the Royal Commission on Higher Education.* Charlottetown: Queen's Printer.

Boocock, S. S. 1972. *An Introduction to the Sociology of Learning.* Boston: Houghton-Mifflen.

_____. 1973. "The School as a Social Environment." *Sociology of Education* 46 (Winter).

_____. 1980. *Sociology of Education.* 2nd ed. Boston: Houghton-Mifflen.

Borg, W. 1964. "Ability Grouping in the Public Schools." Co-operative Research Project No. 557. Salt Lake City: Utah State University.

_____. 1966. *Ability Grouping in the Public Schools.* 2nd ed. Madison, Wisc.: Dembar Educational Research Services.

Boudon, R. 1974. *Education, Opportunity, and Social Inequality: Changing Prospects in Western Society.* New York: John Wiley and Sons, Inc.

Bowd, A. D. 1972. "Some Determinants of School Achievement in Several Indian Groups." *The Alberta Journal of Educational Research* 18 (2).

Bowles, S. 1971. "Unequal Education and the Reproduction of the Social Division of Labour." *Review of Radical Political Economy* 3 (Fall/Winter).

Bowles, S., and H. Gintis. 1973. "IQ in the U.S. Class Structure." *Social Policy* 3 (4,5).

_____. 1976. *Schooling in Capitalist America.* New York: Basic Books.

Bowles, S., H. Gintis, and P. Meyer. 1975. "The Long Shadow of Work: Education, the Family, and the Reproduction of the Social Division of Labor." *The Insurgent Sociologist*, (Summer).

Brace, C. L., and F. B. Livingstone. 1975. "On Creeping Jensenism." In A. Montagu (ed.). *Race and IQ.* New York: Oxford.

Braham, M. 1973. "Is Educative Schooling Possible?" In T. Morrison and A. Burton (eds.), *Options: Reforms and Alternatives for Canadian Education.* Toronto: Holt, Rinehart and Winston of Canada, Limited.

Brandis, W., and B. Bernstein. 1974. *Selection and Control: Teachers' Ratings of Children in the Infant School.* London: Routledge and Kegan Paul.

Brandis, W., and D. Henderson. 1970. *Social Class, Language and Communication.* London: Routledge and Kegan Paul.

Brant, C. S. 1977. "Education for Canadian Eskimos." In R. A. Carleton, L. A. Colley, and N. J. MacKinnon (eds.), *Education Change and Society.* Toronto: Gage Educational.

Braun, Carl. 1976. "Teacher Expectation: Sociopsychological Dynamics." *Review of Educational Research* 46 (Spring).

Brembeck, C. S. 1971. *Social Foundations of Education.* 2nd. ed. New York: John Wiley and Sons.

Breton, R. 1970. "Academic Stratification in Secondary Schools and the Educational Plans of Students." *The Canadian Review of Sociology and Anthropology* 7 (1).

_____. 1972. *Social and Academic Factors in the Career Decisions of Canadian Youth.* Department of Manpower and Immigration, Ottawa.

_____. 1973. "Academic Stratification in Secondary Schools and the Educational Plans of students." In J. E. Curtis and W. G. Scott (eds.), *Social Stratification: Canada.* Scarborough: Prentice-Hall of Canada.

Breton, R., and J. C. McDonald. 1968. "Occupational Preferences of Canadian High School Students." In B. R. Blishen, F. E. Jones, K. D. Naegele, and J. Porter (eds.), *Canadian Society: Sociological Perspectives.* Toronto: The Macmillan Company of Canada Limited.

Brittain, C. V. 1963. "Adolescent Choices and Parent-Peer Cross-Pressures." *American Sociological Review* 28 (3).

Bronfenbrenner, U. 1958. "Socialization and Social Class Through Time and Space." In E. E. Maccoby et al. (eds.), *Readings in Social Psychology*. New York: Holt, Rinehart and Winston.

_____. 1970. *Two Worlds of Childhood: U.S. and U.S.S.R.* New York: Russell Sage Foundation.

_____. 1975a. "Nature and Nurture: A Reinterpretation of the Evidence." In A. Montagu (ed.), *Race and IQ*. New York: Oxford, 1975.

_____. 1975b. "Is Early Intervention Effective? Some Studies of Early Education in Familial and Extra-Familial Settings." In A. Montagu (ed.), *Race and IQ*. New York: Oxford.

Brookover, W. B., and E. L. Erickson. 1975. *Sociology of Education*. Homewood, Illinois: The Dorsey Press.

Brookover, W. B., R. J. Gigliotti, R. P. Henderson, and J. M. Schneider. 1973. *Elementary School Social Environments and Achievement*. East Lansing, Mich.: College of Urban Development, Michigan State University.

Brookover, W. B., A. Paterson, and S. Thomas. 1962. *Self-Concept of Ability and School Achievement*. East Lansing: Office of Research and Publications, College of Education, Michigan State University.

Buckley, W. 1958. "Social Stratification and the Functional Theory of Social Differentiation." *The American Sociological Review* 23 (August).

Buckman, P. (ed.). 1973. *Education Without Schools*. London: Souvenir Press (Educational and Academic) Ltd.

Byers, L. 1961. "Ability Grouping — Help or Hindrance to Social and Emotional Growth?" *The School Review* 69 (4).

Byrne, N. 1972. "Innovation and the Teacher." In N. Byrne and J. Quarter (eds.), *Must Schools Fail? The Growing Debate in Canadian Education*. Toronto: McClelland and Stewart Limited.

Canadian Teachers' Federation. 1969. *School Dropouts: Bibliographies in Education No. 36*. Ottawa: Canadian Teachers' Federation.

Caplow, T., and R. J. McGee. 1958. *The Academic Marketplace*. New York: Basic Books.

Cardinal, H. 1977. *The Rebirth of Canada's Indians*. Edmonton: Hurtig.

Carlton, R. A., L. A. Colley, and N. J. MacKinnon (eds.). 1977. *Education, Change and Society*. Toronto: Gage Educational.

Carroll, J. R. 1950. "Public School Education in Nova Scotia, 1870-1935." M.Ed. dissertation Dalhousie University.

Caskie, D. M. 1979. *Canadian Fact Book on Poverty*. Ottawa: Canadian Council on Social Development.

Cattell, R. B. 1971. *Abilities, Their Structure, Growth and Action*. Boston: Houghton Mifflin.

Chapman, R., and E. Ingram. 1974. "Regionalism in Education." *The Canadian Administrator* 13 (7).

Charters, W. W. 1963. "The Social Background of Teaching." In N. L. Gage (ed.), *Handbook of Research on Teaching*. Chicago: Rand-McNally.

Chekki, D., and J. R. Hofley. 1980. "Women and Inequality." In J. Harp, and J. R. Hofley (eds.), *Structured Inequality in Canada*. Scarborough: Prentice-Hall of Canada.

Church, R. L. 1976. *Education in the United States*. New York: The Free Press.

Cicourel, A., and J. Kitsuse. 1963. *The Educational Decision Makers*. Indianapolis: Bobbs-Merrill.

Cistone, P. J. (ed.). 1972. *School Boards and the Political Fact*. Symposium Series No. 2. Toronto: Ontario Institute for Studies in Education.

Cistone, P. J. 1977. "Educational Policy Making." *Educational Forum* 42 (1).

Clark, B. 1960. "The Cooling Out Function in Higher Education." *American Journal of Sociology* 65 (May).

_____. 1962. *Educating the Expert Society*. San Francisco: Chandler.

Clark, B. M., and M. Trow. 1966. "The Organizational Context." In T. M. Newcomb and E. K. Wilson (eds.), *College Peer Groups*. Chicago: Aldine Publishing Company.

Clarke, S. C. T., and S. Hunka. 1977. "Comparative Views On School Discipline." *The Alberta Journal of Educational Research* 23 (4).

Clayton, R. R. 1975. *The Family, Marriage and Social Change*. Lexington: D. C. Heath.

Clement, W. 1975. *The Canadian Corporate Elite*. Toronto: McClelland and Stewart.

Clifford, M. M., and E. Walster. 1973. "The Effects of Physical Attractiveness on Teacher Expectations." *Sociology of Education* 46 (Spring).

Cockerham, W. C., and A. L. Blevins, Jr. 1976. "Open School vs. Traditional School: Self-Identification Among Native American and White Adolescents." *Sociology of Education* (April)49.

Coleman, J. S. 1961. *The Adolescent Society*. New York: Free Press.

_____. 1968. "The Concept of Equality of Educational Opportunity." *Harvard Educational Review* 38 (1).

Coleman, J. S., E. Q. Campbell, C. J. Hobson, J. McPartland, A. Mood, F. D. Weinfeld, and R. L. York. 1966. *Equality of Educational Opportunity*. Washington, D.C.: U. S. Government Printing Office.

Collins, R. 1971. "Functional and Conflict Theories of Educational Stratification." *American Sociological Review* 36 (December).

_____. 1974. "Where Are Educational Requirements for Employment Highest?" *Sociology of Education* 47 (Fall).

_____. 1975. *Conflict Sociology: Toward an Explanatory Science*. New York: Academic Press, Inc.

_____. 1979. *The Credential Society*. New York: Academic Press.

Cook, G. C. A. (ed.). 1976. *Opportunity for Choice: A Goal for Women in Canada*. Statistics Canada in association with the C. D. Howe Research Institute. Ottawa: Information Canada.

Cooley, C. H. 1964. *Human Nature and the Social Order*. New York: Schocken.

Corwin, R. G. 1974. *Education in Crisis: A Sociological Analysis of Schools and Universities in Transition*. New York: John Wiley and Sons, Inc.

_____. 1975. "Innovation in Organizations: The Case of Schools." *Sociology of Education* 48.

Council of Ministers of Education. 1975. *Review of Educational Policies in Canada.*

Cousin, J., J. P. Fortin, and C. J. Wenaas. 1971. *Some Economic Aspects of Provincial Educational Systems.* Staff Study No. 27. Economic Council of Canada. Ottawa: Information Canada.

Cronbach, L. J. 1969. "Heredity, Environment and Educational Policy." *Harvard Educational Review* 39 (2).

Crow, J. F. 1969. "Genetic Theories and Influences: Comments on the Value of Diversity." In *Harvard Educational Review* 39 (2).

Cuneo, C. J., and J. E. Curtis. 1975. "Social Ascription in the Educational and Occupational Status Attainment of Urban Canadians." *The Canadian Review of Sociology and Anthropology* 12 (1).

Curtis, J., M. Kuhn, and R. Lambert. 1977. "Education and the Pluralist Perspective." In R. A. Carlton, L. A. Colley, and N. J. MacKinnon (eds.), *Education, Change and Society.* Toronto: Gage Educational.

Dandurand, P. 1977. "Education and Power." In R. A. Carlton, L.A. Colley, and N. J. MacKinnon (eds.), *Education, Change and Society.* Toronto: Gage Educational.

Daniel, M., and F. Whittingham. 1975. "Labour Market Experience of Out-of-School Youth." Statistics Canada. *Notes on Labour Statistics 1973.* Ottawa: Information Canada.

Davey, I. E. 1978. "The Rythm of Work and The Rhythm of School." In N. McDonald and A. Chaiton (eds.), *Egerton Ryerson and His Times.* Toronto: Macmillan of Canada.

Davis, K. 1972. "The Relation of Ascribed to Achieved Status." In G. W. Thielbar and S. D. Feldman (eds.), *Issues in Social Inequality.* Boston: Little, Brown and Company.

Davis, K., and W. E. Moore. 1942. "A Conceptual Analysis of Stratification." *American Sociological Review* 7 (3).

_____. 1945. "Some Principles of Stratification." *American Sociological Review* 10 (2).

De Cecco, J. P., and W. R. Crawford. 1974. *The Psychology of Learning and Instruction.* 2nd ed. Englewood Cliffs: Prentice-Hall.

Defleur, L. B., and B. A. Menke. 1975. "Learning About The Labour Free: Occupational Knowledge Among High School Males." *Sociology of Education* 48 (Summer).

Deutsch, M. 1965. "The Role of Social Class in Language Development and Cognition." *American Journal of Orthopsychiatry* 35.

Dobson, R. B. 1977. "Social Status and Inequality of Access to Higher Education in the USSR." In J. Karabel and A. H. Halsey (eds.), *Power and Ideology in Education.* New York: Oxford University Press.

Doherty, E. G., and C. Culver. 1976. "Sex-Role Identification, Ability, and Achievement Among High School Girls." *Sociology of Education* 49 (January).

Dolbeare, K. M., and P. Dolbeare. 1971. *American Ideologies*. Chicago: Markham.

Dollard, J., and N. E. Miller. 1950. *Personality and Psychotherapy*. New York: McGraw-Hill.

Douglas, J. 1964. *The Home and The School*. London: McGibbon and Kee.

Driedger, L. 1980. "Ethnic and Minority Relations." In R. Hagedorn (ed.), *Sociology*. Toronto: Holt, Rinehart and Winston of Canada.

Dryder, E. E. 1972. "High School Athletes and Their Coaches: Educational Plans and Advice." *Sociology of Education* 45 (Summer).

Duncan, O. D., D. L. Featherman, and B. Duncan. 1972. *Socioeconomic Background and Achievement*. New York: Seminar Press.

Dunton, A. D., and A. Laurendeau (Co-chairman). 1968. *Royal Commission on Bilingualism and Biculturalism*. Vol. 2, *Education*. *Ottawa: Queen's Printer*.

*Durkheim, E. 1956 Education and Society*. Translated by S. D. Fox. Glencoe, Illinois: The Free Press.

_____. 1977. "On Education and Society." In J. Karabel and A. H. Halsey (eds.), *Power and Ideology in Education*. New York: Oxford.

Durrie, T. 1972. "Free Schools: The Answer or the Question." In N. Byrne and J. Quarter (eds.), *Must Schools Fail? The Growing Debate in Canadian Education*. Toronto: McClelland and Stewart Limited.

Dusek, J. B. 1975. "Do Teachers Bias Children's Learning?" *Review of Educational Research* 45 (Fall).

Eash, M. J. 1961. "Grouping: What We Have Learned." *Educational Leadership* 18 (April).

Eberlein, L., J. Park, and W. Matheson. 1971. "Self-Ideal Congruence in Five Occupational Groups." *The Alberta Journal of Educational Research* 17 (2).

Eckland, B. K. 1967. "Genetics and Sociology: A Reconsideration." *American Sociological Review* 32 (April).

_____. 1971. "Social Class Structure and the Genetic Basis of Intelligence." In R. Concro (ed.), *Intelligence: Genetic and Environmental Influences*. New York: Grune and Stratton.

Eddy, W. P. 1970. "The Relationship of Role Orientation of Teachers to Organization of Schools." *The Alberta Journal of Educational Research* 16 (1).

Edwards, John R. 1979. *Language and Disadvantage*. London: Edward Arnold.

Eisenstadt, S. N. 1956. *From Generation to Generation*. New York: The Free Press.

Elkind, David. 1969. "Piagetian and Psychometric Conceptions of Intelligence." *Harvard Educational Review* 39 (2).

Entwistle, H. 1977. *Class, Culture and Education*. London: Methuen.

Erikson, E. 1963. *Childhood and Society*. 2nd. ed. New York: W. W. Norton.

Erikson, E. H. 1968. *Identity: Youth and Crisis*. New York: W. W. Norton..

Escande, Claude. 1973. *Les Classes Sociale au CEGEP*. Montreal: Parti Press.

Esland, G. 1977. "Legitimacy and Control." *The Open University Educational Studies* Unit 4. London: The Open University.

Eve, R. A. 1975. "Adolescent Culture, Convenient Myth or Reality? A Comparison of Students and their Teachers." *Sociology of Education* 48 (Spring).

Eysenck, H. J. 1973. *The Measurement of Intelligence.* Lancaster: Medical, Technical Publishers.

_____. 1979. *The Structure and Measurement of Intelligence.* New York: Springler-Verlag.

Fanelli, G. C. 1977. "Locus of Control." In S. Ball (ed.), *Motivation in Education.* New York: Academic Press.

Finley, W. G., and M. Bryon. 1971. *Ability Grouping: 1970.* Athens, Ga.: Center for Educational Improvement, University of Georgia.

Fiorino, A. S. 1978. "The Moral Education of Egerton Ryerson's Idea of Education." In N. McDonald and A. Chaiton (eds.), *Egerton Ryerson and His Times.* Toronto: Macmillan of Canada.

Fleming, W. G. 1957. *Background and Personality Factors Associated with Educational and Occupational Plans and Careers of Ontario Grade Thirteen Students.* Toronto: Ontario College of Education.

Flower, G. E. 1967. "Education." In J. M. S. Careless and R. C. Brown (eds.), *The Canadians 1867-1967.* Toronto: Macmillan Company of Canada Limited.

Forcese, D. 1980. *The Canadian Class Structure.* 2nd. ed. Toronto: McGraw-Hill Ryerson.

French, G. S. 1978. "Egerton Ryerson and the Methodist Model for Upper Canada." In N. McDonald and A. Chaiton (eds.), *Egerton Ryerson and His Times.* Toronto: Macmillan of Canada Limited.

Frideres, J. S. 1974. *Canada's Indians: Contemporary Conflicts.* Scarborough, Ontario: Prentice-Hall of Canada Limited.

Friedenberg, E. Z. 1970. "The Function of the School in Social Homeostasis." *The Canadian Review of Sociology and Anthropology* 7 (1).

_____. 1974. "The Modern High School: A Profile." In S. Fishman, A. M. Kazamias, and H. M. Kliebard (eds.), *Teacher, Student and Society: Perspectives on Education.* Boston: Little, Brown and Company.

Friesen, D. 1967. "Profile of the Potential Dropout." *Alberta Journal of Educational Research* 13 (4).

_____. 1972. "Value Orientations of Modern Youth: A Comparative Study." *Adolescence* 7 (26).

Friere, P. 1970. "The Adult Literacy Process as Cultural Action for Freedom." *Harvard Educational Review* 40.

Frieze, I. R. 1980. "Beliefs About Success and Failure in the Classroom." In J. H. McMillan (ed.), *The Social Psychology of School Learning.* New York: Academic Press.

Gage, N. L., and D. C. Berliner. 1979. *Educational Psychology.* 2nd. ed. Chicago: Rand McNally.

Gagne, R. M. 1977. *The Conditions of Learning.* 3rd. ed. New York: Holt, Rinehart and Winston.

Gallagher, P. 1972. "Power and Participation in Educational Reform." *McGill Journal of Education* 7 (2).

Gallatin, J. E. 1965. *Adolescence and Individuality: A Conceptual Approach to Adolescent Psychology.* New York: Harper and Row.

George, P. M., and H. Y. Kim. 1971. "Social Factors and Educational Aspirations of Canadian High School Students." In J. E. Gallagher and R. D. Lambert (eds.), *Social Process and Institutions.* Toronto: Holt, Rinehart and Winston of Canada Limited.

Getzels, J., and P. Jackson. 1963. "The Highly Intelligent and the Highly Creative Adolescent: A Summary of Some Research Findings." In C. Taylor and F. Barron (eds.), *Scientific Creativity.* New York: Wiley.

Gibbons, M. 1975. "Secondary Education: The Gathering Reform." *Interchange* 6 (3).

Gilbert, S. 1977. "The Selection of Educational Aspirations." In R. A. Carlton, L. A. Colley, and N. J. MacKinnon (eds.), *Education, Change and Society.* Toronto: Gage.

Gillespie, I. 1980. "On the Redistribution of Income in Canada." In J. Harp and J. R. Hofley (eds.), *Structured Inequality in Canada.* Scarborough: Prentice-Hall of Canada.

Gillett, M. 1966. *A History of Education — Thought and Practice.* Toronto: McGraw-Hill Company of Canada Limited.

Gintis, H. 1972. "Towards a Political Economy of Education: A Radical Critique of Ivan Illrich's Deschooling Society." *Harvard Educational Review* 42 (1).

Glasser, W. 1969. *Schools Without Failure.* New York: Harper and Row.

Goble, N. 1976. "Education and Politics: The Canadian Dimension." *Alberta Teachers' Association Magazine* 56 (4).

Goldstein, M. S. 1974. "Academic Careers and Vocational Choices of Elite and Non-Elite Students at an Elite College." *Sociology of Education* 47 (Fall).

Gordon, C. 1975. "Complex Organizations: The Issue of Bureaucracy." In D. Forcese and S. Richer (eds.), *Issues in Canadian Society.* Scarborough, Ontario: Prentice-Hall of Canada.

Gordon, M. T. 1976. "A Different View of the I.Q. — Achievement Gap." *Sociology of Education* 49 (January).

Gosine, M., and M. V. Keith. 1970. "Bureaucracy, Teacher Personality Needs and Teacher Satisfaction." *The Canadian Administrator* 10 (1).

Gould, S. J. 1975. "Racist Argument and I.Q." In A. Montagu (ed.), *Race and I.Q.* New York: Oxford.

Grace, G. R. 1972. *Role Conflict and the Teacher.* London: Routledge and Kegan Paul.

Graff, H. J. 1978. "The Reality Behind the Rhetoric: The Social and Economic Meanings of Literacy in the Mid-Nineteenth Century." In N. McDonald and A. Chaiton (eds.), *Egerton Ryerson and His Times.* Toronto: Macmillan of Canada.

Graham, J. et al. 1974. *Report of the Royal Commission on Education, Public Services and Provincial-Municipal Relations.* Halifax: Queen's Printer.

Gramsci, A. 1976. "The Intellectuals." In R. Dale, G. Esland, and M. MacDonald (eds.), *Schooling and Capitalism.* London: Routledge and Kegan Paul.

Grant, G. 1972. "On Equality of Educational Opportunity: Papers Derived from the Harvard University Faculty Seminar on the Coleman Report." *Harvard Educational Review* 42 (1).

Graubard, A. 1972. "The Free School Movement." *Harvard Educational Review* 42 (3).

Grieger, R. M. 1971. "Pygmalion Revisited: A Loud Call for Caution." *Interchange* 2 (4).

Gue, L. R. 1971. "Value Orientations in an Indian Community." *The Alberta Journal of Education Research* 17 (1).

Hagedorn, R. 1980. "What is Sociology?" In R. Hagedorn (ed.), *Sociology.* Toronto: Holt, Rinehart and Winston of Canada.

Hall, V., and R. Turner. 1974. "The Validity of the 'Different Language Explanation' for poor Scholastic Performance by Black Students." *RER* 44.

Haller, A. O., and A. Portes. 1973. "Status Attainment Process." *Sociology of Education* 46 (Winter).

Haller, E. J., and B. D. Anderson. 1969. "Contextual Effects on Educational Aspirations: Some Canadian Evidence." *Administrator's Notebook* 17.

Haller, E. J., and S. J. Thorson. 1970. "The Political Socialization of Children in the Structure of the Elementary School." *Interchange* 1 (3).

Halsey, A. H., and M. A. Trow. 1971. *The British Academics.* Cambridge, Mass.: Harvard University Press.

Hamilton, W. B. 1970. "The British Heritage." In J. D. Wilson, R. M. Stamp, and L. P. Audet (eds.), *Canadian Education: A History.* Scarborough, Ont.: Prentice-Hall of Canada.

Handlin, O. 1975. "John Dewey's Contribution to Education." In J. Bernard and D. Burner (eds.), *The American Experience in Education.* New York: New Viewpoints, A Division of Franklin Watts, Inc.

Hanks, M. P., and B. K. Eckland. 1976. "Athletics and Social Participation in the Educational Attainment Process." *Sociology of Education* 49 (October).

Hansen, D. A., D. Gold, and E. Labovitz. 1972. "Socioeconomic Inequities in College Entry: A Critical Specification." *American Educational Research Journal* 9 (4).

Harp, J. 1980. "Social Inequalities and the Transmission of Knowledge." In J. Harp and J. R. Hofley (eds.), *Structured Inequality in Canada.* Scarborough: Prentice-Hall of Canada.

Harris, R. S. 1966. "English Influence in Canadian Education." *Canadian Forum* 46 (543).

_____. 1968. *Quiet Evolution: A Study of the Educational System of Ontario.* Toronto: University of Toronto Press.

Harvey, E. B. 1974. "Canadian Higher Education in the Seventies." *Interchange* 5 (2).

Harvey, E., and L. R. Harvey. 1970. "Adolescence, Social Class, and Occupational Expectations." *The Canadian Review of Sociology and Anthropology* 7 (2).

Harvey, E. B., and I. Charner. 1975. "Social Mobility and Occupational Attainments of University Graduates." *The Canadian Review of Sociology and Anthropology* 12 (2).

Hauser, R. M. 1973. "Disaggregating a Social-Psychological Model of Educational Attainment." In A. S. Goldberg and O. D. Duncan (eds.), *Structural Equation Models in the Social Sciences.* New York: Seminar Press.

Hauser, R. M., and P. J. Dickenson. 1974. "Inequality in Occupational Status and Income." *American Educational Research Journal* 11 (2).

Hauser, R. M., and D. L. Featherman. 1976. "Equality of Schooling: Trends and Prospects." *Sociology of Education* 49 (April).

Heathers, G. 1972. "Overview of Innovations in Organizations for Learning." *Interchange* 3 (2/3).

Herman, A. B. 1971. "Effects of High School Program Choice on Self-Concept." *Alberta Journal of Educational Research* 17 (1).

Herrnstein, R. J. 1973. *I.Q. in the Meritocracy.* Boston: Little, Brown.

Hettich, W. 1971. *Expenditures, Outputs and Productivity in Canadian University Education.* Special Study no. 14 prepared for The Economic Council of Canada. Ottawa: Information Canada.

Hettich, W., B. Lacombe, and M. Von Zur-Muehlen. 1972. *Basic Goals and the Financing of Education.* Canadian Teachers' Federation Project on Education Finance (Document 3). Ottawa: Canadian Teachers' Federation.

Heyneman, S. P. 1976. "Influences on Academic Achievement: A Comparison of Results from Uganda and More Industrialized Societies." *Sociology of Education* 49 (July).

Hilgard, E. R., and G. H. Bower. 1975. *Theories of Learning.* 4th ed. New York: Appleton-Century-Crofts.

Hill, W. F. 1977. *Learning.* 3rd ed. New York: Crowell.

Hintzman, D. L. 1978. *The Psychology of Learning and Memory.* San Francisco: W. H. Freeman.

Hobart, C. W. 1970. "Eskimo Education in the Canadian Arctic." *The Canadian Review of Sociology and Anthropology* 7 (1).

Hodge, R. W., P. M. Siegel, and P. H. Rossi. 1966. "Occupational Prestige in the United States: 1925-1963." In R. Bendix and S. M. Lipset (eds.), *Class, Status and Power.* 2nd ed. New York: The Free Press.

Hodge, R. w., D. J. Treiman, and P. H. Rossi. 1966. "A Comparative Study of Occupational Prestige." In R. Bendix and S. M. Lipset (eds.), *Class, Status and Power.* 2nd ed. New York: The Free Press.

Hodgson, E. 1972. "Community Schools." In P. J. Cistone (ed), *School Boards and the Political Fact.* Symposium Series no. 2. Toronto: Ontario Institute for Studies in Education.

Hofley, J. R. 1980. "Classlessness Versus Inequality: An Agonizing Choice." In J. Harp and J. R. Hofley (eds.), *Structured Inequality in Canada.* Scarborough: Prentice-Hall of Canada.

Hofstadter, R. (ed.). 1963. *The Progressive Movement: 1900-1915.* Englewood Cliffs, N.J.: Prentice-Hall.

Hohol, A. E. 1955. "Factors Associated with Dropouts." *Alberta Journal of Educational Research* 1 (1).

Holdaway, E. A. 1972. "What topics Are Discussed at School Board Meetings?" *School Progress* 39 (4). Reprinted in H. A. Stevenson et al. (eds.), *The Best of Times/The Worst of Times.* Toronto: Holt, Rinehart and Winston of Canada.

Holmstrom, E. I., and R. W. Holmstrom. 1974. "The Plight of the Women Doctoral Student." *American Educational Research Journal* 11 (1).

Horner, M. S. 1972. "The Motive to Avoid Success and Changing Aspirations of College Women." In J. Bardwick (ed.), *Readings on the Psychology of Women.* New York: Harper and Row.

Houston, S. E. 1978. "Social Reform and Education: The Issue of Compulsory Schooling, 1851-71." In N. MacDonald and A. Chaiton (eds.), *Egerton Ryerson and His Times.* Toronto: Macmillan of Canada.

Huber, J. 1973. *Changing Women in a Changing Society.* Chicago: The University of Chicago Press.

Hughes, E. C., H. S. Becker, and B. Geer. 1977. "Student Culture and Academic Effect." In B. R. Cosin, I. R. Dale, G. M. Esland, D. MacKinnon, and D. F. Swift (eds.), *School and Society.* 2nd ed. London: Routledge and Kegan Paul.

Hull, C. L. 1943. *Principles of Behaviour.* New York: Appleton.

Hunt, J. McV. 1969. "Has Compensatory Education Failed? Has it Been Attempted?" *Harvard Educational Review* 39 (2).

Hunter, A. A. 1981. *Class Tells.* Toronto: Butterworths.

Hurn, C. J. 1978. *The Limits and Possibilities of Schooling.* Boston: Allyn and Bacon.

Hurst, C. E. 1979. *The Anatomy of Social Inequality.* Toronto: C. V. Mosby.

Husen, T. 1975. *Social Influences on Educational Attainment.* Paris: Centre for Educational Research and Innovation. Organization for Economic Co-operation and Development.

Hutcheon, P. W. 1975. *A Sociology of Canadian Education.* Toronto: Van Nostrand Reinhold.

Illich, I. 1971. *Deschooling Society.* New York: Harper and Row.

Imhelder, B., and J. Piaget. 1958. *The Growth of Logical Thinking from Childhood to Adolescence.* New York: Basic Books.

_____. 1969. *The Early Growth of Logic in the Child.* New York: W. W. Norton.

Inner-City Schools Committee, British Columbia Teachers' Federation. 1970. "Equal Opportunity to Learn?": In *The Poor at School in Canada.* Ottawa: Canadian Teachers' Federation.

Ishwaran, K. (ed.). 1979. *Childhood and Adolescence in Canada.* Toronto: McGraw-Hill Ryerson.

Jackson, E. F. 1962. "Status Inconsistency and Symptoms of Stress." *American Sociological Review* 27 (August).

Jackson, E. F., and H. J. Crockett, Jr. 1964. "Occupational Mobility in the United States: A Point Estimate and Trend Comparison." *American Sociological Review* 29.

Jacoby, S. 1974. *Inside Soviet Schools.* New York: Hill and Wang.

Jain, H. C. 1974. "Is Education Related to Job Performance?" In H. C. Jain (ed.), *Contemporary Issues in Canadian Personnel Administration.* Scarborough, Ontario: Prentice-Hall of Canada Ltd.

Janzen, H. 1970. *Curriculum Change in a Canadian Context.* Toronto: Gage Educational Publishing Limited.

Janzen, H. L., and E. F. Johnston. 1971. "The Use of Reading Tests for Entrance and Placement Testing in a Community College." *The Alberta Journal of Educational Research* 17 (3).

Jencks, C. 1968. "Social Stratification and Higher Education." *Harvard Educational Review* 38 (2).

_____. 1973. "Inequality in Restrospect."*Perspectives on Equality*. Cambridge, Mass: President and Fellows of Harvard College.

Jencks, C. S., and M. D. Brown. 1975. "Effects of High Schools on Their Students." *Harvard Educational Review* 45.

Jencks, C., S. Bartlett, M. Corcoran, J. Crouse, D. Eaglesfield, G. Jackson, K. McClelland, P. Meuser, M. Olneck, J. Schwartz, S. Ward, and J. Williams. 1979. *Who Gets Ahead?* New York: Basic.

Jencks, C., M. Smith, H. Acland, M. J. Bane, D. Cohen, H. Gintis, B. Heyno, and S. Michelson. 1972. *Inequality: A Reassessment of the Effect of Family and Schooling in America.* New York: Basic Books.

Jencks, C., and D. Riesman. 1968. *The Academic Revolution.* Garden City, N.Y.: Doubleday.

Jensen, A. R. 1969. "How Much Can We Boost I.Q. and Scholastic Achievement?" *Harvard Educational Review* 39 (Winter).

_____. 1970a. "Another Look at Culture Fair Testing." In J. Hellmuth (ed.), *Compensatory Education: A National Debate.* New York: Brunner-Mazel.

_____. 1970b. "Can We and Should We Study Race Differences?" In J. Hellmuth (ed.), *Compensatory Education: A National Debate.* New York: Brunner-Mazel.

Johnson, D. W. 1970. *The Social Psychology of Education.* New York: Holt, Rinehart and Winston.

Johnson, F. H. 1968. *A Brief History of Canadian Education.* Toronto: McGraw-Hill.

Jones, F. E. 1968. "The Social Origins of High School Teachers in a Canadian City." In B. R. Blishen, F. E. Jones, K. D. Naegele, and J. Porter (eds.), *Canadian Society: Sociological Perspectives.* Toronto: The Macmillan Company of Canada Limited.

Jones, F. E., and J. Selby. 1972. "School Performance and Social Class." In T. J. Ryan (ed.), *Poverty and the Child: A Canadian Study.* Toronto: McGraw-Hill Ryerson.

Jury, L. E., D. J. Willower, and W. J. DeLocy. 1975. "Teacher Self-Actualization and Pupil Control Ideology." *The Alberta Journal of Educational Research* 21 (4).

Kagan, J. 1969. "Inadequate Evidence and Illogical Conclusions." *Harvard Educational Review* 39 (2).

_____. 1971. "Preschool Enrichment and Learning." *Interchange* 2 (2).

_____. 1975. "The Magical Aura of the I.Q." In A. Montagu (ed.), *Race and I.Q.* New York: Oxford.

Kalin, R., and D. Rayko. 1978. *Discrimination in Evaluation Judgments Against Foreign Accented Job Candidates.* Paper presented at Canadian Psychological Association Conference, Ottawa. (Reported in Edwards, 1979).

Kamin, L. J. 1974. *The Science and Politics of I.Q.* New York: John Wiley and Sons.

Kaplan, H. E. 1977. "Sex Typing in Textbooks Used in the Saskatoon Public Schools." *Intellect* 106 (July).

Karabel, J. 1972. "Community Colleges and Social Stratification." *Harvard Educational Review* 42 (4).

Karabel, J., and A. H. Halsey. (eds.). 1977. *Power and Ideology in Education.* New York: Oxford University Press.

Kariger, R. H. 1962. "The Relation of Home Grouping to the Socioeconomic Status of Parents in Three Junior High Schools." Doctoral Dissertation, Michigan State University.

Katz, J. 1969. *Society, Schools and Progress in Canada.* Oxford: Pergamon Books.

_____. 1974. *Education in Canada.* Vancouver: Douglas, David and Charles.

Katz, M. 1968. *The Irony of Early School Reform.* Cambridge: Harvard University Press.

_____. 1971. *Class, Bureaucracy and Schools.* New York: Praeger.

_____. 1973. "Class, Bureaucracy and Schools." In D. Myers (ed.), *The Failure of Educational Reform in Canada.* Toronto: McClelland and Stewart.

Katz, M. B., and P. H. Mattingley (eds.). 1975. *Education and Social Change.* New York: New York University Press.

Kennett, K. F. 1972. "Intelligence and Socioeconomic Status in a Canadian Sample." *The Alberta Journal of Educational Research* 18 (1).

_____. 1973. "Measured Intelligence, Family Size and Socioeconomic Status." *The Alberta Journal of Educational Research* 19 (4).

Kimble, G. A., and N. Gramezy. 1963. *Principles of General Psychology.* 2nd. ed. New York: Ronald Press.

King, A. J. C. 1972. "Social Class and Secondary School Behaviour." In A. J. C. King and W. W. Coulthard (eds.), *A Social View of Man: Canadian Perspectives.* Toronto: John Wiley and Sons Canada Limited.

Knox, W. E., D. J. Pratto, and C. M. Callahan. 1974. "Domains of Decision-Making and School Counseller Use Among High School Seniors." *Sociology of Education* 47 (Fall).

Kohlberg, L. 1964. "Development of Moral Character and Moral Ideology." In M. L. Hoffman and L. W. Hoffman (eds.), *Review of Child Development Research* Vol. 1. New York: Russell Sage Foundation.

Kohn, M. L. 1969. *Class and Conformity.* Homewood, Ill: Dorsey.

Konrad, A. G. 1977. "A Profile of Community College Trustees." *Canadian Journal of Education* 2 (2).

Kopinak, K. M. 1980. "Polity." In R. Hagedorn. *Sociology.* Toronto: Holt, Rinehart and Winston of Canada.

Krathwohl, D. R., B. S. Bloom, and B. B. Masia. 1964. *Taxonomy of Educational Objective. The Classification of Educational Goals, Handbook II: Affective Domain.* New York: MacKay.

Labour Canada. 1974. *Women in the Labour Force: Facts and Figures.* (1973 ed.) Ottawa: Information Canada.

_____. 1979. *Education and Working Canadians*. Ottawa: Minister of Supply and Services.

Labov, W. 1973. "The Logic of Nonstandard English." In N. Keddie (ed.), *Tinker, Tailor . . . The Myth of Cultural Deprivation*. Harmondsworth Penguin.

_____. 1976. *Language in the Inner City*. Philadelphia: University of Pennsylvania Press.

LaMarsh, J. V., L. A. Beaulieu, and S. A. Young, 1977. *Report of the Royal Commission on Violence in the Communications Industry*. Toronto.

Lane, R. 1981. "Facing Challenges in a New Era in Education." The Halifax Chronicle-Herald, July 29.

Larkin, R. W. 1975. "Social Exchange in the Elementary School Classroom: The Problem of Teacher Legitimation of Social Power." *Sociology of Education* 48 (Fall).

LaVoie, J. C., and G. R. Adams. 1974. "Teacher Expectancy and Its Relation to Physical and Interpersonal Characteristics of the Child." *The Alberta Journal of Educational Research* 20 (2).

Lawlor, S. D. 1970. "Social Class and Achievement Orientation." *The Canadian Review of Sociology and Anthropology* 7 (2).

Lawr, D. A., and R. D. Gidney (eds.). 1973. *Educating Canadians: A Documentary History of Public Education*. Toronto: Van Nostrand Reinhold Limited.

Lawton, D. 1969. *Social Class, Language and Education*. London: Routledge & Kegan Paul.

Lazerson, M. 1978. "Canadian Educational Historiography: Some Observations." In N. McDonald and A. Chaiton (eds.), *Egerton Ryerson and His Times*. Toronto: Macmillan of Canada.

Lerner, R. M. 1976. *Concepts and Theories of Human Development*. Reading, Mass.: Addison-Wesley.

Leslie, G. R. 1976. *The Family in Social Context*. 3rd ed. New York: Oxford University Press.

Levensky, M. 1973. "The Experimental Study Group: A New Undergraduate Program at MIT." *Interchange* 4 (1).

Levy, L. H. 1970. *Conceptions of Personality*. New York: Random House.

Lewantin, R. C. 1975. "Race and Intelligence." In A. Montagu (ed.), *Race and I.Q.* New York: Oxford.

Liebert, R. M., and R. W. Poulos. 1972. "T.V. for Kiddies: Truth, Goodness, Beauty — and a Little Bit of Brainwash." *Psychology Today* 6 (November).

Lind, L. 1972. "The Case for Community Control of the Schools." In N. Byrne and J. Quarter (eds.), *Must Schools Fail? The Growing Debate in Canadian Education*. Toronto: McClelland and Stewart Limited.

Lind, L. J. 1974. *The Learning Machine*. Toronto: House of Anansi.

Litwack, L. 1973. "Education! Separate and Unequal." In M. B. Katz (ed.), *Education in American History: Readings on the Social Issues*. New York: Praeger Publishers.

Livingstone, D. W. 1970. "Alternative Futures for Formal Education." *Interchange* 1 (4).

_____. 1971. "Education Revolution: Promise and Prospects." *Interchange* 2 (1).

_____. 1973. "Some General Tactics for Creating Alternative Educational Futures." *Interchange* 4 (1).

_____. 1976. "Images of the Educational Future in Advanced Industrial Society: An Ontario Inquiry." *Canadian Journal of Education* 1 (2).

Lockhart, A. 1977. "Educational Policy Development in Canada: A Critique of the Past and a Case for the Future." In R. A. Carlton, L. A. Colley, and N. J. MacKinnon (eds.), *Education, Change and Society*. Toronto: Gage Educational.

Loehlin, J. C., L. Gardner, and J. N. Spuhler. 1975. *Race Differences in Intelligence*. San Francisco: W. H. Freeman and Company.

Long, L. H. 1975. "Does Migration Interfere with Children's Progress in School?" *Sociology of Education* 48 (Summer).

Loosemore, J., and R. A. Carlton. 1977. "The Student-Teacher: A Dramaturgical Approach to Role-Learning." In R. Carlton, L. Colley, and N. MacKinnon (eds.), *Education, Change and Society*. Toronto: Gage.

Lortie, D. C. 1975. *Schoolteacher: A Sociological Study*. Chicago: University of Chicago Press.

Lubka, N. 1969. "Ferment in Nova Scotia." *Queen's Quarterly* 76 (2).

Lupul, M. R. 1976. "The Portrayal of Canada's 'Other' Peoples in Senior High School History and Social Studies Textbooks in Alberta, 1905 to the Present." *The Alberta Journal of Educational Research* 22 (1).

Lurd, L. 1972. "The Rise of Bureaucracy in Ontario Schools." *This Magazine* (Summer).

Maccoby, E. E. 1972. "Sex Differences in Intellectual Functioning." In J. Bardwick (ed.), *Readings on the Psychology of Women*. New York: Harper and Row.

Mackie, M. 1972. "School Teachers: The Popular Image." *Alberta Journal of Educational Research* 18 (4).

_____. 1980. "Socialization." In R. E. Hagedorn (ed.), *Sociology*. Toronto: Holt, Rinehart and Winston of Canada.

MACOSA. 1979. *Student Achievement in Alberta*. Report of the Minister's Advisory Council on Student Achievement. Edmonton: Alberta Education.

Magnuson, R. 1980. *A Brief History of Quebec Education*. Montreal: Harvest House.

Manley-Casimer, M., and I. E. Housego. 1970. "Equality of Educational Opportunity: A Canadian Perspective." *The Alberta Journal of Educational Research* 16 (2).

Mann, M. 1960. "What Does Ability Grouping Do to the Self-Concept?" *Childhood Education* 36 (April).

Mannheim, K. 1952. *Essays on the Sociology of Knowledge*. London: Routledge and Kegan Paul.

Marchak, M. P. 1981. *Ideological Perspectives in Canada*. 2nd ed. Toronto: McGraw-Hill.

Markham, L. R. 1976. "Influences of Handwriting Quality on Teacher Evaluation of Written Work." *American Educational Research Journal* 13 (4).

Marsden, L., and E. B. Harvey. 1971. "Equality of Educational Access Reconsidered: The Post-Secondary Case in Ontario." *Interchange* 2 (4).

Marsden, L., E. Harvey, and I. Charner. 1975. "Female Graduates: Their Occupational Mobility and Attainments." *The Canadian Review of Sociology and Anthropology* 12 (4, Part 1).

Martell, G. (ed.). 1974. *The Politics of the Canadian Public School.* Toronto: James Lewis and Samuel, Publishers.

Martin, W. B. W. 1975. "The Negotiated Order of Teachers in Team Teaching Situations." *Sociology of Education* 48 (Spring).

_____. 1976. *The Negotiated Order of the School.* Toronto: Macmillan of Canada.

Martin, W. B. W., and A. J. Macdonell. 1978. *Canadian Education.* Scarborough, Ontario: Prentice-Hall of Canada.

Matheson, G. (ed.). 1976. *Women in the Canadian Mosaic.* Toronto: Peter Martin Associates Ltd.

McClelland, D. C. 1951. *Personality.* New York: Wm. Sloane.

_____. 1961. *The Achieving Society.* Princeton, N.J.: Van Nostrand.

_____. 1976. "Testing for Competence Rather Than for Intelligence." In N. J. Block and G. Dworkin (eds.), *The I.Q. Controversy.* New York: Pantheon Books.

McCormack, Thelma. 1979. "Television and the Changing Cultures of Childhood." In K. Ishwaran (ed.), *Childhood and Adolescence in Canada.* Toronto: McGraw-Hill Ryerson.

McDill, E. L., E. D. Myers, and L. C. Rigsby. 1967. "Institutional Effects on the Academic Behaviour of High School Students." *Sociology of Education* 40.

_____. 1973. *The Academic Impact of Educational Climates.* Baltimore: John Hopkins University Press.

McDiarmid, G., and D. Pratt. 1971. *Teaching Prejudice: A Content Analysis of Social Studies Textbooks Authorized for Use in Ontario.* A Report to the Ontario Human Rights Commission Curriculum Series no. 12. Toronto: Ontario Institute for Studies in Education.

McDonald, N., and A. Chaiton (eds.). 1978. *Egerton Ryerson and His Times.* Toronto: Macmillan of Canada.

McDonald, N. 1978. "Egerton Ryerson and the School as an Agent of Political Socialization." In N. McDonald and A. Chaiton (eds.), *Egerton Ryerson and His Times.* Toronto: Macmillan of Canada.

McGrath, Sr. E. 1980. *An Investigation of the Relationship Between Professionalism and Pre-Service Training of Teachers in Nova Scotia.* Unpublished M.Ed. Thesis, St. Francis Xavier University.

McLuhan, M. 1964. *Understanding Media.* New York: McGraw-Hill.

McMillan, J. H. 1980. "Social Psychology and Learning." In J. H. McMillan (ed.), *The Social Psychology of School Learning.* New York: Academic Press.

Mead, G. H. 1913. "The Social Self." *Journal of Philosophy, Psychology, and Scientific Methods* 10.

_____. 1962. *Mind, Self and Society.* Chicago: University of Chicago Press.

Meltzer, B. N. 1978. "Mead's Social Psychology." In J. G. Manis and B. N. Meltzer (eds.), *Symbolic Interaction: A Reader in Social Psychology.* 3rd. ed. Boston: Allyn and Bacon.

Mendels, G. E., and J. P. Flanders. 1973. "Teacher's Expectations and Pupil Performance." *American Educational Research Journal* 10 (3).

Merton, R. 1957. *Social Theory and Social Structure.* Glencoe: The Free Press.

_____. 1968. *Social Theory and Social Structure.* Enlarged ed. Glencoe: The Free Press.

Mifflen, S. C. 1972. *A Theoretical Framework for the Study of the Relationship Between Teachers' Value Systems and Their Teaching Methods.* Unpublished Dissertation. Indiana University.

Milburn, G., and J. Herbert (eds.). 1974. *National Consciousness and the Curriculum: The Canadian Case.* Toronto: Ontario Institute for Studies in Education.

Miles, M. W. 1977. "The Student Movement and the Industrialization of Higher Education." In J. Karabel and A. H. Halsey (eds.), *Power and Ideology in Education.* New York: Oxford University Press.

Miller, N. E., and J. Dollard. 1941. *Social Learning and Imitation.* New Haven: Yale University Press.

Miller, S. M. 1963. "Dropouts: A Political Problem." *Integrated Education* 1 (August).

Miller, S. M., et al. 1964. *School Dropouts: A Commentary and Annotated Bibliography.* Syracuse, New York: Syracuse University Youth Development Centre.

Mills, C. W. 1956. *The Power Elite.* New York: Oxford.

Milton, O., and J. W. Edgerly. 1976. *The Testing and Grading of Students.* Change Magazine and Educational Change.

Meoller, G. 1968. "Bureaucracy and Teachers' Sense of Power. In R. R. Bell and H. R. Stub (eds.), *The Sociology of Education.* Homewood, Ill: Dorsey Press.

Montagu, A. 1975. "Introduction." In A. Montagu (ed.), *Race and I.Q.* New York: Oxford University Press.

Morrison, J. L., and B. J. Hodgkins. 1971. "The Effectiveness of Catholic Education: A Comparative Analysis." *Sociology of Education* 44 (Winter).

Morsden, L., and E. B. Harvey. 1971. "Equality of Educational Access Reconsidered: The Post Secondary Case in Ontario." *Interchange* 2 (4).

Murphy, R. 1979. *Sociological Theories of Education.* Toronto: McGraw-Hill Ryerson.

Mouctakas, C. 1967. "Creativity and Conformity in Education." In R. Mooney and T. Razek (eds.), *Explorations in Creativity.* New York: Harper.

Munroe, D. 1974. *The Organization and Administration of Education in Canada.* Education Support Branch, Department of the Secretary of State. Ottawa: Information Canada.

Murray, H. A. 1938. *Explorations in Personality.* London: Oxford University Press.

Musella, D., A. Selinger, and M. Arikado. 1975. *Open-Concept Programs in Open-Area Schools.* Toronto: The Ministry of Education, Ontario.

Myers, D. (ed.). 1973. *The Failure of Educational Reform in Canada.* Toronto: McClelland and Stewart.

National Council of Welfare. 1976. *The Hidden Welfare System.* Ottawa.

Neisser, U. 1967. *Cognitive Psychology.* New York: Appleton-Century-Croft.

_____. 1976 *Cognition and Reality*. San Francisco: W. H. Freeman.

Nelsen, R. W., and D. A. Nock. 1978. *Reaching, Writing and Riches*. Kitchener, Ontario: Between the Lines.

Nett, E. M. 1980. "The Family." In R. Hagedorn (ed.), *Sociology*. Toronto: Holt, Rinehart and Winston of Canada.

Newcomb, T. M., and E. E. K. Wilson (eds.). 1966. *College Peer Groups*. Chicago: Aldine.

Nickson, M. 1973. "Current Patterns in the Female Labour Force, Canada 1972." In Statistics Canada, *Notes on Labour Statistics, 1972*. Ottawa: Information Canada.

Nielsen, J. McC. 1978. *Sex in Society*. Belmont, California: Wadsworth Publishing Company.

Nova Scotia Department of Education. 1979. *Public School Programs*. Halifax.

Nova Scotia Human Rights Commission. 1974. *Textbook Analysis: Nova Scotia*. Halifax: Nova Scotia Human Rights Commission.

Novak, M. W. 1974. "Living and Learning in the Free School." *Interchange* 5 (2).

_____. 1975. *Living and Learning in the Free School*. Toronto: McClelland and Stewart.

Nuttall, E. V., R. L. Nuttall, D. Polit, and J. B. Hunter. 1976. "The Side Effects of Family Size, Birth Order, Sibling Separation and Crowding on the Academic Achievement of Boys and Girls." *American Educational Research Journal* 13 (3).

Nye, F. I., and F. M. Berardo. 1973. *The Family: Its Structure and Interaction*. New York: Macmillan.

Ochitwa, O. P. 1973. "Organizational Climate and Adoption of Educational Innovations." *Saskatchewan Journal of Educational Research and Development* 4 (1).

Olneck, M. R., and D. B. Bills. 1980. "What Makes Sammy Run? An Empirical Assessment of the Bowles-Gintis Correspondence Theory." *American Journal of Education* 89 (1).

O'Neill, G. P. 1978. "Post-Secondary Aspirations of High School Seniors in Different School Contexts — A Canadian Study." *The Alberta Journal of Educational Research* 24 (2).

O'Reilly, R. 1975. "Classroom Climate and Achievement in Secondary School Mathematics Classes." *The Alberta Journal of Educational Research* 21 (3).

Ostry, S. (ed.). 1972. *Canadian Higher Education in the Seventies*. Economic Council of Canada: Ottawa Information Canada.

Palos, N. C. 1965. *The Dynamics of Team Teaching*. California: William C. Brown Company.

Panitch, L. 1980. "The Role and Nature of the Canadian State." In J. Harp and J. R. Hofley (eds.), *Structured Inequality in Canada*. Scarborough: Prentice-Hall of Canada.

Parelius, A. P., and R. J. Parelius. 1978. *The Sociology of Education*. Englewood Cliffs: Prentice-Hall.

Parent, A. M. 1966. *Report of the Royal Commission of Enquiry on Education in the Province of Quebec*. Quebec: Queen's Printer.

Parry, K. 1977. "Blood Indians and 'Mormon' Public Schools: A Case Study of Ethnicity and Integrated Education." In R. A. Carleton, L. A. Colley, and N. J. MacKinnon (eds.), *Education, Change and Society*. Toronto: Gage Educational.

Parsons, G. L., et al. 1974. *Career Decisions of Newfoundland Youth*. Report no. 3 of the Committee on 1973 Enrollment. St. John's: Memorial University of Newfoundland.

Parsons, T. 1951. *The Social System*. New York: The Free Press.

_____. 1953. "A Revised Analytical Approach to the Theory of Social Stratification." In R. Bendix and S. M. Lipset (eds.), *Class, Status and Power*. Glencoe: Free Press.

_____. 1959. "The School Class as a Social System: Some of Its Functions in American Society." *Harvard Educational Review* 29 (Fall).

_____. 1962. "Youth in the Context of American Society." *Daedalus* 91.

Parsons, T., and G. Platt. 1973. *The American University*. Cambridge, Mass: Harvard University Press.

Parsons, T., and E. R. Shils. 1962. *Toward a General Theory of Action*. New York: Harper and Row.

Pavalko, R. M., and D. R. Bishop. 1966a. "Peer Influences on the College Plans of Canadian High School Students." *The Canadian Review of Sociology and Anthropology* 3 (4).

_____. 1966b. "Socioeconomic Status and College Plans: A Study of Canadian High School Students." *Sociology of Education* 39 (3).

Pettigrew, T. F. 1968. "Race and Equal Eductional Opportunity." *Harvard Educational Review* 38 (1).

Piaget, J. 1951. *Play, Dreams, and Imitation in Childhood*. New York: Norton.

_____. 1963. *The Origins of Intelligence in Children*. New York: W. W. Norton.

_____. 1965. *The Moral Judgment of the Child*. New York: The Free Press.

Picou, J. S., and T. M. Carter. 1976. "Significant-Other Influence and Aspirations." *Sociology of Education* 49 (January).

Pike, R. M. 1970. *Who Doesn't Get to University — and Why: A Study on Accessibility to Higher Education in Canada*. Ottawa: Association of Universities and Colleges of Canada.

Pike, R. M., and E. Zureck (eds.). 1975. *Socialization and Values in Canadian Society*. Toronto: McClelland and Stewart.

Pincus, F. 1978. "Tracking in Community Colleges." In R. W. Nelsen and D. A. Nock (eds.), *Reading, Writing and Riches*. Kitchener, Ontario: Between the Lines.

Pineo, P. C., and J. Porter. 1973. "Occupational Prestige in Canada." In J. E. Curtis and W. G. Scott (eds.), *Social Stratification: Canada*. Scarborough, Ont.: Prentice-Hall of Canada.

Porter, J. 1965. *The Vertical Mosaic*. Toronto: University of Toronto Press.

_____. 1969. "Social Change and the Aims and Problems of Education in Canada." In A. Malik (ed.), *Social Foundations of Canadian Education*. Scarborough: Prentice-Hall.

_____. 1971. "Post-Industrialism, Post-Nationalism and Post-Secondary Education." *Canadian Public Administration* 14.

_____. 1979. *The Measure of Canadian Society.* Toronto: Gage.

Porter, J., B. Blishen et al. 1971. *Towards 2000: The Future of Post-Secondary Education in Ontario.* Toronto: McClelland and Stewart.

Porter, M. R., J. Porter, and B. R. Blishen. 1979. *Does Money Matter?* Revised Edition. Toronto: Macmillan of Canada.

Prentice, A. 1970. "The American Example." In J. D. Wilson, R. M. Stamp, and L. P. Audet (eds.), *Canadian Education: A History.* Scarborough, Ont.: Prentice-Hall of Canada.

_____. 1977. *The School Promoters.* Toronto: McClelland and Stewart.

Prentice, A. L., and S. E. Houston (eds.). 1975. *Family, School and Society.* Toronto: Oxford University Press.

Pritchett, W., and D. J. Willower. 1975. "Student Perceptions of Teacher-Pupil Control Behaviour and Student Attitudes Toward High School." *The Alberta Journal of Educational Research* 21 (2).

Proudfoot, A. J. 1974. "Interpretations of the B.N.A. Act." In T. E. Giles, *Educational Administration in Canada.* Calgary: Detselig Enterprises.

Quarter, J. 1972. "The Teacher's Role in the Classroom: The Primary Source of Teacher Frustration and Discontent." In N. Byrne and J. Quarter (eds.), *Must Schools Fail? The Growing Debate in Canadian Education.* Toronto: McClelland and Stewart.

Ray, D. 1974. "The Canadian Educational Takeoff: An Assessment, Some Comparisons and Conjectures." *Canadian and International Education* 3 (2).

Regan, G. 1974. "Steps to the Reformation: An Evaluation of the Feasibility of Deschooling." *Interchange* 5 (3).

Rehberg, R. A., and L. Hotchkiss. 1972. "Educational Decision Makers: The Social Guidance Counselor and Social Mobility." *Sociology of Education* 45 (Fall).

Reich, C. A. 1976. "The Last Self." In C. D. Schlosser (ed.), *The Person in Education.* New York: Macmillan.

Reich, C., and V. Young. 1975. "Patterns of Dropping Out." *Interchange* 6 (4).

Reimer, E. 1971. "An Essay on Alternatives in Education." *Interchange* 2 (1).

Reiss, I. L. 1965. "The Universality of the Family: A Conceptual Analysis." *Journal of Marriage and the Family* 27 (November).

Renaud, A. 1971. *Education and the First Canadians.* Toronto: Gage Educational Publishing Limited.

Richer, S. 1974a. "Middle-Class Bias of Schools — In Fact Or Fancy." *Sociology of Education* 47 (Fall).

_____. 1974b. "Programme Composition and Educational Plans." *Sociology of Education* 47 (Summer).

Richer, S., and R. Breton. 1968. "School Organization and Student Differences: Some Views of Canadian Educators." *Canadian Education and Research Digest* 8 (1).

Richmond, A. H. 1973. "Social Mobility of Immigrants." In J. E. Curtis and W. G. Scott (eds.), *Social Stratification: Canada.* Scarborough: Prentice-Hall of Canada.

Rist, R. C., 1970. "Student Social Class and Teacher Expectations: The Self-Fulfilling Prophecy in Ghetto Education." *Harvard Educational Review* 40 (3).

Roach, J. L., L. Gross, and O. Gursslin (eds.). 1969. *Social Stratification in the United States.* Englewood Cliffs: Prentice-Hall.

Rocher, G. 1975. "Formal Education: The Issue of Opportunity." In D. Forcese and S. Richer (eds.), *Issues in Canadian Society.* Scarborough: Prentice-Hall of Canada.

Rodgers, R. H. 1973. *Family Interaction and Transaction.* Englewood Cliffs, N.J.: Prentice-Hall.

Rodin, M., and B. Rodin. 1972. "Student Evaluations of Teachers." *Science* 177 (September).

Rosen, B. C., and R. D'Andrade. 1959. "The Psychological Origins of Achievement Motivation." *Sociometry* 22.

Rosenthal, R., and L. Jacobson. 1966. "Teachers' Expectancies: Determinants of Pupils' I.Q. Gains." *Psychological Reports* 19.

_____. 1968. *Pygmalion in the Classroom.* New York: Holt, Rinehart and Winston.

Rosenthal, T. L., and B. J. Zimmerman. 1978. *Social Learning and Cognition.* New York: Academic Press.

Rossides, D. W. 1976. *The American Class System.* Boston: Houghton Mifflin.

Ruch, C., and V. Young. 1975. "Patterns of Dropping Out." *Interchange* 6 (4).

Rush, G. B. 1977. "Occupation and Education in Canada: The Context of Political Economy." In R. A. Carlton, L. A. Colley, and N. J. MacKinnon (eds.), *Education, Change and Society.* Toronto: Gage Educational.

Ryan, D. W., and T. B. Greenfield. 1975. *The Class Size Question: Development of Research Studies Related to the Effects of Class Size, Pupil/Adult, and Pupil/ Teacher Ratios.* Toronto: The Ministry of Education, Ontario.

Saario, T. N., C. N. Jacklin, and C. Kehr. 1973. "Sex Role Stereotyping in the Public Schools." *Harvard Educational Review* 43 (August).

Sacouman, R. J., 1979. "Underdevelopment and Structural Origins of Antigonish Movement Co-operatives in Eastern Nova Scotia." In R. J. Bryn and R. J. Sacouman (eds.), *Underdevelopment and Social Movements in Atlantic Canada.* Toronto: New Hogtown Press.

Schafer, W. E., and C. Olexa. 1971. *Tracking and Opportunity.* Scranton, Pa.: Chandler.

Schecter, S. 1977. "Capitalism, Class and Educational Reform in Canada." In L. Panitch (ed.), *The Canadian State: Political Economy and Political Power.* Toronto: University of Toronto Press.

Schoenfeldt, L. F. 1974. "Human Differences and Inequalities: Causes and Effects." *American Educational Research Journal* 11 (2).

Schreiber, D. (ed.). *Profile of the School Dropout.* New York: Vintage Books.

Scimecca, J. A. 1980. *Education and Society.* New York: Holt, Rinehart and Winston.

Sears, P. S., and D. H. Feldman. 1974. "Teacher Interactions with Boys and Girls." In J. Stacey, S. Bereaud, and J. Daniels (eds.), *And Jill Came Tumbling After: Sexism in American Education.* New York: Dell Publishing Company.

Sears, R. R. 1951. "A Theoretical Framework for Personality and Social Behaviour." *American Psychologist* 6.

Sears, R. R., E. Maccoby, and H. Levin. 1957. *Patterns of Child Rearing.* New York: Harper.

Seaman, M. 1959. "On the Meaning of Alienation." *American Sociological Review* 24 (December).

Sellick, S. B. 1964/65. "A Study of Male Dropouts in Grades Nine and Ten at Hillcrest High School, Port Arthur, Ontario, from September 1954 to June 1960." *Ontario Journal of Educational Research* 7 (2).

Sewell, W. H., A. O. Haller, and A. Portes. 1969. "The Educational and Early Occupational Attainment Process." *American Sociological Review* 34 (February).

Sewell, W. H., A. O. Haller, and G. W. Oklendorf. 1970. "The Educational and Early Occupational Attainment Process: Replication and Revisions." *American Sociological Review* 35 (December).

Sewell, W. H., and V. P. Shah. 1967. "Socioeconomic Status, Intelligence, and the Attainment of Higher Education." *Sociology of Education* 40.

Sheffield, E. F. 1970. "The Post-War Surge in Post-Secondary Education: 1945-1969." In J. D. Wilson, R. M. Stamp, and L. P. Audet (eds.), *Canadian Education: A History.* Scarborough, Ont.: Prentice-Hall of Canada.

Shook, L. K. 1971. *Catholic, Post-Secondary Education in English-Speaking Canada: A History.* Toronto and Buffalo: University of Toronto Press.

Shuey, A. M. 1966. *The Testing of Negro Intelligence.* 2nd ed. New York: Social Science Press.

Silberman, C. E. 1970. *Crisis in the Classroom.* New York: Random House.

Simpkins, W. S., and D. Friesen. 1969. "Teacher Participation in School Decision Making." *The Canadian Administrator* 8 (4).

_____. 1970. "Discretionary Powers of Classroom Teachers." *The Canadian Administrator* 9 (8).

Simpson, R. L. 1974. "Sex Stereotypes of Secondary School Teaching Subjects: Male and Female Status Gains and Losses." *Sociology of Education* 47 (Summer).

Sissons, C. B. 1959. *Church and State in Canadian Education: An Historical Study.* Toronto: Ryerson Press.

Skinner, B. F. 1938. *The Behaviour of Organism: An Experimental Analysis.* Englewood Cliffs: Prentice-Hall.

_____. 1971. *Beyond Freedom and Dignity.* New York: Knopf.

_____. 1974. *About Behaviourism.* New York: Knopf.

Solomon, L. C., and P. Wockfal. 1975. "The Effects on Income of Type of College Attended." *Sociology of Education* 48 (Winter).

Spady, W. G. 1970. "Lament for the Letterman: Effects of Peer Status and Extracurricular Activities on Goals and Achievement." *American Journal of Sociology* 75 (January).

_____. 1971. "Dropouts from Higher Education: Toward an Empirical Model." *Interchange* 2 (3).

Spearman, C. 1927. *The Abilities of Man.* London: Macmillan.

Spencer, M. 1979. *Foundations of Modern Sociology.* 2nd ed. Englewood Cliffs, N.J.: Prentice-Hall.

Spreitzer, E., and M. Pugh. "Interscholastic Athletics and Educational Expectations." *Sociology of Education* 46 (Spring).

Spring, J. 1972. *Education and the Rise of the Corporate State.* Boston: Beacon Press.

Stamp, R. M. 1971. "Canadian Education and the National Identity." *The Journal of Educational Thought* 5 (3).

_____. 1972. "Vocational Objectives in Canadian Education: An Historical Overview." In S. Ostry (ed.), *Canadian Higher Education in the Seventies.* Published under the auspice of the Economic Council of Canada. Ottawa: Information Canada.

Statistics Canada. 1972a. *Canadian Community Colleges and Related Institutions, 1970-71.* Ottawa: Information Canada.

_____. 1972b. *Student Withdrawals from Canadian Universities.* Service Bulletin 1 (6), Education Division. Ottawa: Information Canada.

_____. 1974a. *Distributional Effects of Health and Educational Benefits.* Ottawa: Information Canada.

_____. 1974b. *Economic Returns to Education in Canada.* Ottawa: Information Canada.

_____. 1976. *Elementary-Secondary School Enrolment 1974-75.* Ottawa: Information Canada.

_____. 1978a. *Education in Canada.* Ottawa: Information Canada.

_____. 1978b. *The Educational Background of Parents of Post-Secondary Students in Canada.* Second Draft. Ottawa: Institutional and Public Finance Statistics Branch, Statistics Canada.

_____. 1979a. *Advance Statistics of Education* Ottawa: Information Canada.

_____. 1979b. *From the Sixties to the Eighties, A Statistical Portrait of Canadian Higher Education.* Ottawa: Information Canada.

_____. 1980a. *Perspectives Canada III.* Ottawa: Information Canada.

_____. 1980b. *Education in Canada.* Ottawa: Minister of Supply and Services.

Statistics Canada in cooperation with the Association of Universities and Colleges of Canada. 1974. *Universities and Colleges of Canada.* Ottawa: Information Canada.

Stebbins, R. A. 1971. "The Meaning of Disorderly Behaviour: Teacher Definition of a Classroom Situation." *Sociology of Education* 44 (2).

_____. 1977. "A Definition of the Situation and Motivation in the Sociology of Education." In R. Carlton, L. Colley, and N. MacKinnon (eds.), *Education, Change and Society.* Toronto: Gage.

Sternberg, R. J. 1980. "Factor Theories of Intelligence Are All Right Almost." *Educational Researcher* 9 (8).

Stinchcombe, A. L. 1969. "Environment: The Cumulation of Effects is Yet to Be Understood." *Harvard Educational Review* 39 (3).

Stuhr, C. A., and E. N. Wright. 1970. "Marks and Patterns of Parental Mobility in a Downtown School." *The Alberta Journal of Educational Research* 16 (1).

Sullivan, E., N. Byrne, and M. Stager. 1970. "The Development of Canadian Students' Political Conceptions." *Interchange* 1 (3).

Tandan, N. K. 1975. "The Decline in the Female-Male Unemployment Rate Differential in Canada 1961-72." In Statistics Canada, *Notes on Labour Statistics 1973*. Ottawa: Information Canada.

Tannenbaum, A. J. 1969. *Adolescents' Attitudes Toward Academic Brilliance.* Unpublished doctoral dissertation, New York University.

Tepperman, L. 1975. *Social Mobility in Canada.* Toronto: McGraw-Hill Ryerson Limited.

Thomas, W. I. 1928. *The Child in America.* New York: A. A. Knopf.

Thurow, L. C. 1972. "Education and Economic Equality." *The Public Interest* 28 (Summer).

Tinto, V. 1973. "College Proximity and Rates of College Attendance." *American Educational Research Journal* 10 (4).

Toffler, A. 1974. *Learning for Tomorrow: The Role of the Future in Education.* New York: Vintage Books.

Torrance, E. P., and K. Arson. 1963. "Experimental Studies of Homogeneous and Heterogeneous Groups for Creative Scientific Tasks." In W. W. Charters and N. L. Gage (eds.), *Readings in the Social Psychology of Education.* Boston: Allyn and Bacon.

Traub, R., et al. 1976. *Openness in Schools: An Evaluation Study.* Research in Education Series no. 5. Toronto: Ontario Institute for Studies in Education.

Travers, R. M. W. 1977. *Essentials of Learning.* 4th ed. New York: Macmillan.

Trow, M. 1961. "The Second Transformation of American Secondary Education." *International Journal of Comparative Sociology* 2 (September).

Trowbridge, N. 1972. "Self Concept and Socioeconomic Status in Elementary School Children." *American Educational Research Journal* 9 (4).

Tumin, M. M. 1953. "Some Principles of Stratification: A Critical Analysis." *American Sociological Review* 18 (4).

_____. 1963. "On Inequality." *American Sociological Review* 28 (1).

Turner. J. H. 1978. *The Structure of Sociological Theory.* Revised edition. Homewood, Ill.: Dorsey.

Turner, R. H. 1960. "Sponsored and Contest Mobility and the School System." *American Sociological Review* 25 (6).

_____. 1964. *The Social Context of Ambition.* San Francisco: Chandler Publishing Company.

Tyler, W. 1972/73. "The Organization Structure of the Secondary School." *Educational Review* 25.

U. S. Department of Health, Education and Welfare. 1972. *Television and Growing Up: The Impact of Televised Violence.* Report to the Surgeon General from the Scientific Advisory Committee on Television and Social Behaviour. Washington, D.C..

Useem, M. 1976. "State Production of Social Knowledge: Patterns in Government Financing of Academic Social Research." *The American Sociological Review* 41 (4).

Vanfossen, B. E. 1979. *The Structure of Social Inequality*. Boston: Little, Brown.

Vernon, P. E. 1965. "Ability Factors and Environmental Influences." *American Psychologist* 20.

Vidler, D. C. 1977. "Achievement Motivation." In S. Ball (ed.), *Motivation in Education*. New York: Academic Press.

Vincent, G. B., and D. B. Black. 1966. "Dropout Is Societies' Burden: Fact or Fiction?" *Canadian Education Research Digest* 6 (4).

Walberg, H. J., and S. C. Thomas. 1972. "Open Education: An Operational Definition and Validation in Great Britain and United States." *American Educational Research Journal* 9 (2).

Wallace, A. F. C. 1956. "Reviatalization Movements." *American Anthropologist* 58 (April).

Wallace, R. A., and A. Wolf. 1980. *Contemporary Sociological Theory*. Englewood Cliffs, N.J.: Prentice-Hall.

Wallach, M. C., and N. Kagan. 1965. *Modes of Thinking in Young Children*. New York: Holt, Rinehart and Winston.

Waller, W. 1932. *The Sociology of Teaching*. New York: Wiley.

Walster, E., T. A. Cleary, and M. M. Clifford. 1971. "The Effect of Race and Sex on College Admission." *Sociology of Education* 44 (Spring).

Weidman, J. C., W. T. Phalen, and M. A. Sullivan. 1972. "The Influence of Educational Attainment on Self-Evaluations of Competence." *Sociology of Education* 45 (Summer).

Wilkins, W. E. 1976. "The Concept of Self-Fulfilling Prophecy." *The Sociology of Education* 49 (April).

Williams, R. 1976. "Base and Superstructure in Marxist Cultural Theory." In R. Dale, G. Esland, and M. MacDonald (eds.), *Schooling and Capitalism*. London: Routledge and Kegan Paul.

Williams, T. 1972. "Educational Aspirations: Longitudinal Evidence on Their Development in Canadian Youth." *Sociology of Education* 45 (2).

_____. 1973. *Cultural Deprivation and Intelligence: Extensions of the Basic Model*. Unpublished Ph.D. dissertation, University of Toronto.

_____. 1974. "Class, I.Q. and Heredity: Canadian Data." *Education Research and Perspectives* 1 (December).

_____. 1975a. "Family Resemblances in Abilities: The Wechsler Scales." *Behaviour Genetics* 5 (October).

_____. 1975b. "Abilities and Environments." In W. H. Sewell, R. M. Hauser, and D. L. Featherstone (eds.), *Schooling and Achievement in American Society*. New York: Academic Press.

_____. 1975c. "Educational Ambition: Teachers and Students." *Sociology of Education* 48 (Fall).

_____. 1976. "Teacher Prophecies and the Inheritance of Inequality." *Sociology of Education* 49 (July).

_____. 1977. "Education and Biosocial Processes." In R. A. Carlton, L. A. Colley, and N. J. MacKinnon (eds.), *Education, Change and Society*. Toronto: Gage Educational.

Wilson, A. B. 1959. "Residential Segregation of Social Classes and Aspirations of High School Boys." *American Sociological Review* 24.

_____. 1968. "Social Class and Equal Educational Opportunity." *Harvard Educational Review* 38.

Wilson, J. D. 1978. "The Pre-Ryerson Years." In N. McDonald and A. Chaiton (eds.), *Egerton Ryerson and His Times*. Toronto: Macmillan of Canada.

Wilson, J. D., R. M. Stamp, and L. P. Audet (eds.). 1970. *Canadian Education: A History*. Scarborough: Prentice-Hall of Canada.

Wolberg, H. J., and G. Anderson. 1968. "Classroom Climate and Individual Learning." *Journal of Educational Psychology* 59.

Wolfgang, A. 1975. *Education of Immigrant Students*. Toronto: The Ontario Institute for Studies in Education.

Wolman, B. B. 1960. *Contemporary Theories and Systems in Psychology*. New York: Harper and Row.

Women on Words and Images. *Dick and Jane as Victims*. 2nd ed. Princeton, N.J.

Wright, R. J. 1975. "The Affective and Cognitive Consequences of an Open Education Elementary School." *American Educational Research Journal* 12 (4).

Wrong, D. H. 1959. "The Functional Theory of Stratification: Some Neglected Considerations." *American Sociological Review* 24 (December).

Yankelovich, D. 1979. "Who Gets Ahead in America." *Psychology Today* (July).

Yates, A. 1971. *The Organization of Schooling: A Study of Educational Grouping Practices*. London: Routledge and Kegan Paul.

Ycas, M. A. 1976. "The Educational Plans of Senior Secondary Students." Discussion paper. Ottawa: Education Support Branch, Department of the Secretary of State.

Young, M. F. D. (ed.). 1971. *Knowledge and Control: New Directions for the Sociology of Education*. London: Collier-Macmillan Publishers.

Zentner, H. 1964. "Reference Group Behaviour Among High School Students." *Alberta Journal of Educational Research* 10 (3).

Zigler, E. F., and I. L. Child (eds.). 1973. *Socialization and Personality Development*. Reading, Mass.: Addison-Wesley.

Zsigmond, Z. E., and C. J. Wenaas. 1970. *Enrolment in Educational Institutions by Province 1951-52 to 1980-81*. Staff Study no. 25, Economic Council of Canada. Ottawa: Information Canada.

Zsigmond, Z. 1975. "Patterns of Demographic Change Affecting Education 1961-2001." Canadian Teachers' Federation, *National Conference on Financing Education, The Challenge of Equity*. Proceedings of a Conference, Quebec City, February 16-19. Ottawa: Canadian Teachers' Federation.

N